From the Heart of a Nation

Our Mother Calls

The Revelation of the Morning Star Over America

by
William L. Roth Jr.

The Morning Star of Our Lord, Inc. is a nonprofit, tax-exempt religious and charitable organization incorporated under the laws of the State of Illinois. It has been established for the dissemination of a miraculous body of work received through the supernatural intercession of the Blessed Virgin Mary under the title of the Morning Star Over America. This organization is solemnly dedicated to all the principles delineated within these written texts in union with the spiritual catechesis of the Supreme Pontiff of the Roman Catholic Church, the Vicar of Christ on Earth. It is the intrinsic role of this Corporation to provide pastoral consolation to those lacking in faith, the infirm, homebound, incarcerated, deprived, dejected and those who are otherwise suffering-humanity for the sake of the Glory of the Kingdom of Jesus Christ.

The Morning Star of Our Lord, Inc.
Springfield, Illinois
www.ImmaculateMary.org

Published by The Morning Star of Our Lord, Inc.
Used with permission.

Publish Date: May 31, 2014

ISBN: 978-0-9793334-3-9

To
My Brother, Timothy

Thank you for sharing a mystery that no one can destroy.

From the Heart of a Nation

Our Mother Calls

The Revelation of the Morning Star Over America

The Mystical Revelation
of the
Morning Star Over America

Official Public Deposit of Works

The following twelve manuscripts comprise the syllabus of the official public record of the Revelation of the Most Blessed Virgin Mary as the Morning Star Over America. The dates of submission of each work to the Bishop of the Roman Catholic Diocese of Springfield in Illinois have been recorded.

In Our Darkest Hour
Morning Star Over America
February 22, 1991 - December 31, 1992 / Volume I
Submission Date: February 9, 2000

In Our Darkest Hour
Morning Star Over America
January 1, 1993 - February 22, 1997 / Volume II
Submission Date: February 9, 2000

Morning Star Over America
Twentieth Century Anthology
AD 1997-1999
Submission Date: November 22, 2010

At the Water's Edge
Essays in Faith and Morals
Submission Date: May 8, 2001

When Legends Rise Again
The Convergence of Capitalism and Christianity
Submission Date: March 13, 2002

White Collar Witch Hunt
The Catholic Priesthood Under Siege
Submission Date: June 26, 2002

Babes in the Woods
With a Little Child to Guide Them
Submission Date: March 18, 2003

To Crispen Courage
The Divine Annihilation
Submission Date: August 8, 2005

Supernal Chambers
A Resurrection Prayer
Submission Date: July 11, 2006

Morning Star Over America
The New Millennium
AD 2000-2002
Submission Date: September 5, 2007

Morning Star Over America
The New Millennium
AD 2003-2005
Submission Date: September 30, 2008

Morning Star Over America
The New Millennium
AD 2006-2008
Submission Date: August 22, 2009

Official Note of Clarification

The official deposit of the revelation of Our Lady under the title *Morning Star Over America* is contained within the first twelve published works, spanning the message dates February 22, 1991 through December 28, 2008. The authors testify that the deposit of revelation under the title *Morning Star Over America* possesses an inclusive character whereby the Most Blessed Virgin manifests a conveyance to Her side through the work, thus gathering all Her children around Her in prayer before the Cross of Her Son Jesus Christ, under the paternal auspices of the Roman Catholic Church. The *Morning Star Over America* revelation is a "private revelation" in accordance with the definition prescribed by the Roman Catholic Church. It holds no requirement of binding assent even in the case of its authenticity. Yet, the Holy Spirit beckons us to accept it so that the world may benefit from our Heavenly Mother's guidance through the authentic witness of the graces subsisting within the Catholic Church. These works are not to be confused in substance or stature with the official Public Revelation and Deposit of Faith sanctioned within the authoritative catechesis of the Church of Rome. The published works of *Morning Star Over America* neither add to, supersede nor supplant, either in part or in toto, the official Deposit of Faith of the Roman Catholic Church. They are a grace of explication through the power of the Holy Spirit, given to assist and focus our understanding of and commitment to the Public Revelation of Jesus Christ. *Morning Star Over America* exists as a subordinate outpouring of grace that subsists beneath the official Deposit of Faith; a particular animation of the Holy Spirit through the benefits of the Sacrament of Confirmation, and an organic, maternal flowering generated as a product of obedient acceptance of that official Deposit of Faith.

Any messages or portions of messages in subsequent works dated after December 28, 2008 or other content, parables, lessons or spiritual treatises related to messages that are not recorded in the original twelve works, are likewise bound under the definition of private revelation, and at present, do not reside beneath the *Morning Star Over America* revelation until such time that they may be specifically elevated by the Church as an addendum to the original work. The Church holds the power to magnify Our Lady's work in this regard through the "sensus fidelium" and its authority to bind. The affirmation of the inclusive nature of the *Morning Star Over America* revelation reflects an explicit welcoming by the Matriarch of Heaven for all people to unite with Her through the special grace of the works and gather with Her in prayer and faithfulness to the Roman Catholic Church. Her presence as the *Mother Star Over America* is not simply a limited grace of significance only to Her two obedient sons. She reveals that She comes to speak to all of Her children with equal emphasis, and with the same maternal authority and motherly compassion; and She petitions our obedient acceptance of Her wise counsel in return.

The subsequent record of Our Lady's continuing relationship with Her two sons after December 28, 2008 is currently recognized by them as a personal gift that remains within the intimate privacy of their personal relationship with the Holy Virgin that can be disclosed or remain secret in perpetuity at their discretion in union with the Her guidance. The Virgin Mother wishes to emphasize that She should not be required to cease any relationship as a precondition for Her to be given venue so that the faith of the Church may be strengthened by the vested recognition of Her motherly guidance as the *Morning Star Over America*. We are encouraged to remember Matthew 5:13-16. For those who would demand that She cease and desist Her intercession before extending their faithfulness and responding in thanksgiving, She has provided a demarcation of "closure" to Her miraculous intercession as the *Morning Star Over America* as of December 28, 2008 so that they too may be unhindered in their acceptance of Her presence for the sake of the conversion of their lost brothers and sisters in our time.

From the Heart of a Nation

Our Mother Calls

The Revelation of the Morning Star Over America

Herald This Grace
Raise the Fanfare for the Queen

Saturday, February 12, 2011
2:13 p.m.

"Now I have come, the Mother of Jesus, the Mother of God, into your presence with joy and appreciation for your obedience to Me and to the mission of the Church. My little sons, it is rare that I might be so elated to speak to mortal creatures with this joy when there are such gross sins and injustices in the world. However, I speak with you openly about My inspiration gained through your trust in God and response to My call. I have spoken to you and your brothers and sisters, your comrades in Christianity for many generations. As you watched in the motion picture 'The Song of Bernadette' last evening, I did not come to her to pronounce doom and gloom. I simply said that it would not be possible for Me to make her happy in this life. It was her understanding of human suffering and its purpose in purifying humanity that made her happy. Her joy was a fruit of her faith, of her realization that the Holy Spirit has come into the midst of men to give wisdom where there is ignorance, to offer the Lord's warning about what shall come if lost sinners do not adhere to the teachings of the Gospel. You have seen that your messages are much like this, and you have likewise taken to heart My messages; you have inherited the same meekness and courage that brought Saint Bernadette to the summit of God's embrace. While this was a good motion picture, lost in the cinema was the content of My messages. Surely it was clear that innocence, self-sacrifice, prayer, service, and suffering bring the hard-hearted to let loose of their obstinance. You saw public officials stand in disbelief, even to the point that they would incarcerate someone who stood so soundly on the facts of what they saw. Yes, they stood against Saint Bernadette until the miracles began to flow. It was then that they started to believe, and as unbelievable as it seems, their belief at first centered on the profits reaped from the visiting pilgrims. The suffering eventually turned to Me because of the suffering of the innocent Bernadette.

My mission throughout the centuries has always been clear to you. It is the same as the mission of the Church. I have heralded the value of prayer and prudence, of humility and self-immolation. Popes and Cardinals abound who have taken seriously My call for greater holiness; and they have preached that the purpose of Christianity is not only for the Salvation of lost sinners, but that they would work together to cure the sick, and to exert their efforts for all the Spiritual and Corporal Acts of Mercy. It is all about this Mercy that the Lord was crucified. He set out to unite Heaven and Earth by His public ministry, and His Crucifixion was the capstone above this Foundation of Love. History has shown that redemption follows the path of purity and righteousness. One can find the Promised Land by denying himself and taking-up the crosses in life that are laid upon him. The converted human soul can be discovered beyond the parameters of this Earth by living with the expectation that the whole of Heaven sees his every act. This is not necessarily a predestination of the soul, but its journey, its walk of life toward the Land of the Living. My Special son, you and your brother have been fortunate to know these things for many decades; and you have not been alone. You have shared the same faith and knowledge that billions of Christians before you have known. Would I as the Mother of God not be remiss if I did not celebrate them, raise them before the exiled world as Saints so many times in My messages to you? Would it not be unfair if I had not hailed them as heroes and conquerors in Jesus when they lived preeminently in His Divine Light for the whole of their years? I stand with them now as they bask in this Light! You have pondered universes never discovered; the history of men has proved that this is the one that matters most to God. You are living what will be revealed as awesome times of miraculous revelation because this is the way it was written. You and your brother, and all who believe in Jesus have been given vision that is widely unknown to those who refuse to believe. This is not something new that I am telling you. It is far and above what most mortal men are willing to embrace. They are oftentimes their own obstacles. They wish to walk with the sight of new birth in their minds, but they are unwilling to open their eyes. This has been the way of the world for thousands of years.

My Special one, this is the reason it has taken so long to bring humanity into these times. It has required the history of the ages, the birthing and development of throngs and choices, the teaching of the chosen ones who would create themselves a record of human achievement according to the Gospels that must be seen by those who are living now. The millions who have traveled to My shrines have come for many reasons, to know their Savior better, to procure physical and mental healing, to lay before their Mother their cares about those they love. I intercede for them and ask Jesus to answer their prayers; and He does so according to the Will of God. We have spoken about books and manuscripts, of poetry and music, of sonnets and reprises, and these are the renderings of inspirited men. They are all good when they lift-up the Son of Man in a way that dignifies His Glory here on Earth and sustains the faith of the masses. Hence, it is in this age of new devices that such people as you and your brother have composed and presented your Marian works to humanity. It has all been a stage of development and attainment, of pondering and reacting. You have walked with faith the same way the Original Apostles agreed to accompany Jesus on His sojourn from place to place. There was tremendous selflessness in what they achieved. Its echo is still heard here in your day. They knew that they needed to embrace what Jesus told them, even to their own mortal demise. As this is not the calling of others who serve in His Holy Name, that they would be martyred in the flesh, it remains true that anyone who suffers or is persecuted while preaching the Gospel is spiritually martyred for the good of the Cross. You have known personally untold people who have offered this gift to God. Remember them with gladness and thanksgiving in your heart, because each of them was special. They decided in their hearts according to their value of holiness what was beautiful. Each of them created beauty; each one measured the beauty of their faith and its resultant actions according to their degree of understanding of what God wanted from them. A beautiful song or heart-touching lyric is unique to its author, and it becomes part of the sacred culture that the Church espouses and teaches every day. Indeed, it is this sacred culture that helps every Christian carry on. All who believe and work for Jesus contribute to this larger culture. They are building the Kingdom that I have spoken about so many times. If you will permit Me to say so, these are the same gifts that you and your brother have laid at the manger and the foot of the Cross with such gentleness, with such care and generosity. The whole world is filled with gifts from faithful men and women to the Christ Child, their Savior Sacrificed on the Cross.

I am pleased by the opportunity to have spoken to you here today about what you have written for your memoirs because we think about the same hopes for a world that seems to be drifting away. I assure you that it cannot drift so far that it cannot be found again. The whole of the seas can be placed into one teardrop of the Son of Man. He realized the pressures and distractions of the world. The Lord God has embraced the same beauty that you have written about, the same individuality of His creatures, the same tenor of confidence by which you live. He knew about the courage of the Martyrs before they ever laid-down their lives. Through the Holy Spirit, He provided for what they would say. He penned their final speeches and valedictory addresses. Jesus has elicited the applause of the Hosts of Heaven from God-loving people here and now. He gives them the inspiration and holiness to achieve their goals on His behalf. This is what He has done for you and your brother through Me."

Sunday, December 20, 2009
9:38 a.m.

"You have come, My children, to Christmas week, and the grand blessings of Heaven will again fall upon the holy. To be sure, you know that you are among them, that you have feasted on the sacrifices of the Saints to make your lives complete, that Jesus has blessed you with profound graciousness in a nation that is so lacking in poise, and that everything we have worked for will come to pass because of these things. Christmas. You have known untold miracles that cannot overshadow its peace. I bring you this peace every time I appear here. I call you to shed the burdens in your minds and those that oppress your spirits, and then you will know what it means to prepare Emmanuel room. My Special son, the Lord's peace comes to you and your brother with vindicating Love. History cannot overshadow the eternity of blessings that you have procured for the world. Sinful mortals cannot impugn your magnanimous work. The tides of time cannot remove

the Grace that I have built into your holy mission for the conversion of the lost. We have seen together many Christmas feasts. You have knelt to pray during every one, all of which you dedicated to Me, so that human arrogance will be destroyed, the unborn will be birthed, the hungry will be fed, the homeless will be sheltered, and the Truth will prevail over the glut of humanity's lies. I ask you to remember that Christmas is the time when many souls are allowed entrance into Heaven from Purgatory. Your prayerful life with your brother the whole year through is the preface to this fact. I will speak to you today with the strains of the peace in which I come. You have given the world another tremendous prologue for your next book because you are open to receive the Holy Spirit. I need not repeat here today how grateful Jesus is for your loyalties to Him. We have long spoken about your years dedicated to the mission of the Church and the purification of the Earth. Yes, it is true that I often come filled with accolades because you have earned the praises of the Father. You must remember that I speak in lofty terms about your contributions because you are raising the weak from their lowly places beneath their own dignity, lifting them from the gutters of the world where they have been cast by the haughty who do not care. You have dignified your brother in ways that others have refused, and for this you have gained the highest Heaven anyone shall ever see.

When I speak about the 'touch' of Christmas, I refer to the moment when the Father sent the Archangel Gabriel to Me, and of My carrying the Messiah in My Womb, and giving Him birth in Bethlehem. I knew the moment that Jesus was conceived in My Womb. It was an instant of ecstasy that no one has ever felt before. In spite of what some theologians have proclaimed, I was utterly aware of what was happening to Me. I was a vessel filled with joy to be the first to touch the Sacred Heart of the Savior of the world. Imagine, during the time when Jesus grew in My Womb, the Sacred Heart was beating inside the same flesh as My Immaculate Heart. We were united there. I was feeding Him as He was nourishing Me. We were inseparable, and we remain inseparable to this day. And, what about this probing beauty that had come upon humankind? What did the Lord ask of men when He was born so uninvited? He was not requisitioned from any king or court of law. His Kingdom existed far from the secular throes of suffering men. It was God who chose to be here in one Man. I was there, I remember. I have pertinent knowledge that an invitation was being made by a God that no one had seen to recognize His beauty in a Son that could be seen. God sent an example of Himself, an Incarnation of His offspring, a teacher and benefactor, a servant and perfect sufferer. He laid-out His Plan for the Redemption of His people in a manger that was as carefully prepared as the ground upon which He would walk. Indeed, the Father knew twenty centuries ago that the world was in need of the renewal that would also renew the whole of Creation from that day. We have prayed about this, My Special son, and we have wept in gladness over what those who have been converted finally came to know. We have seen setbacks in those who have questioned My motives, but they will all be believers in the end. This awareness is coming to everyone alive; they are breaking out of their shells of ignorance and indifference by the hour. Many are yet young in comprehending My role in the Salvation of humanity; they are much like pullets that have yet to know where they are. I reissue My pledge today that your work has not been in vain. I likewise promise that everything you have given to God will be glorified before Creation and vindicated in the eyes of those in doubt.

It has been like a metal filing to a magnet. Jesus was attracted to the Earth because He knew that this was where His mission would be completed. It did not end at the conclusion of His ministry, it was ratified during the Paschal Mysteries. To this day, He works diligently through His disciples, explicating, clarifying, enlightening, admonishing, blessing, healing, mending, overseeing, shielding, comforting, and sharing. We have known this role in the context of the Church since I gave birth to the Head of the Church. We have thought about the sacred possibility that every soul given the breath of life could be touched by the Crucifixion in the same way that Jesus touches the center of the human heart. We have dreamed about days and years to come when there will be no more addictions to material or lust, no more drive to compete with the neighbor, no need for jurists and jails, and certainly no venue for secular palaver to prevail in the public domain.

I once told you that Jesus was born to extinguish secularism altogether. Imagine a world in which the Catholic Church is the center-point of all human endeavors, that all efforts night and day are in preparation for the Second Coming of the Son of Man. He came through Me the first time, and I will bring Him back again. And, just as I meticulously prepared the manger to hold the Son of the Most High, I am preparing the Earth to receive Him once more. We have come very far in that mission, My son. I ask you this Christmas to credit yourself for the wholeness of this gift. Whether you choose to believe it or not, My success here has had everything to do with you and your brother. You have been given to each other by God so that His Kingdom could be spread, and if that sounds self-serving, then this is the way it shall be. While the Father is gracious and giving, He has used you and your brother to advance His own cause.

And, how could it be warm on Christmas Eve when all accounts have told of the inclemency of the day? The same way that you feel spiritual warmth when you hear of good news or when someone is nice to you. How could there be Light in the middle of the night? Because Creation was dimmed by the presence of the King. Nothing can compete with the brilliance of God. If men wince beneath the presence of the noonday sun, they will be driven to their knees before the brilliance of the returning Man-God from Heaven. The weight of human sin is heavier than physical gravity. This is the burden that plagues them the most. It is unseen because it stains the souls of sinners, but its effects can be seen by their victims who are afflicted. You are told about such things as hope, peace, love, and all the virtues that provide the fragrance of redemption to the far corners of the globe. These things are mainly invisible to the eye, but their effects are discernable to anyone, anywhere, no matter the time. We speak of these virtues with the backdrop of those who have passed into history, the likes of Pope Pius XII and John Paul II. It is almost too preposterous a prospect for someone to posit in a question as to whether they led virtuous lives. Of course they did. And, their virtues remain with you, upon and in you. They are seamlessly united with the sacredness of Jesus who is equally within you, and about you, to provide all the strength you require to take you to your elder years. Humanity must realize that welcoming the Prince of Peace means to be thankful that He was born, deferring to His Word, obedient to His mandates, and humble that each of you were chosen to accept. Perfection begins in these things, My Special son. There are some who are 'more perfect' than others, if that seems somehow possible. But, you know what I mean. Acceptance is the greatest degree of perfection that a human being can attain—graciously knowing that whatever happens in this life can be faced with the courage of the Cross. You remember that God does not always provide pathways strewn with roses, but with coarseness and division, with enemies afoot and overhead, and with darkness and doubt. He does not send all of these because they are the effects of sinful men, but He allows whatever happens for the glory of His Son. Even the holocausts served a purpose in evangelizing the Crucifixion.

Born to humanity in a manger so many years ago was the opportunity for everyone given life to be as gentle and generous as the Lord who manifests that life. When all is said and done, the whole of the universes will see that God selected this sphere in the void of outer-space to stand His Son upright and dare take humanity to task. He chose this place to prove that what Adam and Eve committed in the Garden could be reversed. It was by Jesus' birth that God instilled in all men the ability to become innocent again. It was through His Holy Sacrifice that humanity has the venue to prove that they accept. These sacred mysteries will last until the end of time. They eclipse the knowledge of human genius and have defied every attempt of refutation. How could it be that such a simple concept that the birth of a Child could overwhelm every action of billions of people through thousands of years? How could it be true that one whimpering Child could drown-out the malicious roaring of every malevolent monster? Because He is Divine Love. Because He is evidence of the creative genius of the Deity in a single human being. He is thrice-blessed to be one Salvation to a people who will die only once. This is why men speak of a 'good death.' A good death places the capstone on a virtuous life. It means relinquishing the human will to the Father and the Son with the Holy Spirit at peace in the heart. It means living the greatest amount of years for Love, in the Church, toward the horizon of Eternity, and with emphasis on caring for the poor. A good death means that one accepts the New Life in the New World that comes upon those who have served Jesus well. There are many evidentiary signs that someone is on track to a good death. The main indication is that a heart must say, 'Your Will, not mine, O Lord.' A good death means that one accepts the Nativity of Jesus with hope and anticipation, with simplicity and not consumerism. A good death means that one lives a life of perfect poise the way it is preserved in the Sacred Scriptures. And finally, a good death begins when someone becomes old enough to know that their baptism means that they will always be alive, no matter if they remain in or out of the flesh of their own birth.

I pray that My children live many decades. I ask Jesus to provide for them and protect them to be His disciples in the world long into their 80s. I ask all My children to be self-preserving while at the same time being servants themselves. This, My Special son, is the reason I ask you to continue to protect yourself against all the aggressive viruses that are found in the Midwest, and to be careful when you drive and where you go to eat. You have been doing well. It is imperative that you remember how pleased I am with you. I have asked you two main things in 2009. Never be petty about matters of the world. And, always remember that the amendments to humanity must come through the behest of your prayers, that many issues that seem so controversial have nothing to do with what you may have done or not done. Remember to place in your memoirs someday that I always told you that the world is not about you. It is about everyone else, all of your energies focused on making life better for the weak and helpless. Always protracting your thoughts away from what you believe you need if those needs are not in communion with the life of Jesus Christ. I have tried to impress upon you in 2009 that there will not be enough time left before the Second Coming of Jesus for Me to say through My messengers and seers everything I wish to declare about the cultivation of the Earth. Nowhere in history have I said as much as I have to you. The second-most lengthy conversations I had for decades with Sister Lucia."

"Litter and debris imply waste; shards and fragments imply destruction; suffering and death imply redemption."

— William Roth Jr.

The Night of All Remembering
Preface to a Memoir

"Jesus is the procurer of our wisdom and the fashioner of our courage. He comes to us bearing the hallmark of all the lifetimes that will providentially conclude in Him. The chastity of the soul is our ultimate signpost whereupon is conferred our redemption as Christ himself has inscribed His Crucifixion on the breastplate of our hearts. If ever we dare question this fact, let it be only to reasses what more we should do. Why not pray with more passion? Why not believe that there are statelier measures than the changing of the seasons? Why not see each new day as a gateway to the exculpation of our faults by which we defer to the Kingdom of God? Why not downplay our desires in favor of His? Why not become ourselves a new humanity?"

A couple of hours before midnight, across the Atlantic Ocean on a Yugoslavian mountainside, the 14th of August 1989, in the company of tens of thousands of people gathered from the far corners of the globe, I stood before the majesty of the heavens come to Earth. There beneath the veil of a communist night at the first blush of emancipating grace, I encountered the Morning Star presiding over the dawn; a beatific illumination marshaled to humankind by the merciful hand of God. In the glory of that spiritual convocation, the Mother of Jesus Christ revealed Herself, descending from the mystical vaults of Paradise to an impoverished parcel of the world, choosing the obscure and unseen to be the beneficiaries of Her immaculate beauty—and I was there. Medjugorje, a small hamlet in Bosnia-Herzegovina of the former Yugoslavia, has been honorably distinguished in the ages as being blessed by heavenly visitation, and will be hailed in the historical strains of human memory as the centerpiece of the final transformation of contemporary man. That Medjugorian night on the Vigil of the Feast of the Assumption of Mary marked the fulcrum of my life; the demarcation between who I was and what I now will always be—a son, a progeny of a Queen, heir to a Kingdom, and a warrior for a Divinity to which I will always strive. If there can be a grave and being drawn forth from it, or a womb opening to process life into the hands of day, I am among the fortunate ones who have come forth from the dungeon of indifference, from that terminal sleep of omission into a vibrant immortal awakening to the reality of God. My sentiments and devotions have been roused from beneath the pall of inexcusable darkness to be donned in the robes of royalty by a Universal Queen. She has directed my spiritual maturity from the mortal vestibule of existence into the liberating brilliance of divine life in the Sacred Heart of Creation's Messianic King. I have been asked by this beautiful Virgin Mother to manifest within these simple memoirs the dynamic vision that She has composed and sustains in my life, doing so without personal grandiosity or in any relation to myself being a child prodigy or spiritual savant with some kind of over-inflated authority. She wishes instead that I reveal that I am simply a person like any other; a child with a soft heart that has been burdened from birth by a veil of distractions and choices, pummeled like any other, vulnerable to weakness and injury, and liable to misstep, but nonetheless, inherently capable of sound judgement in matters of the conscience. My soul has been providentially cultured with a receptivity to the miraculous overtures from Heaven that are both maturing to the heart of humankind and ultimately unifying at the pinnacle of our common destiny in Christ Jesus. I have pondered deeply what format might be most beneficial for this exposition of my more personal thoughts, perspectives and recollections; and I am not sure it even matters. Nonetheless, my hope is to provide a revelatory contrast where everyone might find their own identification with Jesus and Our Lady in reflection of my own. On the one hand, I understand how difficult it may be to protect an accurate portraiture of the landscape of my life from the irrational distortions heaped upon paladins by sentimentalists; but on the other, I hope to find a balanced arrangement between the burdensome nature of life that each of us endures and the stratospheric vision composed by the Holy Spirit within those children who would be faithful to the King of kings. I wish to be sufficiently intimate to both sides of the fulcrum of that night on Apparition Hill in the former Yugoslavia so that where I stand now may be contrasted with the simple roots of my life which wholly reflect my commonness with the entire body of humanity. I wish that the chasmic gulf which characterizes mankind's detachment from the heavens in our contemporary age be closed. Whether the description of our lives can be differentiated between being blind and given sight, being asleep and awakening, or existing merely as an inconspicuous member of humankind then being given life as a unique child of consequential divinity, I nonetheless experienced the eternal word that reverberates toward each of us through the darkness of our interior solitude. In the flash of its utterance, it told me that life was not some trek of loneliness and separation whereby our existence is without purpose, ultimate revelation, and finally eternal reward. A simple bit of knowledge was deposited into my being from outside the parameters of who I believed myself to be, which then exploded into a transformative power that produced two effects. First, its audible presence definitively shoved to the side and then extinguished decades of relative uncertainty that could no longer sustain itself in the presence of the Truth that had revealed itself within me. A veil was drawn from before the eyes of my soul; distraction and distended confusion were vaporized in an instant of concrete clarity whose life-giving effusions I carry to this day. The interior competition and disarray vanished as if burned away by a galactic blow-torch of a million suns. Interiorly, the battle was won at the outset because personified victory had appeared on the battlefield. I went from helplessness to power, and despondent defeat to certain triumph in the blink of Heaven's grace. And, it is this realization that produced the secondary effect. All that was within me, the better part of my nature, my heart of hearts, the entire deposit of goodness that had been inculcated into my soul during my upbringing came alive all at once. It stood up proudly, inhaled a deep breath of beatific identity, and moved with commanding authority into the dominant position of my interior influence and balance. I went from traitor to warrior in the ranks of the King without hesitation or second-thought because I knew all was forgiven by this Lord of Heaven who wanted nothing but the joy of loving me. It was as if a lording oppressor had been banished from my soul by a great power that would tolerate it no longer; and ironically, I realized in that instant that this oppressor veiling my perception of nearly every perspective that I possessed was my own selfish will. It was not that I was inherently speaking a foreign language detrimental to a correct understanding of God in my life. I was reading authentic words as a Roman Catholic, but I suddenly had access to the dictionary of all those words with the additional realization of the audible inflections of each syllable as our God speaks the language of life. Yes, this is a basic analogy. Imagine no one knowing how to speak English audibly, but we can read fluently. Then, one day a person arrives with a dictionary who can speak the language; who knows all the meanings, conjugations, pronunciations and linguistic inflections. This is the spiritual realms of faith that opened to me. This is the phenomenon or transposition that I experienced —as though I was deaf and could sign, but then could suddenly hear and talk clearly.

Sunday, August 2, 2009
Our Lady, Queen of Angels

"My Special son, it was twenty years ago this month that you embarked on your journey to Medjugorje that changed your way of thinking about the intercessions of God and about your role in the conversion of lost sinners to the Glory of Jesus' Resurrection. Twenty years. Where did they go?* I have them. Jesus has them. God the Father has them. He gave them to you, and you handed them back to Him with good measure and humble service. My children, you must always remember that your lives are a gift from the Heart of God for you to honor and esteem Him. You are not mandated to conquer the world as magnates and kings, but as simple servants of the Cross through which all creatures have been redeemed. Today, My

Special and Chosen ones, I have come to bless you in the dignity that you have shown the Child Jesus and the gratitude that you have shown Jesus Crucified. He will remember you when He comes into His Kingdom, and even before will He grant you the blessings you desire. I ask you not to dwell on how swiftly time seems to be passing, but to realize that your lives are a process toward an event, your redemption in the Cross, that is worth the wait of a thousand lifetimes. Even as you read the pages and reams of My messages from the past 18 years, you are amazed that you have been able to capture them into verifiable documents for history and eternity. This has been no small achievement. I seek your prayers today for the millions who do not understand the value and purpose of life, for those who are committed to teaching the Gospel message without recognition, and for all who tend to the sick and dying. They are uniquely blessed individuals in the eyes of the Lord, and He asks that you elevate them before the Son with respect and appreciation. You have led them to the Cross by your imitation of His life and promises; and for this, you shall inherit fortunes yet unrevealed to the physical Earth. There is no selfishness in you, and everything you promised My Son upon your Confirmation has been kept through the authenticity of your faith. Today, the Angels are with you in a special way because of their awareness beside Me on this date, and you have in you the power of the Holy Spirit to realize their advocacy in the protection of the Church. This is also the anniversary of the date on which the western hemisphere was forced into altercation in Iraq, thus setting the stage for the thesis of many of My messages and prophesies. You have liberated another Middle Eastern country, but the United States has yet to free itself from its imprisonment to lust and materialism. My Special son, I have not the words to tell you and your brother how you are admired for finishing My new millennium anthologies. You have not sacrificed your joy to take the Gospel to the masses. You and your brother have bountiful, explorative, innovative, humble, unifying hearts that know the Truth of Christianity as well as anyone else in the world. We will see that everyone who needs to hear My messages does so; and whether they exercise their own will to believe what I have to say is a matter between themselves and God. We can only enlighten them about the imperative nature of these times in the course of Salvation history. As you review My messages, you can see that we have taken this important theme to them in amplifying ways.

I wish not to diminish the reason I have come to speak to you today, but I must for a moment exclaim on behalf of Jesus and Saint Joseph that the way you repaired your brother's office chair is utterly amazing. There is not another person on Earth who would have spent as much time focused on one chair as you did this one. It is indicative of your drive to complete any mission that you undertake. Indeed, you are correct. He did not break it. It was a product of the way capitalism tries to provide the cheapest product for the most money. Greed broke the chair, the same way that it has broken your nation. It is clear that the Chair of Saint Peter will address the fractured condition of America and the world. Thank you also for attending your brother to the baseball game. The teams are an interesting collection of talent, but it is true that the antics of all the other entertainment at the event was just outright good fun. You have been having fair and cooler weather where you live because of the cyclical nature of the climate. This has been ongoing for thousands of years. It is amazing that so many people hypothesize about such things as having local causes, ones that they attribute to the works of man more than the specifics of the solar system. I am not suggesting that pollution to the air and water are not serious, but they have yet to cause the dramatic shifts in climate that are being discussed by many around the world. You are absolutely right that these are not as important as the spiritual deficits of humanity. There are more immediate issues for world leaders to address than what is occurring at the polar ice caps. We have shifted their attention to the plight of the poor, the excesses of human corruption, and the need for lost sinners to repent and obey the teachings of the Church. Jesus looks at the Earth through the lens of His own Crucifixion. Here where you live and the future you have charted give Him reason for gladness, for knowing in His Heart that His Mother is indeed a Queenly Intercessor for those He came to redeem. Humanity is prone to mistakes, but they can make no mistake about My desire to help them. I wish for you to remember what you gave to Me twenty years ago in Medjugorje besides your heart. You gave Me new hope for the American people, new reason to believe that My adopted children can change, new enlivenment in My intention to keep trying to reach them until all of them hear. Your faith and sincerity in Medjugorje retroactively comforted My Heart on Good Friday, especially when My Crucified Son was laid on My lap. I can now look back at that moment knowing that you stood for life in the presence of His Death. Your love is as resilient as His; your determination to never surrender a soul to the netherworld is just as sound. These are gifts you have given Me that would not have come if you had not answered the call of the Holy Spirit to visit the Saint James church twenty years ago. And, when you said yes to God again in February 1991, you sealed the contract between yourself and the Son of Man, effectively guaranteeing that you would never walk away from that calling to which you have since dedicated every day of your life. And, the prayers that you and your brother pray together emphasize your commitment to the conversion of the lost and the return of prodigal men to the bosom of the Church. When you see all of these things from the other side of time, you will surely know that all Providence has visited you, and that you and your brother were united for God to propagate His Will in ways heretofore unknown in the United States of America. Think about the actual cost of human hope. Do men on Earth expend anything other than their days and years to reach the pinnacle of ecstasy that comes upon their last breaths? Must they burn their joy like firewood to keep these hopes alive, or is it possible to be a happy Christian in the world today? I say that you can retain your joy because of everything I have said to you and your brother in more than 18 years. You have known about the outcome of the existence of man; you have given your life and hours to prove it. Your faith that has been tested countless times has always proved stronger than anything that has tried to impugn it. All the holy men and women who have lived throughout the ages have left in your hands the fruits of their works, and you have harvested them for the present-day Earth to consume. It is a nourishing feast of Truth and consolation that you are feeding them, and you are sowing new seeds for your successors as well. I promise that these successors will be fewer in number than those who have already passed.

You have read the entire AD 2006-2008 anthology of My messages again, and you have a sense for the way it builds into the crescendo that you have called the 'urgency of the message.' If all the world will do the same, nations and peoples will become more holy; they will come to the Church and receive the redemptive Sacraments about which you have written and I have spoken. After all, the Salvation of lost sinners is the reason you are praying right now. It has never really been about your being closer to God than others, or that you have sought favoritism from Me. Your goals have always been tended toward changing those who are ugly on the inside into the beauty of the Paradisial Garden. You must, My Special son, believe that you will be successful along with the Church. Never mind wondering when or if it will happen during your mortal years. You have already reached the heights that Jesus spoke about in the Sermon on the Mount. I continue to tell you to expect miracles in your lifetime because this is what all men of good will should expect. I am a miracle; your faith is another miracle, and every conversion to the Cross is a miracle that you will reap by your dedication to My Son.

Something you should work on, however, is how to respond to people. There will be an utter landslide of scandalous questions to attempt to discredit your work. You will be heckled and ridiculed, rejected, socially indicted, labeled as heretics, lambasted with accusations of devil worship, and on and on. I will attempt to defer this as long as possible, but it will eventually come."

I told Her that I was unafraid.

"I know that you are unafraid, but you must be prepared."

I asked, "How can I best prepare?"

"I will answer that question with the most important response that I have ever given a living human being. Reject your own pride. Do not believe that even in all you have done for Me and your devotion to the Church that

you are worthy of an ounce of respect. Do not anticipate being welcomed like prophets, but be prepared to endure the scoffing of assailants that will make the public demonstrations in Iran and America look like picnics in the park. Yes, there will be plenty of people in the world who will support you, but they will be vastly outnumbered. I will do My best to try to prepare you for the onslaught that Jesus has thus far shielded you from. Your workplace has been a dose of that preparation, but only about one in a thousand as ugly. Your works are capable of standing on their own."

* - Our Holy Mother was touching my heart in a special way with the words She chose today. This is part of Her closeness with me. The phrase "Twenty years. Where did they go?," is a maternal allusion to a line out of one of my favorite songs by Bob Seger, "Like a Rock."

When my brother Timothy and I made our pilgrimages to Medjugorje in 1989, we sensed that our previous lives were meant to pass into history. We were touched by the Holy Spirit, and our minds began to focus on the miracles of God and His agendum for the transformation of the Earth. Upon returning, we found that life was devoid of the miraculous overtones we felt in Saint James parish because almost no one around us knew of its existence or could accept into their perception the transcending magnitude of such a supernatural event. Divine intervention has been evacuated from the sensibilities of the intellectual modern man. Our Lady's mission is such a contradiction to our humanistic temporal mind-set. Nonetheless, She wishes to encourage our state of affairs into a beatific relationship between Herself and Her children until that last reticent child succumbs to Her grace. She comes with special blessings for humanity so that our hearts and spirits would commence an immersion of the Earth with the fruits of the spiritual labors that She initiates. We have spent years conversing with the Mother of the Lord on Her terms, shouldering the yoke of responsibility for transferring Her perfect sentiments into the greater world. And still, She continues to teach about the ways of men, of the hope by which millions have lived throughout the ages, and what made that hope real. The Most Blessed Virgin's purpose is to remain with Her children until the Father says that we have finished, and the reason is to instill in us the grand vision to which the Roman Catholic Church has ascribed for twenty centuries in the face of all opposition. She is instilling a vision of future Glory into the present day world of man, and it is our willingness to believe through a courageous faith that informs us about the manifestations of God in the here and now, and in our Afterlife, and in all the eternities and histories ever spoken about by angels and contemplative men. There are obviously more questions than answers about human existence, and no one is immune to the natural curiosities about the Church, the Will of the Father, the meditations that move Him most, the treatment of the lost and unfortunate in a world of plenty, and all the rest. Our Lady's dialogue is about assuring us that Jesus hears every word we utter to Him, and each one is blessed because speaking to Him implies a living faith residing in us, seeking the betterment of all facets of our existence. We cannot offend Him or bring Him sorrow or pain by explaining how our hearts feel. If He sees discomfort in us, He will bring us peace, if we allow it to come. There are mystical reasons for everything that the Blessed Virgin has asked us to do, and there are likewise practical applications that deal with our spiritual growth. She wishes us to never feel alienated from Her; to please open our hearts to Her in every way, and She will tell us everything about which She has become aware as the Queen of Love. Even as She is the Mediatrix of all Graces from Heaven, the Father owns certain wishes and motivations that will be known solely to Him until the Return of Jesus in Glory. We must remember that no matter the stupendous nature of Our Lady's station, She is not part of the Most Blessed Trinity, hence She shares a great deal in common with us as being also a created human being. Yet, She does have access to the center of Truth and the Seat of Wisdom as the Matriarch of Wisdom; therefore, we should feel free to ask Her whatever we wish in matters of faith and morals from the platform of our deepest prayers. Through

Her, the heavens seek from us a perfect life, no matter what anyone believes to the contrary. But, it is a perfect life that is beautifully human. We are exiled from Heaven due to the failures of Adam, and we have been told the story of the redemption of humanity. Our Lady helps us be stronger people, as Christians, and also more patient and calming, more goal-oriented and directing, and peaceful of heart. She helps build our self-confidence in issues affecting our heart, self-image, and strength in the societies of the Earth.

Saturday, October 3, 2009
Virgin Mary

"My little children, you are both so holy and likeable, and you know that the Father has deigned that His people should change from their errant ways before it is too late. My purposes are to touch those who are far from God, to awaken My faithful children to the awesome graces that are about to come to you. You will see your enemies vanquished by the power of the Cross. I have altered the tone of My messages to assist in adapting humanity, that they will look at My messages to you and recognize Me in them. I come to repeat the fact that My appreciation for you and admiration of you are overwhelming. You look at the world with much greater hope than you did before I came speaking to you, but you also realize that the will of your brothers and sisters is oftentimes contrary to that of the Father. I have asked all My messengers worldwide to exercise patience while He reaches them through My miraculous touch. I do not mean to frighten anyone through My messages, but to express the concerns and matters that must be addressed. Every generation has its responsibility to renew the holiness that leaves when former generations die. This has been the mission of the Church for centuries. You have given Jesus your greatest amount of good hours. I am duly honored that you commit your acts to Me, that you remember that all suffering is redeemed in the Cross, and that you have the patience that I have requested to see this journey through."

The Queen of Heaven daily offers good wishes upon our wholesome memories to the delight of the Angels who have supported us through the years. She appreciates our welcoming Her into our presence each time we pray for the conversion of anyone whose will contradicts the Will of God. Our intentions become Her intentions. She has spoken to humanity across the ages about the fusion of our intentions with the prerogatives of the Father so that our work always tends toward the accomplishment of the common good that serves the Church and makes the world more holy. During these years of revelation, She has brought humanity an enlightenment that it requires to realize that Jesus is with us in charismatic terms. She has given us reason to believe in miracles from Heaven again, and the extraordinary manifestations that emanate Light that we would not otherwise have recognized as signs from our Heavenly Father. There is a significant amount of practical power that comes with our faith in that we advance the common good by our regular daily chores. When Jesus says that we are called to feed His sheep, He means both spiritually and physically. We give them the Word of Life to keep their faith alive, and offer them the food from our tables to nourish their bodies as they grow in time. We know, therefore, that our faith is embodied not only in what we pray for, but in our manual labors that uplift the poor in seeable and discernable ways. Our Christian faith is a testament of action fortified by eternal vision that makes us practitioners of the Word of the Lord to the ends of the Earth, willing into being by our own allegiance to the Cross a better world for all who suffer. Millions who have no knowledge of human Salvation ask, "Why the Cross?" Why does God allow certain circumstances to exist and forces that seem to oppose His Kingdom to prevail, at least temporarily? Why do certain victims die in reckless accidents, and their families and friends inquire why their Guardian Angels did not protect them? Our Lady has given the reason. They are required to live prayerfully, soundly, safely, and intelligently about issues that tend to place human life and limb in peril. If they refuse to do so, they testify wrongly to onlookers and survivors that Jesus does not truly care about their welfare and safety. A great deal of bitterness against the Lord is manifested because someone was either injured or killed in an accident, such as a house fire, and those who loved the victims blame God for someone else's sins of commission or omission, whether it be sloth which produced faulty machinery or greed which generated unsafe heating systems. And, it is even more bewildering that the children of God would lift prayers for their personal safety, then climb into racing machines and drive them over 200 miles per hour for the sake of entertainment.

This can be taken to an even more enlightening plateau. Even as we know that nothing is impossible with God, how should we respond to someone who says that a minister prayed for another twenty years of life, but was found dead on the floor of his office three months later? Did God not hear his prayers, therefore He does not exist at all? Yet, the minister ate a horrible diet and refused any suggestions about a lifestyle that would lend to a longer life, then prayed for twenty more years as if he had no part in the request. What do we suppose such things as this do to those who oppose the existence of God? As a practical matter, the minister should have accepted his part in bringing himself to such ill health; that is the first thing. The second and most important is that he should also have known by reason of Scripture that most people live 70 years, and longer only if they are strong. This is suggested in the same Holy Word that he professed to preach. The larger ramification of this is not whether he did not protect his health or whether he did not live to be 90 years old, but what his lack of spiritual reason did to those who looked to him for wisdom and counsel. He did not receive the fruits of his prayers, some say, because he was not in touch with God after all. And, what of all the television evangelists who have received millions of dollars from impressionable and needy human souls who thought their contributions would suffice for their repentance before the Father? The answer is that they were still separated from the Sacraments that foster their reunion into the Paradise to which they aspire. Our Lady has said there exists a stark contrast between the people mentioned and the Roman Catholic Church. The Church is not considered to be evangelical, but instead a mystical body of evangelizers, for a specific reason. It is mainly because it is the Holy Spirit that calls lost souls to the Cross, made tangible and communicable through the Holy Mass, and not any one preaching person whose message is devoid of those Sacraments. There are many ministers who speak to their congregations as if they are talking to people who have not yet been converted. The reason they do so is because the Holy Spirit within tells them they are looking at people who are empty. The heart and mind know that something is missing, but they do not yet know that it is the Manna of Life. Those ministers cannot put their finger on the vacuum they see before them every week. There is no concentric Bread of Life in churches separated from the Original Catholic and Apostolic Church; and this is the emptiness they see, the void that all of them recognize in one another as non-Catholics. Anyone can be a nice, caring, sharing person, even those who do not believe in God. However, being congenial and sharing does not make someone a Christian. Further, being a Christian in name does not make someone Catholic. The point in all this is the one that all the Popes, priests, Martyrs, and mystics throughout the centuries have attempted to prove; that without the Holy Sacrifice of the Mass, there can be no true allegiance to the Cross, no understanding of redemptive suffering united with the Cross, and no vision into the glorious reward of dying with Jesus Christ. The Holy Mass is the centerpiece of the Crucifixion that has saved those who believe; hence the dichotomy between vision and blindness, light and darkness, and unity and division. True Christianity is Roman Catholicism circumscribed by all who are in allegiance to the Vicar of Christ in Rome. In this, it is not those who simply recognize who he is, or who consider him a good person and the like, but all who acknowledge that he is the Holy See for the world on behalf of Heaven, and all who take the necessary steps to convert to Catholicism of their own accord. This is the witness of my brother Timothy who experienced the transcending majesty of the Apostolic heritage pulsing and consuming him on Christmas Eve 1977 through the power of the Holy Mass. He attended the Banquet of the Living with me that night, but as a non-Catholic he was not fed; he did not take Holy Communion. His soul knew that it had reached the healing springs where his thirst for the Lord would be quenched, but he was not allowed to drink. And, history records the rest of the story in his conversion and subsequent calling by the heavens to witness and suffer for the conversion of mankind through the miraculous intercession of the Morning Star Over America. Our Lady repeats over and again this pathway to glory through the Church of Rome because She wishes to reassert Her commitment to all Her children to lead humanity to the Feast Table of the Lord while there is still time. This is the witness; this is our witness; this is the testimony of two millennia of Saints. And, our portion is the suffering that Satan heaps upon those who proclaim this unvarnished Truth. He despises anyone who augments his defeat. He slanders and mocks those who bear this Truth because he wants everyone to believe that our alignment with the teachings of the Original Apostolic Church will do nothing more than drive us away from God's favor at the point of his sword. Satan is unequivocally wrong. He is the master of deceit and the merchant of hatred.

To underscore the reason for these thoughts, I refer again to the teachings about human suffering of all the Pontiffs throughout the last two-thousand years. Non-Catholic preachers and all who think like them have never drawn the connection between suffering and the sanctification of humanity through our seamless unity with Christ Crucified in the Most Blessed Sacrament from the Altar. They believe that they should dress in their best clothing on Sundays and gather to sing and pray as though they are shielded from any of the pain that took Jesus to His death. And, for the most part, Satan leaves them alone because he knows that they have hardly any power to convert lost sinners to Salvation in the Cross and make reparation for the sins of their peers. Although She loves all Her children to every end, Our Lady has said the Protestant churches and all others who oppose the Roman Catholic

Church do veritably nothing to purify the world in the ways Jesus commands. This is clear by the way we see them backslapping one another in their so-called sanctuaries and in public places where they gather. They have a sort of blind ignorance about them that is lacking in the Wisdom taught by the Saints about reparative suffering. These statements of the truth are not about derision of anyone or trying to force negative thoughts into anyone's minds about them. It is rather a manifestation of reality from the perfect perspective of God who is the Truth above every mortal man; a Truth that humanity desperately needs to know to be inspired to change for the better, notwithstanding the sacrificial repercussions that must be endured. Those outside the Catholic Church do not understand fasting, and they also have a skewed vision of what Jesus told the world about the Triumph of the Cross. And, for all this discussion, the main issue at hand is that they refuse to come to their Blessed Mother because Her presence is much too Catholic for their protesting nature. As convoluted as this darkened perspective has become over the past 500 years and into the 21st century, Our Lady has told us to remember with compassion that most of these well-intentioned, yet misguided, people will go to Heaven. How? The suffering of the Roman Catholic Church will save them! The Roman Catholic Church is Christ purifying and saving the world through the hearts of His people impeccably united with His Sacred Heart at One Table in the same Sacrifice. This should be a great clarifying grace, as the spiritual focus of most all Our Lady's messages to my brother and me since 1991 have been on the unchurched, particularly those who see themselves as its active enemies, such adversaries as radical secularists, intellectuals, agnostics, feminists, and atheists. In time, it will become apparent through the varying levels of focus of all Her messages. They range from giving due praise to the Catholic faithful, rebuking disobedient Catholics, admonishing those who detest the concept of spiritualism, and bringing the awakening of the heart to the benign souls who simply do not know the difference.

Our Lady dispenses a tranquil, easy feeling about the transpiring of the harsh days of our mortal existence, knowing that all we have been accomplishing; the slow and determined changes we seek for the world, all this is happening an hour at a time. There is a sense of inevitability in everything in Christianity, especially the fact that what we despise about the Earth is dying, and all that we see as the perfecting of humanity is coming to life. This is the reason we have always referred to our mission as a harvest springtime, as contradictory as it sounds. But, Our Lady has told us much more. It has been Her abundant honor to tell us that behind the scenes, Jesus is creating the future that will hold the true "shock and awe," the rapturous inspiration for the millions wondering where they will see a final departure from the horrific evil in this world. Yes, the Church is marching onward, and all the rituals, liturgies, and prayers that touch Jesus' Sacred Heart are being conducted to the joy of the Angels. If we can see the breadth of life according to Her wise lessons, we will be better able to determine the effectiveness of its length according to the Divine Love we profess. America recently saw an airplane that was apparently landed on the surface of water after it became disabled in the air. It was not necessarily a miracle the way we acknowledge them to be, but it was an auspicious outcome to what could have been a terrible tragedy. Talent, physics, location, and opportunity brought the incident to a good ending. However, the miracle is that so many are seeing the hand of the Lord in it. For this, we are always grateful. Does it take a flock of geese or body of water to make men realize that God's intervention is accessible to even those who do not believe? The Virgin Mary has told us before that God dispatches Nature in many ways to upend and sever, to spin, wreck, realign, combust and combine. All in all, it is indeed the prayers of the faithful that manifests all such incidents. Jesus determines where these prayers will take hold, which times and places, what in the universe must be touched to help His flock believe more deeply in Him. Does it require a sparkling rainbow in the skies after the funeral of a beloved journalist, or simply a blooming flower, or a newborn baby? Yes, the stirring of the heart by the Holy Spirit happens through them all. But, Our Lady personally asked my brother and me to consider what twenty years of messages will eventually do, and a dozen works, and a New Millennium that has opened in the United States with the upbraiding of everything that closed the last century? Can we daresay that the Will of the Father is working and purifying us through our actions? If so, then we will all know in time, after each of us has fully accepted our role in His plan, that it required our collective faith in the Cross to bring the world to fruition in the perfection He so desires.

There is a thought that should soothe the reticence of anyone who has an aversion to tendering their sacrifice to the benefit of the world. Once we enter Heaven, we will have the freedom and the power to relive the sweetest moments of life again, and we will be given the joy of everything that eluded us so that we could concentrate on the Salvation of God's people. In the sacrifice, we lose nothing. We must remember the words of the Metropolitan of Lourdes who told Bernadette upon her passing that she was now in Heaven and on Earth. Indeed, she lives the New Earth. She was given the delight of her dreams. And, in our pilgrimage, Jesus will not allow anything that we do to lead us down a path of regret. This is why so many people have accused Him of not answering their prayers. He is preserving their joy, a reward filled with surprises. I can now sense the agendum of God and the synopsis of Creation as Christ unfurls it toward the destiny of His Cross. Our Lady is presently preparing to dispense this revelatory tidbit of knowledge to every soul given the breath of life; and what we do with it remains to be seen. Will we re-convert the United States of America with courageous devotion? Basically, this is why She has been appearing, to cultivate God's divine nature within us before the reckoning, to align our sentiments in preparation for the Apocalypse so that we will find something within our essence that will stand and proclaim its identification with Divine Love once all that oppresses it has been annihilated. She wishes that we not find ourselves vacant of all goodness once the veil of our lives is drawn back from the eyes of our existence.

She wishes our holy determination to rise like an invincible power in allegiance to the King of Creation. Our Lady is announcing the curtain call of mortal humanity upon the Earth through Her miraculous appearances. This moment is imminent.

Sunday, April 12, 2009
Virgin Mary

"What can I say about the indescribable beauty of the pages you have written? You have outlaid the profound holiness of your heart there, and the spirit of your own awakening in letters and sentences, admonishments for the world, and aspirations for what the future will bring. I weep happy tears instead of sorrowful ones when I read the content of your heart because I know that you belong to Me. And, this is the essence of eternal joy for all peoples. Someday, please tell them that I have said that Jesus is as satisfied that His lost brothers and sisters would come to Me as if they went directly to the Holy Cross because He knows that I will take them there Myself."

Think, dear Lord, about what we think.
See our pain with the glow of your eyes.
Bring us back from the troubled brink.
Safeguard our faith below the dark skies.
Upon your sea crest, we shall never sink.
Healed by your Sacrifice, together we rise.

-William Roth Jr.

The Roots of Our Dilemma
Religious Pluralism, Moral Relativism, Pagan Secularism

"To celebrate kindness and grace, the spirit of peace and the letter of the law, for the expungement of sins, chastity of the flesh, the purification of the soul and the advancement of wisdom: these are the things that make humanity whole, that pave the way for joy, for the truth to be told, and for righteousness to inundate the nations."

Regrettably, we look at a world that is tending toward chaos in nearly every realm of its present existence, not wishing to admit that what we most fear might actually be occurring. The spectrum of humanity's response to this descending tragedy is indeed revealing. We see our markets rip-roaring in volatility as traders frantically search for the last cent of profit for their portfolios, sensing that financial armageddon could ensue at any next moment, and hoping they have the prescient foresight to vacate the playground before the teeter-totter is displaced from its fulcrum, tossing us collectively upon the ground. Our parents send their children to be educated in America's institutions of learning, but find that they must maintain the vigilance of the world's most renowned sentinels so the character of their children is not corrupted by the swine swill of so-called progressive revolutionaries whose agendum is to depose every tenet of virtue professed for the last 5,000 years. And, on nearly every other front, these same young people must concurrently fight their own personal battles against the hedonistic influences of the progeny of the 1960s sexuality crash who could not have cared less that they were abdicating their responsibility for the future virtue of western civilization which is now collapsing under the dead weight of their licentiousness. The machinations of honorable statesmanship have ground to a halt as partisan factions battle over a second and a third agendum for America, neither the preeminent vision of God, conspicuously absent any true defense of human dignity, respect for unborn children, or deference to two millennia of moral thinking bequeathed to us by some of the greatest minds to ever ponder human existence. It seems that only in the realms of increasing our personal wealth do we strive for the highest accomplishment. We hyperventilate over wealth and possessions as if they are the goose that laid the golden egg walking too close to the frying pan. Rare few wish to impede another's right to accumulate as much money and precious materials as can be secured within their burgeoning coffers. The reason?—most people are well aware of the measure of their "stuff" and they harbor a subliminal outrage at the possibility that anyone might dare challenge them on the day their own ship might actually come in, as remote as that possibility probably is. This reminds me of an old college buddy who used to scarf down our carry-out pizzas as if he was inhaling them so that he could satisfy his appetite before everyone else caused him to run out of pizza. I found myself trying to match his speed-eating skills, afraid of not getting a second piece, before I realized the monumental injustice in it and addressed the situation by never eating pizza with him again. In like manner, it seems that the rich are just as afraid they are not going to get a big enough piece of the economic pie to satisfy their lust for wealth and power. In a polar opposite vein of selfishness, there are those who have willfully disregarded every opportunity, educational and communal, that this great nation has ever supplied to them, and have thus failed to prepare themselves to become a noble contribution to anyone. Yet, masses of these people stand, wail, perform, petition the government and sometimes riot about some mythical oppression as if they are entitled to an ever-increasing share of the fruits of others' labors through some secularly divine national right of entitlement. No one is entitled to another person's charity, nor are they entitled to the nation's charity without their own best contribution. Charity ceases to be the voluntary sacrificial gift of the giver when the gift is extorted from a person by another party. And, then there is so-called homosexual marriage. Only the damned would call the Most Blessed Virgin Mary a bigot when She tells us that this abomination is directly fomented by the Devil Himself. Five thousand years of the wisdom of God invested in the union of man and woman for the propagation of humanity into Thy Kingdom Come; the cradle of human civilization itself plummeting from the heights as the bow breaks because satanic plunderers sawed the limb from the towering redwood of Divine Revelation; not now realizing they are in free fall into the abyss. There is not a sane thinker in America who is not now standing beside our cultural sidelines surveying the hellish chaos, wondering how we descended into such a state of societal dysfunction and outright moral rot. Millions pray to the God of Abraham and His Messianic Son, and gather in congregations on Sundays, seeking the strength to endure while petitioning with sacrificial hearts for their children to bypass the seedier parts of life, having the parental wisdom to know that the present day world will consume their children's happiness like a devouring beast. Then, there are the truly enigmatic ones; those who maintain that being a Christian means repeating the metronomic delusion that everything is not so bad, intending to intone a secular salvation where we offer no conversion of heart to Jesus Christ, but instead gather in unity with flowers as if at Woodstock, and somehow receive the anointing to bypass the consequences of our actions unscathed, notwithstanding that we have already heard the thud and the grinding of metal as our ship of state gouges out that inhospitable shore and founders itself upon the rocks. For the record, the Holy Spirit was nowhere near Max Yasgur's dairy farm on the Feast of the Assumption in 1969. It seems that we refuse to accept that every statistical measure of cultural stability related to our children, save one, shows that we are losing civilization as Christ would have it. Our secular institutions of primary education are fighting tooth and toenail to maintain the focus of their children upon the rudimentary skills needed to be of service to humanity for the rest of their lives, yet they make way with applause any agendum that advances a sexual and moral revolution under the guise of multiculturalism, while willfully ignoring piety, virtue, honorable tradition, purity, nobility, moral order, and sacrificial love in the process, as if these attributes are irrelevant to people of such progressive sophistication as themselves. Our colleges and universities are lost in a self-created nightmare that they do not have the vaguest idea how to awaken from, inculcating a meaningless "tolerance" for every affront to moral principle that can be advanced, and trumpeting our cohabitation with outright evil through their strains of social diversity. If they see a noble tradition, they will set about uprooting it from the tender fields of the planet as if they were releasing Holocaust survivors from a death camp. Then, our children commence across their thresholds of indoctrination carrying lifeless mantras as their ideological banner, prepared to stand for nothing but the delusions of socio-political, cultural and atheistic revolutionaries. Can humanity not see the synonyms: Diversity-Religious Pluralism, Tolerance-Moral Relativism, Godlessness-Atheistic Secularism? But, the Sun of Truth still shines on those who wish to bask in its rays because *unity at the expense of morality cannot withstand the test of virtue.* It is the Vicar of Christ alone in union with His Hierarchy who are drawing millions of young people internationally every two or three years to the World Youth Days held across the globe to counteract this darkness and to teach virtue, moral courage and the true meaning of life to the impressionable souls of God's children. Indeed, where else would they ever learn of it? The Most Blessed Virgin Mary Herself is gathering tens of millions beneath Her Mantle of miraculous intercession to turn the tide of history back into the direction of Jesus Christ and the wisdom of His Original Apostolic Church. No secular government, code, society, organization, or institution is even attempting to effect such elevating grace in this barren world. Indeed, no other is defending the complete spectrum of virtue and moral reasoning with as much courage and, at the same time, disdained so profoundly. And yet, our society is collapsing nonetheless because of the sheer numbers of cackling peanut galleries with media megaphones who disregard, disparage and disrespect the Church instituted by Christ Himself. An abominable weight of sin and derision is being placed upon the great works of the Church, and it is obscuring the path to deliverance for vast multitudes. Humanity will never be able to justify before Jesus Christ our neglect in upholding the sacred mandates He gave us from the Mount of Olives and Crucifixion Hill.   There is no pragmatic or philosophical reason for our having allowed society and the Earth to deteriorate into such a depraved condition.   We might make frail attempts to explain-away our passivity in the wake of the onslaught against our unborn children by saying that we could not take-on city hall.   However, I am convinced that Our Lord would have us forthrightly take down city hall with all the brainpower and righteousness we can muster to restore the world's order of love and dignity of life that the Father commands.   God would support any dynamic that would better enforce His ordinances before a people who have so brazenly shunned them for thousands of years.   This is what I see occurring in the not too distant future; for there is coming a reckoning so massive that it will be too large to grasp within the confines of the rational human mind.   Most people will side with a winner, no matter who it is; but as of this moment, it seems that most people are only acknowledging the crucifixion side of Christianity, the side that would ask them to contribute their sacrifices.   They are not seeing that there is Easter Glory for those who do.   There is a Triumph approaching that will become so visibly profound that every last syllable of criticism against the Roman Catholic Church will be erased from the vocabulary of spoken tongues.   The enemies of Catholicism cannot fathom a Victory that could be so overwhelming as to leave them speechless and begging for forgiveness at the same time.   And, I tell you, it is coming! I have already seen it.   I have lived it.   I have stared into its Face. Behold, there is no stopping it.   It is just a matter of when God says 'enough,' and transforms these days of Divine Mercy into the blazing heat of Eternal Reckoning.   Jesus is willing and prepared to call their renegade folly to an end.   On the day the Almighty Father decides to pull back the veil, it is over.   While human egos seem to be invincible before us now, they will be annihilated in an instant with the pain of ripping bandages off of a thousand scabs.   The inevitable purging of Creation of all that corrupts it is on humanity's doorstep, its entrance delayed only by the Divine Mercy of the Savior of the world and the prayers of the faithful. Even as the story of redemption is unfolding as Christ would endure it, the proverbial slow motion train wreck is occurring for everyone to see. Unabashed immorality, brazen heresy, aggressive derision, celebrated sin, and earth-shattering blasphemy. History will bear out the story of the descent of sinful man into the pit of the ages unless we find the courage, each and every one of us, to step back from the commissions and omissions that are destroying us individually and collectively as a nation, and instead become a holy people of unity and conviction within the noble boundaries of our most holy presentation of ourselves, all defined by the Dogma, Traditions, and Teachings of the Roman Catholic Church. A huge segment of humankind is in a state of complete rebellion against the authority of the Almighty Father to form their souls to participate in His Glory, lest they be lost forever to the desolation of Hell. Masses numbering in the tens of millions in this country alone humble themselves before nothing and no one, subjecting themselves only to their own guiding demigods. And, many of those demons do they serve. They obey nothing but their bipolar whims in the moment, their souls led to the slaughter by the purveyors of darkness entrenched throughout our culture, all holding amplified megaphones of influence. They embrace no responsibility for their conduct and the fruits of their actions in the syllabus of society and the pristine fields of others' lives. They are without form, function or future in the eternal Kingdom of God, and thus they will never pass beyond the gates of that everlasting Paradise. While time and the spirits of wickedness treat them kindly to pursue their epicurean and progressive ideals, they are deaf to the tolling bell that announces their end, whereupon they will be thrust before the reality of Creation outside-of-time which they never cared to sacrificially engage. And, there they will stand, naked, with the diary of their fruitless existence testifying in bold-relief that they were too arrogant to accept that even Jesus Christ Himself could command their obedience to His Holiness as surety for their entrance into His Kingdom.

It is clear that millions of people have asked the Lord for the conversion of the world. And, millions more have laid their petitions upon the many altars of the globe, especially at the locations of the Virgin Mary's great shrines. Our Lady has said that She will intercede until Her intercession is needed no more. Until then, we are not to become hopelessly distracted or seduced by the horrific conditions in the United States regarding our government and its economy. These things have always ebbed and flowed through time. We must work hard in holy ways, provide in the most constructive ways, and prepare ourselves spiritually, no matter what may come. Notwithstanding what may come in the future through the turbulent tides of time, it is presently appalling to realize how some of our fellow countrymen are trying to survive now. And, these terrible conditions are precipitating the grotesque sin of individuals taking their own lives, which is a blasphemous and evil usurpation of the gift of life. This is why we must pray with a passionate heart for those whom we may not know, and especially for those serving in the military who are bringing themselves fatal harm and taking the lives of others as a result of their traumas. Do we realize how repulsive suicide is to the Father of Life? Imagine what it feels like for Him. He has been forced to ask each of these people whether His Grace and Spirit was insufficient, whether His Son and His Mother were not effective in defining how He loves His creatures to the ends of the Earth. They leave grieving children and other relatives who then question the motives of God, when God has not started these terrible wars. And, we know the rest of the story. When we read the news reports and see how the secular world is driving us toward a hellish oblivion, we must not grovel in the pit or become embittered by what we see. Think instead about all the Light that comes when the Pope or a Prelate reprimands the instigators of this diabolical darkness for starting wars of death and aggression, for doing nothing to stop abortion, for propagating the wickedness of same-sex unions, for the social engineering of the consciences of children, away from the pure and holy courses of their development. Yes, the spring will arrive, and the world will seem bigger and brighter. To hasten that day, we must prosper Our Lady's messages of warning to those who are perpetuating the darkness, and stand in holy defiance before their backlash. We must prosper the mission of the Church and convert lost sinners to the Holy Cross. We are writers and speakers, doers and composers, laborers and builders. We have everything at our disposal to keep manifesting the message of Salvation to anyone we please in a country that still protects those rights. The promises of the Gospel are real. We can expect miracles to happen. We have every right to demand from our Savior the gladness of heart for which we pray. It is His Will. He told us that if we believe in Him with all our heart, mind, and soul that He would give us our dreams and aspirations. Time will tell us whether each of our dreams is in accordance with the Father, in leading our brothers and sisters to the Cross, and bringing peace and joy to wanting lands.

Our Lady told me in 1991 as one of Her first orders of discipline, "*If you and your brother disagree one more time, there are going to be serious consequences.*" Although She was mainly referring to the damage our relationship would sustain by our own actions, Her warning did not preclude actions on Her part as a disciplinarian, and we knew it. We learned early on in our relationship that She has the power to command consequences where we wished we would have listened and obeyed. This is part of Her motherly discipline that She is not afraid to implement. Nevertheless, I was stunned by Her exacting expectations as we took disagreement to be an accepted norm in human relationships. But, She said, "no," there is only agreement in the loving Truth; the rest is the playground of pride, dissension, arrogance, and lack of love. And, what have been the consequences to humanity during the centuries of simmering disagreement that we are now trying to band-aid with innumerable versions of religious ecumenism? For five hundred years, Christianity has been dismembered by sinners who believe they have a better prescription than the Original Apostolic Church for the unity of civilization beneath the Cross of Christ. In fact, those separated from the Catholic Church do not even have a universal vision of inclusion within their thinking; the one people consuming the Bread of Life at one Table of Faith. Every person who believes in the concept of religious pluralism has given up on searching for the preeminent Truth of the Ages which will bind us together in solidarity as the family of man. Their debilitated faith has been blinded by the intimidation of charlatans who do not care enough about suffering humanity to initiate their own unity beneath the Cross upon which their Savior died. These deceivers are simply another generation in a long line of moral cowards who are puffed-up with pride, and have thus forfeited the entire legacy of Jesus' Crucifixion, Death and Resurrection in order to avoid their own cross which comes by declaring that there is Truth in a Church founded by Jesus Christ, alive and breathing as on the first day He walked from the Tomb! Rather than surrender in humble conversion through the Original Apostolic Church, they desire instead to see every future generation languish in uprising and revolution, squabbling and rioting, war and pestilence, disease and death. They refuse to surrender into a united powerhouse at one table of faith unless everyone kneels to their phantasies before a throne on which they are seated. They believe Christ instituted a democracy instead of a Kingdom with a Crucified King. They refuse to humble themselves to achieve the beauty of humanity at the pinnacle of our purpose in loving God as His endearing creation. Indeed, if religious pluralism is acceptable, why would there ever be any need for conversion to anything? And, that is the point. If there is no singular Truth, then why Jesus' declaration of there being one table of faith; why the requirement of conversion? And, if there is no need for conversion, why would anyone evangelize; why make disciples in any nation, let alone them all? If there is no singular Truth to be testified to every living person that has repercussions for our future, then what is it that Jesus Christ found so important that He would not relent even to the point of being crucified on the Cross? Religious pluralism is the fatal compromise of a Faith so ethereal and supernatural, so boundless and eternal, resilient, peaceful, heart-warming, unified and purposeful. We have identity in the ultimate truths of the Gospel emanating from the hierarchical institution of sanctifying sacramental grace that He instituted with His Spirit. Worldwide unity and fraternity is in this singular, uniting Kingdom of Faith that has been flourishing from its Seat in Rome since Peter set foot on its pagan streets. Religious pluralism is nothing more than a grand, watered-down compromise between people who would rather fight like the dickens against one another than surrender in service and sacrifice for the reward of Christian unity in its most perfect form. Religious pluralism depletes and degrades our unity of purpose, our vision of the unseen landscape of the Holy Spirit, our fraternal strength against the evil legions who seek to drag us all into hell, and our stabilizing power to defend the universal principles impaled into the Earth when Jesus thrust the Cross into the soil of the Holy Land with the weight of His own broken body nearly two thousand years ago. Once belief in an indivisible, singular Truth was fractured; once the Church was divided by ideologies, sects, and persuasions; once Jesus was forced to say, "Why did you doubt?," we as a unified body of faith began to sink beneath the torrential monsoons poured-forth from the ego-stricken mentality of pseudo-theological men who have surrendered their will to nothing but themselves. Then, to quell the fratricidal disagreements instigated by those who would not surrender for the sake of love, the Truth was dragged through the latrine of human pride, chided to descend from Her place of beatific supremacy, stripped of Her modest composure and forced to grovel in competition with the beasts, when all She aspired to do was come down from Heaven to lay down Her life to save us. The insuperable Truth of God was forced to wear the striped-pajamas of a dignity unfit to live. And, Our Lady tells us, "*If you and your brother disagree one more time, there are going to be serious consequences.*" And, those consequences will evidently come because moral relativism has stepped up to play its diabolical part, for the relativists believe if you cannot see the overarching Truth that is so high above us all, then surely they must be able to make up their own personal version for the here and now. Their audacity tells them that no one can instruct them what to do or hold them accountable to any conduct or belief. Moral relativism is the lie generated by people who have accepted religious pluralism. It obscures every unabridged principle that God ever wished to reveal about Himself by stirring them into a rancid mishmash of human pride at war with every sacred reality the Holy Spirit has deposited into the age of men through His Original Church. And finally, pagan secularism rises from the stirring sea of darkness and runs rampage without the restraint of conscience brought by the moral order of the Holy Spirit. Dead souls begin their reign. Pagan secularism completes the destruction of Faith by taking advantage of the disunity wrought by religious pluralism, and exploits a world vacant of soaring principle for the sake of material gain, sexual pleasure, societal stature, and the lust for power which comes through the consolidation of wealth. It is blind to the future age of Glory where all men are judged upon the harvested fruits of the vineyard left in their stead. This is why the world needs to recognize the Rock of Truth upon which it can build again. The Sacred Hierarchy of the Roman Catholic Church was instituted by the Holy Spirit as the antidote for this crumbling "diversity." The Mother Church stands alone as the last bastion of civilization in the face of the worldwide community of nations that are blindly headed toward certain destruction without God's miraculous intervention. No other save the Church of Rome has defended virtue, matched to the revelations of reason and history, or articulated the guiding principles that underpin social cohesion revealed by God Himself through His Son. This Church alone has endured the heart-wrenching struggles of two thousand years of sinful humanity overcoming its darkest hours. The Catholic Church has been given the keys to hold bound the unalterable Truth, and loose the world from an exilic nightmare of existence defined by the collective atrocities of mankind at his worst. Yes, the Catholic Church does declare that She is the sole repository of the Definitive Revelation of the Son of Man. She is the authority over the legacy of Jesus' Kingdom on Earth, and His one to come. She is the testator before the Throne of God through the sacrificial lives of Saints and Martyrs who never subscribed to any compromise of their Savior. They beckoned for a conversion that the Church still resounds in its dogmatic voice. The Catholic Church brings into this age both the Truth and the faculties and fraternity to raise the most formidable force for the transformation of human existence that has ever been contemplated by man. And, it is Our Lady who is convening this moment of victory in the souls of all who will humble themselves enough to listen to Her. Yet, it is becoming increasingly apparent that secular Americans mistake peacefulness and quietude for idleness and non-productivity; and they equate prayerful meditation with psychosomatic illusion. However, their opinions are not in agreement with the facts. In truth, our Christian faith creates a spiritual buffer-zone, separating us from the obscene fallout of the material world. This is what makes our redemption in the Cross so fruitful, reassuring, restorative, and meaningful. It makes our environment one that reflects the confidence to which Our Lady refers. The identity we have found in Jesus comes from our awareness that the Holy Spirit changes our entire constitution and makes us more enduring creatures than we ever thought possible.

October 31, 2010
Virgin Mary

"My darling little children, the secular elite are too busy smithing words, turning phrases, and spinning yarns to pay any mind to the reality of Christian conversion; they are headed for the demise that is rightfully theirs. We have implored them through much greater eloquence than they will ever know to open their lives to the sacred mysticism by which all blessed men thrive. I have spoken to you about your unity in Jesus, and therefore in the Father, through the Divine Love in which you were created. I bring you grand benisons that portend good things, that foretell of a future that is wrapped in the Glory yet to come. It is My joy today, My dear sons, to remind you that you have been set upon the pathway to redemption because you have always believed; you have always grasped the concept of the reconciliation of the Father and His creatures through the Crucified Son.

Why must this be so? Why so much suffering? Why such true fashioning of grated feelings to reach a land filled with such peace? Because you will know that peace through your own fellowship with its Prince. All men must follow the footsteps of the One Who Is, the one 'I Am' of all that has been given from the limitless Heart of God. This is the reason we pray. It is all about reconciliation that is founded upon confession and forgiveness."

Religious pluralism is generating moral relativism, which leaves the highest ideals and principles of a noble humanity fractured and isolated, where atheists and pagan secularists who have rejected God outright can either marginalize them or extinguish them altogether. It is oftentimes very difficult to perceive where this triple-headed beast is plying its wares within our lives because evil often possesses a clandestine nature where it secures a hiddenness in plain sight within the attitudinal structure of our post-modern culture. We are a society that is completely submerged in indulgence at the expense of every last scintilla of moral restraint. And for this to have happened, Christianity had to be forced to the shadows, marginalized, lest Her call for fasting impede their gluttonous feast. How was She banished from our sight? In thousands, nay millions, of increments of lowering our heads and walking away from the battle because we did not want to be accused of creating a disturbance. We stood for nothing, either publicly or loudly enough to be a force for good. We walked away from the Cross because we did not want to be crucified there. In an atmosphere where the sacrifice to align with definitive moral truth has been totally forfeited to placate every metaphysical whim that could possibly be conceived by the human mind, the world is left in a state where only heroes have the will to respond; and it is Our Lady who is raising them to maturity. Satan loves to use the artifice of conflict to his advantage. He knows Jesus' brothers and sisters desire to maintain the peace of God in and around them. He knows we wish to be compassionate, peaceful, patient, and charitable. He also knows that those who serve his hedonism desire the peaceful status quo of their wealth, stability, and popularity, provided by the subservience of others that they indenture around themselves. Thus, when one brings the Truth of the Gospel head-to-head with this darkness, the Evil One not only makes sure conflict ensues to shock the souls of God's children in the fight, but further, to enlist those who are controlling a dead society to punish those who dared to challenge their status quo of darkness from which they profit. Then, the lies of Satan begin to ring: 'You need to respect their beliefs. They are allowed their opinion. Don't force your religion on them. You should be more peaceful and not cause such a lack of peace.' The children of Christianity in our contemporary age have been disarmed by the lie of religious pluralism; and they cower at the slightest whiff of conflict that Satan generates against their testimony to the Truth, brow-beating them into believing that their spreading of the Gospel is ill-founded if it has caused such a disturbance. They have forgotten that Jesus said that if they have hated Him, they will also hate you; and for the simplest of things. And, that hatred has taken on many faces and facets in our present age. Outright lies about your actions and motivations will become commonplace. Stories will be spun about you that could never be sold to the most despicable tabloid, but they will be believed anyway. False witnesses will appear in droves. Your friends will abandon you. Your families will forsake you. Your intentions will be misconstrued; your words twisted opposite their meaning; all but the most heroic of your faith leaders will stand silent; everything will come together to ensure the assassination of your character, even among your fellow faithsians. This is the way of the Cross of Christ when the Truth is brought into full confrontation with the darkness of the age. But, Our Lady says that this is reason for the greatest rejoicing in Heaven because the Son of Man has appeared again in the fullness of His spiritual countenance, and He will begin to respond to every prayer you ever uttered! As if one would need a more practical example, let us consider the secular American workforce. If you speak the truth of the Gospel, defend your faith in the Roman Catholic Church, and stand-up for principles of decency in any secular corporation in America, no matter how gently you do it, you will either be disciplined or fired before nightfall after being blamed for the conflict that will be generated by the enemies of God who hear your words. They do not want their mad dash for wealth and power to be impeded by any yoke of fairness or decency. Jesus Christ is not a conducive element to the secular culture of American business, and is damaging to the decorum of the business environment because He is hated and rejected with as much venom today as on the day He was killed. Secular America believes that Christianity has no right to assume any place of public prominence in our society or in the machinations of our economy. And, heaven forbid anyone tell rich overlords of their responsibility to serve the least and refrain from erecting additional barns for their opulent wealth. In other words, the most godless human being in the office would throw a fit, blame you for forcing your religion upon them in "their" workplace, and demand a showdown with the leaders who take their part, compromise away their faith if they have any, and decide based purely upon monetary reasons in order to maintain the orderly machinery which sustains their wealth and power. Our leaders always believe that any disturbance which has a facet of Christianity involved must be blamed upon the Christian. They, too, believe that Jesus Christ has no place within their organization, and they will crucify any of His followers as their first order of business because they just cannot endure the conflict "the Christian is causing." The King of Heaven has no place to lay His head in our day, and has multiple crosses prepared for Him. It is a unique and rare leader who will stand by the Truth of Christ in these situations.

Saturday, January 2, 2010
Virgin Mary

"There has been no question that your workplace has been a hellish place to go. I only ask that you see it for what it is, not that it makes it any easier, but that you see the corporate atmosphere for what it has become all over the United States. It has worked its way into your religious workplace

by reason of the secular dispositions of your worldly leaders. It is grotesque that such undeserving people would give themselves hundreds of thousands of dollars in bonuses. It is profane and unfair. Such is the way of corporate America. Imagine the banking industry giving a million dollars' bonus to leaders who take their industry into insolvency, and using taxpayers' loans to pay those bonuses. This is the kind of capitalism that I have denounced in this holy place for the past 19 years. It will change permanently when it ends, and its demise is coming."

None of this is a cynical analysis. It is the state to which religious pluralism, moral relativism, and pagan secularism have brought us; and it is the way Satan is controlling much of the American economy, forcing the virtues of Christianity to the margins in favor of the crass elitism of the most despicable and greedy human beings on the planet. Is there any other explanation for the explosive growth of compensation for senior leaders compared to the average worker's wages which have become all but stagnant over the past 40 years? Additional barns, indeed! And, to add insult to injury, only the most courageous religious leaders overcome the temptation to side with the corporate leaders, whereupon the faithless remainder admonish their flocks to not be so aggressive with their faith in these environments out of respect for their employers. In other words, Christians are intimidated to be silent and accept Christ's Crucifixion in daily increments of godlessness that they endure with Him every single day of their lives. Is it any wonder how things have gotten where they are? Do we have to ask ourselves why Christian evangelization is all but dead on the vine? It is hard for us to admit that the societal fulcrum has tipped us into near paganism quite some time ago, and that to retrieve our lost innocence, we are going to have to fight like history's greatest Catholic Saints to suspend the Divine Justice of God upon us all. A capitalistic mafia is in charge of the economic arena; and they sit in most positions of power, are polished and well-spoken, congenial and humorous, wear business suits, eat the most impressive fares, and go home every night to the most plush accommodations imaginable—and the legacy of their contribution to the Cross of Jesus Christ before the Throne of God someday is the farthest thing from their minds. They are fattening themselves for the day of slaughter, just as Saint James said in chapter five of his biblical writing.

Saturday, June 27, 2009
Virgin Mary

"My dear little children, I come to speak to you about sanctifying humanity because a time will come when many will wish that they would have changed. Now is their time to act. You must remember that I love you in your holiness, but I love all lost sinners especially in their weaknesses. I do not disembrace My children just because they are wandering other paths, walking away from the Truth, or blinded from seeing the Cross. I remind you both that I see your brothers and sisters in a light of forgiveness and compassion that they do not offer one another. They are much too quick to judge, much too hasty to make summary decisions about how they have been offended in their state of ignorance. We can reach them; the Holy Spirit can permeate their hardened hearts. You know that this will happen because you trust Me, you believe what I have been saying to you for so many years. There are yet uncovered inequities that have yet to be dealt with by the righteous. I mean that those who follow the Cross must remember that as grotesque as the conditions in the world appear, there are much worse conditions that you have not yet seen, far more degradation and depravity. And, through your prayers and efforts, you are preventing impressionable young souls from falling deeper into mortal sin and misbehavior. I cannot overstate the impact the Holy Rosary has on changing the status of life here in America. I ask you to pray for the elderly and poor who have no way to escape the awful heat and squalid conditions in which they are forced to live. Even as you have seen the places around the globe where young children are huddled in shacks and caves, there are tens of thousands of paupers now sleeping on blankets in the park, under water towers and bridges, and inside old appliance boxes they have found behind American merchants' stores. They have been abandoned by their parents, dismissed from their schools,

and they have become addicted to drugs and sex as ways to earn enough money to eat a meal or two a week. Yes, this is in the same United States where you see so much money wasted on material things, where your countrymen take pride in showing their products to other patrons around the world, and where millions of dollars are spent launching machines into outer-space. We have discussed these matters before, and I mention them again today to induce you to pray for the victims of these things."

None of this is of any great revelation to the Christian faithful; these are the daily facts of our lives in union with Christ. But, for those who do not see so clearly, it would benefit them if we describe additional societal dynamics that are such an affront to the redemption of our culture from the inevitable flames of Hell. Where should we start? Most anywhere, really. Abortion, homosexuality, lesbianism, pornography, prostitution, same-sex marriage, gender reassignment surgeries, transgender dysphoria, premarital relations, cohabitation outside of marriage, divorce, unwed pregnancies, drug abuse, alcoholism, suicide, legalization of illicit drugs, flesh cutting, piercing, tattooing, lawlessness, capital punishment, decadent entertainment, cage fighting, the African-American gansta culture, drive-by shootings, binge eating contests, spring break debauchery, high school sports factories, university-sanctioned porn festivals, socially engineering students by faculty, and on and on. And, then there are the godless state lawyers litigating punishment upon both the Catholic adoption agencies for failing to promote the leftist immoral revolution of family deconstruction, and also the conscience-driven pharmacists who refuse to facilitate the killing of unborn children by cooperating in pharmaceutical means of death. What about the ACLU attempting to strip every last vestige of Christ's salvific Crucifixion from public view?—and even when failing in a particular court case, an aforementioned Cross in honor of America's war veterans is torn down anyway in the stealth of the night by Satan's hordes, whereupon secular judges refuse to allow it to be re-erected, even though the law stated that it could remain there as it had for decades. Let us speak of homosexuality for a moment, not to argue its moral dimensions because those have already been measured clearly within the biblical teachings of Christianity. But rather, what happens to all post-modern arguments supporting homosexuality when our scientists eventually discover the physiological and psychological root causes of sex-same attraction, and they initiate protocols that correct the abnormal condition? Think about it. What happens when we finally discover the root cause of the abnormality and figure out how to prescribe treatment to place human development back onto the path intended by both human biology and God? What happens when we discover the broken part, as we eventually will, and move to deliver these poor people from their affliction? Will its advocates then utter "whoops," and rejoice at the opportunity for the healing of their brothers and sisters? What if the cure is a gestational therapy for the child in the mother's womb? Does not a near prophetic feeling come over you at this very moment knowing the reaction? In our current state of moral inversion, the delusional hordes will ironically wail for the choice of the child in the womb, the same child they refuse to admit is present in the case of abortion. They will argue and legislate for the right of the child to have the choice to remain afflicted simply to justify their independence from any recognition of the moral precepts of the Christianity they hate; and they will butcher any sense of intellectual reasoning to vindicate their insane positions. They will trumpet their responsibility to speak for the voice of the child, wishing to rescind the decision of the mother because they will realize that there has never been a mother in the history of creation who desired her child to be born afflicted with the condition of being sexually attracted to a member of the same sex. Think about it. There has never been a mother in the history of the world who desired that her child be born with the burden of homosexual tendencies. Every mother has been heterosexual and would partake of the cure for her child, rendering true same sex attraction extinct from the Earth, leaving nothing but the pornographic poseurs who truly have no same-sex attraction, but who willfully abuse their sexuality nonetheless for nothing more elevated than to satiate their desire for hedonistic sexual experimentation.

Saturday, June 4, 2011
Virgin Mary

"Let there be no mistake in what I am saying here. The events of this past week that took place in the local courthouse are directly from the bowels of Hell. There is no such thing as the union between two people of the same sex. This is despicable and ruinous; it gives young people the wrong impression about the purpose of their gender. It validates the indefensible. It brings shame upon a land that professes to believe in the Christian Gospel. And, it was signed into law by a Roman Catholic governor. You already know that this is why suffering continues; it goes on to open the eyes of the blind, those who will not see what the Lord wants them to envision with their eyes of faith. We pray for all who are committing these atrocious acts, not that they will be destroyed, but that they will be enlightened by the power of the Father to put them in their place, to raise them from their dungeon of darkness, to wrest them from the grip of the devil, to reclaim them from the clutches of the world's secular evil. Thank you and all who are praying for humanity to awaken from their slumber, from their indifference and error, from their outright rejection of the teachings of the Church."

It is not lost to me the reaction that many will have to the content of my words. Many will attach a tone to them that I did not relate because it will assist them in their refutations to characterize me in the most derisive light. Many people contort themselves into all kinds of shapes, trying to get their words into a container that cannot be assailed. And in doing so, the seriousness of the Truth becomes so obscured as to be nonexistent. The salt truly does lose its flavor. Our Lady has told me instead to be unafraid of speaking the unvarnished Truth just as She does, lest our culture descend into holocaust and these people enter the fires of Hell. Someone must tell them with such laser clarity that their souls cringe toward conversion. The world is filled with leaders who wish to be nothing more than proper and measured, pandering for approval, never causing a stir, never seeking the conversion of others except through some roundabout veiled personal accident.

They always make sure that the true power and authority of the Gospel is couched in some vague pastoral language where no one would ever be put-off or offended should their audiences ever bother to read their words at all. Their articulations rarely engage anyone because they redact the Truth behind an obscuring secular propriety, afraid of going to the Cross to share Calvary with our Crucified Master. While I am never a subscriber to offensive verbal attacks in personal situations unless Satan is present in his most viral form seeking to blaspheme and destroy, we must nonetheless be prepared as Christians to answer in every situation that is laid before us. We must give reason for our faith. We have the authority of God to speak to His Creation, to engage it and subdue it, even from the first strains of Genesis! We must tell the world that it is all for Love! It is for the opportunity for everyone to experience the beauty and affirmation that comes only from God, a sanctification for which they have been searching their entire lives, and that suffering would be no more. Satan must not be allowed to rampage unchallenged; which means we must be unyielding in our advocacy of the Truth, launched into the world clearly, wholly, concisely and powerfully, without abridgement or cowardice. "Proclaim the Gospel from the housetops," he said.—*Pope John Paul II 1993 - Cherry Creek State Park, CO.* The validity of this perspective is confirmed by asking how it is possible that 60 million unborn children have been slaughtered in their mothers' wombs in the United States of America where over 60 million professed Catholics live, along with tens of millions of Protestant Christians? How is it possible, I ask? It is because there has been no true leadership on any housetop in the past 50 years, and we have sunken so low in the darkness of spiritual stagnation that we refuse to accept that actual pagan infanticide is occurring right in front of our eyes. Religious pluralism, moral relativism and pagan secularism have gutted us of our convictions and that portion of our humanity that should be horrified and ready to fight to the death to defend the world from such evil. It is the same evil atrocity that was perpetrated during the Holocaust of World War II, the same demon of death, present again in full view of a humanity who has no more willingness to engage it than the German populace against Hitler. Who is going to be the Winston Churchill of the Roman Catholic Church, who is willing to fight, to engage the carnage? Our Holy Father can only do so much if his army will not climb out of the foxhole. All the Saints of Heaven are waiting to be called to the Earth for the battle. Our Lady has prepared millions in Her boot camps of miraculous grace. Can we hear the echoes of President Abraham Lincoln about his General, George McClellan, during the Civil War, "If General McClellan isn't going to use his army, I'd like to borrow it for a time." If we do not stand up for the Gospel and move to convert our society into something more palatable to God, He is going to purge the evil from this land with such horror and destruction by His own divine hand that the survivors are going to have no recourse but to plead to Him in prayer for their survival. And, those who do not believe this have simply yet to realize the hideous situation we are in and the passion for justice that the Heavenly Father possesses. You see, He fought to the death through His Only Begotten Son; and He won! The heavens will not compromise with evil; they will destroy it without mercy and to the glee of the Angels and Saints once this age of Divine Mercy is culminated. In our state of darkness, mankind has forgotten the examples of history and what God will bring upon a corrupt world to save it from being completely consumed. Saint Joan of Arc stands as a righteous beacon to a history littered with the ghosts of fallen nations and conquered kingdoms, placed into the dustbins of time because they refused to be life-giving agents to the world. If peace comes naturally, men will be rewarded supernaturally. If peace comes in the aftermath of war, is it compromised by the spoils? Probably not. Sometimes defending righteousness on the battlefield is sufficient evidence that your enemies are the only ones without reason. We conduct a constant interchange with our own sense of conscious awareness and our environment, the ecosystem, our neighbors and friends, the transcontinental mass of humanity, inorganic nature, the vile crassness of our partisan affairs, the forces of stagnation and change, our historical connection to the past, the uncertain future, and everything else that shapes, impacts, and influences our opinions, the way we present ourselves, our key impulses and reactions, and how we perceive the frameworks and values of everyday life. Surely we can find some time for God, the Master of Truth, who watches the universe sovereignly and yet from within, waiting for us to accord Jesus the Lord our fullest attention and purge ourselves of the rest.

Sunday, May 3, 2009
Virgin Mary

"My sons, let us join our hearts and prayers in homage of the Deity and assist in the sanctifying of the world. We are having remarkable impact on opening their eyes to the outer limits of the human experience, and we shall in the end drive them into the open where they can be easily seen and judged. I will after the publication of your next book continue My messages about the Sacraments and an entire economy of messages about the purity of human faith and the Salvation of the lost. Therein, you will hear and see some of the most awesome strains to convince your brothers and sisters that the Cross is real that you will weep with joy. Thank you for standing strong against all the matters you see in the world, on television, and elsewhere that prove to you that the climax of the American culture must be near. You are facing a future where you will be strong because I have armed you with messages and miracles to awaken your lost brothers and sisters from their secular comas. I also see that you are surprised that your Metropolitan in Chicago upbraided the new United States president about matters of morals according to the teachings of the Church. Let us see whether Cardinal George's advice translates into prudent moral decisions by the president. This is the kind of intervention for which we have prayed. His counsel to the president was not unlike your writing. The president is not prone to evil, but he is influenced by evil because of those who surround him. In other words, he has sold-out his moral choices to achieve the office of president. I have confidence that you and your brother know that you will also teach American leaders and the electorate about the Truth as it is known in God.

Americans thirty years ago used to talk about the moral majority. They called it the silent majority. Sadly, that majority is no longer as moral as it used to be. My Special son, it is your love for Me that keeps Me coming here. You have both been working for Jesus like tremendous machines. Thank you dearly for your prayers, and for taking special care that your new book is another one for the ages."

Suppose an owner of an orchard had a tree that began producing less fruit, and of diminished quality, than the prior year. Whereupon the next year its condition further deteriorated to the point that he realizes he must take action because the ultimate outcome is inevitably a barren tree that would be good for nothing but kindling in his fireplace. So, turning his attention to the tree, he fertilizes and cultivates the ground around it, prunes the overgrown branches, and applies pesticides to defend against harmful insects. But, after providing all this care to this tree, the next season it produces less than the last. If the man's vision is only as wide as the spectrum of applications he has administered to the tree, his efforts to save his fruit are hopeless. Yet, if his vision were to become wider, he would see that a neighboring landowner, who cares nothing for the natural landscape or the man's trees, has built a facility where toxic waste was being dumped onto the ground, ultimately poisoning the small creek that ran near the tree where it was gaining its nutriment. And, thus it was dying because of the pollution. This simple parable is about perspective. While the culture of the United States is more complex than a single landowner attempting to save the life of a single tree, the lesson of the interactions in our culture in union with that part of our being that is growing into a more enlightened and noble people is quite apropos. The reason the landscape of our lives is diminishing in its manifestation of good fruit is because cultures die in seasons and generations from the depleting forces inflicted upon them, not in minutes and hours such as a mortal attack would generate. Hidden forces rage in the unseen undercurrents of our lives for years and decades before the sustaining strength of society's fruit-bearing agents are depleted enough for us to recognize that we are being starved for the robust nutriments that we require to keep civilization alive. Presently, there are multitudes who are awakening to the fateful realization that the fruit of our nation no longer tastes sweet, and the leaves are beginning to change midsummer before their time. It is almost a trite cliche to say that none are so blind as those who will not see. We are a haphazard conglomeration of peoples from differing parts of the globe with adversarial ideologies, splintered allegiances, and disparate economic classes. Yet, we are all going to arrive at the exact same place in time—our passing from this life into what is beyond. We are curious to a fault regarding every mystery in the galactic skies above, on the tips of the highest mountains and what lies in their cores. The silent depths of the deepest trenches of the seas conscript our curiosity, as do the lives of any individuals who wish to obscure any part of their private existence from society's prying eyes. And, it is ironic that we could not seem to care less about what is behind the veil of our passing into the grasp of death. In truth, it is not so much that we do not care, it is rather that we ultimately do not want to know because that knowledge creates uncompromising demands in our lives for which we refuse to take responsibility. Nothing is worse than an ignoramus who is presented with the facts, but continues to disbelieve anyway. It is the worst kind of contrary human being. Willful ignorance, pride, arrogance; attributes of a humanity without life, existence which is dying and plummeting into the abyss. These people are the neighboring landowners who have erected their sewage-spewing facilities in the midst of the vineyard of God. The American nation professes a pledge of allegiance and an ideal of indivisibility. What does indivisibility mean in the context of what we are witnessing in our fractured societies? Is it inseparability from the highest truths of our existence? Is it a pledge to be united to the most transcending principles? Is it imitating and professing the most noble tenets of the human species? Social commentators parrot the phrase "...our way of life..." Does this mean nothing more than that anyone can do and say anything they want without any responsibility to the whole or the common ideals we envision as an enlighten species of creatures? Does it include the inner-city slums created from the spiritual blight impressed upon our children by our culture of broken families and the failed educational systems that have prepared them to contribute utterly nothing to their fellow man? Does it encompass the colossal disparity between economic classes generated by the outright theft of the nation's resources by the top percentiles of the rich? Is the description that our commentators are defending meant to include all those forces which diminish, degrade, and destroy our unseen qualities of virtue, self-restraint, productivity, civility, and human dignity? Is "our way of life" really meant to include the slaughter of over 60 million unborn children in their mothers' wombs? Really? This is exactly what pagan secularism tells us. Action absent virtue. Willfulness unchecked by nobility. Sacredness targeted by hostility. Purity mocked into shame. Charity extinguished by the death of conscience. Spontaneity lacking the moderation of moral principle; and life forced to step to the side so that death can skewer its gruesome legacy into our heritage. When we function by these dysfunctional definitions, the whole of society is subject to the pollution of the most rogue, despicable forces that could ever be dreamed up by wicked men because the freedom to choose is "their right," and "entitlement" is the ship they are waiting to board. This is how nations collapse into the darkness of the ages. And, the atheists scream, "Don't you dare bring your Christianity anywhere near me!," not realizing that they are going down on the same ship as everyone else. Well, we are beginning to live their satanic dream, and God is not going to allow it to continue. He will save the righteous and toss the left-over damned into the eternal fires of Hell. The argument is always put forth that Christianity is not needed for man to be noble and of right conduct, whereupon vaunted atheists of seeming good character are trotted-out to posit that Christ is an inconsequential manifestation of man's imagination. But, never is it admitted into evidence that their crime scene has been tainted by the influence of other forces, namely by the environment of good Christian people and the aura of the Church in which each of them grew up. They fail to admit that they matured and were formed psychologically within the very framework of order imbued within our society, sustained by Christianity; the culture of moral and judicial principle, influenced in hundreds and millions of increments of simple grace throughout their mortal lives. All the principles of human dignity, freedom, liberty, virtue and the rest were secured and brought before them through time by the genius of Christianity. They possess facets of goodness only because Jesus arrived first. Any goodness that they possess has been formed in them by the Holy Spirit incognito through the Christian halo of grace that surrounds this planet upon which they have walked. It matters not whether their families may have never been religious, or that they may have grown up on foreign continents hostile to Christianity. Their civility and good-heartedness is part of the spiritual warmth they assumed by being born on a planet where the raging inferno of God's Heart burns from the Seat of Christianity in Vatican City. It would seem that atheists would be the easiest to transform into the beatitudes of Christ's Life because their souls are so frigid and absent of meaning beyond human mortality. The smallest glimmer of miraculous grace should have an enormous impact upon their perceptions. But, their thoughts are intellectually worldly. They are humanists who love their sins more than the promises that Our Lady's miraculous intercession portends. And of all the irony, it is the gaining of unity among those who already know Christ that seems to be the actual impossibility because Protestantism prudishly sniffs at mystical grace and walks away upon realizing that nearly every supernatural intervention of God is calling like a clarion for them to convert to the sacramental graces of the Roman Catholic Church, which their protesting heritage demands they reject. Therefore, what is God to do? This is why religious pluralism is the most damaging aspect of the unholy trinity. It divides Christians and obscures the Truth. It soils the billboard of Redemption that the Holy Spirit is writing on. And, while not depleting the power in itself, it impedes it for a time, because God is merciful before the day of justice. Our benevolent Father is extending this mercy through the appearance and intercessions of the Mother of Jesus where She has asked us to come together to pray for the wholesale conversion of the world's sinners, the souls whom are needed to complete the mission of cleansing the Earth according to the decrees of the Lord and the content of Her messages. It is clear that there is indeed a prefigured plan for reorienting humanity in the themes of sacrifice, even as individuals around the world tend to drift into clusters according to their biases and physical needs, and then become incarcerated by their misplaced ideas about the meaning of life. Their prejudices collect them into sects and groups in which they feed off one another to strengthen their error. It has taken miracles throughout the ages to break them loose from these bonds, and it is no different in these closing days of the world. Yes, the miracles are coming, with the Morning Star Over America being one of them! When the world seems inconceivably vague and hard, when the clarity of our thoughts blurs into confusion and beyond recognition, when the cold shroud of uncertainty creeps upon us for no apparent reason, we must remain footed in the serenity of the Cross. The crassness of human life cannot dim the sheen of God's stardom that still comforts our forbears from generations past. We are told that Jesus Christ stands beside us and simultaneously within us. How malleable we must become! All we need to do is focus our eyes on the heart, turning our attention to the keystone truth that has laid claim to our meandering lives. This is the presence that prolongs the daylight and soothes the night! This is Jesus who has spread the undying sureness of Divine Love across the annals of modern men. This is the Savior who has raised our souls to the stature of royalty before the grand parade of the ages.

Our Virgin Mother engaged a discussion with me one day during my prayer of the Most Holy Rosary regarding the word "probabilism," a term that I had never heard before. I was shown how it had two completely different meanings, depending upon whether one recognized the moral order of the Church. In secular philosophy, probabilism is the doctrine which was introduced by the Skeptics which posited that certainty is impossible, and that probability suffices to govern faith and practice. Now, the definition taken by the moral thinkers within Roman Catholic theology is somewhat different. It supposes that definitive knowledge of the truth is possible, and that in cases of moral doubt, a person may follow a soundly probable opinion concerning the morality of an action. For Catholics, probabilism is the view that when in personal doubt about how to act morally, humanity may follow any reputable authority recognized by the Roman Catholic Church, wherein the definitive truth resides. In the two definitions of this concept, we see the contrast between moral certainty and moral relativism, between the religious and the secular. In other words, within one word are two definitions that completely contradict each other. The secular doctrine that certainty is impossible and that probability suffices to govern faith and practices is false because the doctrine of Christianity is absolutely certain. If all human acts are measured against the New Covenant Gospel, there would be no questions about moral absolutism. Now, we are faced with all kinds of exceptions that detractors of the Church have conjured that are not directly addressed in the Sacred Scriptures relating to the actions of mortal men. It is more than sufficing to say that the Holy Spirit guides any well-formed Christian conscience, but the variable is always the definition of "well-formed." God gives us reasoned intelligence about the morality of man because He desires our purification in all things righteous, that we become the likeness of His sinless Son. Whenever clergy and other Catholics are asked why they take positions about certain human acts, it is oftentimes difficult to point to a certain scriptural passage because the Bible is actually the bag of seed into which evangelizers have dipped their hand to thereafter sow across the landscape of man. Oftentimes, we are asked to determine the nature of the plant without necessarily being able to inspect the seed which died in the soil to give the plant we see its life. And, that is the great mistake for those who refuse to recognize the Most Blessed Virgin's miraculous intercession because it is not talked about in the Bible with sufficient apparency to transcend their intellectual confusion. They will not recognize the forest of conifers covering the hillside as being just that because they are looking for the original pine cone that is responsible for hundreds of them being there. Yes, the seed from the original bag possesses the DNA of the Holy Spirit, and the offspring of that seed also is of the same spiritual genetics. Further, non-Catholics have always been critical about the promulgation of the teachings in the Catholic Catechism. We have seen that the Church and the Congregation for the Doctrine of the Faith have infused flowering miraculous knowledge into the new Catechism while citing as many evidentiary scriptural passages, or "seeds," as possible. They are denoted with various asterisks which cross-reference those citations, most of them at the bottom of the page on which a particular tenet is discussed. What do we do about those who claim not to be able to find substantiation for the Catechism in the Old or New Covenant? Taking a horse to water but not being able to make it drink is one way to look at it, but this metaphor does little to address the problem. Evangelization must take on a face of asking graceful, pointed questions of them about their reservations and intellectual impediments. Should we not help them reconcile their stumbling blocks and assist them with the further evidence they require? Should we not equally cite their hypocrisy? All around the globe, Protestants and others lean on verbose sermons from evangelists who are trying to persuade their hearers to accept their version of the Gospel, not based on what the Catholic Bible declares, but oftentimes on one altered by a secular king. Our Lady says they are worshiping from a text that has been amended without the assistance of the Holy Spirit. It may sound as if the text is the ancient original in the complexities of its Reformation-era grammatical constructs, but this is a deception. They also depend on the interpretation of their Bible by their so-called ordained clergy, who are themselves out of touch and untethered from the historical veracity of the Original Mother Church of Christianity. Can we see the hypocrisy in this? They require the Catholic Church not to listen to the Hierarchy and Magisterium. Yet, they have their own levels of structural power and teaching. There are almost incalculable numbers of them, tens of thousands of non-Catholic denominations, all with their own power structures, whereupon they depend on their church elders to interpret situations where they are confused about matters dealing with the issues of modern society, the composition of their particular disciplines, their approach to their sacraments and families, and many more. Yet, they denounce and castigate the Hierarchy of the Roman Catholic Church for being the custodian of the Holy Spirit's Theology of Probabilism. Only in the Roman Catholic Church will you find those who are capable of speaking about questions of morality when there seems to be ambiguity in a certain moral conduct. Why? Because the Holy Spirit comes to people who have given their lives into union with the Original Apostolic Church to specifically dispense the Wisdom of the Father for the ever-changing world. It is obvious that these recipients are generally ordained priests, but in cases such as the miraculous intercession of the Queen of Heaven, many of Her seers and messengers are privy to the same spiritual enlightenment from the Throne of God in a very special way. One of the main examples of this disconnection is the growing acceptance of the exercise of such sexual depravities as same-sex "marriage," transgenderism, homosexuality, and lesbianism by many Protestant churches and their sympathizers, while the Roman Catholic Church continues to teach the Truth of the Gospel handed-down by Jesus Christ. Can we see the glaring contrast in the two views on probabilism after one rejects that an ultimate spiritual authority even exists on the Earth? For there to have ever been a chance for unity among the nations and between peoples in the last two millennia, a strategy was required for approaching people who do not believe that there is a knowable definitive Truth. Jesus knew this from the beginning. Hence, who do you believe the principal officer on Earth is for that Truth? Yes, the Vicar of Christ, the Pope in Rome, the modern-day Successor to Saint Peter. He is not an authoritarian, but someone who helps interpret theological Probabilism, even to the most difficult and obscured limits. And, Christ is the Holy Arbiter. Here, we see that the charism of Papal Infallibility in teaching Christian Truth has been the key to God's strategy for the propagation of human Redemption all along. It was upon Saint Peter himself that Jesus declared the Rock of His Church, that His Apostle's Faith might never fail. If the Pontiff is rendered infallible in faith and morals by the power of God, religious pluralism is unmasked for the lie it is; moral relativism vaporizes before certainty, and pagan secularism is converted into brotherhood with that portion of humanity who already heeds our Holy Father's moral guidance. In this does the world find peace and unity with Christ beneath the Cross, awaiting the new springtime of heavenly beatitude upon the Earth.

Before the Sunrise
Preparation for the Light

"Dear Lord Jesus, you are the Incarnation of infinite goodness having come into the physical world for our reconciliation. You have chased away the darkness with your Heraldic Light. You have awakened and purified your people to whom you have dedicated your life. Let our prayers reach your ears from our lowly place in exile, where you watch over us and make way for our entrance into your Eternal Kingdom. We ask that you remember us when you come again, and never allow us to stray from your side. Keep us forever holy; be our beatific conscience as we walk this narrow path. We pray for all souls who have found you, for the millions who are still seeking, and especially for those who turn their backs on you. It is only through your heavenly grace that we can guide them into your sacred presence. Amen."

My home town of Ashland, Illinois during my youth was your typical depiction of Americana at its best. Five simple sole-proprietor gas stations, two family-owned food markets, a couple of car dealerships, and a minor sprinkling of taverns; a pool hall, its own high school and grade school, and a wholesome decorum of peaceful security surrounding the meanderings of life in a small Midwestern village. To this day, I fondly remember leaving the keys in the cars and the doors to the house unlocked, and often wide open when no one was home, not harboring the faintest apprehension that any thieves might barge in. I was born in 1961 on September 20th in Springfield, Illinois at the hospital where my mother worked, and was baptized into the Roman Catholic Church a few weeks later on the 8th of October. My parents moved to Ashland in 1962 with myself and my oldest sister, who was born in December 1959. I would later get four more sisters between 1963 and 1970. My father was returning to his hometown roots after serving a stint in the Navy and his attendance in college, while my mother accompanied him from Springfield after they were married in January of 1959. The home they chose for their family in Ashland was a large two-story dwelling with a barn on a couple of acres directly across the street from Saint Augustine's Catholic church on the western edge of the village. It now seems rather providential, considering how influential this simple proximity to the seat of my faith was in preparation for the more recent events of my life. The church was a rather large structure for such a small community of Catholics. While being the center of our weekend reverence, the parish property was also a playground around which we would play hide-and-seek and the other games of childhood. I remember the stately wrought iron bell tower that had weathered the decades pealing out the call of our worship across the village, and the day when its rickety structure had to be taken down. They removed the bell before its demolition and placed it at the base of the tower next to the church building, probably because it weighed so much that no one wanted to move it any farther. They forgot to inactivate the manual clapper, which posed too great of a temptation for several of us. On dozens of warm summer nights, we would challenge one another to see who could ring it the most times before becoming afraid of being caught by the local constable for disturbing the peace. The young boy who had the record of well over twenty-five gongs went on to be the police chief of a large city in west-central Illinois. Being a curious youth, I explored anything about the church that drew my attention. I recall as a very small child standing on the kneeler in the pew, watching the parish priest come out of a side door and on numerous occasions disappearing behind the large main altar containing the Tabernacle, and then walking out from the other side. At that age, I had never stepped foot in the sanctuary, seen the sacristy, or been behind the altar. And, that was enough to inflame an amazing curiosity in me as to "what was back there?" So, I explored and came away impressed by the wiring and unfinished materials that composed its unseen interior structure, not to mention awed by the humongous fan installed in the outside wall behind the altar, which was the only source of ventilation for a church that had yet to have air conditioning installed. It was many a Sunday in the summertime where my father had sweat dripping off his nose because of the heat as he and others raised as many side windows as they could which were not painted shut. With this same youthful curiosity, I wandered beneath the church on several occasions, into its basement through an outside door that was never locked. I found old crates of altar wine that looked as if they had been there for fifty years, and remember wondering who in their right mind would drink that old nasty stuff now. On one excursion, I wormed my way beneath the floor of the sanctuary into the dirt crawlspace under the main floor of the church and crawled to the vestibule at the front door along Main Street, thinking that no one had probably touched the ground I was crawling over since the day the church was built —my own catacombs, as it were. I giggled while imagining what it would be like to be beneath the floor during Sunday Mass and banging on people's feet as they sat in their pews, making them think the dead were rising. I reminisce about those times now and wonder what Jesus thought watching from the Tabernacle, the unique sight of some little urchin rooting around in the subterranean bowels of His church. I never disturbed anything during my reconnoitering because of the respect that I was taught to have for the church. Even when the older altar boys were taking swigs from the altar wine before Mass, my conscience would be screaming to me that what they were doing was wrong. I was called a wimp several times at declining these occasions. At a very young age, I was in awe of the Tabernacle enshrined within the architecture of the main altar. It was a place into which "man did not go." The greatness of the Eucharistic Host informed my innocent conscience that it was beyond me, and that I should invoke good discipline which precluded its touch with my hands. I knew the Tabernacle was where God resides on earth, almost as if it was electrified with holiness. It is hard to describe this feeling, which I still possess to this day. The confines of the Tabernacles of the Catholic Church are veritable locations of Heaven on Earth, environments of absolute perfection where patiently rests the

King of kings for our adoration; and woe to those who transcend beyond that veil steeped in unrepented sins. They violate the Beauty of the Ages with as much corruption as an abortion doctor stripping a child from a mother's womb. The thing that most characterizes my youth is that I was comfortable with the Church. I saw it as somewhat my possession, almost the way one would consider the perimeter of their personal bedroom. I fondly remember the weekend Masses seated with the families that grew in faith through the years alongside us. It is funny how everyone seemed to sit in the same general location within the church every Sunday throughout the generations, almost as if they were religiously right or left handed. I remember Mrs. Mary Kay Gardner always processing her children to the second pew from the front on the right side, if not the first pew itself. She was a lady of great devotion, long-suffering, peaceful, and kind. She was my first-grade teacher and one of the most blessed women I have ever known. For all that I might ever accomplish, I think my efforts are paled compared to the holiness she achieved by being simply who she was. She struck a pose of grace that so closely resembled the aura surrounding the Most Blessed Virgin, and I am thankful to have known her. There were also the Newells from whom I first learned of Our Lady's appearances in Medjugorje, the Flinns, Copleys, Reisers, Devlins, Dineens, Meyers, Brandts, Mahoneys, and dozens of others whom I remember just as affectionately. All took their devotion to God and to His Catholic Church seriously; all raised their children to be reverent, holy, and heartfelt. Saint Augustine truly cared for the families nestled beneath the reach of his intercessory patrimony.

From this foundation of faith, life in Ashland resonated for us, maybe not in a particularly evangelizing way at the time, but rather in the way each person recognized and engaged those around them from a natural poise of respect and encouragement. And yes, the ornery ones were there too; perhaps others you might speak with would place me in that category a time or two. But, we met to praise God on Sundays and holidays; we were herded as children to catechism classes on

Wednesdays, and we joined one another at chilli suppers, ice cream socials, and other events throughout the year. We buried loved ones, united to celebrate marriages, baptized our infants, and greeted with happiness each successive priest who came to consecrate the bread and serve us with his love. I remember Father(s) Vincent Heraty, Bernard LaBonte, John B. Kennedy and Joseph Murray, along with the many visiting priests who served us through the years. It was a time, if one can believe it, where the administrators of the public school system deferred the after-school hours to the Church on Wednesday evenings, that the children not be absent from their times of religious instruction when they might have been drawn to scheduled organized school functions instead. This is the Americana that the United States used to know. Our family life possessed this anchoring in the Church due to our proximity to it—there really was no excuse for missing Sunday Mass right across the street—especially when my father was so intent upon his responsibility to raise his six children with the decency that faith engenders. Religious artifacts dotted our home life. My father was an excellent craftsman and woodworker when he was not working his normal schedule at the telephone company, which included as much overtime as he could work because he had so many mouths to feed. Our home was adorned with many pieces of furniture made by his hand, and others repaired that were damaged by ours. My parents made the mistake of giving me a child's tool set for my fourth birthday. I used the small screwdriver to loosen screws on everything in sight. It was not until I proceeded to use the hammer to pound dents into the corner of the walnut dining room table, and employed my screwdriver to remove the screws from the bottom hinge of the front door, leaving it hanging in the wind from the top hinge, that my days as a tradesman came to an end. I always said that if they had gotten me a ladder along with the tool set, I would have made it to the top hinge of the door also, causing it to come crashing to the pavement. Mysteriously, several tools went missing from my tool set after the door and table incidents. I was never punished, I guess it was because they never dreamed that I would actually begin to employ the tools for their purpose. Atop our television set rested a wooden figurine of Our Lady of Guadalupe carved by my father. He also chiseled an engraving of the same image in a larger size that he wished to place into a shrine. There is a popular painting of a young man in his wood shop carving a statue of the Virgin Mary whose hand is extended in blessing over him as he works. I think of my father when I see this picture and remember the faithful artifacts that he has produced to glorify God and to show his love for our Blessed Mother. I am proud of him for doing these things because it taught me where our devotions should be placed, that there are things beyond our sight that deserve our respect, and to which we must give reverential deference. While our home was not littered as an ostentatious shrine of religious paraphernalia, it was adorned with the scents of our faith in the books that laid on the end tables, a picture or two on the walls, a holy water font on the door frame, and the statues of Jesus and His Mother upon our bureaus and desks. There was also a plaque that my father placed on the wall at the top of the stairs near our bedrooms, bearing the prayer of Saint Francis. That plaque is from where I learned to memorize this beautiful prayer. Maybe Saint Francis was listening all that time and decided to petition God to enlist me into the Franciscan Hospital Sisters where I served for the better part of my career as a technical computer analyst. I resigned from the Hospital Sisters on February 11, 2013 not knowing that Pope Benedict XVI would concurrently announce his resignation from the Papacy of the Roman Catholic Church that same day. It was an amazing grace upon returning home from my last meeting at HSHS that day, to turn on the television and see the breaking announcement that the Holy Father was stepping down as the supreme leader of the Roman Catholic faithful. I experienced a deeply intimate communion with the Holy Father and Our Lady's miraculous intercession as this confirming impression was marked into my life. It was a great signal grace for me that my life was being miraculously choreographed by the hand of Providence.

My sisters and I were taught from the time we were infants to pray, and it began like this: "God bless mommy and daddy, and brother and sisters, grandma and grandpa, aunts and uncles, cousins, and friends and enemies, and make me a good child. And, a special prayer for mommy." Then, we would recite the Our Father, the Hail Mary, and the Glory Be. As we grew, our prayers matured to include the Holy Rosary which we would usually pray together with our father on Tuesday evenings when my mother worked her one day a week schedule at the hospital as a registered nurse. Her limited schedule outside the home was believed to be of the utmost importance so that she could care for us personally as we matured. Yes, it sometimes seemed like being forced into a death march being called from our play to the living room to begin the Rosary on those evenings. My father used to call Tuesdays the "bad day at black rock" because we were not allowed to have any friends over or go anywhere after school on those days. He ran a little tighter ship than mother. I can remember to this day one of my younger sisters sitting with arms crossed with her bottom lip sticking out, pouting because the praying of the Rosary was the last thing on the planet she wished to engage that night. Ironically, it is this same sister who now possesses some of the greatest affection for Our Lady of any of us. These times in the evening were very special as I look back now. They were not only times of enculturation into a life of prayer, but also opportunities for my father to form our consciences by speaking to us about how to look at ourselves, our responsibilities, and our relationships with one another. He made Jesus present to us through the concepts he related. The number of times I heard him say, "Now, how would you act if Jesus were sitting in that chair right over there?" are too numerous to count, but that thought alone brought the unseen world of Our Lord's presence into our daily lives. It enlivened our consciences to the Holy Spirit and the presence of the unseen Kingdom of the Almighty Father. I have related before several of my earliest memories that I can recall from my childhood. The first was my Grandma Roth's visitation in the first week of January 1964 when I was lifted up by someone that evening in the funeral home so that I could see her peacefully reposed in her beautifully adorned casket. I was just over two years old; and although a vague memory now, I can still remember seeing her lying there. It is such an uncanny thing to recall something from so early in my childhood. I sometimes wonder whether it is God's answer to my grandmother's prayer that I would somehow always remember her. As very small children in the mid to late 1960s, I remember riding out into the countryside to visit Grandpa and his dog "Brownie" on his farm; and as we passed the cemetery along the old country road, my father would always summon our attention and lead us in offering a prayer for the departed souls who rested there, and to remember Grandma. It was such a simple act of faith and devotion, but I was impressed by it deeply. It got to be that during the occasions when he might have forgotten or been distracted, my sisters or I would remind him to say our prayer if we had passed the cemetery without intoning it. Another heartfelt memory is sitting on my father's lap as a tiny child with his arms around me reading the Bible. On one particular day, he pointed out an image on the inside cover depicting the Most Blessed Sacrament and describing to me what it was. I remember this early event clearly because it was the first time I made the association between the Bible and what was actually happening when we "went to church." As a result of that descriptive moment, the same reverential aura began to surround that Bible that I felt toward the Tabernacle. Anyway, we were taught to pray, especially the Rosary, and were exposed to the foundations and substance of our Catholic faith in dozens of subtle, and sometimes not so subtle, ways during our upbringing. The subtle would be the simple statue of Our Lady of Guadalupe sitting for years atop the television set that drew our attention, not only because of its intricate beauty of craftsmanship, but what it commemorated and how it called for our complementary acceptance of the actual miracle of Our Lady's apparitions to Juan Diego in Mexico in 1531. It opened us to the possibilities that God could employ, should He so choose. From our father, we knew of the Most Blessed Virgin's appearances at both Fatima and Lourdes. Hence, the miraculous intercession of the Virgin Mary became an accepted portion of our faith-upbringing, at least for me. The not so subtle ways were the demands for our weekly attendance at Sunday Mass without excuse, the insistence of my serving as an altar boy every morning at the 7:45 a.m. Mass during the Lenten seasons, and the periodic directive on Saturday afternoon to get across the street so the Catholic priest could hear our penitential confessions. We were encouraged to fast the hour before taking Holy Communion at Mass, which left us watching the clock to the minute, hoping to finish our cereal before the t-minus one hour bell struck. We would even play a little fast and loose with the timing by figuring that we did not actually "receive" the Eucharist until forty minutes past the hour so we could eat up until twenty minutes before Mass began. We observed the obligations for Holy Days, were given penances for the days of Lent, such as refraining from sweets and eating between meals to abstaining from watching television for forty days, which seemed to be the worst penance of all for the first week, after which it did not seem to matter that much because we found other things to do. Quite candidly, I never thought it was quite "fair" that my father continued to watch many of his favorite programs after we were hustled to bed, but I would imagine his penance was imbedded in enduring the six of us the rest of the time; so he deserved his moments of peaceful relaxation.

As a part of our enculturation within the Catholic faith, on August 3, 1971, just before my tenth birthday, my father enrolled myself and my sisters in the Central Association of the Miraculous Medal which is a particular movement founded in 1915 by Father Joseph Skelly, C.M., a Vincentian priest from the Congregation of the Mission founded by Saint Vincent de Paul in 1625. The charism of this movement was to make known the apparitions of the Virgin Mary to Saint Catherine Labouré on November 27, 1830 in the Apparition Chapel of the motherhouse of the Daughters of Charity in Paris. During these series of apparitions, the Most Blessed Virgin Mary manifested a vision to Saint Catherine. The event is described by the

Association of the Miraculous Medal as follows: *Our Lady was standing on a globe, with dazzling rays of light streaming from her outstretched hands. Framing the figure was an inscription: "O Mary conceived without sin, pray for us who have recourse to thee." Then Mary spoke to Catherine: "Have a medal struck upon this model. Those who wear it will receive great graces, especially if they wear it around the neck. Graces will abound for persons who wear it with confidence." The vision then seemed to turn to show the reverse of the Medal: the letter M surmounted by a cross with a bar at its base; below this monogram, the Sacred Heart of Jesus crowned with thorns, and the Immaculate Heart of Mary pierced with a sword. With approval of the Catholic Church, the first medals were made in 1832 and were distributed in Paris. Almost immediately the blessings that Mary had promised began to shower down on those who wore her medal, and soon all of France was clamoring for what the people referred to as the "Miraculous Medal."* I received one of these medals upon being enrolled in the Association by my father. Although I was very young, I treasured it, always believing that it was something that came directly from our Holy Mother that possessed great power. I began wearing the "Miraculous Medal" that August, and have had it on a chain around my neck almost continually since that time. I would even place it in my sock during all the basketball games I played throughout my grade school, high school, and college sports careers. Many people would dismiss this medal bearing any significance upon the mystical relationship that I have with our Blessed Mother and Her revelations as the Morning Star Over America. I declare instead that the miraculous intercession that I have experienced in my life through Our Lady is a testament to the promise that She extended to humanity in November of 1830: *"Have a medal struck upon this model. Those who wear it will receive great graces, especially if they wear it around the neck. Graces will abound for persons who wear it with confidence."* This small medal was my first physical connection with our Holy Mother. After receiving it, my heart took greater notice of the stories of Her appearances. I found a book on my father's book shelf about the Tilma of Our Lady of Guadalupe, and another about the apparitions of Fatima in 1917 and the prophecies that surrounded it. Suddenly, the statue atop the television took on a greater meaning. I would often lay in bed and deeply ponder what it would have been like to be there in those times to witness those miraculous events, and to be so close to the Hosts of Heaven. I remember seeing the movie, "The Song of Bernadette," which recounted Our Lady's appearances to Bernadette Soubirous in Lourdes, France, and having to fight back tears because of the emotions I experienced through the television screen. Whenever I would read or see anything about these supernatural events, my heart would well up with a feeling that would bring me to tears. It felt real in the moment to me interiorly, almost as if I was transcending back through time and observing the events firsthand through the book or television program. No doubts or calculated discernment ever entered my mind; I believed these events as if I was there and had witnessed them for myself. But, it was always the "If I had been there..." I still had a sense of separation from these events; that they had occurred so long ago to such good people, and that I was mesmerized by such a beautiful occasion of heavenly grace. I always felt detached by time as if all those opportunities were beyond me, but so happy for those who were able to be there, even the bystanders. I thought, how blessed they must have felt. It is the same way I felt when reading the Bible about Jesus' life. The sensation was as if I was reading stories of a history from which I was separated.

As I grew older into my early teens, I developed a determination whereby I would set goals for myself to overcome personal things that I did not like to do or were difficult to accomplish in the realms of my faith. I persevered in reading the entire Bible in this light. I reread the Baltimore Catechism; I dived into the spiritual writings of certain religious leaders and the Saints; and I read the Vatican II documents over the course of several years. This attention toward religious themes was not according to any agendum or inward calling that I noticed, but simply an occasional focus in the times when I was least distracted by school and sports. Like I said, I was comfortable with the Church, and the themes of religion were a natural part of our lives. In the beginning, I saw these things as being character challenges which did not necessarily come from a voracious appetite for anything religious, per se. But, my attitude subtly changed as my heart began to be stimulated by all that I read and the simple acts of penance I performed. An example were the multiple times when I would finish washing my hands in the bathroom and quickly leave the room, forgetting to shut off the light. Half-way across the next room, I would hear the call of my conscience, telling me that I had forgotten to extinguish the light almost as if it were a completely separate "will" within me to whom I must conform. In each of those moments, I recognized the moment of decision. I could disregard the call or instead respond and retrace my steps to shut out the light. When I did not respond, this voice would become incessant in its urging until I was forced to retreat, just to quiet my heart again. This same theme often occurred within many circumstances, and I became conditioned where I rarely allowed myself to ignore the voice inside me. I now realize that this interior calling, this voice, was actually inspired by the heavenly hosts who were sent to acclimate me to the preeminent Voice of the Holy Spirit in preparation for my obedience to the Queen of Heaven. Another instance of a challenge brought by my conscience occurred in my early teens when I read in the Bible where Jesus asked His disciples why they could not remain with Him even one hour during His Agony in the Garden. I considered that I had never done that for a full hour, except when Holy Mass ran long on a particular holy day. So, I ran across the street that day, determined to sit before the Most Blessed Sacrament in the Tabernacle for a whole hour to the minute. The first fifteen minutes went pretty smoothly as I said my prayers, but then I began paying more attention to the watch on my wrist. The minute hand never moved so slowly. When I finally reached the end of the hour, I decided to stay even longer to show Jesus that I was there not just to see if I could sit still for an hour, but to show Him that I was there for Him. It is funny how it has never been difficult to sit for an hour before the Most Blessed Sacrament since that day. Many other exercises in spiritual discipline that I engaged bore fruit in the same way. I remember being deeply touched by the writings of Archbishop Fulton Sheen and his visionary insightfulness into the Life of Christ. I like to say that the writings of SS Augustine and Aquinas were enlighteningly revelatory to me, and initiated a sense of contemplation into their mystical thoughts. I used to spend hours lying in my bed at night, just thinking about things and how they related to this grand structure that I sensed was surrounding me. It was like looking at yourself now as you passed through the grade levels of your primary education. You can always remember that you had been in lower grades, and that you understood more than you did the previous year. I could also see those previous grades through which I had traveled, and I recognized the greater circumference of my perception by comparison to earlier times. Although this wisdom was really of a very simple nature, it was the solid foundation upon which my soul was maturing. It was the "good soil." I always believed things needed to be done right. I craved interior discipline because of its challenge, and would demand things of myself simply because I did not want to do them. But, I abhorred being disciplined or put upon by others, especially when I could discern no legitimate reason except it simply happened to be "their" will at the time. I could easily inflict personal sacrifice upon myself and could tell myself "no" interiorly, but having anyone burden me with their whimsical will brought about great interior disturbance and would well my anger. My soul craved its freedom while my developing conscience provided the check on its direction. Early in life, I realized that I had to be disengaged from my whims and obedient to the voice within me to have any semblance of peace. I knew that capricious desires created spiritual burdens, and realized there were really only two options; comply with my conscience or snuff it out by the continual ignoring of its call. The latter I refused to do because I believed there was no honesty in it. I was not going to lie to myself, just to feel comfortable doing something that I knew was wrong. I sought to be the master of my being, and was unaffected by the herd mentality of my passions or those of others. I used to play mental games where I would be confronted with a situation, and would assume different postures of perspective and play-out the consequences of each in my mind. I guess you could say that I was naturally contemplative. I was continually thinking "down the road" from the perspective of the future, looking back. If someone was looking at a situation from one direction, I would present opposing viewpoints in order to bring a more comprehensive light upon the situation when I knew they had not thought deeply about what they were saying. In most cases, I was already "down the road" looking back, and had already deduced what I thought was the most appropriate course of action; not based upon my whims, but upon an honest evaluation of the facts and eventual consequences. This led some to believe that I was contrarian by nature. Again, this is a description in hindsight, as it was not an agendum on my part or anything I consciously knew I was doing at the time. My actions were simply a natural response to what was going on interiorly. The more difficult part was not in the protecting of my heart from my personal whims, but rather insulating myself from others' bad choices and their willful attacks against my heart and the freedom of my being. My sense came from my exposure to the thoughts of the Saints and the discipline of my parents to remain on the correct path. I believed the words of the Saints when I read them because I always realized that they had proven themselves through their sacrificial lives, and that they were smarter than me. And further, I did not want to be ignorant of what Jesus wished me to think. As for my parents, I always knew that I was responsible to obey them in everything they had taught me. Some believed that I simply always wished to be right. In a sense, this was true; who wants to be wrong? But, that correctness was not a self-centered obstinance. All I believed had come from someone else. I wanted to be in association with the holy people I was reading about, even if I would never be as heroic in sanctity or as sacrificial as they were. It was not only me who was believing these things to be correct, but centuries of great people to whom I was conforming my thoughts and ideas. It was like a beautiful picture being built within me, and I wanted nothing but the most brilliant character of goodness to be incorporated into my edifice of identity. And, when I did not conform, my conscience became my worst burden. Much of this description is in hindsight, because at the time when I was chided for being stubborn and thinking that I was always right, I was hurt deeply and accused myself of being arrogant and prideful, causing me to try again to be more quiet when I possessed a contrary view than was presented to me. There were times when I would begin certain religious books from authors who were not Catholic. It never took long to toss them aside after just a few pages, not because I did not like non-Catholic things, as I did not have an opinion of any Protestant world at that age, but because those writings and perspectives were noticeably bland to me, and even sour-tasting to my sensible attention, without my even understanding what might be sweet or sour. They were words without the conviction of sacrifice. There was no heroism in any of them. There was no Cross. It is as if the great Saints got to my mental constitution first, and no one could compete with them. I have always said that most of us are caught in a confining web of who befriended us first or offended us last. A spontaneous discernment occurred through my strong interior conscience; my heart knew what added to my inquisitiveness about God and what did not. I guess I was as stubborn interiorly as others thought I was in daily conversation. For example, what if you were building a house and had a pneumatic air-nailer in your hand, and a person walked up to you and asked if you wished to use a stone from their rock garden to beat nails into the wood? You would look at them incredulously and hold up the air-nailer, which would render the purpose of their query moot without your ever having to say a word. I enjoyed the spiritual challenge to my soul that my reading provided, and thought that this was the way for me to live more fully according to the spiritual inclinations that I felt within me. My contrarian nature was pronounced, but not in opposition to my religious faith, but rather against the world and any force that urged me to go along with any crowd that was absent of Jesus from their thinking. My father often asked, "If everyone is running off and jumping in the lake, are you going to also?" I got into the thoughtful habit of contradicting everything that I encountered, which was actually a very prudent attitude to have, since nearly everything that is presented to us in our contemporary age comes from the depths of worldly darkness and temptation, which needs to be contradicted. The Cross is the sign of contradiction. I possessed a seemingly natural "check" or filter through which I sifted everything I encountered. To this day, my aversion to the herd mentality is definitive and pronounced, unless it is in the direction of the Roman Catholic Church and Our Lady's miraculous intercession. Beware when all speak well of you. Beware of the frenzies and fads created by the media and popular culture. Beware of anyone attempting to obscure the Faith for the sake of some hollow false peace. I even hold suspect those agendas by Catholics that diminish, overshadow and lead people away from embracing the motherly intercession that our Holy Virgin is dispensing throughout the world. They are wolves. Her assistance to humanity in this age is paramount and necessary, but not required if one already subsists in Christian perfection. Our Lady once admonished me to remember that any time thousands of people gather in one place, such as at our great sporting events, it is incumbent upon us to ask for what purpose, and determine whether it is for the Glory of God in communion with His Will, or if it is just another of the many missed opportunities to draw the world closer to Christ Jesus through the Mother Church.

I would consider myself as being a rather insecure child and very shy throughout my teens, although very strong willed because I was being incessantly prodded by my conscience interiorly. I had very high anxiety in being pointed out in a crowd, and abhorred having to get up in front of any class at school, although I could play on the basketball court in front of any number of spectators and not feel the twinge of nervousness. I was always cognizant of doing what was right, lest I would have to travel through the day carrying the heaviness of nonconformity within my spirit. Additionally, I knew what being punished was all about since my father, being the woodworker, crafted a nice unbreakable wooden paddle which rested atop the refrigerator within reach of any immediate need of "attitude adjustment" as he would call it. My sisters and I were good students in school, not because of any advanced intelligence, but because our mother and father expected nothing less, and no excuses mattered. They attended parent-teacher conferences and told our teachers that they needed to be informed immediately if our deportment was not adequate. I remember my father telling us that if we got in trouble at school that we would get it double when we got home. Thanks be to God that he never had to make good on that promise. Good grades were our responsibility, paying attention in class was required, completion of homework was expected, and misconduct was punished. We were taught to respect and obey authority; and in our small town school, this was very easy because of the outstanding character and intelligence of our school administrators and teachers during our childhood. These were times before our educational institutions descended into secular pagan indoctrination. These were times when during the Christmas seasons we would put on pageants commemorating the Birth of Jesus in our public schools with students playing Mary and Joseph while the rest of us narrated the scenes with religious Christmas carols from the bleachers. Imagine an entire grade school body of students singing Silent Night in a darkened auditorium as cool blue lights bathed a scene of a manger before which knelt the Virgin and Saint Joseph. We lived seeing the Peanuts character "Linus" standing before us on a spotlighted stage, declaring to the world the birth of the Prince of Peace in the hallowed tones of Sacred Scripture. It was a beautiful time that is unheard of today because of the followers of Satan. There were so many good people who projected goodness both in their public and private lives during our childhood. Themes of discipline were prevalent throughout our growing up. My father had a signal where he would stand on the door stoop and whistle very loudly as a call for us to come in from our play, no matter where we were throughout the neighborhood. It was always funny when we would be playing a half-block or so away, and my sisters and I would hear our father whistle; we would drop what we were doing immediately and run for home, yelling back to our friends that our father was calling. They would always be looking at us incredulously, not realizing the far-off whistle was our signal. But, woe to us if we did not respond to the calling of our father. It was not that he was ever mean; he just meant business when it came to obeying him. Discipline could be swift and somewhat severe, such as when I had gotten a new motorcycle at fifteen years old and was told not to take it out of the yard. My parents went out to dinner one evening in the summer, and I decided to take it for a short spin down a country road that was a couple of blocks away, just to see how fast it would really go because I could never quite open it up within the smaller borders of our yard and pasture. Well, I did find out how fast it went, but so did a neighbor who told my parents that I had been out of the yard. I was not able to ride my new motorcycle for a couple months that summer. My father never did offer my keys back to me. I had to go ask him for them to ever get them back. Another time when we were younger, he used to tell us repeatedly to put our bicycles and tricycles in the garage in the evening. You can imagine a yard filled with the toys of six children. We rarely remembered to put them away unless prodded or if a big storm was brewing where we would later have to retrieve the trash cans from down the street. Then one day, they all seemed to disappear. We thought surely someone did not steal our bicycles in Ashland, of all places. After looking high and low, we found them in the barn, placed there by my father because we did not obey his command to put them away at night. He had collected them all and chained them to a stall in a dark corner of the barn. He believed that if we were not going to take care of them, we were not going to be able to have them. It is funny how it was over a week before we ever realized that they had disappeared. I can still hear him; "Don't slam the door; don't run in the house; don't throw the ball in the house; don't bounce the ball in the house; don't jump on the couch; don't jump on the bed; do the dishes; take out the garbage; back up from the television," and oh yes, the best one of all, on the phone when mother called him at work when we were being ornery and she could not control us, "You are going to get it when I get home." A couple of times after these phone calls, we dropped the paddle behind the refrigerator so he would not be able to find it when he got home. It was not any different in regard to our conduct at Holy Mass on Sunday. I remember a month of consecutive Sundays in my childhood years where I was told during Mass that I was "going to get it" when I got home for my conduct. And I did, except for the last Sunday when I ran home as fast as I could and put on as many pairs of underwear that I could find in order to soften the blow. I remember sitting in the living room, getting the "talking to" before the punishment, and my legs were falling asleep sitting in the chair because the multiple pairs of underwear I had put on were too tight and were cutting off the circulation to my legs. Ironically, on that Sunday, my father relented and I was never punished for my conduct in church again. Sadly to this day, I have never really realized what I was doing wrong during those times, except for the sibling antagonizing that often went on amongst the six of us. I do not wish anyone to perceive my father as some kind of dictatorial tyrant who reigned punishment at the drop of a hat because that would not be the truth. I hold him in the highest respect and admiration for how faithful a Catholic he has been throughout his life, in good times and bad. He is probably the single most sacrificial man I have ever met for the sake of his family and his God. He is a very honorable man who loves his family deeply, and has been very aware of the active role he was required to take in the formation of his children. He was determined that we would not grow up as hellions on his watch. We were taught to respect authority, perform the duties we were asked, and if we decided to do something, to do it well. We were never allowed to simply quit things that we started. My father was somewhat shy in personal situations, but composed, almost stoic, in his public capacities as a member of the school board and mayor of our small town, although he was never afraid to assert what he believed to be the truth in a given situation. He was very analytical and contemplative. I always thought he could have been an excellent engineer if he would have had the opportunity. It was an amazing combination in his personality. I remember during the early 1970s when students were rebelling against the school board due to the dress code at the high school, as they were across the nation. After the students made their self-centered presentation at the meeting, challenging the traditional norms, my father cut through their entire argument and stated, "This has nothing to do with what you wish to wear, it is simply your attack upon authority," and he was right. My father was a structured, respectable, ethical person who knew the importance of forming his children to be able to discipline themselves. He was honest to a fault, generous as appropriate in our family of eight, and deeply respectful of the Church. My mother, who was a convert from Protestantism, one time stated in the heat of a moment that father loved the Church more than he loved his own family. And, I remember the Bible verse popping into my head at that moment where Jesus said that anyone who loves family more than Him was not worthy of the Kingdom of Heaven. I thought, "Of course, he should." My father worked as diligently and as fluently as he could to enforce and reinforce the Catholic faith into our lives without offending my mother's Protestant predisposition because it was deeply ingrained into the fiber of his being by his parents and the times in which he grew up in the post-depression era. You could say that we had characteristics of a somewhat ecumenical household. At the same time he was invoking discipline, he provided for and participated in our lives to heavenly degrees. I remember in first grade we were studying the opening of the space age in the United States and our teacher told us that we could build rockets and bring them in for show-and-tell as part of our lessons. This was well before any scale modeling companies built rocketry replicas. Well, my father helped me build a four foot tall Saturn V rocket out of large index cards and manila folders from scratch, complete with removable capsule and a lunar module with retractable legs hidden inside the body of the rocket, just like the real orbiter. It was an awesome scale model for a seven year old. Unfortunately, I also remember carrying my rocket to school that morning and another of my friends walking up with his, which was nothing more than a toilet paper roll with some ragged cut fins attached to it with scotch tape and a string of colored paper streaming out the bottom simulating fire. It was apparent that he had made it completely by himself with no assistance from anyone. I remember him lowering his head and hiding it from everyone's view upon seeing mine. His pain struck my heart deeply even at seven years old; I pondered how something so nice from my father could turn into such a painful incident for another person. In truth, I wish I had his simple rocket today so that I could enshrine it with the dignity it deserved then. It is how Jesus sees many of the things we do for Him. To Jesus, my friend's rocket was as majestic as the real Saturn V thundering from its launchpad before the gaze of a nation of awestruck spectators. But, this was how my father participated in our lives. He always helped us generate the best that could be created. Our Halloween costumes were ingenious and huge every year, often winning the annual parade awards. He built playhouses, track and field equipment, poured a concrete basketball court next to the garage where my backboard and rim hung, and helped me restore an old Mustang automobile into driveable condition. He remodeled my room with a study carrel and a wall of bookshelves; helped me build model airplanes and ships, woodworking projects, and a whole range of art projects that our school would require of my sisters and me. One day, he walked in the door with over twenty model kits that needed to be assembled as a requirement for my Cub Scout merit badges, and it was neither Christmas nor my birthday. I spent hours on end gluing together and painting these models atop my study carrel. I enjoyed the intricacy of these types of tasks, but mostly because I was anxious to get to the finished product. When we did things, it was always the best we could accomplish together; and it was all because of him. And of course, it was my mother who always made sure that our innumerable activities and accomplishments were transported and placed in their appropriate places, whether it was at our school or before the public at large. She was deeply concerned that we cut the correct pose and not bring disrepute or scorn upon the family. She would take us to swimming pools in the summer, attend all of our sporting events, make sure we had treats for school holidays, and monitored the play of an entire population of neighborhood children for years on end.

As I grew up, I was always involved in the local sports teams, particularly basketball and baseball. I remember my first day at summer little league baseball between second and third grade. I really looked up to the older boys and how good they were at hitting, fielding and throwing a baseball. When they passed out uniforms that night, I received one which looked like an old woolen rag. It was missing buttons, and several letters from the town name were gone from the chest of the jersey, but I did not care one bit. I was more enamored with the real-life stirrup socks that simply had a loop at the bottom and the brand new baseball glove that my parents had gotten me. Our coach asked me what position that I thought I would like to play. At that time, everyone seemed to want to be the pitcher, but due to my shyness, I thought that was a position with a little too much visibility, so I settled for second base because I thought that it was a pretty short throw from second base to first base if the ball was ever actually hit to me. In the summer, friends were always coming over to our house, and we would hit baseballs to each other for hours on end, practicing and spending time together. Yes, we broke several of the neighbors' windows in the process with our errant throws and reckless hitting, and placed dents in many other things, including cars and trucks. It seemed as we grew older and stronger, the yards in which we were playing became smaller and smaller. A home run did not simply mean another point on the board, it meant retrieving the ball from the neighbor's yard after it had bounced off the facade of their house, their vehicle or garage door. We were playing one afternoon when one of my friends hit a baseball over my head and directly through an elderly lady's window immediately behind me. Well, my eyes and head turned to watch the flight of the ball through the plate glass window; and when I turned back around, everyone on the field was running for a place to hide. I was more concerned about getting the ball back as it was now rolling around inside the lady's house, and no one wanted to go to the door to retrieve it. Our athletics matured through those days, and eventually we fielded some very good teams which created many fond memories for us. On October 28, 1972 on a drizzly overcast Saturday, several friends and I were walking through a nearby cemetery that morning when one of the boys whose father was the town mortician said that it was bad luck to step on the newer granite full-length tombstone caps. I told him that he was crazy and proceeded to jump up and down with both feet upon the grave cap, challenging his declaration of some illusory fate. It was not two hours later that I sustained a broken leg while playing pick-up football in the same yard where the broken window occurred. I fractured my right femur, which sounded like a tree branch breaking, after an older friend tackled me and I fell in an awkward way upon it. I remember that my mother was hosting a garage sale that day, and that she and my father loaded me in the back of our station wagon and transported me to the Memorial Medical Center in Springfield, some twenty miles away. The injury never really hurt, either when it happened or anytime during the trip to the hospital. I laid in the hospital in traction for six weeks into December before a cast was placed on my leg, which I was required to wear for another six weeks. Then began the intense months-long rehabilitation of the severely atrophied muscles which had not been used in nearly four months. It was February before I ever returned to school on crutches, although my teachers visited me on numerous occasions to help me continue with my studies while I was recuperating. I still do not believe in "bad luck" from some ominous unseen force, but I do believe that there is an order to the universe and a respect and reverence required for the true and holy where we are mandated to effect reparation for offenses such as my disrespect toward the sacredness of that burial plot. I have no idea where my conscience was that day, but I realize that there are consequences to be paid for infractions against the sacred, either by me or by those who are chosen to sacrifice and suffer in reparation for the sins of the world. This is why fasting, prayer, self-denial, and sacrifice are so powerful for others. I would like to ask: Can you imagine the price that will be exacted for the violation against the sanctity of the human life of unborn children, if six months of my life were required for the act of ignoring the sanctity of a grave site? Woe to those who are advocates of abortion!

Later that summer of 1973, my mother came home one day and informed me that I had a new paper route, along with the responsibility of delivering newspapers every evening after school and early Sunday mornings. I did not have any input on whether I wanted a paper route or not; I was simply told that was what I would be doing from now on. The last thing I wanted at the time was any more chores to perform. Well, I delivered newspapers every day and collected the money from my subscribers on Saturday. It turned out in hindsight to be a very good experience. I learned to pay bills, handle monetary receipts, fulfill responsibilities, interact with the bank, and be held accountable to do a job well. I accumulated substantial sums of money for a child of twelve years of age. The entire family helped in the delivery of the papers when the times were difficult, such as when the weather was inclement or I was late in getting home from basketball practice after school. I learned very good lessons through this paper route. My thinking was relatively young and immature at that time, and while my sisters and parents were often helping me carry my responsibilities, it did not dawn on me to compensate them for their assistance. I was simply in a routine where I was taking care of the monies, worried about making the newspaper company payment, and collecting extra funds for what I desired in food at the local diners or candy and soda from the grocery store. My perspective was not wide enough to recognize the contribution they were making; and at the time, I did not receive much mentoring on the dimensions of the situation. What happened the previous day was out of sight and out of mind on the day I was collecting funds from the subscribers. Then, one afternoon, my young sister asked to borrow some money. I lent her the funds, expecting repayment to be part of the deal. After some time, she asked for more money, and I told her no and a frustrated argument ensued about her previous debt, which she could not pay anyway because she had no job, as she was even younger than me. My father came to my upstairs bedroom and tried to mediate the situation, where I told him angrily that she had not paid back the previous loan. He looked at me sternly, left the room, and returned some minutes later and threw a hand-full of money at me and said, "There's your God!" His words struck me like a lightning bolt, and from that day and that moment of grace, I have never relented in being generous, even past the point my circumstances would permit. I never want to be accused of that again in this world or the next because my God is Jesus Christ, and I do not want anyone to ever suspect through my words or conduct that this is not so. These are the kinds of lessons that I learned the hard way, in that my parents were often not anticipatory of the possibility of these confrontational situations or insightful enough to realize a teachable moment before these consequences could occur. Our insight as a family usually came after the altercation and our considering what caused it. For me, these occasions were simply more fuel for the contemplation that was ongoing within me. I would hold onto incidents and ponder them for great lengths of time, contemplating my place and responsibility in them. I was relentless at accusing myself of guilt, and rarely passed it on to anyone else unless I was convinced that I was in the right. Maybe this was where I generated my seemingly abnormal sense of insecurity. It was always easier to admit that I had done wrong, even if I had not, and tell myself that I would try to do better next time. My soul wanted to be at peace, but I could not understand why our family life had to be so disruptive at times. I could never seem to just brush away the sorrow. Thoughts would play in my mind until they were reconciled into some kind of understanding which restored a sense of interior peace, which usually meant admitting that my conduct was somehow the cause that I needed to remedy. As with most families that I have observed, we were not a family that had any eagerness to apologize for our parts in disruptive incidents. Open repentance does not seem to be a grace that our contemporary culture values, and I guess we were victims of this cultural omission along with the many other examples we see. In fact, I rarely remember anyone ever telling any other that they were sorry for anything. Although it was usually apparent through our demeanor and reformed conduct, our handling of offenses against each other was usually to submerge them in our psyche, then forget and go on, rather than addressing with contrition the one we may have hurt. Yes, most of us went to confession, but the further personal reconciliation within our family was very difficult, almost as if one were entering a minefield that was best avoided. In the beginning, we were never conditioned and disciplined to truly talk honestly and respectfully to one another without someone becoming defensive or offended in the process. Our differences were usually characterized by cold silence and an avoidance of subjects altogether. But, our maturity in Christianity finally brought us to realize that there is something wholly regenerative about being able to face those whom we have hurt and extend our sorrow and our promise to be better in the future. Without this recognition and allegiance to the Holy Gospel, along with the meeting of hearts, admission of guilt, and request for forgiveness, the manifestation of unity and love is burdened by an interior isolationism. This separation obscures the vision between hearts, the knowledge of one another, the trust in the best motivations of the others, to know and to believe, to purge and renew, to bind and become one. I believe these are things that every family should come to understand so that they can come upon the strength to corral and subdue the forces that would tear their families apart. And, it all happens through Roman Catholic Christianity. Only through the power of the Sacraments and the cohesion created through family prayer of the Most Holy Rosary can a bastion of strength and dignified protection manifest itself by the power of God.

As my sisters and I encountered our junior high and high school years, the forces of the world began to invade our home life to a greater degree. Our parents became more apprehensive of the relationships my sisters engaged in and their activities while outside their immediate supervision. While many young people my age were negotiating the lifestyles which offered drinking and carousing, my conscience was too powerful to allow myself to venture very far into those societal boweries. I do not claim to have been an angel; I had difficulties negotiating this period of time because I wished deeply to maintain my friendships with my peers and not be thought a prude, but I knew what a slippery slope it was to begin the habit of ignoring the call of the conscience and forsaking obedience to the truth. Once one slips the first time, the second is so much easier to justify; and from there, it becomes a habit, and finally the conscience is killed. One's acclimation to compromise occurs almost instantaneously because the mind starts generating warped justifications to overwhelm the conscience. My relationships with my female classmates were good. Yet, I avoided deep emotional attachments with any of them, mainly because I was very shy around girls. I also did not want to place myself into the position of having to fight against being drawn into situations I knew were not appropriate, and then having to battle any puritan reputation leveled by my male classmates. So, instead of participating in these societal norms of high school life, I became focused more deeply on sports, particularly basketball which I had played in organized fashion since third grade. I began to get stronger upon entering junior high and high school and spent hours upon hours, day after day, with a basketball in my hands. A day did not go by where I did not spend time shooting and dribbling on my home court, at neighbors' houses, at the school or the municipal parks. I remember the winters where my friends and I would remove snow and chip away the ice from the pavement so that we could play a pick-up game. We cut the fingers out of gloves and wore them so our hands would not freeze. It is amazing how hard a frozen basketball actually is, and how much it stings trying to catch a crisp pass from another player.

We pumped-up the ball with extra air just to get it to bounce in the freezing weather. Yes, there were broken windows, jammed fingers, busted lips and turned ankles by the scores. My father erected lights so that I could practice even into the night. Father Murray, the Catholic priest who lived across the street, joked with me after Mass one Sunday about how he could not get any sleep because of the thump, thump, thump of my basketball bouncing at all hours of the night. Sadly, his comments never made any impression upon me at the time. I did not realize that he might have been subtly making me aware of the situation in order to get me to stop at a decent hour, so I just kept playing whenever the urge stuck me. Many older friends stopped by late in the evening if they saw the lights on, sometimes close to midnight, and asked to enjoy an informal game of twenty-one or three-on-three. In truth, I do not think many of them were stopping so much to play basketball, but because I had five attractive sisters. I had many different friendships and relationships with my peers in Ashland. My oldest sister had entered high school by this time, which allowed me to become acquainted with many of the older boys.

It was during late 1975 and early 1976 that my dearest friend, Timothy Parsons-Heather, moved into my personal sphere of life. He was a good friend to several guys that I had begun to befriend as I began widening my life into the community through my paper route and working with local farmers, clearing weeds from their soybean fields and storing straw and hay bales into their barns. My delivery of the daily newspaper took me peddling past the local ice cream shop that had pinball machines and a fooseball table. And, since I always carried a pouch-full of quarters, I would stop regularly to play these machines and eat cheeseburgers and ice cream. There were always several older guys there who allowed me to play the different games with them, probably because I was there so often that I acquired fairly good skills, and they needed a good partner on their team to win the games. Anyway, through these acquaintances, I became better friends with Tim whom I had already known for several years, as I had delivered newspapers to his mother and father in the Ashland trailer court where he also lived at the time. Our first meeting was actually in about 1973-74 as I rode my bicycle to their door one day, burdened by the weight of the newspaper bag hanging from the handle bars. While trying to balance the entire contraption against the stairway so that I could dismount and climb the stairs to place the newspaper in the mailbox next to the door, Tim popped out the door in front of me, said "Hi!," and reached to get the paper so that I did not have to risk everything crashing all over the ground. From that day forward, he would often barge through the doorway at the exact second I arrived and retrieve the paper as if he was watching out the window for me to show up. In truth, he probably heard me banging my bicycle against the stairway everyday as I came in for a sometimes uncontrolled "landing" against it. I have fond memories of those initial moments of our meeting. He was nearly eight years older than me, and a student enrolled at MacMurray College in Jacksonville, Illinois; and over the course of several months, he became more available within my scope of friends. My parents were still fairly protective of me at that age, even though I was expanding my interaction with several of the older boys. Neither my sisters nor I were allowed to run the streets unsupervised, even as hospitable as Ashland was during those days. We had specific times when we were required to be home in the evening. Permission was required for wherever we went; to the park, the store, the local baseball games in the summer or to friends' houses to play. It was not until a couple of years later in the summer of 1976, after my graduation from junior high school, that Tim asked if I wanted to go with him to the Jacksonville Speedway to watch the stock-car races where several local men participated on Saturday nights. Tim was the public address announcer for the weekend races, so my parents allowed me to accompany him. I was able to watch the event from the scoring tower in the middle of the track at the start-finish line that night. It was the 200th anniversary of the July 4th weekend for our nation, and there was a special schedule of races for the holiday. The tower room was filled with huge trophies for the evening, and as each race was won, it was my job to pick out the correct trophy from the pile so that Tim could bestow it upon the winning driver as he announced accolades to the crowd over the public address system. I never felt so important; a part of something much larger than anything my simple life had been so far in our small village. As these experiences of childhood rolled on, every day was spent riding my mini-bike repeatedly around the pasture, playing basketball, mowing the lawn, weeding the garden, picking up walnuts and throwing them, and swimming in our backyard pool. There were neighborhood friends at our house continually, especially because of the swimming pool and probably my sisters. In the evenings, Tim and I, along with other friends, would travel to neighboring towns to eat pizza or get hamburgers from McDonalds, and then exhaust the night riding around the town and countryside, laughing and talking until the time arrived when my parents expected me home. It was rather providential in hindsight that Tim was drawn into my sphere of living, despite the wagging tongues who thought that our friendship might be somehow based upon illicit motives of an older man befriending a younger boy. There has never been any truth to those slanderous concerns. Despite the fact that Tim seemed to be friends with nearly everyone, our growing relationship was our response to our future calling together as witnesses to the miraculous intercession of Our Lady. We engaged in very meaningful conversations about life and truth compared to the horseplay that usually ensued when others were with us. Timothy was extremely kind and generous, probably the most selfless person that I had ever met. He never let me pay for any of our activities, movies or meals. And, he displayed to me the greatest respect and attention, even though I was so much younger than him. We would sit for hours driving around laughing, joking, listening to music, but most of all, talking about every subject imaginable, many having to do with religious themes, which resulted in Tim's conversion to Catholicism. As I entered high school that fall, I spent quite a lot of my time with him, which had the added benefit of protecting me from becoming involved with the more negative social elements that high school usually presents. Being with him was a comfortable place where I could more easily avoid getting into any trouble from my parents. He was almost the older brother that I never had, being that I was an only son in a family of five sisters. In June of 1977, he joined our family at Saint Augustine's church for my grandfather's funeral where he played taps at the cemetery interment. It was the first time he had ever experienced the Catholic Mass, as he had grown up within the Methodist church alongside his parents. Later that fall, Tim bought a new, black and gold, 1977 Firebird Formula. Being a sixteen-year-old boy and having just gotten my driver's license, I thought it was the most awesome car that I had ever seen. I quickly made it my job to make sure that it was always clean. I spent many hours washing and polishing it so that it never looked in any way other than new. Since I lived in a family of so many children and relatively little means, it was so special to have something nice. This made me always wish to keep the things that I received as new and clean as when I first received them. Dents had to be fixed, vehicles must be clean, and the yard had to be mowed, although I was not too worried about the weeds that grew in the garden. I did have my limits. Tim made me feel as if his Firebird was actually my first car. He gave me a set of ignition keys and allowed me to drive it anytime I wished. It was a pretty heady time being a sixteen year old driving one of the most beautiful muscle cars of the day. This is how our relationship developed: kindness was returned for kindness, and respect was the order of how we dealt with each other. Some, including my parents, thought that Tim's generosity was inordinate, but they failed to realize that it was the definition of his character learned from his upbringing, and that he was as equally generous and engaging with all those who showed him the slightest bit of friendship. In my case and without my parents' awareness, our friendship was maturing in the providentiality of God's future grace through the Most Blessed Virgin Mary. Our friendship floated along through the year beside my interaction with my other friends and the high school sporting activities. On Christmas Eve of 1977, Tim accompanied me to Midnight Mass at

Saint Augustine's parish. It was a transformational experience for his Christian faith, which led him to enter the Roman Catholic Church through the pastoral guidance of Rev. Father Joseph Murray. He was baptized into Catholicism on October 7th of 1978 and received the Sacrament of Confirmation twelve months later on October 28th, 1979 along with the rest of the catechumens who had petitioned for entrance into the Faith, with my father serving as his confirmation sponsor.

Sunday, September 20, 2009
Virgin Mary

"Now little children, I have come on this beautiful day to offer My Love in ways to which you have been inclined throughout your lives. My Special son, I offer you My good wishes on the occasion of your 48th birthday. You have for 20 years dedicated the meaning of your life to Me and Jesus, to the conversion of lost sinners, and to the benefit of the Lord's Kingdom here on the Earth. I know that you welcome your birthday with happiness, knowing that it is another year of your commitment to the Holy Cross and the Salvation known to men through Jesus' Sacrifice on Mount Calvary. Please be aware that God is fully-knowing of your own sacrifices for the sake of the exiled world. Do you remember in March 1991 when you and your brother were exiting an automobile at a fast food restaurant in Peoria, Illinois and a young child asked out of the blue, "…is that your Mother?" What was the young child seeing? He saw Me there with you and your brother, hovering above you, watching your every movement as you prepared for the preparation of all the awesome works you have so far compiled for Jesus. The little child was given the grace of seeing Me so you would know that I was there. He told you so. I know that you do not dwell on these kinds of things in your books, but that is fine; they are signs to let you know that I am always with you. It was as much a gift for the boy as it was for you. He became a Roman Catholic priest. My visit with you today is to remind you of the blessedness by which you have lived. This is appropriate on your birthday. If you think about your decades of life, you know that the first one and part of the second were formative, as any person

grows through. You then became intensely aware of My presence during high school and college because I supplemented your prayers for success with Mine. And, I was happy and pleased that you became successful in all ways academic that have brought you to this day. The beauty of the universe is with you now. It is Me. And, the true happiness that all men will eventually seek is the Holy Spirit in your heart, the Paraclete of God who is taking you to new heights of Wisdom. This is where your true happiness has always resided.

I am remembering every day to pray for you and your brother, and I ask Jesus to ponder new ways to innovatively spread My messages across America and around the globe, while at the same time allowing you sufficient venue to complete the last book of the 20th century with relative anonymity. You are marching now toward the last quarter of the year 2009, and as you say, you will enter yet another decade of the new millennium. Thank you for your true faith, My child. Mere words cannot explain how Jesus desires you to be righteously proud of your service to Him. You will receive many authentic signs, wonders, and blessings as the years pass to help you understand the nature of your elevation in Jesus' Most Sacred Heart."

So, one can see how our lives came together in our social life and also in the life of the Church concurrently in our youth. Over the next ten years, Tim and I remained close friends as we each engaged our unique paths of life, seeing each other periodically between our responsibilities; he in public service as the executive director of the county housing authority, and myself in college, through graduation, and progressing into my career in the newly blossoming computer industry. Timothy would periodically visit me at college and keep in contact by telephone. I was recruited to play college basketball at Eastern Illinois University, and spent one semester there before transferring to MacMurray College in Jacksonville, Illinois. There had been a head coaching change at EIU between the time I had been recruited and the fall of 1980 when I arrived which caused the terms of my status as a walk-on to change. My studies at MacMurray College were difficult, as I had chosen the more technical fields of information technology, or computer science as they called it at the time, and also mathematics and technical physics. I had no formal plans or direction for my education or career at the outset; I was simply floating through the stated curriculum that I thought would interest me and provide challenges; challenges which were also numerous for my faith in a small Methodist setting. I recall the class *Luther and the Reformation* which I took during my sophomore year. Like I have related, I only possessed rudimentary knowledge of the Protestant Reformation at that point, as the issue was never addressed in our religious instruction or upbringing. We were taught from childhood the truths of the Faith and not about all the philosophies and ideologies that might oppose it. Yet, I possessed a solid anchoring for my age in the historical breadth and basic thinking of the Catholic Church and the origin of its Dogma and teachings, in conjunction with the lives and mystical charisms of the Catholic Saints. So, when I was confronted with the vitriolic rhetoric of the Reformation and also the misinformation about the Catholic Church regurgitated within this course by the Lutheran professor, it was a daily crucifixion of my heart and emotions. My soul was screaming in anger and pain every day at having to sit and listen to the desecration and mischaracterization of the Original Apostolic Church from his lips, and also endure the sorrow I felt at those in the class being misinformed with such half-truths, confusion and darkness. I remember not ever saying much during that course because I was so insecure and shy, but mostly because I did not know how to respond confidently during class in a way that would matter before the professor's authority and my final grade. He had an entire arsenal of polished rebuttals with which to level at me should I have raised my head. My defense of the Catholic Church came in my final assignment where I launched my rebuke of Martin Luther and his so-called reformation of Christianity, while defending the keys passed to Saint Peter, albeit it was written from my simple perspective and righteous indignation as opposed to being a footnoted theological treatise. I did not know how to write, but I did know how to say what

I thought. The professor simply critiqued my assignment, saying it sounded more like a polemic than a constructive or defensible exposition, although he gave me an A- on the paper. Nonetheless, the simple truth was related that was never forthcoming in his class. This experience gave me a much wider perspective of how differing peoples were being impressed with ideas that were detrimental to the advancement of the Christianity in which I was being nurtured. Until that time, I thought Christianity was just Christianity, and that everyone understood the faith in basically the same terms. Little did I realize that the segment of Christianity that claimed to be Protestant did not understand any of the mystical or sacramental perspectives that the Roman Catholic Church has held for nearly two thousand years, nor were they postured to come any closer to the original Bread of Life from the Catholic Altar. It was like watching a 100 meter dash where a huge segment of the competitors were crouching in their individual starting blocks pointed in the opposite direction as if they were going to run the race backwards at the sound of the gun. There was no way they could ever finish the race in victory by assuming such a diametric position.

As I approached the end of my junior year, I had nearly completed my major requirements for my degree in computer science; and I happened to be scanning a class schedule hanging on the wall in my professor's office when it occurred to me that if I buckled down and filled my schedule during my senior year with physics and math classes that I could leave college with a double major in computer science and technical physics, and nearly acquire a major in mathematics also. Again, I was presented with a choice where I could either relax and spend my senior year enjoying the lighter side of the collegiate experience or discipline myself to accomplish something greater. I remember deciding not to be lazy and take the easier path, but instead to accomplish what was possible that others may not so easily choose to do. It was simply another moment of consistency in how my mind and spirit engaged life. I considered what most people would probably do, and I chose the opposite because the difficulty presented an opportunity for my character and identity to reflect a more honorable path of life. Maybe it was my contrarian nature again, or maybe my drive to carve out a uniqueness to my life, but I was spurred interiorly to attempt achievement in these ways. My conscience was always asking me who I wanted to be. How did I want to be seen when all was said and done? It constantly pushed and nagged me, just as in those moments where I was prodded to shut off the bathroom light in my youth. I was encouraged by my conscience to expand the dimensions of who I was, and not retreat into flippancy, mediocrity or even sloth. So, I engaged my senior year in college and the demands of my schedule while also spending leisure time with a younger female co-ed with whom I fell in love. She was a very smart and beautiful young lady who had an innocent playfulness and an uncanny confidence. She rarely, if ever, became jealous or insecure over anybody or anything. She was not in any way affiliated with any religion, but was open and accepting to accompany me to Holy Mass on numerous occasions. Our relationship lasted through my graduation and into the next year whereupon I was heartbroken to realize that our bond could not withstand the distance and separation while I engaged the workforce and she remained finishing her final years in college. But, I still carry fond memories of our time together. Thereafter, I refocused my life with my friends and co-workers, engaging the local night life and spending evenings and weekends playing sports for the next several years. And, in all this, I never lost the respect for my Catholic faith or the Church itself. As I think back through all these times even into my early childhood, I cannot ever remember an instance, absent of a single time or two of being sick, where I missed Holy Mass on Sunday. Through my childhood, high school, college and into my adult working life, there was never a time where I had forsaken the call of my conscience and disavowed my obligation to Sunday Mass or the Holy days. The liturgical life of the Catholic Church was ingrained and infused into my life as intricately and precisely as breakfast, lunch and dinner, although it was never something that was forced into my thinking or anything I consciously created within me; it happened almost unawares and naturally through the unfolding of my life and the example and discipline of my parents. Even during my years in college, every Lent I would attend daily Mass at the church next to the campus, a Lenten discipline I accepted from my parents during my youth. To describe more clearly how deeply my heart reveres the sanctity of the Catholic Church, I can testify that I have been blessed by God with never having entertained a single negative thought in my mind about the Roman Catholic Church or its Dogma and teachings throughout the course of my life. Never a moment of consternation; no adversarial inclinations; no conversations, no frustrations and nary a thought in opposition to it. Every thought has been to defend it and conform to it. I have never challenged or confronted its teachings on sexuality, the male priesthood, liturgical observations, confession to a priest, or any of the other areas of confrontation that detractors have with the Church. I have never entertained a single moment of interior debate about any of these things, not even in passing. It is as if my mind has never been allowed to contemplate an opposing perspective regarding the Church, not by way of any mental oppression, but through a dispensation of preeminent beauty that has trumped anything that would dare oppose it. I have always had a beautiful luminescence within my interior vision enveloping the Church which nothing could compete with. I have never asked Our Lady about this phenomenon, but I have always wondered whether it was a particular grace in preparation for Her miraculous intercession in my life and Her revelations as the Morning Star Over America. I can describe how I believe this luminous nature developed and was nurtured. Imagine having a large room filled with objects, including boxes of different sizes where each one would fit inside another that was a little larger. Now, consider someone asking you to retrieve just the boxes from the pitch-black room of objects and one by one place them within the others until there was only one box left in the room with all the others inside it. Also, consider that you did not know what a "box" was. The process of selecting and placing all boxes inside the others would be a nearly impossible, complicated and time consuming task if you were left alone to accomplish that feat. Your mind would be flooded with a herculean dilemma. What is a box? What is the size compared with all the others that could be possible in the dark room? Does the object you pick up even matter in the dimensions of your task? Can you simply throw the object to the side and ignore it? Have you placed a ball inside a box, then a bicycle on top of it? This is how it seems that most people find themselves sifting truths from life. But, this is not the way it occurred for me. I do not see my life as having had to undergo this sifting process and the contradictions and chaos that are generated by it. I did not make any decisions about each object's worth, or where they went or in what order. I was handed only boxes out of the darkness in their correct order throughout my life through the integrity of my parents, the wisdom of the Church, and the insightful vision contained within the writings of the Saints, all at the orchestration of my conscience through the docile and accepting obedience of my heart. I benefitted from the wisdom of the ages because my heart was "open acceptance" in matters of the Catholic faith without exception. And further, I was surrounded by some of the most reverend, holy, saintly, traditional examples of the priesthood that ever lived. I respected the Church far and away above me, matched with my respect for my elders and superiors, such as my teachers in school. I never had an instance where I had to discern which box went where or whether I should choose to discard it altogether as a useless object in the grand scheme of universal redemption. There was no pollution of the integrity of my vision of faith. I was never confronted with the personal biases of individual theologians or the progressive views of lukewarm laypersons in religion classes. I did not have to endure any competing entities before my faith had matured enough to defend itself. All has been orderly and congruous, organic and symmetric. I have not once interiorly debated the wisdom in the teachings of the Church as if I did not want to comply with its tenets, nor do I understand the audacity of those who do, other than their hearts are polluted, distorted and dysfunctional. It is so easy for me to see that it is all based in their pride and arrogance in opposition to the King of kings, for should they surrender themselves, all would become clear. They have the boxes from their room stacked incorrectly and additionally interspersed with objects that are not boxes at all. Their interior structures are not built on solid foundations. My heart has peacefully accepted from the beginning everything the Catholic Church is; my vision has grown in communion with the great Saints, and my conscience has instructed me to comply and obey without ever raising my head to challenge the Dogmas that the Church proclaims. My conscience has never told me to retrace my steps in regards to the structure of my faith, as it did to demand that I turn out the bathroom light. So when I do raise my head, it is to declare all that the Catholic Church professes and teaches with honor, pride, and the force of beatific conviction. I am a child of God who has always lived within His Apostolic Church; I have the right to speak! After all, who in their right mind confronts and challenges the legacy and tradition of something so breathtakingly beautiful, instituted by the King of Creation 267 Popes ago, of such longevity, truth and honor, filled with the stories of the greatest giants and legends to have ever suffered for righteousness while breathing the air of this world? If societies long for the genius exhausted ages ago, herein it still lives. If the world pines to see that courage long-forfeited to the cowardice of worldly expedience, herein does it breathe in the souls of the greatest of men. And if darkness lays its pall over the beatific vision of nobler times, then from this Bastion of Divinity does the Light of Christ beam out of the night of the coming ages. You see, the Catholic Church already stands proudly behind the doorway of tomorrow's horizon, there awaiting the appearance of man in each of his days in these realms of exile. I never paid much attention to people who were in conflict with the Catholic Church because for me it was always a matter of ignorance or their prideful ego overriding their heart, and most of their good sense. Their positions were always rooted in selfishness or their desire to engage in the seductive nature of the world at the expense of doing what was right and pure. I never understood the argumentative and dismissive nature of these individuals. I understand why the Most Blessed Virgin often refers to them as reprobates. And no, She is not unkind for stating exactly who they are, nor is She anything but the greatest advocate for the diversity of holiness within the sacred unity of God's divine Providence beneath the Cross. Everyone is encouraged to join the Sacrifice! I always contend for the Original Mother Church based upon an honest review of its history, while protestors are nearly always offended in some way or another about how put upon they are by its sacrificial disciplines. They neither love the Church nor the family of man enough to make any sacrifice of themselves for anybody but their friends and families, or the esteem that comes from preaching to their choirs. Sinners do as much. It is always about them. They ignore the idea of One Bread at One Table of Faith. They eschew actual Christian unity at the Altar of Sacrifice. My sense regarding those who state that we are not sheep and that blind obedience to the Dogmas of the Church is irresponsible is that I have cast my lot of faith and the essence of my being with the original Apostles and all the giant Catholic Saints that the Church has produced. I cast my lot with the Virgin Mary who stood beneath the Cross. I stand in the footsteps of their lineage. I want to be in their company for all of time and throughout eternity. I would tell the doubters that they have simply couched their rebellious natures in some kind of vain justification that rings, "I'll decide" without their ever having calculated whether they have enough troops in the battle to win. [Luke 14:31] They profess allegiance to a doctrine that is a mere 500 years old. Catholics surrender to one that has graced the Earth for two millennia. Consider all the Saints who are on the side of the Catholic Church with the testament of their lives: Augustine, Jerome, Polycarp, Ambrose, Alphonsus, Gregory the Great, Aquinas, Catherine of Sienna, Mother Teresa, John Paul the Great, Teresa of Avila, John of the Cross, Francis of Assisi, Therese of Lisieux, Catherine Laboure, Bernadette, Padre Pio, Mother Teresa of Calcutta, Lucia; the entire Litany of Saints, the Martyrs, the Successors of Saint Peter, the original Apostles, all the holy women, the Queen of Heaven, and a whole unnamed history of honorable men and women whose staid courage describes their allegiances to the Holy Spirit through the Church instituted by Christ Himself. Their "boxes" were also aligned in the order of beatific grace, and I honor them, I petition them to assist us in this our finest hour. How does any person stare into the eyes of these holy legions standing in the fields of honor beyond the sunsets and declare that they stand against these giants of the ages and what they died for? I ask again, how? It is decadent foolishness based in the willful rot of human pride and outright ignorance. While I always realized that there was a cacophony of voices which claimed to be speaking for the Church and deciphering for humanity what it truly means to be a follower of Christ, I realized early on that there was a unifying harmony in the voice flowing from the legacy of the Roman Catholic Church's greatest Saints; an exact thunder of accord that could be easily heard and felt in the contemporary articulations of the Magisterium, especially the Popes throughout my life. Hence, one could actually be confident in extending not blind obedience, but a fully-informed, confident, strong, and heroic allegiance to the Vicar of Christ and the authentic message of the Gospel that flows from each successive Pontificate. It is all one voice, one echoing, one reverberation through the ages from the Burning Bush to the appearance of the Archangel Gabriel, to the Manger of Bethlehem, to the Cross of Calvary, the Evangelists, the Saints, and the Universal Apostolic Church to the final breath of the last Roman Catholic. It is the Voice of God to the human species through His Son Jesus, the Christ, by the animating power of the Holy Spirit. In the end, no other Voice will be resonating in triumph over the test of time and the altercation with the diablerie of the mortal ages, except the spiritual oratory of the Roman Catholic Church. We await that great day in joyful hope for the Second Coming of Our Savior, Jesus Christ. And atop all this, when Our Lady greeted me through Her immaculate intercession, all this honorable allegiance to the Church became a personal "beatific love" for it. My being stood up. Love for the Church is a love for the history of humanity redeemed; all the faithful people, compassion for their sacrifices, admiration for their devotions, all transcending back to the focal point of one Savior and one Virgin Mother on a mountaintop called Calvary where the world was split to the core and saved from damnation.

My faith-filled upbringing, spiritual curiosity, and intellectual development manifested this internal kingdom of Catholic faith within me. It is now fortified with sacrificial pilings and angelic ramparts erected across the breadth of my maturing vision, my budding view of history, and my place in it. I feel an intimate communion with history's giants who reach beyond the boundaries of the material world at every faithful step I extend into the temporal unknowns; guiding, encouraging, admonishing, and defending. If I suffer, so be it; many good people have endured onslaught for the sake of the truth. If I am victorious, praise be to God for allowing me a foretaste of His Dominion. If I am slandered, I am in good company with the Saints who faced sinister swords instead of sniveling swagger. If I am uncertain, I know that each step I take is in the direction of God's Will because the most intuitive geniuses of Christendom will intercede on my behalf to make it so. Within a "beatific keep" so sacred in the recesses of my interior solitude lies invincible my identity as a child of God. I have always known this since I was old enough to form a sentence. If I was asked how I arrived at this place; what was the most important thing that allows me to now reside in such confidence and certitude, I would remind everyone of those days that I heeded the call of my conscience and retraced my steps to shut out the bathroom light. Over and above all that I knew about the Church and the lives of the Saints, our attendance at Holy Mass as a family, and the blessing of my upbringing, it comes down to those intimate moments of personal decision when I invoked the sacrifice of my will to comply with the voice I heard within me. The voice of God always calls us to the sacrifice of our will until the day our will mirrors the Will of Our Lord. On that day, it is not sacrifice; it is not diminishment; it is power and glory; it is no longer we who live, but Christ who lives in us. The Christian conversion of the human person is not like searing it with a fiery brand or affixing an embossment to the surface of the soul, but actually dismantling and reconstructing the entire constitution of our spiritual identity. Crucifixion and Resurrection. The Roman Catholic Catechism describes a radical reorientation that occurs the moment the mind and heart are consecrated to Jesus Christ, so much so that the old self is supplanted by the divine framework of our new irreducible nature. We often speak about the fibers of our being as though we are made of divisible components comprising the essence of the self. This may be true for our physical body, but our soul cannot be diluted or dissected this way. We either belong to God wholeheartedly or not at all. There can be no fractures or fissures in our commitment to redemption if we expect the Lord to resurrect us when we die. The human soul does not enter Heaven in phases. Hence, our conversion to the Cross and dedication to the Church consist of our willingness to be remade as though to be born again, shedding our original birth like crawling out of a shell. The whole concept of fullness is made of this because the Holy Spirit fills us to overflowing with the grace and peace of our Eucharistic King. And, in this is the New Earth.

Our Lady gave me a simple perspective about this coming New Earth as we spoke one day. She acknowledged man's use of the word "chemistry" as defined in our dictionaries whereby we describe the science dealing with the composition, properties, and transformations of substances and elementary forms of matter. Chemistry is the definition we use to circumscribe our body of knowledge of the composition, change and manipulation of the matter that surrounds us. Within our mortal framework of existence, all matter is fluctuating, moving, transforming, balancing, being constructed, rent asunder and manipulated. Hot and cold are balancing each other in a battle for equilibrium. States of matter are vibrating and revolving, playing out their altercations. All existence is seeking its place of ultimate fulfillment. Our Holy Mother gave me another word to highlight a beatific concept. The word is "chemisis." She defined "chemisis" as the final composition of the created world; the completion of all chemical, biological, and natural reactions and phenomena relating to organic and inorganic matter. It is a word whose definition is unknown to scientists because they have yet to fathom the realms beyond their measuring devices and the moment that none of them will ever be needed again. Chemisis describes the environs of the New Earth at the Second Coming of Jesus Christ. At present, every atom and molecule of matter is fulfilling its purpose of assisting the God of the heavens in redeeming His children. Creation too suffers in the image of the Son of God. Hence, at the Second Coming of Christ to fulfill and finish the great Sacrifice of Redemption, Creation itself will become complete; transformed and released from its sacrificial service to the transformation of human souls. All will be reconciled in the peace that Christ completed upon His Crucifixion.

Sunday, October 24, 2010
Virgin Mary

"I have given you a new word with which to describe to your readers and listeners about the consummate state of the exiled world. You are all moving toward the 'chemisis' of the Earth. It was pronounced this way by Jesus on the Cross. As sure as the Salvation of men was assured upon the Crucifixion, Jesus fixed all Creation in time to be perfected with the heart of the redeemed. It is not unlike the photograph of the perfected soul that I spoke about years ago. When this Earth is supplanted by the New Earth, there will no longer be a need for chemistry as you know it. All that is physical will have been permanently refined into the ultimate chemisis about which I speak. It will be complete, but still alive. It will be fully prospered and grown, but not subject to the reversal known to mortal seasons. There will be spring, summer, and autumn simultaneously. And, there will be winter only for those who want it. Do you understand this derivation of this new concept? Its derivation is the Resurrection, and it will be effected when Jesus returns again in Glory."

If anything can be gained from my revealing this brief synopsis of my reflections upon my life and childhood development, I would hope that everyone would see how blessed I was to be protected in an environment that reflected the truth at me while I was searching and listening to my heart, trying to locate it within myself, and myself within it. I would imagine if I were to continue pondering other dimensions that I could write hundreds of more pages of perspectives and ponderings that I engaged over the years, but all of them would have the underpinning that I have already related. The Catholic Faith which I have never questioned or rejected is the basis from which I have experienced everything. It is the solid foundation beneath me that cannot be razed. And, that entire foundation was miraculously confirmed as the universal Truth when the Most Blessed Virgin Mary commenced Her miraculous intercession in my life. If my words are to hold any benefit for those who might read any of our works, I would ask everyone to believe and accept that they are also loved, accepted, and blessed by God, just as I have described in my reflections. Conversation with God and the Heavenly Hosts is what prayer is all about. The truth surrounds us every day, trying to make an imprint upon us. Every opportunity exists for each of us that was present in the beginning for me. I am not unique; "We are unique!" Our Lady's messages have the power to realign all the "boxes" within any man. Everyone has a will and the complete autonomy and power to invoke that will toward the end for which God created us. There is a narrow path which leads to Paradise; a path I desired to remain upon throughout my upbringing, but it is to the credit of so many others who sacrificed, fought, and prayed that I remain there, including all of my family who brought their faith in Jesus through time to be deposited in my soul. What a familial legacy given to the corridors of time! It is the great gift, the pearl of unlimited price, that they gave to me. This is how Christianity has survived through the ages, propagating through time and the souls of men to their posterity, unstoppable, like a tidal wave bearing a pearl on its crest. If you are not on this narrow path, find it here in the intercession of our Heavenly Mother, and point your feet with determination in the direction She is leading. Heed the Morning Star Over America. Take a second look at the majesty of the Roman Catholic Church. Kneel and ask the King of Heaven to inflame your conscience with a resonant voice of guidance, then listen and obey its strains of sacrificial beauty. Ask Him for the courage to read the works of the Morning Star Over America and defer to them so that good order may be restored to your being. Everyone can stop and retreat to "turn out the bathroom light." Each of us can choose to do good, no matter the cost, no matter the sacrifice. Each of us can invoke courage and make ourselves part of the best and most noble part of humanity. There is no power in the universe other than your own will that can stop you from moving into the Light of the Queen of Heaven. The Virgin Mary is your Mother! Her messengers are not special because they have received spiritual gifts; they are special because they believe and pray according to the truth that She speaks. The Father of Lights dispenses the realization of His Presence in response to the order of graces that man builds between Heaven and Earth through the disciplines and sacrifices of self-denial, the reorientation of vision, and the prayers that elevate the heart into the beatitude of the Father. A sailing ship moves swiftly across the water only after the sails have been raised. Prayer is the raising of those sails. Contemplation is the calling of the winds. Orienting our entire interior disposition into conformity with the Roman Catholic Church turns our ship into the breezes, billowing the sails with motive power in the direction of the redemption of our souls. Sailors and shipmen have never protested the wind, they have ridden those gusts and zephyrs, the gales and tempests, to undiscovered shores and lands where new nations were created, treasures were discovered, where possibilities flourished, and new beginnings were bestowed upon themselves and their posterity, all for the Glory of God. And, Our Lady accompanied them all, bringing Her Son to humanity for the redemption of His people. She says, "Ahoy, My children! Greetings from the Kingdom of Heaven. The Creator of the Universe, your loving

Father, sends His indulgent blessing in the Name of His Son, Jesus! I bear the good news that He has dispatched the Messiah and His angelic legions to deliver you, bearing gifts of the greatest joy from on High because He loves you! He is not coming to conquer you, but to bless you with His Glory and repatriate you into the palatial estates of your true homeland, the Paradise where He reigns by one Word and one Law: Love!"

Awakened by the Dawn
Medjugorje Breaks in My Life

"Heavenly Father, through your infinite wisdom, grant us the blessing of your peace throughout our lives. Hone our spiritual vision with a sense of comprehension of the abounding presence of your Will. Through knowledge and servitude, let us realize beyond hesitation that our every gift to others is a prayer to you. All in all, make us the people whom you always wanted us to be, and grant humanity the grace and dignity that preserves the holiness for which your Son was crucified. Our Lady of Perpetual Help, always remain at our side. We ask this through Christ Our Lord. Amen."

It was 1987 when I was called by one of the women of the parish to her home. At the time, I was facilitating the high school religion class at Saint Augustine's church and thought that maybe she had some information that pertained to the classes. I remember standing at the door and her handing me a copy of a book about Medjugorje and telling me that the Most Blessed Virgin had been appearing to six children in this Yugoslavian town every day since 1981. In that instant, my mind exploded. I felt almost a panic of euphoric anticipation overwhelm me. I realize now that it was Our Lady invading my soul in preparation for what She would ask of me a few short years later. All the stories that I had read, the accounts of witnesses, and the testimony of religious authorities about Her appearances in former times all came into the present and hit me with a wonderment and a joy that I cannot describe. I felt like a little boy who had been found or one who had no longer been left out. It was as if God who was once way up in the sky outside my reach was now on our planet where He could see and hear me. I sensed a spotlight shining upon the Earth like a laser beam which caused me to immediately begin to wonder how I could get into that Light so that I could be seen. I thanked the woman for the book and ran home and immediately read it cover to cover. The words of the book jumped off the pages. A door in the heavens opened for me, and I was determined to climb through it before it had a chance to close again. I retrieved my Rosary and began to pray it that night. Even though we had grown up praying the Rosary, it had been a couple years since I had recited it; and I had forgotten a few of the mysteries, although I remembered that they were categorized into Joyful, Sorrowful, and Glorious events in Jesus' life. So, I made-up mysteries as I prayed that night. I did not have any sense of opportunity to travel to Medjugorje, nor were there any places where I knew to find more information other than in the book I was reading. Therefore, I was pretty much on my own to orient my life according to the intentions that our Holy Mother was articulating to these children, whom I had never met and most people did not know. I just knew that simple children upon enduring such persecution with no gain in material or prestige rarely, if ever, lie. So for the next two years, the events of Our Lady's daily appearances were always at the forefront of my thoughts, wondering what She had said and what events were occurring. We must remember the internet was barely a figment in someone's futuristic imagination at that time, and the newspapers surely refused to publicize any apparitions of the Virgin Mary. I prayed my Rosary often and continued to practice the disciplines of the Church and participate in the Liturgies. My intentions reflected the orientation of my relationship with the Church. I never prayed to receive anything, but rather to know what I should believe and do to help me become a better person. I never petitioned Our Lady to display any manifestation or miracle because I thought it displayed a certain presumptuousness, knowing that I did not deserve such gifts. I just wanted Her to know that She had my attention, that I wanted to be good, and that I was trying with all my heart to obey Her, no matter what that meant. I never desired or wanted anything from Her, just that She would keep me on the path that would please both Her and Her Son. My orientation was of waiting for Her next command and praying for the world as She asked in Her messages. Even though I was mindful every day of Her appearing again in Medjugorje, thoughts of actually traveling to a far-away communist country were far beyond any sensible reality for me. I would have more likely considered entering the space program for an excursion to the moon as an astronaut.

Then, unbeknownst to me that it was the anniversary of the death of Saint Bernadette of Lourdes, on April 16, 1989, I began attending daily Mass. Soon afterward, something changed. After almost two years of engaging my career, the night life with my friends, the sport of go-kart racing, and boating and partying on the lake, all the while still fulfilling my religious obligations, the voice of my conscience ignited and began calling me toward Medjugorje in a way that I never considered before. It said, "Now is the time for Medjugorje. If something so great is happening in this world in your time, then you must participate and witness to it." I had received a special edition newspaper which chronicled the story of Medjugorje that also had advertisements for pilgrimages to the small hamlet. Upon scanning the several groups, I chose one, called, paid my money and was given my departure date that fell during the week of the Feast of the Assumption of Mary in August. On Mother's Day in May, my grandparents came to Ashland to have Sunday dinner with us. My grandfather leaned over during dinner and told me that the house next door to them in Springfield was for sale. At that time, I did not have the faintest notion of looking to buy a house, but within two weeks, I had agreed on a price and providentially closed on my new home on May 31st, the Feast of the Visitation of Mary. As my August departure date arrived, I was settled and ready to engage my travels across the ocean. The day of my arrival in Medjugorje brought a heightened sense of what I had been interiorly experiencing all along. I knew and could feel that I was now beneath the supernatural "spotlight," open and apparent before the eyes of God's providence; close enough to feel the warmth from the fire. It was as if through the passing of one night's travel, I went from a relatively undefined, freewheeling state to a definitive, conscripted conviction; from wandering amiss to knowing the north of the compass.

My faith exploded past the inanimate parameters of being merely a belief system assimilated from childhood into a comprehensive, revelatory acceptance of God's unseen Kingdom. Everything that I had ever read, known, and believed about the Catholic Church and the legacy of Christianity into our time became a living thing that stood and began to breathe in front of my eyes. The immovable and stoic was moving and interacting interiorly with my heart. The static became uniformly electric. It was as shocking to me as it would be for one to live in the redwood forest since birth, accepting the beauty of its natural magnificence, and suddenly one day all the trees beginning to walk and talk, transcending anything you had ever supposed about them. I have always characterized my reaction as running 100 miles per hour with my hair on fire, and in an instant coming to a screeching halt before something that whisked the idea of running right out of my brain. And, there was also great joy and peace in coming to realize the actual purpose of my life. I had found why I was born and that I would never return to the life I had known before. The interior affirmation I felt was beyond what I could have ever imagined for myself, like an athlete enduring sacrifice and arduous training for many years, finally feeling the roses of ultimate victory lightly falling upon his upturned face. There was reward through the simple existence of the tiny village of Medjugorje. Everything that I had spent my life believing only through the strength of my logical intellect and determined faith; the disciplines, the sacrifices, the penances, the obedience, always trying to do the right thing; I could feel the pleasure that God had for it all. And in turn, I felt compelled to show the God whom I could not see that I now knew He was there and that I loved His Son for His Sacrifice to save us. I could see the power and beatitude in all the facets of the Church that I had read about and participated in. I had an immediate and advanced affinity for the Saints and all they endured, and why. I understood with far more precision the genius of Roman Catholicism and how I had been participating in its miraculous heavenly grace all along, without realizing that there were such transcending depths; heights that human beings had not begun to fathom. A door had opened within me; one that I always knew was there, but thought would never be opened until after I had died. All the metaphors one could imagine are summed up in that my Catholic faith was now alive and breathing, not assisted or on life-support, but self-sustaining from within by the power of the Holy Spirit who had finally revealed Himself to me. My awakening was not from a previous self-created nightmare as some people experience, as if I was jostled into a land foreign to me. I was awakened to the exact reality that I was participating in interiorly; I did not have to be jerked around into a new way of looking at the world or my life. My ecstatic soul screamed at the top of its lungs that I had been right all along to believe and obey my Catholic fathers; like throwing my fists in the air in victory and crying out—"Yes!" — complete and total affirmation by the supernatural power of Heaven for all that I believed and understood, indeed, all that I was! The trepidation felt in the phenomenon whereby people hedge against their faith publicly in order to be accepted socially was incinerated in me. I felt a courage that severed all these bland attachments to social approbation. From that moment on, I could not have cared less what any mortal sinner thought about my faith-filled convictions because I had experienced the grace of God, and I knew that the desire to be united with Him in the beauty of the ages beneath Jesus' Cross was the only path to success that life would ever bestow for any of us. If there were one hundred teams that were all prepared to enter a tournament, how would you feel going into the games knowing that you were on the team that would never be defeated? The pearl of great price was lying within my grasp and, for me, everything else had already been put up for auction, including what anyone else might think.

Upon returning home, it was difficult for me to share my experiences about my pilgrimage without crying, which was a particular cross for me. It was several years before I could even speak about some of the most intimate moments of grace that Our Lady dispensed to me because the feeling that would well-up within me would overwhelm my senses. Any time I would turn my interior focus toward those most revelatory moments, the Light of Jesus' suffering became so bright and the Truth of His Kingship so clear that the composure of my emotions could not withstand it. This mystical phenomenon occurs periodically to this day. There are realities within the heart of humanity that are beyond the sensible imagination of men; beauties that lie behind doors that most people do not even know exist within them. God can open any of these mystical thresholds at the blink of His Will and bring humanity to its knees in jubilation or destruction. This is why He patiently waits, nurturing our change of heart through mystical events such as the miraculous appearance of Our Lady. He wishes our hearts to be reoriented in advance of the ultimate revelation of Glory, that we would feel the joy of knowing that we were with Him in the hardest times as opposed to finding, inadvertently or not, that we were His enemies instead. Subsequent to my pilgrimage to Medjugorje, there was very little guidance or support from anyone on how to sustain the newfound elevation and animation of my Catholic faith. There was a pronounced sense of detachment from my previous life and all the things that had held enjoyment for me. When friends were heading for happy hour, I was entering the vestibule of the church to offer my prayers at Holy Mass and receive Our Lord in the Most Holy Eucharist. I sensed inside me the new path of my life which no one was going to deter me from engaging with all my heart. I knew with clarity the purpose of my life, but I did not know which direction to go. There was a vagueness brought about by how huge I recognized the challenge to be in a thoroughly secular society. In October, I was visiting the local Marian center when suddenly, out of the blue, I was given the directive of leading a Rosary group at the center. I have always thought it was rather providential that the man who spontaneously tapped me to begin this prayer group was the same doctor who cared for me in 1972 when I had broken my leg as a child. He was a man of special grace who has been instrumental in spreading the word of Our Lady's appearances in Medjugorje across many states to thousands of people. He had traveled to the shrine several years earlier and had developed an itinerary of public talks and slide shows to relate to everyone the great grace that was being dispensed to the world there. By November, and as a result of the witness of both myself and my sister who had accompanied me to Medjugorje, Timothy Parsons-Heather and my father together made a pilgrimage to the shrine. During the week of their trip, I had scheduled a return trip to Medjugorje at the beginning of December. The night Timothy and my father arrived home, I mentioned that I was departing again in three weeks. Timothy immediately spoke up and said, "I am going with you."

It was during this trip spanning the Feast of the Immaculate Conception of Mary in December 1989, while standing outside the home of one of the Medjugorje visionaries, Vicka Ivankovic, that my brother and I were beckoned from the crowd of pilgrims to come into her residence for a private meeting with the visionary. I was astounded and a bit nervous being pointed out in a crowd because I had merely expected to stand along with all the others and listen to one of her talks that she often gave to the pilgrims. As my brother and I hurriedly climbed the outdoor steps, the crowd seemed astonished and turned our way, wondering what was happening and why we were being called into the home. We entered Vicka's living room where she was standing, radiantly smiling. I felt an amazing sense of anticipation and a deep thankfulness for being blessed to personally meet this beautiful young lady. Neither my brother nor I could speak her language, and she could not understand ours, neither was there a translator. We embraced as if we had always known one another, exchanging sibling affections and smiles, then she placed a hand atop each of our heads and began to pray in her Croatian language while we bowed our heads and prayed silently with her. After she finished, she beamed at us with her huge smile. Timothy then leaned toward her and kissed her on the cheek, while I kissed her on the other. She smiled even more radiantly and deferred her gaze downward and blushed. We then said our goodbyes and proceeded out the door toward the balcony steps. As I came out of the house and moved toward the staircase, I remember the entire crowd to the person staring at us with wonderment written across their faces. I could sense that they were all curiously interrogating our demeanor, wondering what we had just experienced and why. It was a very profound moment of transcension, going from an anonymous face in the crowd to being the object of focus for so many people that I had never met, especially as shy as I was. As this entire scene was passing before me like watching a movie, I possessed a rapturous feeling of peace within me where I wanted to simply walk away with my brother across the countryside, away from the crowds. I do not know the prayer that Vicka lifted to God, but from that moment, I have felt a personal identification with her. She is my little sister, and I pray for her often. The burdens she carries to be such an instrument of grace are beyond the comprehension of most people. Our Lady has told me and helped me realize that mystical gifts come through the diminishment of the flesh and the endurance of suffering. My brother and I returned home after celebrating the Feast of the Immaculate Conception in one of the most mystically vibrant places on the planet. We both offered our sincere consecrations to the Immaculate Heart of Mary that day and promised to live as She was asking everyone. During our stay, I purchased a large 3-foot tall statue of Our Lady at the foot of Mount Krizevac, or Cross Mountain, where the townspeople of Medjugorje erected a cross in 1933. I carried this statue on the airplane and set it next to me on the return trip to the United States. I remember one very special lady who was deeply touched by our trip. As we flew out of the country that morning, she was looking out the window of the airplane with tears streaming down her face, staring into the sunrise, watching the miracle of the sun from her seat. I was struck watching her nearly ecstatic communion with God, wishing there was an entire world of people just like her. She thanked me in Chicago after our landing for bringing our Holy Mother home with us. I hope she someday realizes how prophetic her words were that day. My travels to this Marian shrine produced no objective or outward supernatural signs for me personally; I did not see the miracle of the sun, although I watched in amazement as other people stared into its blazing radiance and described the spinning colors and dancing movements. I witnessed an entire crowd of people watching the miracle of the sun who simultaneously cried at the exact same instant, "the sun disappeared! It's gone from the sky!" On a day with a bright blue sky, the sun disappeared from the sky—for them. One of the people who personally witnessed this was my brother who was standing right next to me at the time. I asked him to explain to me what he was seeing, and he simply said, shrugging his shoulders, "I do not see the sun in the sky. It is gone. I only see blue sky." I did not see any signs in the sky, crosses spinning, appearances of heavenly beings or miraculous healings, but I experienced a deeply profound interior light within my soul that to this day I cannot truly explain.

Upon returning home, my newly fortified faith posed a glaring contrast to the normal cadence of our family life. Most believed what we related about Our Lady's appearance, but they could not grasp the feelings of exhilaration that we were experiencing, which gave some pause as to whether we were becoming zealots and moving into the realms of unbalanced religious hysteria. This is a common theme that many people have experienced when faced with others noticing the awakening of their faith and the reality of God, especially through Our Lady's miraculous intercessions. For me, it did not matter; my spiritual compass was not coming off north for anyone. I knew the truth of what I had experienced; I know the Mother of God is appearing in Medjugorje through the graces of light I continue to carry within me to this day. Over the course of the next several years, I believe all the members of my family ultimately made their own pilgrimages to Medjugorje to experience the great grace of Our Lady's intercession. From December 1989 through the beginning of 1991, Timothy and I returned to our workplaces and groups of friends, trying to keep alive the grace of our faith in the normal course of our days. It was very difficult during these months as the forces crescendoed against our new enlightenment in attempt to pull us back into the secular cadence of life. My attendance at daily Mass was paramount in supporting my strength of conviction during this time. I do not think that I could have withstood the temptations and attacks against my new devotions without my daily reception of the Bread of Life. I knew Our Lady wished the entire world to know of the message that She was delivering through Medjugorje, but there was very little actual support or acceptance forthcoming from anyone in the Church, except for the small group of individuals who had either made their own pilgrimage to Medjugorje or who had believed the testimony of others with their entire heart and were trying to live the messages. So, all through 1990 and into 1991, our small groups prayed the Rosary together while my brother Timothy whom I saw periodically lived fifty miles away in Beardstown, Illinois.

Sunday, September 20, 2009
Virgin Mary

"I have been attempting to continue My awakening of the Saint James parish in Medjugorje because some of the pilgrims who come there are only looking for miracles without sacrifice. They are looking for proof of God's existence instead of new ways to honor Him. You have seen and heard of those who go there and return home to lukewarm lives. You know that I call all pilgrims to Medjugorje, but each one must take to heart what they see and hear there. They must come home and live active lives of supernatural faith in the seed of new meaning that is implanted in them. My son, I am having little success with most American pilgrims. It is the kind of culture to which they return in the United States. It is steeped in secularism and secular humanism, in materialism and consumerism, and in selfishness and pride. These things comprise the American credo, that they are free to choose whatever lifestyle or belief system they choose. We know that this is not the case when it comes to remaining loyal to the Cross. All of this works against the movement of Americans to the mission to which you and your brother have given your lives. You have created a deposit of works that is massive to those who have never heard of Me. And this weekend, you have been an electrician, carpenter on the attic floor, auto mechanic in the garage, furniture mover, and messenger for the Mother of God. What a life!"

This is the description of my life and how I arrived at the February doorstep of 1991; nothing particularly extraordinary, life as normal as any young man my age, nothing beyond the capabilities and sentiments of any person; nothing beyond the faith or reason of anyone given the breath of life. I simply possessed an innocent openness to the Catholic faith from the beginning, a childlike inquisitiveness about God, and a deference to anything that He might choose to do miraculously or otherwise. And, above all, I trusted my own heart because everything I had ever known about Jesus and His Church had been validated by Our Lady's mystical grace. My Catholic faith was the soil that the Holy Spirit had been cultivating my entire life, unbeknownst to me. And, Our Lady had now planted it with seed and fertilized it with the reality and power of God, coupled with the "miracle-grow" of possibilities engendered within the power of Her miraculous intercession. I have always thought the parable of the sowing of the seed on rocky soil or good, or among the thistles, was glaringly applicable to the great gift that the Holy Spirit is dispensing through Our Lady's appearances in Medjugorje, and indeed, Her many other intercessions throughout the world. The soil of my soul was prepared for Her grace; nothing impeded it, while I was intimately aware of the secular thistles of 1990 that tried to grow up and choke my newly awakened faith. I also painfully encountered the rocky soil in all those I met who purposely displayed their haughty indifference, who derided Our Lady's intercession, who refused to defer to any evangelization of Her messages, and who with passive aggressive avoidance attempted to stifle and extinguish any cooperation with the Queen of Heaven's agendum to reach Her children to save them. Sadly, several of these people were Roman Catholic priests. There is no bitterness toward these people, simply a recognition of Our Lady's heart-wrenching sorrow as She is required to endure them with such patience and grace. It truly does not have to be this way, if man would simply display the faith that he claims he has. She told me one time that the indifference of one atheist kills more hope than all the tyrants who will walk the face of the Earth. And, it is even worse when it is a person professing faith or one of its leaders who is the culprit displaying so much faithlessness. They say they believe in the Holy Spirit, but reject everything the Holy Spirit does. Purposely ignoring and impugning Our Lady's miraculous intercession is devastating to the evangelization of the Catholic faith because that intentional aggression testifies to the world that our faith is not the authentic directive of God, but merely a debatable mantra spawned from an illusory mind. This cowardice tells the world that God is an entity that, if He exists at all, never truly interacts with His Creation or commands anything. And further, it dismisses Him to nothing more than a point of concern after having passed from this life, if ever at all. Our Lady wishes me to relate through this description of my early life that there is nothing that sets me apart in any way from anyone else in the human family. I have possessed no advantage, aptitude, esteem, opportunity or inherent gift that has not been freely dispensed from the Cross to every other person given the breath of life. I am normal; not in the estimation of those employing deranged worldly judgement, but normal in the sense of how God intends His children to approach Him. I believe, I accept, and I obey the Testament and Traditions of the Original Apostolic Church that the Virgin Mary reigns over as Mother and Queen. I believe in the many contemporary instances of the Most Blessed Virgin's miraculous intercession throughout the world, and I have been rewarded for that obedient acceptance. This is my Christian mantra and my example that I carried into my sleep on the night of February 21, 1991, a night where the seed planted by the Mother of God broke the soil with colossal concussion to launch the Morning Star into the skies over America. Upon the cock crowing, a beaming light was brought forth to brighten the soul of man, to shine, heal and convert, to prophesy and lead humanity into the revelatory age of our spiritual greatness. My eyes closed that night to a worldly identity that I would leave behind at the break of dawn, not destined to awaken to the tragedy of our vessel of dreams being interred beneath the waves, but risen to the christening of hopes for a new Creation; the sunrise where a starving population would feast their eyes on an entire field of ready-to-harvest grain glistening in the morning sun. On that new morning, a diary would commence that would record the authentic intervention of the heavens into the lives of two men, that humanity would be awakened in preparation for the Second Coming of the Son of Man. I hope that these pages describing my life will be seen as coming from my obedient compliance with Our Lady's request to record the perspective that I possessed leading up to the commencement of Her revelation as the Morning Star Over America. She did not come to my brother and me because we had done anything exemplary—She simply knew that we would believe and trust Her, as if we had any other choice before the revelation of such majesty. She knew that we would need Her daily assistance to complete the work that She would ask us to accomplish. Yes, She knew Her beauty would be enough. There are no spiritual gifts outside the power of the Holy Spirit; He alone who unilaterally decides whom He will bless to suffer in communion with the Savior of the world. For my part, I simply hope that I have fulfilled and will continue to perform my solemn duties acceptably. When all is said and done, we must remember the scriptural response, "I am no more than a servant..."—a child who aches inside to one day hear, "Well done, my faithful one."

> *Listen to Jesus' voice calling in the night. Hear the yearning in His sacred timbre, beckoning humanity to invoke His Crucifixion.*
>
> —William Roth Jr.

Saturday, December 26, 2009
Virgin Mary

"Today, My children, My Immaculate Heart beats the rhythm of gratitude that you have again dedicated another year to the conversion of lost sinners. It is not that you have nothing more to do, not that you would be unhappy with less redeeming things, but that you already know the outcome

of the world. You have yet to see it with your eyes, but like your fellow Roman Catholics before you, the images in your heart about Peace and Justice keep you focused on the reconciliation between Heaven and Earth. Heaven will prevail, this is for certain. What remains of the Earth the way you see it now is according to the willingness of humanity to change. They have required the Holy Gospel from the First Century, and they still need the intervention of the Church to remind them to keep looking forward, past the veil, beyond the parameters of their exile, and into the eyes of God. You have attested your agreement that this time must come. You have proved that you believe The Word. My Special and Chosen ones, think about this for a moment. You were carried to Medjugorje on the hope that you would be closer to the Father and uniquely united with Jesus. You were curious about these miraculous things they call apparitions and interior locutions because you knew they originated from the unseen realms. Remember that you did not come to the Saint James parish of your own accord, but that I called you there. It required your time, faith and resources, which you gladly invested. Look here! Look where you are now. The passing of time has proved that your original interest was more than curiosity, but a mission to enhance the integrity of your religious faith. In other words, the Lord asked you to heave the rock of faith over the hill, and He created the gravity that led it to the feet of humankind. All you need to do is show Him one thing, that you believe that He will react to your faith in Him, and the whole of the heavens will answer. It is not unlike the thunder whose percussions shake more rains from the clouds.

You have learned a great deal about human emotions and battling secularism even from the last twelve months. It is fitting that you feel satisfied that you have accomplished everything that Jesus set-out for you. I am unsure what I can properly say to commend you for what you have written. It is deeply spiritual and uplifting. It is not too negative. You have learned from My messages during these many years that the modern world must be destroyed in order to rebuild it again. And, you are seeing the destruction every day, material and spiritual. Please do not be shocked by what you see unfolding as time continues to pass. You have become accustomed to seeing the tragedies that are caused by human beings and Nature alike. It is here in this home that so many facets of the world will begin to change. You have been the epicenter of creative amendment that is spoken about in the Scriptures. There is no room for sadness for millions around the globe because of your kindness to Me. When you occasionally look at your deposit of published works, you can discern an agenda from Me that appears to be directed at anonymous people. All those whom you have met and the many you will meet in Heaven will benefit from My intercession. The sentence structure and cadence of My words are unique to Me. This is what the language experts will see. Even as I gave a brief Christmas message in Medjugorje yesterday, everything I have said and plan to reveal there indicate the leading of humanity to the Morning Star Over America.

You are also seeing the beginning of another decade, the second of the new millennium. There will be another large segment of the world's population pass into Jesus' arms in the next decade, just as in all those prior. I seek from you the assurance that you will accept the Lord's Will as it pertains to this because some of them will be close to you. It is a tremendous victory when redeemed souls see the face of God. And, there will be more wars break out here in this world, more starving and diseases. It is always the same as long as unrepentant sinners reject the message of the Cross. The Holy Spirit will propagate the Gospel message through your holy heart, and you will foster the mission of the Church by your obedience to Me. What we have given each other cannot be taken away. The life you have devoted to Jesus, all the months and years, are for the consecration of humanity to His Most Sacred Heart. This is the irreducible genius that God implanted in you from a very young age. You have loved in His likeness. You have inherited and perfected it. And, you have multiplied the good virtues that made the Saints glow with priceless joy when they closed their eyes in death. They bequeathed everything they did and said to the Church and ultimately to the collective souls who comprise it. Do you realize what this means to Jesus? Hence, I come today with My happiness to share with you. From 1991 through 2009 is a long time for you. It is only one breath for Me, but *you are with Me in every way. You know that 20 centuries is a brief time compared with the Eternity of Heaven. My messages here have been about the length and breadth of human expression with righteous overtones, and this is what you have passed-on to your brothers and sisters in your books. As I have said before—all for the glory of God!*

I ask that you do not see the passing of the new year as any significant demarcation because you are on a seamless journey to Heaven. It is important in the sense that you are getting closer to living in Paradise, but it is actually just another number. We are unsure how many more there will be, but suffice it to say that something significant is going to occur in your natural life span that awakens the world to the Truth. If you shall come with your brother to Heaven before Jesus comes again, know that it will not matter. You have already done enough for a thousand lifetimes and an infinity of returns of the Son of Man. Life is to be lived one day at a time. I am always with you, and Jesus has never left you. I am pleased that you occasionally write such quotations as that which appears at the opening of today's message. Please ponder the coming spring that will be here presently, and know that the warmer days are ahead. Winter will not come again for another year! I am so uplifted that you have an appreciation for recorded music. It is a unique way to comfort the human spirit and show your love for God. Each person on Earth has been given a special gift. The matter of discovering it is left to the human heart, to the availability of great mentors and masters, and to the desire to discover the 'self' that connects you to the creativity of the God of your fathers. This is the reason why your brother enjoys the works of the classics. I know that you like them too. Puccini and Dvorak were listeners of the spirit of peace as it relates to the consolation of the heart, even in the crass inclemency of the secular world. There is beauty in everyone, if only it can be brought out. As I have told you before, it is usually excavated from the depths of the soul by deep suffering. I simply ask that you remember how much I love you."

The Glorious Morning
February 22, 1991
The Feast of the Chair of St. Peter

"Dear Lord Jesus, place within the circumference of your care all who are broken and alone, the outcast and ostracized, those castigated for teaching your Word, and the millions who are in their last agony in reparation for the sins of the unconverted. We hold in our hearts the grace of your Crucifixion through which all human endeavors are sanctified. The restitution owed for the transgressions of men has been paid by you, and we are liberated from the culpability of Adam by our imitation of your love. Give us the fleetfootedness to shine your torchlight into the darkness, and make of us whatever glorifies your holy name. We ask this through Christ our Lord. Amen."

There were very prophetic elements to the lives of my brother and me in the years leading up to Our Lady's open intercession to us that we did not realize at the time they occurred. We were normal worldly boys who nonetheless had a deep underpinning of the Apostolic faith in my case, and an impenetrable sense of friendship and decency in his. I did not consider myself an author or aspire to be one, yet I remember sitting at my study desk in my bedroom in the early 1980s composing an outline for a book that I thought should be written. I could not write then, nor do I believe myself to be much of a writer now; and I did not like English class even in the slightest, although I did pay attention. My biggest claim to writing was a three page book report in junior high school that had long been lost to the flames of the trash burner in our back yard. Words such as honor, devotion, virtue, and many others of like subject matter were written on my outline. I was consumed with what they really meant, although I never presumed I would ever write a book because I would not have known where to begin. I simply thought that I should highlight what should be written about by someone. There was also a similar moment when Tim and I were together during a later period when I blurted out that we should write a book about all the things we often talked about. I never believed what I was saying; I was simply boasting, but I knew somehow the fleeting things we spoke about should be captured, knowing that once the conversations left our lips, they floated off, dissipated and were scattered, lost to the breezes of further dialogue. I never spoke with anyone else about the things Timothy and I engaged in our conversations. I believed that the themes of our conversations were important enough to place into print so that we could remember our thoughts someday when they might mean more.

Then, the day of February 22, 1991 arrived; and with it the reconciliation of my life and all my previous thoughts into a single coherent vision, with a meaningful purpose for my past and a direction for the rest of my life. Not only did the event of the Most Blessed Virgin's intercession make sense, but my life made sense; I made sense; all my thoughts made sense, even my earlier sentiments of capturing the meaningfulness of the day onto a written page made sense. Her presence ignited a reconciliation within me, a living dream of spiritual animation. The future was no longer hidden in some undefined, obscuring mist. When recalling my perceptions and self-identity preceding those initial days, I recognize a clear demarcation between the way I viewed life and how I see it now. My former perceptions seem so long ago in another life. I was a blind man who was suddenly given sight. A blind man may have a puppy described to him all day long, but what does he think, not only at having a puppy placed in his lap, but also given sight to see the precious animal for the first time? I was sensibly and emotionally overwhelmed, shock and awe, by all that was impacting my mental constitution, and my physical and spiritual sight as well. I was encountering supernatural graces, mystical phenomena, confirmations and "coincidences" so far beyond the ability of the most stern contrarian to refute; all coming out of the realms of improbability at my sense of perception like a deluge. Life became openly unhinged from the conscripted boundaries of what human beings take for granted as being "normal." Thereafter, I began to endure the accusations of being "abnormal," in need of psychiatric help, and worse, under the influence of the devil. Then, the suffering inflicted by others commenced. I gained a great perspective on how ostracization and division occurs. I witnessed how Satan moves through entire groups of people and manipulates their thoughts to condemn what they cannot explain or control. Our Lady's appearance was more normal to my being than my previous existence. I was released from the darkness and deception to an extended degree. Boundaries were wiped away that I did not even know existed until they were breached. And, even from the first moments that morning, I sensed a transcending heavenly purpose that was beyond my ability to ignore. I could see the inevitability of history because I was engaged with the same Virgin Mother who stood on Mount Calvary outside Jerusalem 2000 years ago. The history of time was suddenly compressed to a point of being irrelevant because I was factually communicating with this same reverent Mother. And, somehow this compression extended forward as if the Second Coming of Jesus were already upon me, and there She still stood with open arms. From the first night, I never believed that our Holy Mother's intercession was a casual or singular event, nor a reward for something that I was doing right, although I loved Her with all my heart after my pilgrimages to Medjugorje. I did not see it as a solitary matter of happenstance, but rather as an entire panoramic, structured, decisive renewal of existence that had worldwide ramifications that would lead to the conversion of millions. I perceived instantly that the dimensions of Her transcension far exceeded anything I happened to be experiencing in the moment. Every last scintilla of my will that I could imagine invoking against the truth of Her presence was vaporized. I believed! I was convinced to the deepest recesses of my being. My soul knew for the first time what it meant to be faced with something and someone for whom I would gladly give up my life. One segment of my mental constitution was completely focused on how to obey Her more profoundly and accept more deeply, while the other was experiencing an earthquake. Amidst a mental explosion occurring to the boundaries of my thoughts, there was impenetrable stability in my convictions. I was not scattered or unsure; I became confident, impenetrably focused and determined. Nothing more true had ever happened in my life, and it meant more than anything life could offer me. Our Lady is of a beauty so majestic and tender that we are thrust back into the innocent sentiments of early childhood before Her immaculate grace. My soul realized in a blinding flash, as if a veil was drawn away, that She is my Mother from whom I had somehow been separated. I felt like a child who had been taken from his family who was suddenly reunited with his Mother whom he remembered loving more than anything in the world. It was an actual sense of reunion with a Mother I knew intimately. I had been overshadowed and enveloped by an actual canopy of Divine Love that had detached from the greatest imaginations of man and descended with clarity and reality around my being. I was Her child, and my soul knew it. Amidst all these profound soul-shaking reverberations, I quickly gained an ominous sense that very few would ever accept what my brother and me would relate. I felt it acutely and painfully, and had it confirmed to ever greater degrees as the days progressed forward from those first moments in February 1991. I carried a great apprehension, knowing it is too easy for people to dismiss mystical claims as the delusions of unbalanced minds. The work of faith is their own, and many stumble in exercising that faith in the moment that it is called upon by God because we are too often rationalists who demand that God anchor His revelations in the material parameters of the world so we can grasp them for support not requiring our faith. Our Lady guided us for over twenty years through a peaceful, meticulous process of living life, calling daily upon our faith in order to generate the material parameters that everyone could grasp as a foothold of belief. Morning Star Over America has material parameters in the form of twelve books that no human being had the capacity to generate, especially my brother and me. But for many, it will be so much easier to disbelieve and discount without ever reading them, or at best, reading only until they reach that first sentence they do not agree with. In my experience, most people cannot transcend their fears without having something concrete to hold on to, and once the dissembling commences, it requires elevated levels of individual strength to maintain one's spiritual composure in the verity of the unseen realms of the Holy Spirit. That is why it is so easy for children; they simply believe what they are told and begin to function according to that new information. Small children routinely do what they are asked and believe what they are told. Frail humanness claimed the judgement of many of those near us in the beginning; and then between them in their doubts, they formed a collective where the evil one thrashed and stirred, causing great fear and commotion on their part, and pain and rejection on mine and my brother's. There was no physical evidence at the time to offer anyone as proof to calm their fears. Words were not enough. Trust was out of the question. There were not twelve books and thousands of pages of supernal truth, but only the text of a message given every day and the claims from my brother and me that we had received them from the Mother of God. I could not work a miracle or hand them a golden crown from atop Her head. I only possessed an ecstatic enthusiasm that was bursting from every pore of my being. Sorrowfully, I was not able to quell the fears of those who could not conquer their growing skepticism. They disbelieved simply because they could not find the courage within themselves to accept. I understand the chasm they had to cross because I was already standing firmly on the other side looking at them across the expanse that grew wider by the day. My determination was unfazed by those who were chiding me to admit that the phenomena were from evil origins because Our Lady was dispensing graces upon me to keep me unwavering. I grieved at being attacked, but I could not profess what was not true. Unbelief thrived like a virus throughout the group that surrounded us. I could not say a word that was not twisted into a lie and thrown back in my face. It broke my heart as I began to fully realize my lot in the ranks of visionaries throughout history. Few of them, if any, had ever been believed from the outset. I realized the Gospel warnings were going to play-out in my life, and I was not prepared for the emotional attacks, notwithstanding Our Lady's support at every step. From those initial days forward, suffering and torment became the portion that my brother and me were served from every imaginable direction. Our hearts were pummeled. We were verbally attacked, emotionally browbeaten, questioned, prodded, intimidated, scorned, slandered, accused of being gay, received scathing denunciations and vitriol on the telephone recorder, and ultimately harassed through the internet; groups were organized against us, priests were enlisted who guided everyone away from us, spiritual directors and pastors counseled parishioners against our work, all but four members of our 50+ member prayer group fled from our presence; and a man who said to us privately that he would always stand with us, not three days later walked out with the rest who could not accept and thereafter stood shoulder-to-shoulder with those who ridiculed us. And, all of this is a blessing that we cling to, knowing we suffered defending Our Lady's honor. It was an amazing revelation into the life of Our Lord for me. I understand how Palm Sunday turned into Good Friday in the short span of a week, and I am so blessed to have suffered these indignities for the sake of the Truth which still lives in our hearts and our deposit of works. Timothy and I were only acceptable if we surrendered our testimony and either admitted we were making up the messages or yielded to counseling to be detached from Satan's diabolical delusion. Great efforts were expended to separate my brother and me, while Our Lady was telling us to let nothing divide us. I have heard too many people pontificate that if the circumstances around a given intercession do not bring peace, the intercession is not from God. Never have I heard one of these people say that peace comes after one invokes their faith and believes. It never comes to rest on those who do not. The disturbances caused by faithless bystanders who refuse to invoke their trust in God must never be respected as criteria in determining the authenticity of anything related to the intercession of the heavenly hosts. It is a paradox in the arena of discernment. While peace is a fruit of the Holy Spirit and a sign of authenticity, it is found in the hearts of those who believe, no matter what worldly circumstances swirl around a given intercession. Even in light of what happened and what my brother and I endured, it is a blessing that so few believed in those initial days. God allows human weakness for His Glory. From a discernment standpoint, the intercession we experienced would have been suspect, though not definitively, if everyone had believed as passionately as my brother and me from the initial moments. The opportunity for the scandalizing of Our Lady's work would have been far greater, and Morning Star Over America may have never been manifested. The faith of humanity plays a great part in the manifestations of the Holy Spirit. God does not throw pearls before swine. My brother and I have shared very intimate moments with Jesus in His Passion. Those insights are breathtaking. A mystical event was initiated by Heaven which was beyond human intellectual capacities so that it might never be claimed that sinners were responsible for it. We too are sinners; we are not responsible for it, although our Holy Mother praises our obedient faith. Transcending into the realms of accepting the revelations of the Holy Spirit is not an intellectual exercise of the mind; it is a path directly through the Sacred Heart of the Crucifixion. It requires an invocation of faith and a surrender originating in the deepest recesses of the heart where the binding mental constructs of the mind are obliterated, and where suffering and obedience meet in the perfection of the human soul. There is confusion and disturbance around every authentic intercession, except in the heart of the recipients. It is there that one will find clarity and serenity, oftentimes beneath great suffering and pain heaped upon that gentle heart. God dispenses a great impenetrable rock of undeniable truth into the center of a visionary's heart which is non-negotiable before the judgement of Eternity and the relativistic self-autonomy of men. And, when that rock is encountered, the world fights against it by either trying to prove it is a fantasy unworthy of credibility, or by assassinating the character of the messenger. No messenger can carry that burden without miraculous interior graces from the Holy Spirit. Only the Son of God Himself could do it alone.

Atop the difficulties in believing by religiously minded people, the secular world is at an even greater distance from the truth. The faithless chide everyone to believe that miraculous interventions by the heavenly hosts are nothing more than sentimental musings from unstable people, unworthy of attention until they become too convincing, then worthy of contempt and derision once it is understood the message applies to them. I did not know how to describe our experiences in cognitive dimensions at the outset because they were not an event of material parameters like describing who was present at a birthday gathering. I equate the dilemma with trying to describe your first love to someone who has never experienced being in love. How does one describe that happiness? Eventually, I matured to the concept Our Lady was trying to teach me all along. The work of believing belongs to the individual person. It is their sacrifice to make. It is their trust to invoke. It is their obedience to offer. My concern is not to audit the response of anyone to see if they are measuring up in their devotion, although I am overwhelmed with joy and thankfulness when I see it because I know how happy it makes Jesus and our Holy Mother. The vision of Her joy ignites within me when I see the faith of others. There is a psychological phenomenon that occurs whereby if a person knows you are trying to convince them of something, they sense power over you, and will "force" you to convince them by withholding their compliance until you grovel beneath their patronage. Their sacrificial faith is the commodity they withhold.

Saturday, July 4, 2009
Virgin Mary

"My darling sons, your Mother comes to speak to you on this independence day in the United States, a day of rain, darkness, and cool temperatures. I bring the brilliant Light of God to lost creatures everywhere, and I offer My blessings, My intercession, and My compassion and

humilities. When you think about what this month means in your lives, you will be amazed. We have been waiting for the coming of July 2009 for decades; America and the world have hungered for the finishing of My messages that will transform and renew them through Jesus' Most Sacred Heart. When you speak of the finishing of the Mass and the mission of the Church, you cannot omit the implications that My messages here have and are about to have on the conversion of lost sinners. My little ones, you are too close to your work to know what lies in your hands. You have had too many daily doses of toil and disappointment, too much persecution and pain. It would seem that you must now take a broader perspective about God's intentions for you, and think peacefully and righteously about the gifts He has dispensed to humanity in this place. Men have spoken for centuries about the grand stations and architectures that have stood on various grounds, and this place is no exception. It has changed from prairie to village, to homeland and residence. When I spoke to you last year about having appeared here in 1865, I knew then that I would be giving this message to you now. Yes, you have been subjected to the soiling of your name and the impugning of your dignity from doubters everywhere. Your sense of worth has been devalued by those with whom you have worked and prayed. Once, a man stood and said here in this very building that he was taking his prayer group and going somewhere else, and this resulted in the fracturing of their unity with Me. Indeed, it was the initiation of their own suffering, losses they would sustain so they could see the Cross from which they walked that day. Another doubter went to Medjugorje and colluded with still another doubter to defame your work here with Me. But, they failed, and the pilgrim who thought she was doing God's work called you evil in His name. The Father loves her nonetheless, and you know of the unspeakable tragedies she has suffered to take her own soul back to the Crucifixion. My sons, this is a weekend and ensuing week that will mark history with indelible blessings because you have remained side-by-side for Me, you have given your lives without complaint so that I can effect the mission of the Church. Be gratified that you have done these things, and know that you have joined the long line of sufferers who have propagated the Holy Gospel that humanity could be redeemed.

My Special son, I come to you in a reflective tenor today because I can see what I wish you to see; that you and your brother are days away from placing the exclamation point on your faith in God. Your own deaths will be as beautiful; all the remaining days allotted to you are provided in His Book, and you must come to better understand what a sacrifice this has been. Whatever goes on through the days, where you work, with whom you work, how much money you make, and all the rest are all supplemental things; they are part of your march toward the Glory about which you have spoken and written for many years. Your hearts have been broken by the arrogance of other men. It seems as though your prayers have been ignored. Your fellow citizens have been callous, indifferent, and even meanspirited against the very work that has comprised your mortal lives. You are better for all of this, My sons. You cannot see it now, but you have ascended to heights that you would have never reached if your lives had been marked by any more ease. The everyday ritual of telling God about life, remember the Father hears you, and He still lends you His ear. Yes, He embraces all of your worries and woes; He deigns that you see them through the lens of the Cross. He heard every prayer that Jesus uttered in Gethsemane and those He offered from the Cross. Why did the Father not intervene? Why did He not rescue Jesus from the Sacrifice He was born to endure? Because this is the way men are refined. God's Heart was as Crucified on the day Adam and Eve spurned Him as Jesus' Body was ravaged on the Cross. He wishes you to take Him in through all ways physical and spiritual, and you have done your part well. You have been good and faithful servants. God has always been the essence of perfect sanctity, as has Jesus and the Holy Spirit. Knowing this, you have seen that such divinity can be brought to sorrow, the innocent suffering for the guilty. This is what you have done for the Blessed Trinity, for the conversion of the wicked, for the propagation of the Church, the uplifting of the poor, and the esteeming of the Saints. Take to the Lord in prayer all your doubts and inquiries about why life must be this way, and He will answer you.

My Special son, it is My intense hope that you will never blame yourself for the way conditions have been in your workplace. If you must blame anyone, it would be a departure from the Truth if you did not blame Me. When you responded affirmatively to My call, you became a target of Satan's hatred. It has been a hellish 18 years for you because of your compliance with My wishes. Should I have warned you more clearly about this? There are no regrets for those who are unified with Jesus on the Cross, but I have all along planned on this independence day to apologize to you for the life that has been heaped upon your soul. I am truly sorry. It has never been about whether you are too emotional or whether your pride has caused you to bear so much pain. It has been about the gruesome attacks you have endured to reflect the perfection of the Cross, a process that you have shared with your brother for many years. I know that you tell him that you are proud of him, and he understands what you mean. However, I bid you to remember that the praise and glory belong to God. Your brother was born for the purpose that is coming, and you must remember that he would never have accepted the fruit of his own life if he had done anything less. You have been a good teacher for him, a good mentor and friend, a holy companion and supporter. Let Me make this clear so there is no mistake. It is you who have believed and served. You have suffered the gauntlet and the isolation about which you have spoken. When your special petition arrived on the Altar at Medjugorje, it was not dead on arrival, but it was crucified there. It was united in the Sacred Heart of Jesus and enlisted in the ages for the purification of the world. Everything you have prayed for will occur. I ask you to trust that you will live everything you have ever prayed for. Jesus can change time, suspend the ages, reinstate them, move and mend hearts, heal every illness, and dissipate any darkness. The fact remains that exiled humanity is still detained by time, and for good reason. I have called upon you and your brother as the Lord has had Me do, and you said yes. You agreed to help without counting the cost, even as you are now seeing what that cost has been. It has been in many ways too much, too expensive for the taste of dignified men, too much awkward and disenchanting for two Illinois friends who could have prospered in so many other ways. This is why I am reflective today. I know what you have given Jesus. I understand your pain and suffering. I know that you have looked at the gifts of the Saints and

Doctors of the Church and realized that you are identified with them. I pray for you every day. I weep because you are saddled with the agony of living only for the Church. You have this in common with tens of thousands of priests. Simply said, you are Love in the likeness of Jesus."

Nevertheless, beyond all this mostly irrelevant discussion of the parameters of disbelief, in those first moments, I was inspired to capture our experiences with as much detail as possible as a way of sharing the grace I was experiencing for those who would invoke the sacrifice and believe in future times. I sensed the opportunity to provide Our Lady with a venue to dispense a comprehensive record of the facts that might be so overwhelming that it would become like an anvil, impossible to destroy or dismiss, and would ping a beautiful note every time it was struck. My sense of history was crying out to me interiorly in a way my conscience had never spoken to me before. There was such an urgent fire within me, driving me toward a path that I had never conceived in my thoughts. I heard an interior voice pressuring me to consider how many intercessions were recorded only in their messages, and not instead through a record of convincing panoramic faith that testified to as many facets of the events from the first moments by the chosen participants. This is how it began, this is how it continues. I recorded as much detail of our experiences as felt comfortable, initially because I knew how hard it would be for me to remember with concise recollection what was transpiring. Anyone's personal testimony has little influence after the fact in most situations, and is easy to dismiss, even in a secular court of law. However, a written, factual, diarist journal recorded during the events always stands the test of time, even in the face of contrary witnesses testifying from memory long after the fact. Hence, my sense was to "capture" the moments and lock them into time in a comprehensive record for history. My efforts were to concretize into physical evidence that which I did not possess in those first stressful days. And, by doing so, it has allowed the authenticity of Our Lady's grace to transcend the veil into the applicable senses of those She wishes to touch.

My intentions were confirmed by a good and holy priest who asked me a few short days after February 22 whether I was "recording everything." Our Lady used this subject to teach me something profound. My initial senses were driving me to obey in a scrupulous, fearful and indentured way, as if I was an anonymous slave, afraid of doing something that was wrong. She told me one night that I was "not required" to record the events any longer. I was thrown into an unstable quandary about the worth of what I was recording. Could the voices in me have been so wrong? The fear engendered in my obedience was forcing me to ponder relinquishing my efforts because I believed that not being "required" meant that I should stop. Even though I pondered these thoughts, my conscience was still prodding me relentlessly to continue. In the midst of my uncertainty, I continued recording the events and messages, even though I was not "required" to do so. This is an example of innumerable spiritual lessons that our Holy Mother has allowed me to grapple with over the years with many different subjects and conditions. Ironically, She helped me understand that She was never asking me to quit my writing. She simply said I was not required to, just as no one is required to believe in private revelation from anyone. She tested whether my devotions were actually my own. Both myself and the world have been blessed abundantly because my brother and I continued; and blessed are those who accept, believe and obey the revelations of the Morning Star Over America, although you do not have to. She wished to impress upon me that She saw me as Her child, not Her slave; that love is a gift, our lives are a sacrifice of love, and all that we do is a gift to God, not an extorted compliance to some lording tyrant. She placed my devotion within the parameters of being a free act of my love for Her, not a conscription based in fear of Her majestic authority. I was "not required" to be anything more than Her loving child. Accepting and embracing Her, and loving Her Son, was enough. Everything else is the "sacrifice of love" to the benefit of augmenting the conversion of the world. This is the testament of the great Saints; extraordinary love and sacrifice for the propagation of the Mysteries of the Holy Gospel. Our Lady's lesson tempered my obedience to be founded in love, not based in fear of making a mistake or not contributing enough. I have done every single thing She has asked without exception over more than two decades simply because I love Her, not because I was required to perform any more special duties than living my simple compliance to Her Son. Her lesson settled my soul into a deeper relationship with Her where I could feel Her affections more deeply, unimpeded by my unrefined temperaments.

My experiences in Medjugorje had convinced me that our Holy Mother had been trying in a special way for over a decade to convert mankind into a more faithful state of allegiance to Her Son. At that time, no one in the United States had witnessed the full-bore abominations of terror, secularism, and the morally rotten descent related to human sexuality in our society. The 1980s were relatively puritan by today's standards. There still seemed to be a sense of great hope for prosperity, good fortune, peace, and advancement radiating from our culture, even as materialistic as it was. Less than two years before, I had experienced my first encounter with the mystical grace of the Blessed Virgin in my pilgrimages to Medjugorje, but the opening of Her miraculous intercession in my life, and that of my brother Timothy, advanced and magnified the realms of God for me to exponential degrees. I was changed and awakened. I felt the purpose of Her intercession exceeding anything I could have hoped for humanity. I sensed the "chance" for the world to be confronted by something that would stop us in our tracks and force us to reevaluate our existence before it was too late. It is all about what the heavens want. They desire that we be reunited with them both here and now, and in Heaven someday, and not be lost to oblivion for Eternity because we were too stubborn to accept the time of our visitation and conversion into the Sacred Heart of Jesus. Human beings can damn themselves, and for a whole lot less than what people might imagine. The heavenly hosts desire us to know them so that we will love them and want to be with them forever in the realms of eternal life after our sacrificial sojourn in exile. This Afterlife is defined and embodied in Jesus Christ the Messiah, who is the Sacrificial Lamb of the Cross, our Savior and Redeemer. No one enters Heaven without accepting Jesus Christ and His Sacrifice as expiation for their sins—no one! But, we must realize that none of us knows when that final opportunity for Divine Mercy is granted to a person, and whether they have accepted it. Therefore, we cannot judge the ultimate destination of any soul simply based upon the perceptions of the life we have seen them live in the material world. Nevertheless, nothing should preclude us from cautioning against those things that Sacred Scripture states will make us unfit for Eternal Life. It is a narrow path, after all, which leads to redemption. I believe more than anything else my soul was in shock at having revealed to it realms that I only grasped through an intellectual faith before the day our Holy Mother made Her apparency known in my life. I realize now that there are other dimensions to faith besides its intellectual component, although you would be hard-pressed to convince most academicians and theologians to respond to those other mystical dimensions which include Our Lady's miraculous intercessions. They think they "know" enough to get into Heaven when, in actuality, Our Lord is looking for their seamless identity with the prescience of His Spirit and the courage to clothe themselves with His sacrificial nature. He is looking for their willingness to be led. It is almost impossible for a human being to describe the overwhelming power in the grace of the Queen of the Universe. But, that is who She is; a Queen who reigns beside a King in His Majesty in realms we can only pray to enter. We talk about Her grace, and others try to write their perspectives either from their learning or their moments of prayerful intuition. We seem to be fluent in our scrupulous orthodoxy when we are speaking what we believe about Her grace. But coming face-to-face with Her royal eminence is impossible for a sinner to grasp without being humbled and changed. We become speechless in awe and usually in tears at the sight of such beauty. Pride is vaporized. All the orthodoxy seems to fail. Learning is rendered meaningless. Words cease to suffice. It is a love so infinite that man does not know what to do with what he is witnessing in comparison to our personal state of sinfulness. Imagine being offered the most delicate flower in the universe which radiates a love for you that is indescribable, something so beautiful that you burn with a raging passion to have it caress you in the most intimate recesses of your being, but you fear allowing it to touch you because you know your sins will cringe its beauty into tears. Oh, how She has suffered in Her Son's Passion! One is caught between the desire for Her infinite touch of consolation, and yet, dominated by a repulsive inhibition that tells you what you see is beyond your ever embracing it. You feel a mystical paralysis. And, even in the midst of this description or this dilemma, this beautiful Mother is yet so compelling, so riveting, so inviting, so lovely, so healing; you know that She has already endured the greatest horror, the most piercing pain, the most surreal indignity, that somehow you can find yourself worthy to hide in the wounds of Her Immaculate Heart. You know She has the power and the desire to accept you despite all you are. It is not that we are ever acceptable in those revealing moments, but Her grace makes us acceptable for the purpose of our conversion and transformation into the Absolution of Her Son. Her presence is cleansing and reparative. And, we realize that it is all by the power of the Calvarian Sacrifice in which She was enveloped on that first Good Friday, standing at the foot of the Cross while Her Son was executed because men were so evil. In the factual history of man, a Savior was born upon this planet from the Womb of this Virgin, was crucified, died, was entombed and rose again on the third day. I repeat, that is factual history. Anyone who claims otherwise is under the influence of the Antichrist. An ultimate engagement with fallen humanity occurred within the Holy Virgin's Immaculate Heart as She gazed at Her Son hanging on the Cross. In those moments, She held us tenderly, even in the knowledge that our sins were His Cross. She sustained our onslaught against Her Child because She believed His words that the meaning of His entire life was the redemption of His Father's creation. And, to this day, She strives to convince us to become children who will one day be proud of ourselves for being so good, if we but obey Her and begin to pray. We do this by accepting Jesus as our Crucified King, converting our hearts into agreement with everything He spoke and did, and allowing Her to teach us to become strengthened in virtue so that we can become like Him in every way our faithfulness can generate. This does not mean we will match our Lord's masterful stature as the preeminent Savior of the world, for there is only one Lamb of God who has completed the one Sacrifice of Redemption. Nevertheless, it means that we become His brothers and sisters, lifted-up in His image by His choosing us as family through adoption. If we die with Him, we will live again with Him. That is His promise. We are admitted into the mystery of Trinitarian beatitude that has always existed from before the foundation of the world. We are given definition as being something larger than mortal. We are returned to the dignity in which we were conceived by our Creator, not as renegade weaklings, but as unimpeachable children within the domain of His Infinite Reign. This is why Our Lady is given infinite joy by our acceptance and great return to our original identity, and that She can hold us again in Her arms as the newborns of Paradise. She beckons all to come to Her. She will cleanse us, place us in the lineage of holiness, and present us before the Son for the absolution of our beings, no matter what we may be guilty of; just as any mother would do with any child she has borne. It is surely true that the Nativity of Jesus Christ is a testament to the love and faith of the Fair Maiden who gave Him birth, Our Lady of the New Covenant whose grace and energy have capsized humanity's pride. We are drowning in our own nakedness and being rescued by Her blessings, while She continues teaching us the ways of God, coaxing us to change, soliciting our prayers, inspiring our meditations, and admonishing our wrongdoings. The Blessed Virgin Mary must have knelt beside the Bethlehem manger with peace in Her Immaculate Heart, knowing that the Incarnation of the Son of Man made Her likewise the perfect servant as the Savior whom She bore. Mary is the Sacred Vessel whose intercession has made all the difference in the identity of Heaven as we shall see it in Eternity. Her converting kindness in this world and the next has elicited the Divine Mercy of Jesus to delve deeply inside His own Wounds to find forgiveness for our sins. While Jesus is the bravest Man who ever lived, the Mother who knelt beside Him in prayer and stood by Him during His most painful hours is the most perseverant of any woman, the longest-suffering and most enduring of them all. And, we owe Her our lives here and beyond our exile as much as we accept the Crucifixion of Her Son for the remission of our sinfulness.

What Our Lady has done for me as an example and child of the Father far outstrips the piffling definitions that fanatical secular humanists are trying to shape into humanity's perceptions. I am a child, Her child, who has been given the antidote to their secular poison through the miraculous intercession of the Morning Star Over America. I have been inoculated with a baptism of the entire blast of Catholic grace, pile-driven into Calvary by the Messiah on the Cross since the day of October 8, 1961 when the waters of the baptismal Sacrament streamed across my forehead and down past my ears. Both myself and my brother, along with my fellow faithsians, are part of the two millennia legacy of Roman Catholic giantness, birthed into existence by the Immaculate Queen of Heaven with all the grace She possesses. All the rogues of this world called to the fore at the same moment would be turned back and driven to their knees with one glance from Her beautiful eyes. They have no idea who they are dealing with. But oh, how I wish they would come and look at Her anyway. If it is possible for a Saint to be charming, let it be said that the Mother of Jesus is the incarnation of charm par excellence. Our Lady surpasses so many dimensions of humanity and motherhood personified that She seems miraculous Herself. Nowhere have I seen another mother listen so attentively to her children's concerns. The Blessed Virgin looks us straight in the heart with Her welcoming eyes and mystical gaze, peering deep into our souls; and She speaks not just about the culture of the exiled world, but about the beauty beyond the celestial skies. We are absorbed by Her compassion for those who are lonely and the millions who suffer in reflection of Our Lord on the Cross. And, it is through Our Lady's endearing command and exquisite poise that we understand the holiness of God in human form. After all, besides Her Son, Mary is the only other sinless person born into the physical realms. The Blessed Mother wants us to believe that we are all visionaries in a beatific sense, that we can see our victories through Jesus on the Cross, and classify and categorize our priorities so prayer is the focal point of our lives. Our Lady has made clear that humanity is ill-prepared to take on our most wrenching challenges without spiritual love nourished by the Holy Eucharist. She speaks clearly about the sanctity of our faith in God. Any ambiguity we feel about our mission here on Earth is unfounded. Our thirst for holiness is not an unquenchable desire, but the wellspring and purpose of life. The Virgin Mary would have us believe that there is a pontiff in every man, perhaps a Pope Anthony Magnificat or a prelate or doctor, a teacher or writer, a philosopher or poet. What we make of what She sees matters most to God, not whether we cede our potential to our weaknesses or fail to recognize the grace in our own humanity. The immaculate being of the Most Blessed Virgin Mary reigns above the frail vagaries of sinful mortals. Our cinematic and performing arts fail to depict either Her beauty or Her eminence because we fail to consider what truly composes the spirit of a perfect woman and mother. We approach Her depictions in order to identify with Her more easily as sinners, and thus define Her in our image instead of Her own. Instead, we must seat ourselves on the plateau of feminine perfection and never descend from that pinnacle one micron. We must truly come to know Her as a living, breathing Matriarch with the combined power, grace, authority and maternal instinct that exceeds the collective grace of all mothers to have ever graced this planet; one who has processed through life at our side from the moment we were given the breath of existence. She precedes our birth and already succeeds our death. Every step She witnesses. Every sentiment dedicated to Her She guides. It takes a recognition of the totality of desolation experienced by Her and Her Son during His Life and Passion to be focused on the reality of Her pristine excellence, Her monumental suffering and the transcendent power of Her Immaculate Heart and soul. We must see Her not as simply another version of the female species who experienced certain tragedies in Her life, but instead we must witness and then testify to the absolute perfect woman conceived by God Himself, the consummate beauty of femininity and motherhood, the paragon female creature; unmatched, unrivaled, venerated past the portals of Creation itself. She is God's feminine magnum opus. Every woman who fails to at least make an attempt to imitate Her grace has been a failure to the human race. That is why motherhood is on a plateau all by itself. Motherhood is the pinnacle imitation of the Virgin, while virginity is Her image. Humanity must rise to Her with arms raised above our heads like infants flailing for the embrace of their mother instead of trying to pull Her down into some caricature of sinful humanity in order to make Her more palatable to our acceptance. She is the mystical epitome of what every woman is supposed to be without excuse; pure, gentle, maternal, graceful, and strong in all of these. It will be a sobering revelation on the day our mortal characterizations of Her are transformed before our eyes into the full-spectrum revelation of Her eternal soul and the powers and beauties She possesses. Then, those hands will fly out above our heads, flailing toward Her, beckoning to be lifted to where She is. With all due respect, blind people do not make very good art critics, nor are they exquisite painters. But, it seems this is what happens when protestors characterize the Queen of the Universe for the rest of us. Can a Protestant ever describe the Most Blessed Virgin accurately after having spent a lifetime rejecting who She actually is? I am intimately cognizant of the incongruity between how many portray our Holy Mother and how I know Her. She is so often portrayed as nothing more than a meek push-over who never broaches subjects that would offend anyone. It is believed that She would never confront the arrogance of sinners or utter a word in a way that addresses the personal beliefs of reprobates in a strident manner. This is not the Mother that I know. While Her meekness is perfect and overwhelming, it is a paradox to realize that She will not accept any excuse, whimper, glance, sentiment, word or thought that is not the Truth. She has no use whatsoever for the attitudes of unrepentant sinners, knowing She will ultimately help them to the cleansing baths of their own suffering. Redemption of Her children is eternally serious to Her. She will crush anything that impedes our conversion, especially our obstinance. There is no negotiation with Her in order to keep back for ourselves any sinful tendencies or slothful druthers. She demands the absolute conversion of the hearts of Her children because She knows that is where our power, happiness, healing, strength, conviction, holiness, and eternal life reside. She will not allow us to say "no" to eternal redemption without a confrontation of biblical proportions. Her miraculous intercession is the beginning of that final confrontation with humanity; the Triumph of Her Immaculate Heart will be its culmination. She is going to win our personal acclamations of Her fortitudinous wisdom. We are going to finally admit that we can be perfect in love; and we will show it to Her through our prayers and sacrifices, or through our reparatory suffering. If mankind were to be oriented in thinking according to the wisdom of Heaven, we would realize that it is impossible for Our Lady to offend sinners, no matter what She says, because the offension is a characteristic that we own. We generate the offense within us because we are not in alignment with Heaven. Our Lady has no part in that. Should anyone refrain from speaking the Truth of human salvation because it happens to offend someone? Should we mince our words and obfuscate the reality of true evangelization behind some watered-down relativistic pluralism because someone may find that they are not in alignment with the Truth of the Gospel mandates? Indeed, this has been happening far too long. Jesus was crucified because He spoke uncompromisingly, firmly, clearly, and unyieldingly. He worked miracles with the effect of crushing His opposition; and those miracles hastened His Crucifixion nonetheless. If we speak clearly enough and are not afraid to engage the darkness, we also will be opposed, even by those closest to us. "If they hated Me, they will hate you," He said. I can relate that Our Lady has never offended me, not because She has not strictly administered discipline upon me or stated the truth that I needed an attitude adjustment at times. It is because the "me" who would be offended by Her unyielding truth is crucified at the revelation of the disparate contrast between Her Glory and my incongruent vision. The Divine Truth borne within Her presence confirms to me that my rebellious human ego is a seductive, dictatorial enemy of my eternal future—as is yours. I still have my ego which needs to be crushed from time to time, but during the time I am in Our Lady's mystical presence, it is annihilated. I love Her, I obey Her; She tells me the Truth, I accept the Truth, no matter what it is. What do I have to give to Her except my love? I have no piece of my ego or willful attitude that She is interested in. She revels in the precious sentiments of the heart and everything from that domain that is generated by the Holy Spirit. She swells with euphoria and satisfaction upon witnessing authenticity of spirit, our original demeanor as innocent children. There is no ego that is any match for Her. There is nothing that any sinful mortal can force upon Her, accuse Her of, take from Her, or do to Her. After the mystical imprint of meeting Her, She is not concerned about those who walk away because She knows they will return famished for Her beauty like a prodigal child. The Most Blessed Virgin will not hesitate to call anyone's bluff, be they pagan or Prelate, not because She is concerned about the hand they are playing or what they feel they can win, but because She is always holding the royal flush, the winning hand, no matter what game one of Her children wishes to play. It can sometimes be perplexing to hear the call for the extinction of the human ego because we find it difficult to reconcile a place for the action of the human will when exercising our human functions of choosing, influencing, and creating. We do not wish to be stripped of our dignified power and thrust into the pit of uncertainty and seeming helplessness. We believe that the ego being extinguished means we must be meekly silent about our opinions when confronted with immoral, and even horrific, situations. This is a misunderstanding of our identity and responsibility in this vineyard. Innumerable are the people who reject Christianity, then snipe at how prideful and arrogant a Christian is when that person of faith refuses to comply with a particular situation or argument. We should not misconstrue the exercise of the will as always being a manifestation of the debilitating selfish ego. The ego can die and be reborn with the identity of Christ. Everyone should know that while there is a human ego that conscripts us to darkness and forces humanity to depletion and destruction for the sake of personal gain, there is also a spiritual ego, or identity, that feeds upon the wisdom of God and is potent, powerful, fearless, unyielding, prophetic, and eternal. The spiritual will functions through the Cross, absent of every motivation and accolade other than the identification with the Sacrifice for the redemption of man. Spirit crushes ego because it does not want its worldly satisfactions. This spiritual persona when fully matured and sanctified in the Sacrifice of Calvary is the essence of the Spiritual Father in lordship over His vineyard, rightfully capable of animating and articulating the work of human redemption. This is the identity of the Vicar of Christ, the Pope in Rome, and all who are in communion with him. It is the identity of the faithful Catholic.

It is ironic that we can immediately sense in great intellectual detail what it means when someone says that hell is about to be unleashed on earth. We sometimes tremble at the thought of how ominous the times seem to be, and that the final holocaust is probably far too close for comfort. Yet, we seem to be dead of conscience if someone were to tell us that the Creator of the Universe is about to unleash Heaven on Earth and what that portends; a Heaven that will obliterate with unyielding determination every last scintilla of opposition that has ever existed against His Catholic Kingdom; consuming the wicked, the hate-filled, and the vile to the roaring acclamation of the Saints! Just wait until Creation hears this ecstatic earthquake of human and angelic euphoria! All the stadiums of history, from forums to coliseums to amphitheaters in their days of glory, from twenty-first century sports stadia to colossal entertainment venues roaring with applause, from victorious battlefields to commencement ceremonies and ticker-tape parades with their jubilant throngs; billions strong from the arena of human history, all thundering in a single ovation of victory—"Hosannah to God in the highest, praise to Christ the King!" Where will the atheists and archenemies of God and His Crucified Christ find solace then? Where will they find a seat? Talk about standing in a furnace of eternal shame; fifty yard line, on a logo of the Eucharist before they are escorted by angels from the celebration into the darkness where they will wail and grind their teeth. Mercy will have been completed. They will have made their choice. The number who surrendered in humility to the Savior of the world will have been recorded in the Book of the Living. The dawn of the Day of Justice will break, and judgement will be administered in response to the multiple millennia of horrors heaped upon the children of God by Satan and his minions, down to the last renegade who spits at the Roman Catholic Church. In the grand scheme of human redemption, our lives now are the plenary opportunity granted by God to prepare ourselves for His grand Judgement of humanity. We must endure, petition, sacrifice, hope, pray, believe, obey, proclaim, defend, advance, secure, heal, feed and confess; and love in the image of Christ and His Mother in preparation for this great moment. No matter what any sinner thinks, it is not a violation of Love to announce the prophesied lot of the unrepentant wicked who will be damned. Sacred Scripture states it clearly. Jesus spoke about it urgently, and bled for it copiously. We plead with everyone who will listen that they not challenge their ultimate destiny and ride their prideful arrogance all the way into the fires of Hell. Repent and be accepted again! Virtue becomes the identity of the children of Mary. We battle in a world of yet unrepentant thugs who are trying to confirm into social acceptance that the Truth proclaimed by Catholics has no right to any audience before the ages, especially in the public arena where these haughty vagrants presume to dominate socially and politically. Somewhere in the psyche of modern man, we have developed an idea that we can negotiate Eternal

Truth simply because we do not wish to subscribe to its prescriptions. The yoke of faith and virtue seems too heavy a burden to bear. Yet, the Truth is like the sun rising in the morning; there is nothing man can do about it. Look how many do not like the sun because they wish to profit from the darkness. God did not create man to bow to any of these fascists; to no authoritarianism not prescribed by His beatific grace. No sinner has the right to define any society outside the boundaries of the revelations of the Holy Gospel. We have the right, nay the obligation, to be as courageous in our testimony as we are inspired by the Holy Spirit of our God to be. We have the duty to bring the Truth to humankind, even if we might be banished, exiled or killed as a consequence of their rejection. Indeed, the world is flush with the signs that portend the end of the ages, the most pronounced being the general extinction of the original faith of the Apostles and the facts of their teaching from within every cultural institution, societal medium and most religious denominations. What is left of the faith heralded for centuries is undergoing a mutation at the hands of the secular world that is rendering it impotent and incapable of saving anyone or building anything. It is being replaced by the calculated ideologies of materialism, secular humanism, moral relativism, and religious pluralism. These forces are taking advantage of a society whose contemplative depth has become so shallow that few really care what these concepts mean or how their rotten fruits have any relevance to their lives and futures. Materialism is distracting people like the serpent of the Edenic garden. Secular humanism pulverizes the spirit soul within men. Moral relativism is born of an egocentric arrogance that refuses to submit to the Sacrifice. And, religious pluralism is an abomination that is touted as the only possibility in a world of so many who live by their own definition of religion, even if all but one are disjointed from the witness of every authentic Saint the world has ever produced. The contemporary justification for this menagerie is that the Truth is malleable to each individual person according to the times and places where we act out our lives. Relativism rejects the idea that any

Truth binds our assent before the Throne of God. Human beings generate these fallible perspectives about life, mainly because the clarity of our vision is limited by the finite demarcations which bound the here and now. We lose our grasp on the unquestionable Truth that reality bears upon mankind the instant time closes the present moment behind us. When the facts of existence leave the present, they no longer seem to be present to defend themselves before the fallible estimations and biases of sinners. We can see this in how many great traditions are being wiped away without the smallest twinge of conscience. Indeed, does Scripture state that there will be those who persecute you and believe that they are giving glory to God while doing it. These people believe they are serving great future legacies where their actions will someday be hailed as evidence they were geniuses before their time. Sadly, they will only be condemned as the destroyers. The answer is not in a culture that mocks moral responsibility. Spin is nothing more than an intellectual lie spewing from someone who does not have the courage to face the truth head-on, or the retribution after proclaiming it. Just what are the limits on an American's freedom to choose? Does any segment of the population really have the freedom to plunge an entire nation into depravity and immorality? The hip-hop moguls and superficial entertainers seem to think so, and woe to them. Innumerable cohorts of false idols have caused so many little ones to stumble that it is beyond comprehension how deep is the ocean they are going to be thrown into, necklaced with the millstones of justice. [Mark 9:42] There is a Truth that is beyond the contorted justifications of men. We must search it out or we will be lost in the smoldering carnage of this world and the flaming desolation of the next. Universal Truth puts the skids on religious pluralism and hails the original Mother Church from which the Wisdom of Heaven first poured forth. She alone has dared to proclaim Jesus' words with the intent in which He spoke them. If our spirits are not connected to this ultimate reality through His Apostolic Church, we see clearly neither before our births nor after our deaths. And, the information that is transferred to us in the writings and recordings of men separated from this Deific Truth is inevitably skewed according to the fallible opinions and agendas of these sinful mortals. For example, what future generation could ever look back on the punitory reporting of the American secular media at the beginning of the 21st century and get an honest depiction of the actual integrity of the Roman Catholic priesthood? Let's face it, we live in a society where we are impressed by nothing of any more depth than billboards and the pixels of televideo screens. Our contemplative attention span is very small, if existent at all. We will not think deeply about the logical consequences and repercussions of our beliefs on a macro scale. Is this not the reason why every governing system throughout history has fallen to rot, revolution, and ruin? Great parts of the world are in the midst of rioting revolutions as these words are being composed because of the vacuous nature of the ideologies reeking death upon them. And, the people in their midst know it, but do not see the Light of Christ as their salvation. The vineyard belongs to Christ the King; the United States of America belongs to Christ the King under the consecrated stead of the Immaculate Virgin Mary; and the faithful are its stewards awaiting His triumphant return for the fruits of His people's love. As assuredly as the Jewish people were given a promised land, so too have we been given a vineyard as their spiritual progeny. We are commissioned and ordained by the Creator of all things to encourage humankind through every venue to accept Jesus Christ through the Church that He instituted on Earth for the salvation of man; not by way of a generic pluralistic, self-indulgent, protesting Christianity, but through the hierarchical Roman Catholicism of sacrificial love that has stood tall for twenty centuries with its seven-fold flush of Divine Sacraments. No one has been sent by God to claim any other authority, advance any other doctrine, conscript any dominating obedience, demand any groveling servitude, or preach any other ideology except that which has been revealed by His own Divine Will through the Holy Spirit animating His Original Apostolic Church. The destination of the redeemed is that place of unity beneath the Cross of the human being who proved Himself to be the greatest

Man to have ever lived, and yet live He still does! The sacred repository for all this wisdom is the Roman Catholic Church. That is why the miraculous intercessions of the Most Holy Virgin Mary throughout time are so auspicious and so Catholic, and now so urgent in these final days. These, Her final interventions, are a plea for this closing generation of mankind to open its eyes to the birthplace of human redemption which rests in Her. The great power of the Holy Spirit is bathing humanity with grace and truth at the behest of the most gentle Creature ever to have been given the breath of life. This is the unvarnished and undeniable truth that I have encountered in my relationship with Her; the same truth that She is trying to get Her Church to accept with definitive and vocal allegiance throughout its hierarchy. The Church Triumphant—those in Heaven—could not care one whit about anything that opposes their King. They will not dignify or condone evil works because they all fought and died in their witness to Christ Crucified against such evil. They are clothed in power and perfection, and they know that everything that opposes His Divine Will will ultimately be annihilated and shoveled like chaff into the eternal furnace. Heaven is Triumph and Victory! The Heavenly Hosts and Saints have complete focus and absolute determination to wipe away every enemy that refuses to surrender to the beauty of love and forgiveness, allegiance and sacrifice, devotion and piety. That is why the Saints petition, intercede, and cry from the heavens into the echo chamber of men's hearts, hoping those reverberations will buckle our knees in humble contrition before Jesus' great Sacrifice.

None of this should be seen as strident or fundamentalist, although that is the indictment that is normally hurled to obfuscate the voice of anyone attempting to draw humanity into the folds of deific grace. Unimpeachable declarations of the truth are assailed as radical because sinners do not wish to comply with the sacrifices required of them to prove their sacrificial love for humanity. They are shocked by them because they are so far removed from any faithful rationality, standing instead in the complete darkness of their own miserable soul and cringe in opposition when the light shines out upon the path they know they should take. The rejection brandished by others should not impede us for a moment. We are not pacifists! We do not have to comply when they demand that we keep our Christianity in some private hidden sphere of society, lest they throw a fit. We do not have to be silent with somber faces to the ground when faced with successful congenial people wandering around in the dark, headed toward damnation. Yes, even prominent people can have no appetite for holiness or confession of their Savior. So many have bartered away their souls for the sake of the passing things of this world. What does it profit a man to gain the whole world and suffer the loss of his soul? What does it profit a man or woman to become a Senator of the United States of America, and then advocate and defend the slaughter of unborn children? Being a senator will not save either of them. Many have killed their moral consciences so long ago that they cannot remember a time when church pews were normally filled to capacity across the country. Our contemporary society has been cultured into such a darkened state of indifference regarding our ultimate destiny before the judgement of the Almighty Father that it has become fashionable to mock and slander any declaration of virtuous conviction as coming from a religious zealot, unworthy of anyone's attention. We are afraid to stand with those lone souls proclaiming the truth because we believe somehow they should not have created such a stir. How often do we hear that they should have somehow shown their faith by their humble example alone, instead of speaking words of truth that caused such disruption? These excuses are as innumerable as raindrops in a hurricane. I have said before that all Satan has to do is create a ruckus and it will be blamed on the one speaking the truth of Christ Jesus. There is a reason that most every prophet in history has been killed, and most faithful evangelizers marginalized by their contemporaries. Evidence abounds because "...Light has come into the world, but people loved darkness instead of light because their deeds were evil." Slanderous rebuttal and social ostracization are always the weapons brought to bear against spiritual magnanimity. Pain and suffering are the only weapons our adversaries can bring to the battle; it is all they can wield in response because their humble contrition is out of the question. Our Holy Mother wants everyone to know that the Gospel is not as accusatory as they believe it to be; rather, it is to their ultimate joy to be shown the path out of their valley of tears; it is the most liberating thing on the planet. God called it the pearl of great price for a reason. He is trying to save us from this searing bath of exile by loosening our held-fast perceptions that there is nothing more significant to existence than what we see; that we are enslaved to a servile nightmare as nothing but animals in a global survival of the fittest menagerie that huge portions of the world's population are losing.

If scientists could prove the existence of God, spirituality would be reduced to a hypothetical laboratory experiment, devoid of the mysticism that humanity needs to be elevated from the depths of the common and ordinary. God reveals Himself to the Earth on His own terms; we will never discover His identity in a test tube or petri dish. The Father is uncontainable, but His Spirit can be isolated inside the human heart as a knowable and approachable conceiver of Creation. This must begin with the desire to in fact search for Him and sense the need for reaching out for wisdom beyond our years that cannot be divulged anywhere else. Our forefathers would have given life, fortune, and limb to have been able to see for only a moment what awaited them beyond their lives; when in fact, we already know what they yearned to see. It is found in professing our religious conviction in the revelations of the Messianic message, for this is how we are touched in unprecedented ways by supernatural powers beyond our own realms. If we give ourselves to Christ Jesus to every imaginable degree by our willingness to sacrifice for Him, we will embark upon the journey that will take us to the beatific heights heralded in the Scriptures. It is obvious that no theoretical equation will ever be this transcending. The reality of Christianity that is staring right into our eyes is telling us that our lives are not all about money, entertainment, luxury, travel, sensuality, celebrity and prestige on the one hand; and capitalistic servitude, imprisonment, drug abuse, broken families, poverty, promiscuity, abortion, and three jobs plus tips on the other. There is the opportunity for humankind to be elevated like royalty above all of this. But, we must cooperate as a family in obedience to our Heavenly Mother. The holdouts must convert their hearts. The dead weight of indifference must be lifted. The rich must stop pilfering the fruits of the entire vineyard into their storehouses; the slothful must engage their truest contributions. If one would claim that it would take a miracle for this rearrangement to occur, then so be it because our witness to the Morning Star Over America is one of those miracles. And, if this rendition of God's almighty affection is not good enough, then peruse the other 20 centuries of Roman Catholicism and witness the lives of millions of bigger-than-life Saints whose mystical relationships with God and Our Lady might pale ours by comparison. The Holy Spirit has been alive and working the length and breadth of salvation history. God is real and He is listening; and He would respond if we would bother to speak to Him with one voice as His family. He would end the suffering with one sunrise if we would stop sinning. He will work contemporary miracles as great as those in the days of old if we would display our truest faith first by tendering our complete allegiance to Him in advance. He is not in a contest with humanity to see who will blink first. But, if that is the game mankind wishes to play, He has already closed His eyes and opened them again on the third day for the sake of letting us win. It is our moment to believe. The world as we know it is swiftly bending toward a Reckoning that is imminent. It has taken just over two millennia to bring Creation to its fullness with the Gospel preached throughout the entire Earth. Everyone knows the name Jesus Christ. Humanity has endured atrocities and horrors of almost unimaginable proportions throughout time. And now, finally, we are witnessing the closing days of the mortal world; the allotment of exile that God has given to His creatures to glorify Him and work-through our conversion. This is our time! We must bask in this sunset of opportunity and invoke all that is right and just, to align ourselves, even if only for the sake of self-preservation, with the beauty of the Gospel because we are about to be called to account of how we have administered this sacred vineyard of our Creator. There is not a person among us who cannot look around them and see someone who is lost by the ways they act and what they believe. Millions are those who are sitting under the nearest tree, stuffed to the gullets with all the grapes, announcing their last belch of audacity, right in the face of the returning King. How many do we see on the wrong path, even if we are only considering the material world and how to have some semblance of successful independence? We must reach to them to help them realize that there exists an unseen spiritual pathway that must also be tread for the sake of eternal freedom beyond the grave. And, it will only be Jesus Christ who will grant that ultimate dispensation. So, what must change? Everyone must pray from the heart to convert the definition of who we believe ourselves to be; while on our knees we must stand, and orient how we will choose to approach life so that God can make something more beautiful of us than what we display now. If we will not let Him teach us what to believe, we have no future. We must accept the sacrifice that comes with the transfiguration brought by virtue. We must be willing to forfeit everything that the secular culture tells us is true because, quite frankly, those who reject Christ and have embraced the alternate universe of moral relativism are lost and are leading us toward social and eternal damnation. They are faltering and failing right before our eyes; and everyone with an ounce of moral conscience still alive knows it. We must enter into a battle to regain the supple nature of our soul immersed in the Truth of God. We must become filled with grace. Only then will society realign itself with its fruitful purposes before the laws of the mystical universe which will one day appear from behind the veil with cataclysmic thunder. We must awaken ourselves from the faithless, tamped-down perspective that Christ's Second Coming is irrelevant simply because we cannot yet be sure that it might be tomorrow. Our Lady would rather we prepare ourselves as if it were tomorrow. Can we see the difference? If you have faith to invoke, invoke it now. If you have a prayer to say, lift it this day. If you need to experience the grace of conversion, call up your courage and darken the door of the nearest Catholic Church because Our Lady's flush of miraculous intercessions worldwide prefigures the Second Coming of Her Son. She preceded Him the first time, and She is now anointing our time with Her presence in preparation for His grand entrance to redeem His people. As we look at our world so lost in violence, atheism, and mockery of all that is holy, it is easy to see that it is just as in the days of Noah when the crowds and leaders mocked him for obeying his God and building an ark. They were swept away as Noah watched from the confines of God's security. Our Lady is the Ark of the End Times; She is the security.

In the face of such a daunting mountain that strips the hope of lesser men, my confidence in God's triumph comes through what eye hath not seen nor ear heard, but has been revealed to us in the august Queen of Heaven. I have experienced the utter joy of our Heavenly Mother as She comes to speak to Her children, whether it is in the dead of the winter snows spread upon the ground, during the white flakes falling, or beneath the blazing summer rays baking man's existence as if God's displeasure were scorching the planet. She asks that we ponder tomorrow and what good news and new strength will come if we but respond to Her miraculous intercession. She asks us to see the unfolding of life in all the ways of grace, whether it is winter, spring, summer or fall. She wishes us to know that She will reach down from Heaven and live the days of our lives one at a time with us, just as She did on Earth. Although She has spoken thoroughly about the horrible condition of humanity and its reckless course, She says there is still hope. Many times before, She has foretold the dangers that men face when they do not approach the Holy Cross in contrition before their Savior. Lest we surrender everything we have promised to believe, we must accept that Creation is taking the form of dignity that the Father has planned. It seems that there is little consolation during stressful moments to think that everything will someday be righted, but even those moments are closing the gap between the present and the Glory we shall inherit. This beautiful Queen comes to give assurances to humankind and the promise from God that when we invoke the Gospel we are serving according to our pledge given to Him upon our baptism and confirmation, and especially through our consecration to Her Immaculate Heart. Who could have known that we would be so blessed, that the United States and the western world would have been enlightened by the Holy Spirit in such remarkable ways in the span of our heritage? We have spoken about the economy of Salvation and the intensity of our belief in God in proper ways, indicating our willingness to invest the remainder of our years assuring that His Will is done. The Mother of God wants us to understand the personification of beatific love manifested by Her Son Jesus, and to realize that it is both our success and our destiny. It is our only success. She has been waiting two millennia to teach this generation the meaning of the personification of beatific love. She has been sent by the God of our fathers through miraculous overtones to invoke His Name through the endless power of the Holy Spirit. The personification of beatific love means that the Love of God can live in the hearts and minds of mortal sinners. This is exclusionary of sinners who perpetually break the rules and commit the worst sins of impurity and blasphemy against His Holy Word. It is about the rest who are living on Earth who are prone to sin, but who do not fall to temptation and who avoid the occasion of sin. When Jesus told the Apostles and disciples that each one should be perfect as He is perfect, He was speaking to those whom He recognized as sinners. This made them unlike Himself who was incapable of sin. This is the same thing as a diamond telling a rock to shine with facets as awesome as its own. This means that what the Father determines to be perfection is what defines the perfection of men. If heretics refuse to repent and are ultimately slain in the end by the righteous at the command of God, it is a perfect act. Saint Joan of Arc, too, was a sacrificial witness to the perfect righteousness of God. Begetting children is a perfect act. Rebuking one's enemies and forging peace pacts are perfect acts of beatific love. The personification of this love is what the enlightenment of the spiritual conscience is about. There does not have to be context and relevance for beatific love to live in the material world because it is irrevocably capable of existing on its own, for its own reward, for its own glory. Then there is the man. The man, any man or anyone, any soul who is given to the Truth. There exists both inside and outside of time the essence of 'man' that makes him simultaneous; something that describes something else. In this, man is material and the eloquence of material, flesh that lives-out the prudence of the Father's Will in every way possible. Our Lady has seen and spoken about these men and women many times throughout the years. They are called Saints! We too reach this personification of beatific love when we internalize the meaning and excellence of redemptive sacrifice. The waves and echoes of our perfection ripple through time in ways that we cannot yet see. In the overall image of what human beings are meant to be and supposed to accomplish, the Saints have forged a discernable pattern of that perfection. Why am I describing this? Because we must begin to see ourselves as venerable beings in the eyes of God so we will stop taking seriously what cold-hearted sinners think of us. Worldly beings and creatures are selfish; they are stubborn in their error, they are consumed by pride, and they are unwilling to share the pardon and forgiveness that they require from those they offend. Therefore, when we speak about the personification of beatific love, we include the excellence about which Our Lady speaks, about which we have read in the Sacred Scriptures and witnessed in the lives of history's greatest Saints. Do we remember some of the strains? 'If there is any excellence...' This is a question posed in the Word of the Lord.

The answer is that there is indeed excellence. It is there because of all the reasons outlined heretofore, and for more and better reasons than those. There is excellence because the Father has placed in our hands the tools to create divine excellence in ways that have not yet been defined by any lexicon or lines of purpose. Excellence, like beatific love, is whatever the Father says makes His Kingdom complete. When He says that people shine, He is not speaking about the reflection of light off their skin. He refers to the awesome softness of the spirit and kindness of heart that is of old, tendered to humanity by the Martyrs who laid down their lives, by the Saints who served and suffered, by the children of those who knew only to raise children as their means of glorifying His Kingdom on Earth. Shining implies that there is some essential light that reflects from the surface of these souls. The emphasis of life, the determination to satisfy righteous curiosity, the drive to discover the Teacher of Salvation, all of these are facets from which this essential light is reflected and repeated. When good men speak highly of creatures for whom the Lord has died, they are telling of the eternal greatness that has captivated the world throughout all times and places. Jesus died to save good men and those prone to commit evil acts. It is our commission to tell the good ones that they cannot live in silence just because their reward is irrevocably imminent. There is such a thing as retrofitting the human spirit with the conscience of the Gospel, and this is what sharing the Word of God is all about. It is indeed about feeding the poor and tending to the needs of those who are lacking, but it is even more about telling these souls the reasons why. In this way, saying thank you also means saying 'I love you.' And, it means that saying 'you are welcome' also means saying 'I love you.' Fashioning for human fate a future of victory gives living beings a purpose for rising in the morning under the guiding hand of God. If we see these things in other people, we are seeing wise innocence. We are seeing mature beginnings in little hearts that are too tender to hate. This is what makes simple people look upon messengers and seers as contributors to the conversion and salvation of lost sinners. There are thousands of these humble souls around the world. They are committed to tremendous goals that resound the power and innocence of the adolescent Christ. Our Lady is witness to their kindness and bravery in single swipes of genius. They are here and all around, and they will make a difference in the world before their mortal years are through.

There is a sense of urgency in what our Holy Mother has told us through the years. Our prayers and patience provide sufficient action and thoroughness to suffice that urgency. If the Son of Man does not return before we are taken into Heaven, we should know that we have established a record to be followed by the Faith Church succeeding us until He does. Our faith builds sky-scraping castles here on the ground where our forbears have tread and our successors will walk. We have painted a picture of beatific love across the skies where the Morning Star is poised, night and day, through good times and bad, through floods and droughts, through the wailing of men and their ecstatic joy. This is the reason that all those innocent people are reaching-out on their own, far advanced of their years, to conquer material things so they will be prepared to be champions in the spiritual realms. They are like all those who have gone before in grace in that they will never forget the sweet taste of victory through the bitterness of the years. By all means, if Our Lady were standing before a class of graduating children, She would never tell them that they are not special. She would say that inside each of them lives the heart of a giant that is calling-out to be fed. She would say that their commencement apparel becomes them. It is fitting that they be decked in dignity for the lessons they have learned, for fighting the good fight, for finishing the race. She would tell them that they are special because they are the legitimate heirs of a God-given Truth that must be shared in all ways and in all nations. Speaking in first person, She would say, *"You have inside you seeds that were planted there not the first day you attended school, but the very moment you inherited the breath of life. You have lives that will be lived-out in the world and before a world that is broken, and you must help good men fix it. You must take all the wisdom that you have gleaned from your experiences here and build on it, make humongous righteous mountains out of simple 'good will' mole hills. You must change the world and the destiny of humanity! You must chart the course by which your own children will travel the worthy path of human achievement if that achievement makes the world a better place. You must not agree with other men just for the sake of harmony, but you must foster harmony when that agreement upholds the principles of Truth. You must blaze new trails and pore-over the workings of your predecessors to blend in your own lives a fitting way of life that takes all with whom you work toward the horizon beyond which your reward and redemption lies. You must stare into the sun with eyes peeled, and then emit this same light into the night with the bequeathal you have gained. Yes, My little children, the personification of beatific love is the most important mission you will ever attempt because it is all about the renewal of the self. It is about identifying with the same genius that created the universe and the prodigies that replicated it for the advancement of human excellence."* These are not just hollow words; they are words that the material world seems too busy to hear. These are sentiments that will make a difference in who succeeds and who does not. There is a great question that the children of Mary are asking, and I have the answer. The answer is yes! Before the end of time, the Queen of Heaven will appear to all Her children simultaneously to tell us that Her Incarnate Son will presently return. She will introduce Him as more than the miracle worker whom we have been told about in writing and the spoken word. She will remind us that our victories in Him are the only true ones that matter. She will share with us the same sense of anticipation by which they lived on Holy Saturday and in anticipation of Pentecost. Salvation history has proven that God can only speak the Truth. The Truth is this: Jesus is waiting, all right. He is poised and prepared for entrance into His earthly Kingdom with Justice and Judgement. If we are standing in the Light of the Crucifixion, do not be afraid! Woe to you, however, if you are cowered in the shadows. The Second Coming of Jesus Christ will be like a massive flood that will flush-out all people everywhere, the good and bad, the timid and courageous, and the meek and mighty. This Return of the King will be about making goodness the reason for the creation of man. It will be about giving valor to the timid and preparedness for the meek.

But, until that awesome moment of the Parousia, the Revelation of the King, we must surrender our epicurean fancies and realize the finest things of life lie in the sacredness of God. Is the virgin a lesser being because she sacrifices carnal pleasures? Is the young man of temperate comportment truly missing out on the excesses of the daredevil? No, the virgin and the temperate man are among the greatest of beings because they have invoked the nature of God through their sacrifices for the redemption of man. They are traveling the narrow path of Christ. Our interior identities must be restored, circumscribed once again by the boundaries of virtuous self-restraint where grace rises set-apart from the indulgent frivolity and selfish tyranny of sinners. Contemporary American history is being jack-hammered with a consistent, unrelenting assault on the conceptual foundations of the human identity, clothed in the holiness of the finest hours of its history. News flash! Right-wing pundits are as lost and impotent as the blathering wretches defending the satanic fortress of the left. Western civilization once grounded in the Judeo-Christian spirit is collapsing into the dust bin of history for a whole host of reasons which can ultimately be synthesized down to one glaring premise. We have terminally destabilized our society by letting everything that confirms, supports and stabilizes the moral virtues of man to be driven from our public consciousness and our hearts, and with it our sense of duty to the moral foundations of our society and the formation of our children. As a nation, we have abdicated our responsibility to mold our children in the restraining virtues of Christianity beginning in the anarchy of the societal revolution of the 1960s, and now coming to the perfection of evil in the gansta incubus dominating the African-American subculture. The greatest generation transformed into a nightmare overnight through the subversive elements that detested moral rectitude. Virtue, tradition, and moral reason were replaced by a delusional hedonistic beast that breathed a manifesto of false liberation from its frothing lips. And now, conscience destroyed, this monster has given us the wholesale slaughter of unborn children, impurity, sexual licentiousness, pornography, the destruction of marriage and the family, drug-abuse, alcoholism, sexually transmitted disease, familial grief, suicide, hopelessness, epidemic drop-out rates, violence, crime, drive-by shootings, theft, graft, political tyranny, and cities that rival the warlord atmospheres of our worst overseas enemies because our children have been gangsterized by black entertainment moguls for the sake of money. Woe to those who have led the little ones astray! It truly would be better had they draped millstones around their necks and thrown themselves into the depths of the Marianas Trench than to greet the coming Reckoning the way they are. We took for granted the entire underpinning of our national greatness that was bequeathed to us from the sacrificial shoulders of our grandparents and great grandparents. The national cache of civility, virtue, courage and honor went to the battles of World War II, and the magnanimous spoils of their victory were thereafter pilfered by renegade, demonic revolutionaries that had been lying in wait for their chance to perform a utopian transformation of our country into a secular, socialist, atheistic nightmare. Satan grabbed our country in its moment of victory and throttled our nobility out of us, one drop of compromise at a time.

We are hypnotized by a gilded narrative that America is a stately oak that stands proudly in the meadow of human affairs, but we refuse to awaken to the reality of what is just beneath the literary bark. The moment of concession is swiftly approaching where we will be driven to our knees in realization, forced to acknowledge that our national identity has become rotted to the core, the heartwood sustaining our goodness long eaten away by the ravenous mites of godlessness one person at a time. The noble and honorable contingent that is left suffer the four nightmares of the secular world that have nearly completed their destruction of the United States of America: Media, Politics, Education and Entertainment. And, the Master of the four is Power brought by wealth. We somehow live with the misguided idea that the prosperity and protection that surrounds us, the civilized atmosphere of virtue stabilizing our society, is some permanent, immutable emanation of the physical environment that each of us has been born into by destiny, much like our feet can touch solid ground no matter where we step. But, the sand is shifting, and Americans are beginning to realize that the narrative does not match the reality of their lives. We must understand instead that the cohesive qualities of any great nation are the fruit of the faith of generations of people who sacrificed and suffered for the good, who matured their families in the graces of God, and who had a vivid vision of their ultimate destiny before the merciful judgement of the Almighty Father. They fought out of hellish darkness in their ancestral homelands, most landing in poverty in a new world, nearly all suffering the desolation of war, hardship, ill-health and relatively early death. Cell phones, designer clothes, sports cars, celebrity. Where do these fit in the character of who they were? Yes, they came to carve-out a place where all good things could come to their posterity, but their entire definition of "all good things" came from a completely different universe of devotion. Their hopes for their future came from their hearts, tempered in the forge of human suffering while passionately petitioning the God whom most of them now see face to face. Americans of our contemporary generations have been almost free from want or care compared to any of our forebears. We have never had to fight for our survival, to fight for our soul of existence, or the definition of what the world should become, as if it were about to be overrun by barbarian hordes. Sure, we have fought wars against foreign foes, most of whom were no match for our military and technological capabilities. But, we have not been confronted since World War II, or maybe the Cuban missile crisis, with an existential threat to our very existence, with enemies crossing the border of any state or town. Yet, is it only because we have not been looking in the right place? The threat that portends the extinction of America is not a foe from foreign lands on the globe, but rather, holocausts that are generated when human souls become vacant of the spirit of God and surrender to the most base animal instincts, guided by the raw intellectual capacities of the human creature. Evil can possess unimaginable genius. And, in this, every town and city in the United States of America has already been overrun. The Spirit of God and His Wisdom is like a buoyant life preserver that our countrymen have worn since the day the first explorers landed. But, we have now tossed that buoyancy aside in favor of enormous millstones placed around as many necks as possible. Do we actually believe that the right to choose is so sacrosanct that good people are required to sit aside as the most despicable humans "choose" to destroy the public moral consciousness and our civilized atmosphere along with it? Talk about plucking your own eyes out. Do we have to stand by with our hands in our pockets, watching the infanticide of this nation's children? How tall is a pile of 60 million infant corpses? Two, three Freedom Towers high? Ten? Many believe that we are required to defer to the most vile human beings as they exercise their so-called personal rights to be as evil as they want to be, that all of us are required to live by the lowest common denominator of their moral rot. This is no prescription for the greatness of any nation, only the testament to its extinction. Fertile landscapes alone do not portend greatness; it is the people who must be great—of heart and holiness! We must believe in One God announced by the Prophets, revealed in the Messiah from Bethlehem, and testified to by an entire lineage of Christian Saints who accepted that this King died to save the world. Otherwise, we have failed every generation of Americans that ever tilled the ground, dug a ditch, raised a barn, tended to livestock, taught a child, built a business, worked a mine, poured an interstate highway, laid a railway line, flew a jet fighter, drove a tank, stormed a hill, died on a battlefield, ran for office, preached a sermon, road a bull, raced a vehicle, sang a song, composed a symphony, nursed a patient, carved a mountainside, rocketed into space, fought for justice, or declared with hope that it is possible to imitate the Son of God as His brothers and sisters. *Blessed Lord, please change the hearts of my countrymen before it is too late for them to be saved! If you must place America on the pyre to save them, then let the flames rise to the heights of our purple mountains!* The radicals who came of their diabolic age in the 1960s, along with their progeny in like stead, have matured their evil and eradicated the cohesive moral enlightenment of an entire nation; and we are now living their nightmare that we are going to awaken from in a cold sweat, finding it to be true. The heroic parents and clergy who have fought this tidal wave of immorality over the past sixty years are solely responsible for the remnant of decency that still lives in the traditions of love and morality within our contemporary American families. And, it is this salting of virtue that must not be allowed to lose its taste, that is providing the remnants of social stability that yet sustain our nation. Christ the King will not go quietly into the night to the jeers of the damned. He cannot be expelled from this world by anyone. Crucifixion could not keep Him exiled from His Creation. And, if there comes a day where only one Catholic might be left standing, God will resurrect an entire New World through the Faith of that one Catholic and defeat every single one of His enemies. If I am that voice, then I announce the inevitability of His New World! This is the power our God has, authority over ages and times, and who is allowed a place in them and for how long! Blessed are they whose homes are filled with peace, whose families are touched by righteous grace that comes from the heart of the Father in ways inexplicable and beyond the logic of men, for the universal sharing of love, capable of dismantling the Earth and reassembling it again. It would seem that the important issues in human life are clarity and direction, perspective, values and beliefs, identification and association. These are indicators of the inward aspects of the individual, but they do not address the condition of the soul. Everything that permeates the designs of man on a sensitivity scale fosters our self-actualization and sufficiency, but the most critical decision we will ever make is how we will judge ourselves before the Father who created us. What do we use as criteria? It is not always as difficult as it appears. All we need is for the Holy Spirit to give us the proper rhymes and reasons, clefs and registers, and we will sing with such dimensions that we will begin to wonder who we really are. How we vocalize these strains is the essential element telling whether we have truly lived or just existed. It has a sweet cadence too, like a child's hand rustling through a jar of jelly beans, or someone reaching into a paper bag of carpentry nails, getting ready to hammer down a sheet of plywood. There is something about hearing the rolling and rattling that is like music to human ears. In the process, we interpret social values based on our own biases and beliefs, but we are not permitted to do so when they deviate from the sacred divine. Abortion is one of them. No matter what criteria we apply, killing the unborn disenfranchises entire societies of the human race whether in America or across the world in foreign lands. Women have no right before God to kill the children in their wombs, no matter how they got there. No person has the right to kill, destroy or pollute. The righteous have the right to legitimate self-defense. The thuggery and sloth of the inner cities is loathsome. The excesses of the daredevil are the public testament of the fool who disrespects God's gift of life. The words of the slanderer who impugns the moral sanctity of a nation are snake-vomit falling from the lips of the damned.

These issues, among many, have made the Earth a sore spot in Creation, where secular paganism holds out in opposition to beatific truth. We must not be so complacent as to believe that Satan cannot be fully entrenched in the consciences of those who are looking directly into our eyes and smiling as if they are our friends. We must not be taken aback to realize that in this final era that Satan has even infiltrated the hearts of some of the highest leaders; congressmen and senators, presidents and their cabinets, media moguls and merchants, actors, corporate heads, and yes, even pastors, nuns and priests. The Prince of Darkness has convinced millions through the sorcery of the secular void that it is an offense against charity, human dignity, and freedom of choice to impede him from completing the destruction of the last Christian conscience on Earth. Have we stopped to consider what will be left? Who will teach virtue and the sacred identity of man then? Who will defend the least of these? The fanatical drive to legitimize acts of homosexuality and enshrine so-called same-sex marriage throughout the western world is directly from the soul of Lucifer. It is proof of his existence. The devil has deceived an entire spectrum of political, cultural, entertainment, and religious leaders in our country. First, with the outright murder of abortion, and now with an attack on the institution of marriage and the moral foundation of America itself. Divide and conquer. They made a collective out of an abomination and called it a class, and now they are fighting for equal rights for that class. Every excretion of evil that is seeking legitimacy is now adopting this formula of destruction beneath the big-tent banner of political ideology. An outright hijacking of America is occurring. Immoral terrorists have taken over the airliner of our nation's morality, have bound and gagged all the righteous passengers, and are now targeting the last vestiges of moral tradition from the cockpit of their death laden craft. And, the societal leaders in the control tower have radioed to them saying, "The sky is blue and the pattern is clear. Have a nice flight." We are witnessing the total capitulation, even approbation, to this satanic abomination by nearly every secular principal and most supposedly religious in our society. These cowards and millions more under their leadership have been cowed by hollow accusation of bigotry from those who have sold their souls to the Antichrist. They have rejected the Holy Gospel; they are crucifying Christ! It is the ultimate peer pressure, the complete, focused, dominant conscription of the public consciousness by the devil through the levers of the cultural mechanics. Those who are spreading this evil think they are giving glory to the most noble part of their humanity when they are actually descending into the darkest pits of hell. They are submerged in a lie that will destroy their soul. There is a definitive, diabolical psychological inversion occurring in the secular mentality that is absent the Light of God. They are purveyors of damnation, and they will not stop until the Christianity that humanity has known for 2000 years is finally exterminated from the planet. Their sinister mentality will turn its fascism with full force, and without apology, toward the historical tenets of Christianity in order to rewrite the Gospels into a text absent of Light; in fact this is already being attempted. No faithful priest, pastor, nun, or layperson will be spared the onslaught. The secular world cannot reconcile the purity in the Gospel of Jesus Christ with what it is peddling about human sexuality and the foundation of the family. Thus, the manipulation of Christianity itself is imminent and inevitable within their itinerary. These deluded souls are being driven by the devil to reconcile their cognitive dissonance by exterminating their moral conscience which necessitates their eradication of the moral voice of the entire nation, lest they stand convicted before the ages. This process has been advanced through his surreptitious deceit and outright lies for decades. The consciences of the secularists have been destroyed. Their souls are dead, and through their "new progressive light" which is actually the darkness of hell, they are trying to imprint the consciousness of an entire western world with the legitimization of death in any form that suits their choice. Even as I write on this day in 2013, it is ominous the number of legislative dominos across America that are falling in the direction of a secular blessing of this abominable collective. They have already fallen into the desolations of abortion, divorce, sexual immorality, mercy-killing, and a whole host of other nation killing phenomena. And now, secular legislators believe the scales have finally tipped in favor of the curse of so-called same-sex marriage as being the new definition for unions in the American culture and are running headlong to get in front of the parade. I tell you, it is not a parade that they will want to be leading on the fateful day of the Son of Man! Hell is real, and every one of these people risk being condemned into those eternal fires! Jesus Christ is infinitely merciful—to those who repent. The idea that we are simply too lovable a creation for God to ever throw His enemies to their destruction is preposterous. He is giving humanity the chance to "choose" Heaven, to don the yoke which is easy, to sacrifice for the sake of His Kingdom, obey His Commandments, accept His Beatitudes, plead for His Absolution, pray to sustain His goodness, and adopt the vision which throws off every last vestige of Satan's darkness. But, look at how humanity now jeers at Him; look at what mockery comes from mankind's lips. We live in a country where our religious leaders have negotiated away this undeniable message of the Gospel. We are afraid the reprobates will scoff and sneer at us for having such a metaphysical message that to them is nothing more than religious fantasy. We are afraid of the machinations of their persecution which include their control of our systems of justice that are now becoming evermore tainted with their judgements of godlessness. It is no different than the way the crowds addressed Noah as he built the Ark. Well, the rains came and so will the chastisements to close out this final age, and these same crowds will be wailing and gnashing their teeth at the justice that will have come upon them. They can mock me all they wish for warning them of their destiny, but it will descend nonetheless, absent their conversion. This is not arrogance; this is a prophetic warning and a confident testament to the Victory of Christ and the Triumph of His Mother because I have seen the Morning Star Over America and Her Son, the Christ. Arrogance is in those whose pride will not allow them to repent at having so casually tossed the Faith of the Apostles into the gutter of societal contempt. Our country is being split down the middle, a separation of the spiritual Christian sheep from the secular atheistic goats. This winnowing is a providential signal of the return of Jesus Christ. Our homeland is at the doorstep of the Reckoning. God is not going to allow evil to obtain the ultimate triumph, solely for the sake of the sacrificial victims who have surrendered their lives through prayer and penitential suffering for the deliverance of the many. His unrecognized and unseen plan of redemption is occurring through His Mother beyond the vision of the secular world who would benefit from it if they would choose to convert their hearts before it is too late. What do I say to those faced with same-sex inclinations? No more than I would say to myself as a single man. You are not the victim. Christ is the Victim! Stop your wallowing in cowardice. Our Lord gave you a burden to bear for the sake of redemption just as He has for every other child of the Almighty Father. Look around the world at the suffering borne by the innocent. You are not given a dispensation from the purity of Christ, and you are not alone. He allowed your burden, your thorn in the flesh, not so that you would surrender to it, but that you would conquer it and bring your baptismal garment unstained back to Heaven in honor of Him. No one enters Heaven without a cross. Everyone shares in the Crucifixion that has saved us all. Invoke the nature of God through the sacrifice of your passions. Subdue your flesh and comport your identity with the purity and sanctity of the Most Holy Trinity! In Christ's Sacrifice, you will find healing, self-control, purity, power, and deliverance. Carry your flesh as Christ carried human flesh up the side of Calvary to the place where He conquered it. Die with Christ so that you can be resurrected with Him.

In the center of this frank assessment of American culture, perhaps one of the most remarkable things the Blessed Mother ever said to me was after I had been to sacramental confession and reminded Her that I was deeply sorry for my sins. Our Lady responded that She had no idea what sins I was talking about. I was astonished by Her response because I realized that I had not truly accepted that the Sacrament of Penance had wiped them out, rewriting the record of my past. There is so much goodness unfolding around the world, so much hope and inspiration, if we know where to find it, and so much potential for joy in all things comely and beautiful. We are God's gift to one another, with helping hands and consoling hearts; we are friends of spiritual confidence and the extension of everything holy that humanity has the foundation to become. There is nothing maudlin about this. I have always said that if you show me a man who never weeps, I will show you a man devoid of compassion. In this sense, innocence does not imply vulnerability. We see every day the paradox of Our Lady's urgent calling to be more enduring and to encounter the days of life one at a time, while simultaneously being mindful of the purpose of them all. The constancy in what we do rests in the diversified ways we examine and compare ourselves with Christ Jesus and the Heavenly Father's eternal perfection that has nullified our deep-seated errors. We are drawn-up to Jesus by way of the Cross to all things miraculous and perpetual that we hope to see someday. My hope has always been that we can defer to everything the Lord asks of us, and then we can say that we are worthy of summoning the Angels and Saints upon whose prayers, blessings, and intercessions we passionately rely. Everything we yearn for; the good fortune we desire, and whatever we hold-out for comes through the same hope springing forth from the faith of our fathers, knowing that deep inside our best kept secrets is the recipe for fulfillment that God has implanted there. We will never see or capture it without Him. Without the love that comes from On High, we would be too shortsighted to envision the grandest of what life can be. We might become giants among men in all other ways, but if we fail to clothe ourselves in the raiment of the Father's saintly blessing, we will never shine like Jesus Christ. Instead of being stepping stones into Paradise, we will remain like scattered grains of sand, idle to the universe, with no wisdom or grace to foster a better world. Is this what the heirs of our Lord's Resurrection foresee? I don't think so. Christians expect far greater substance out of life than simple mortality, much more than the fiery arches of offensive weapons or the grim images of such things as school book depositories and hundred-year floods. We know that mortal life has exhaustible texture, that it can be rough or smooth; sometimes intense, gutting, craggy, cruel and unseemly, and even suffocating and overbearing; but most people do not know how to touch or view it with any sense of understanding what to look for. Fortunately for us, everything we will ever need to know about Christianity is that we can walk as believers before seeing, making our way beyond the most startling moments, perilous threats, thunderous valleys, deepest forests, and darkest nights to arrive safely in our eternal homeland, to turn back the years and defy the ages; ultimately discovering that our eyesight was perfect all along. Our Lord's call to suffering must be something of greater value than all the gold and precious metals on earth, more healing than any salving balm, more tasteful to the palate than a thousand sweet confections, more capable of slaying the evils surrounding us than a glistening saber's edge, and more brilliant than a million magnifications of the glaring midday sun. So why is humanity so afraid? What makes men so reticent, fearful, and resentful when summoned to bear their crosses? What are we worried about? The fact is, we are perpetuating the defeat of Satan through the same redemptive agony that took our crucified Lord to say on the Cross that the whole created world, its final legacy, and whatever else might come, were finished. It is true that Christian moral piety consigns us to the utter pursuit of spiritual holiness, and most of us are still tapering ourselves away from the manipulations of the world while growing in our appreciation for the Church. It is said that humankind cannot achieve complete oneness with Heaven while living exiled on Earth, but the Holy Mother tells us differently. Our Lady says that we can manifest the kind of genuine love and charity that prepares us for redemption while we live these very days and hours. The only thing holding us back from believing this is our own self-doubt about the princely value of the human soul. Our faith must become like wildfires too vast to extinguish, cascades of wisdom for the parched curiosity of men, and whirlwinds to expel the stale pride of the billions of unbelievers around the globe. Our flesh may be waning as we speak, but our eternal spirits are ever-growing, ever-reaching, ever-striving for this higher form of life. This is the Gospel to which Our Lady calls the world through Her miraculous intercession. This is how She has taught my brother and me to look upon the world. Capitulate to nothing that is not of God. Aspire to the highest realms of Truth. Love your enemies enough to tell them the truth. And, leave the world upon your passing the scent of your loving and righteous heart.

The Revelation
of
Morning Star Over America
A Supernal Sonnet

And God said,
"Let these creatures stand erect above the beasts of the ages.
Give them the intellects to speak and the hearts to unite.
Enlighten them with My Spirit,
Give their hearts vision,
Inspire their souls to My Throne,
So their voices may proclaim to the universe
That I love them."

Sunday, August 23, 2009
Virgin Mary

"My children, while you are aware of your blessings, it would seem that you are yet unable to grasp the magnitude of the gifts you have given the Deity and humanity on the Earth through your completion and dissemination of My messages as the Morning Star Over America. You have said it correctly. What deposit of works could be for anything other than comprising the miracle that has blessed so many souls? What motivation must there be in the dedication of two lives and a thus-far collective 37 years to ensuring the conversion of wicked men? The Holy Spirit is the origin of all this, My children. Two of My children have given over 18 years of their lives, yes indeed, even 20 each since your pilgrimages, and the world is more the blessed for your faith. You have arrived at a moment in the years when it is all right for you to exhale a breath of relief that your genuine selves are for the propagation of the Cross and the refinement of everything yet to be polished by the Man who died there. We must think about this accomplishment in grand terms, and you must remember each and every day and hour that you granted the Father in the completion of your work. Every Hail Mary, every heartbeat, every keystroke, every moment you have walked forward wearing the excellence of the Cross has made you Saints still residing *on the Earth. My children! You are the children of the Mother of God! You are the adopted progeny of the Most Perfect Woman ever created. You are the brothers of the Only Perfect Man who ever lived. And, it is with honor that God sees you here with Me now, willing to devote your hearts and lives to listen to what I have to say, when all the rest, all the societies and secular sects are out there somewhere, running about the globe, looking and hearing only what they choose, researching meaningless conclusions, distracted from the things that really matter. I wish for you to remember that yesterday was the Feast of My Queenship on which you placed in the hands of Archbishop Lucas and Saint Mary Jane Kerns My messages for AD 2006-2008. And, I ask you to remember it because of who these two people are. Imagine how they are looked upon by the Lord. And, in light of this, the Lord has spoken to them through your faith in His Truth.*

What this means, My sons, is that you have joined the ranks of believers who are of a nobler race, of a lineage of servants about whom you have read in biographical anthologies, about whom you have heard of miracles that have no explanation, whose names are mentioned in Eucharistic prayers, whose life-skills and talents are hailed before the masses, and whose ranks you shall join when your earthly journeys are through. I have dictated grand and evocative messages to My children to the far corners of the world from this humble place in central Illinois. I have been factual and eloquent, uplifting and upbraiding, professorial and motherly, and most of all, gently admonishing. We know what needs to happen to make humanity pure. We know what is wrong, and I have said on many occasions what must be effected to address it. You have become incomparably unique children of the Matriarch of Humanity by your obedience, and yet you do not see how; you cannot grasp what it means to be in your shoes. You are too humble, and you see yourselves as too ordinary. Not any more! What has happened to this world that changes by the hour, that intensifies by wars and depletes from human excesses; what future has been wrought through My supernatural narrations will bring peace and light, just as I gave Jesus to the world in Bethlehem. My Morning Star messages are so historical in nature that it would take the entire collection of human theologians thousands of years to dissect them. And, this is why most of them will never try. They will say, "Oh no, not me. I am not up to that charge!" The same miracles that will overcome the lost and forsaken will likewise bring them down, and they will see themselves ultimately as did Saint Thomas Aquinas, as praying little children again. Open any page of My messages beginning February 22, 1991 through December 28, 2008 and you will see a reflection of God's devotion to the Church. My Special son, it is holy and awesome that you have permitted this gift to transpire. You must be humbled by what I have said today, but you must also be proud."

Sunday, December 13, 2009
Virgin Mary

"Welcome to the Immaculate Love to which you are drawn, and from which the Fruit of My Womb was birthed into the world. I have compassion for those who suffer, and I have pity for the many who do not yet know God. It is My honor to come bless you and speak the strains of holiness to which you are so devoted. My Special son, your writing is becoming so awesome and panoramic that it may eclipse your other works. I have told you that the Holy Spirit comes to you when you ask, when you wish for dreams to share with those who are living in darkness, waking them into the Light of Eternal Truth. Your deposit of works has now superceded most of My other messages in the world, and this has occurred here in the heart of America where it is needed most. What kind of hypocrisy do your opponents believe is acceptable? I am the Patroness of the United States of America, but your fellow citizens and brothers in Christ believe that I have no right of persuasion here. What utter nonsense. It only makes sense that the Morning Star Over America would eventually arrive. It is logical and follows every tenor of naturalism laid-out in the books of the Bible. What would the future hold if I had not spoken to you and your brother beginning the final decade of the Twentieth Century? Yes, helplessness and hopelessness. Think about two of the most emphatic instances of intercession that the Lord gave the Earth as the last century came to a close. They began ten years apart. Medjugorje and the Morning Star Over America. My Special son, you

realize that I am the Miracle that humanity is seeking. I told the Archangel Gabriel that I was compliant with the Will of God because My Heart was inspirited with Love for humanity. It was as innate to My Being as life itself. The rest is left for good souls like you to explain. This could be the focus of your memoirs, along with all the grand and supernatural propriety that you have gleaned from My presence. You can intermingle the ethereal and the practical to show the world what a refining experience being a Christian is. You are given to the excellence that has made Saints of your forbears, and in this, you cannot fail. I ask only that you remember that you are the reason for this. Not Me. Not all the unseen aspects of Creation that you can only imagine. It has been your desire to build-up a better world through the mission of the Church. It is a product of your demands that humanity do better. This is what the Holy Spirit has implanted in you. The record of your life story will do much to convert the masses. Your books, your prologues, and My messages need a personal face not from Me, but from you who have seen and heard Me. This is why your first Diary is such a miraculous piece. It is filled with stories that help humanize your experiences, like speaking to all the small miracles in the first days in 1991. Even you and your brother tend to lose sight of what happened back then, but you will always believe it. You know what you saw. You remember the miracles. You have concrete knowledge of witnessing them. Everyone would want to know what you thought. What impact do you believe that such things have on the dispensing of My messages?"

I responded, "They are details that no charlatan would have had the imagination, creativity or composure to have dreamed up."

"And, this is why I have done it. I never once believed that it was necessary for you. You are certainly aware that these supernal manifestations cannot be expunged from time. Remember that our final goal is not to make your brothers and sisters believe for the sake of knowing that miracles exist, but what the true motivations are behind those miracles. They are asked to come into full communion with the Roman Catholic Church. There are no relevant miracles anywhere else."

Sunday, December 6, 2009
Virgin Mary

"My little sons, there are times when the Mother of God weeps because I have seen so much passion lived by My children, and this is one of those occasions. You work daily for Jesus because you love Him. You have faith, you are filled with the Holy Spirit, that the Kingdom of the Father is alive in you, and that your role in the history of Creation has been united with everything that is eternal. You are witnessing for Heaven in a world in which you are participant disciples. There is Glory waiting for you, and it is clear that it has already been seated with you. Today, you are near the end of another decade, the first of this new century and new millennium, and you will see the fruits of the labors of the Church and your efforts on My Son's behalf handed to those who hunger for righteousness. I am sure that you cannot calculate how many times I have urged you to have patience, but you will soon know that it was a good calling. You see the condition of the world and the degradation of the moral fabric of America. We have more to do as the new decade opens. My Special son, there are many pretty strains and thoughtful images. You know that there are endless stories yet to be told. There are homilies yet unspoken, admonishments to be made, clarifications to issue the masses about faith and morals, and instructions for the disciples of the Church. I have brought My Motherhood into this home, into your hearts. I have maintained your union with your brother. It is clear that the two of you have done your part to live in peace. If you take another look at your collection of works, you will see that the fruits of your union have been righteous.

I ask that you ponder for a moment what exactly separates humanity from the unseen world. How many worlds are there that cannot be seen? Or, is it one massive world composed of smaller spheres? Or, is there anything of discernable shape at all? When men speak about rectifying everything that is wrong, and of reconciling this world and the next, can it be true that they are comparing seeable Creation with the spiritual realms? My intent is to suggest that Heaven, as you know, is boundless, but it has parameters so as to exclude everyone and everything that is not in it. This seems like an oxymoron, that it is a paradox, but it is a sacred mystery not unlike the inexplicable Trinity. I have told you that Heaven cannot be described by words on a page. It is vastly too beatific and overwhelming to the senses. Even those who have been shown Heaven while here on Earth have been unable to describe what they have seen. The fact that you cannot see Heaven at this moment is evidence that you are exiled from a place that exists separate from the world of men. However, this 'place' is everywhere except Purgatory and Hell. The point I am making is that you are situated inside Heaven now, but in a particular location that precludes you from seeing and knowing it. Anyone who is filled with the Holy Spirit is in this station, which means that those who do not believe in Jesus and the Deity are not even partly in Heaven now. Do you understand this dichotomy? I am saying that a person living on Earth can be located in the heavenly realms next to another individual who is not. This is very crucial to what you believe as a Catholic Christian, and it is even more crucial to your comprehension of the conversion of the soul. Your part as a baptized Christian is to maintain your balance of spirit, your uprightness in the Gospel Truth, so that you are always the perfect image of The Christ who walked here before you. You are held upright by the heritage and posterity of the Church and the dedication and service of all believers who preceded you.

I have given messages around the globe for centuries to close the gap between those who believe and those who do not. It is clear that the Sacred Scriptures serve this purpose, but too many modern men see the Bible as an antiquated history book for the weak of mind. The Church teaches that everything that humanity needs to be saved in Jesus' Crucifixion is written in the Holy Bible. Everything someone needs to be delivered to Heaven in His Paschal Resurrection is delineated in the New Covenant. These things are as true as the sunlight is bright. However, the new millennium has brought with it a different kind of insolence. Mankind has searched for and discovered new ways to sin. They need miracles to set them straight. I knew this at the wedding feast of Canaan, and I know it to this day. Do you remember what My Son said when I asked Him for more wine? Yes, He said, "My time has not yet come." He knew that I was asking for a miracle. He said to Me privately that day, "One day, all the world will know that you are their miracle." And, here I am. I speak in reflection of Jesus' hidden proclamation that day. He was seeing in His Sacred Heart all the generations who would live and centuries that would come, and He knew that He would respond with blessings upon this world at My behest."

It has been twenty-three years since Our Lady began Her grand intercession in our lives as the Morning Star Over America. I suppose there are innumerable opinions on what kind of people my brother and I should be based upon the sentimental historical depictions of visionaries and seers by religious biographers. In reality, we are still the same people, the same personalities, the same sense of humor, the same seriousness about the facets of our lives. What has changed is that our perceptions are far more keen after having been matured by our Virgin Mother's view of Creation. Prayer with Our Lady has changed us because we have been close to Her and listened to the wisdom that flows from Her lips. She has formed my brother and me to a far greater composure in the Holy Spirit than we would have otherwise attained in the struggles of life alone. She has strengthened our sense of what is right and true from the purview of Her maternal divinity, and reoriented our vision to see life completely in the context of the redemption of humanity in a world that is quickly approaching the close of the mortal age. Indeed, what is the value of gaining all the materials, accolades, and comforts of the globe and finding at the last that they were of no more worth than a ball of mud compared to a perfectly-cut diamond the size of the planet. Our exile from the fullness of God is temporary. Soon Eternal Life will replace it for all of us, if we are found worthy. Mortal existence will be overshadowed to a degree that we will wonder if it ever really existed at all. There are multitudes of people who will read the words recorded in the Morning Star revelation and dismiss them, often with prejudice, because they will not be able to reconcile their current beliefs with the declarations that Our Lady levels from Her knowledge of what will greet us outside of time. It is difficult for them to assimilate a wholesale change in their perception because their vision of the world is mortally dimensional, subject to failure, circumscribed by the parameters of only what they can see, hear and touch. They have held errant perceptions for so long, in collaboration with so many other lost souls, that they feel entitled to their darkness as their personal truth that no one has the authority to impugn. None of them can readily see beyond their passing. And, they have never met an intimate compatriot who has risen from the dead to tell them what is in the hereafter. Quite frankly, many have been impressed by protesting wolves and charlatans who have evangelized a false Gospel absent the Cross of Jesus Christ. Prosperity-gospel evangelicals are wolves in the finest robes. Most people outside the Catholic Church cannot grasp the concept of sanctification of the soul or their responsibilities to effect it by their conformity to the image of the Crucified Christ. This is why they are at a loss when explaining human suffering along with the testament of a loving and merciful God. It is a paradox to them. Our Lady explains all of this to us in a way that piques our heroic nature. Once we come to believe the true eternal power that our prayers possess, not just in assuaging our God's supposed anger at sin, but in our playing a sacrificial part "in filling up what is lacking in Christ's afflictions," we will come to experience the reward of being with Christ in the Glory of His Cross. It is a gift to be given the power to mark the ages of man, to augment glory itself, and adorn the halls of eternity with the most significant and triumphant sacrifice a creature could enjoin. It is elevation, magnification, expansion, and creation which emanates from perfect serenity, composure, and the ultimate comfort of Deific Love. Angels and Saints are reveled into permanent stirrings of ecstasy by the prayers and virtues displayed by man while in this region of sacrificial exile. Jesus has declared to the Father that we are worthy, and the Father has concurred. Hence, it is easy to worship God in the ultimate thanksgiving when face to face with Him. But, it is triumphant to extend that worship while in the darkness, simply through the invincible power of the heart. That "raising power" of the heart is man's miracle. And, we can see how many cannot, and will not, make that leap of faith. They cannot invoke any sense of victory, no transcending movement into greatness. Hence, we do it for them through our prayers and sacrificial intentions. We carry their spirit into those heights upon the wings of our faith. And, God responds. Morning Star Over America is His response to the prayers of millions of people for those who need a miracle to believe; millions of Rosaries lifted to Him, contemplations of His Life wafting to His Throne, children petitioning greater virtues from themselves and the many, for unyielding strength, constant determination, ever-faithful devotions, and lamentations of deliverance from those chosen to suffer for us all. God is real. Jesus is alive. He is interacting with humanity by way of His Divine Mercy with any heart that wishes to quit the world, tender the faith, and reach for His hand. My hope is that each person would desire to draw close and follow the example of my brother and me which is a testament, not only to surrender and obedience, but to the sacrifice that allows faith to become knowledge. We believe in the authenticity of the Roman Catholic Church as being the original Mother Church instituted by Christ 2000 years ago. We believe in the Most Blessed Trinity whose Second Person became Man. We believe the Bread from the Catholic Altar is the authentic Bread of Life spoken of in Sacred Scripture. We believe in the intercession of the Angels and Saints, particularly witnessed through our work. We believe that the Most Blessed Virgin is our Heavenly Mother who is the great, final Intercessor before the great day of the Lord. We believe it is most beneficial that every heart defer to Her motherly guidance. She is not an option; She is the Ark of the New Covenant. She is the Queen of Heaven and Mother of God. She is the Woman Clothed with the Sun, depicted in the Book of Revelation. Our Lady gives each of us the permission to completely detach ourselves from everything we have ever believed about life, every tradition, every familial bond, every cultural custom and idea about life, so that She can rebuild us in the beatific order, in the image of our original dignity, in the image of Christ. He is the Redeemer worthy of all worship who extends everything good that man has ever tasted. It would seem that the United States of America has a great distance to travel to find His favor again, but that chasm can be transcended in the blink of an eye, in one great invocation of faith. One wave of revelation can roll across this land from sea to sea, much like a tsunami swells and inundates any shore its strikes. If the citizens of the United States can grasp for a single moment that the Morning Star Over America revelation is authentic, that their God has actually pierced the veil and allowed His Mother to extend to them Her Immaculate Heart, the world will never be the same. We will thunder as a collective humanity toward redemption like a shuttle blasting from its launchpad into a clear blue sky. We will realize that the plurality sought by those who reject the Catholic Church is the lie that it has always been, generated as a negotiated truce with all those who have refused to tender their obedience, even after God has blessed the world with so many astounding and revelatory miracles. Anyone would have thought the great Miracle of the Sun in Fatima, Portugal on October 13, 1917 witnessed by 70,000 people would have been enough to permanently transform the world and bring His Kingdom to fruition. But, such has not been the case because of the stoics who believed instead that it was not worthy of their belief. Hence, we suffered the horrors of a twentieth century filled with unimaginable human misery, desecration, blasphemy, war, pestilence, and death. Pure inhumanity. Our Holy Mother has little regard for the melting pot as a description of the culture of the United States. She is not afraid to point out that there is very little unity occurring amongst the expanding populations within our national borders. In fact, it is getting worse. Only in Christ will our identity not be stirred into an unrecognizable porridge where copious amounts of rhetorical seasoning has to be continuously added to somehow make us believe it tastes better. Only in the Kingdom of Jesus Christ is every unique thing about our identity individually exalted before the whole of Creation, much like a single diamond lying in a treasure chest filled to the brim with other multi-colored diamonds, sparkling at the discoverer who cannot decide which one he wants to pick up first. It is only in the Roman Catholic Church through its Sacraments that each chunk of coal is transformed into a breathtaking diamond. This is a definitive truth that is irrevocable.

Everyone but the atheist and the idiot harbors an anticipation of what awaits us past the veil of our mortal passing. Being thrust before the judgement of the timeless ages of men has not dawned upon those who mock our Heavenly Creator. And, nearly everyone else thinks it is too good to be true that He might open a door in that veil in advance of that final moment of truth. Yet, that is exactly what Jesus is allowing in the miraculous intercession of His Mother. The single most beautiful creature of Paradise is revealing a vision of what is behind that veil, what awaits us; the love, the glory, the perfection, the healing, the purpose, the deliverance, and the freedom. It is all there. It is for us according to the judgement of our lives. But now is the time for the faint of heart, the doubtful, the obstinate, the faithless, the wicked, and yes the atheist, to see and to know that there is a greater destiny than to be lost to the ages because of the stubbornness of human pride. Now is the time of their great opportunity, seeing contemporary testimony from authentic messengers of God who are worthy of belief. No human being on the planet is capable of self-creating the wisdom that Our Lady's words magnify. No person possesses the magnanimity to surrender their lives for decades without respite with no return except slander, abuse, ridicule, isolation and torment as the reward for delivering Her messages. No one offers their lives for their enemies outside the grace of Christianity. Neither is there anywhere a person's determination to succeed so long term, able to generate so much patience, indicative of such unimaginable fortitude, so long-suffering, for no monetary or celebratory reward. And, neither were my brother and me of such character if we had been left to our own designs about life. It is all the work of God through the Most Blessed Virgin Mary. We had never conceived such depth of devotion, such purpose or meaning as our Holy

Mother coaxed from us—all for Love. And, we realized it all just by looking at Her. The spiritual luminescence in Her eyes penetrates to the deepest recesses of the soul and is enough to convert the entire planet because you can see the suffering of the Crucifixion in Her gaze; all the power of Calvary is in the sparkle, all the Triumph of the Resurrection in the commanding serenity that no force in Creation can disturb. She personifies and radiates Her Son like a perfect mirror, and the human soul is drawn to that refuge like a filing to a magnet, to that place of rest awaiting the final deliverance of humankind. We experienced an activation of the visionary heart, almost as if it were a complete substitution of beingness. And, once in the pull of Her spiritual magnetism, nothing else possesses greater attraction that would draw us away. Through Her we find the greatest, most intimate love for the Savior of man. This is the field of influence that the heavens wish us to fall into, into the grace of God, much like a comet falling into the gravity well of the sun. This is the effect that occurs at our Holy Mother's many shrines where Her children kneel in humble obedience, soliciting Her loving succor. Her children are like incoming comets that are drawn by Her maternal attraction, swinging around the Son with plumes of divinity that everyone can see. Our Lady and Her grace have been the stabilizing genius in our lives that generated the entire collage of grace surrounding the centerpiece of Her messages to us. She has been the rock-solid encouragement, the hope-generator behind everything we are asked to dispense to this suffering world. She has all the beatific capacities that make giants of men and titans of paupers. She can inspire any man to beatific heights that lie only in our dormant dreams. So, it is to our betterment that we partake of Her wisdom, each and every one of us, by drinking from the font of Her encouragement as the Morning Star Over America. Now is the time of our great awakening to the reality that we have a destiny in glory the moment we choose to bow before the Messiah who has wiped our sins away, because if we do not, we will perish as fools without glory as the most reproachable creatures that ever drew breath. Pride and obstinance will get us nowhere but thrown into the fires of damnation. Trepidation from the fear-mongers toward Our Lady's intercessions comes from those who are profiting from the status quo of worldly indifference and religious cowardice. The human ego believes it to be a terrible thing to be told what it must do. These cowards love to be obeyed, rather than to obey. They obey only their own ideas, and then, only if there is profit in the demand. We can feel rebellion battling our humility every day we are required to submit to things demanded by others. Yet, God commands nonetheless, and only because He so passionately desires our return to Him to share His Glory. Indeed, in the name of justice, God will damn the unrepentant wicked who have rejected His merciful overtures for conversion. There will be no excuses that will matter. Christ is the only Savior who is the ultimate authority over life and death. His commands are not a product of domination or slavery inflicted upon anyone, but rather a heartfelt petition to accept redemption by offering a simple "thank you" to Him for voluntarily suffering a horrible Crucifixion that He could have chosen to avoid altogether. That is why the Holy Mass of the Roman Catholic Church has been humanity's "thank you" for 2000 years. It is the only place where we as a body of mankind, in unison, offer this collective worldwide gratitude. The yoke is easy and the burden is light in the knowledge that the rewards are eternal. Not one person would be offended to be told that they must go to the store to purchase a lottery ticket, lest they never win. And, oh how fast would they run if presented with the winning numbers. Jesus will force no one to purchase the ticket, while presenting the numbers to everyone. He requires that act of obedient submission from each person who will be granted Paradise. The Heavenly Father forces no one to enter Heaven, and He provides astounding revelations such as Morning Star Over America to show everyone that Heaven is real. In these moments of His Mother's undeniable presence, He allows everyone a stunning display of the composure of His Kingdom in a manner that preserves the integrity of our act of submission. While it was His Will that humanity be exiled from Heaven, it is our will to accept His Son's Sacrifice that will allow our admittance once again. Every heart tastes the Sacrifice or they will never see Heaven. The human ego recoils at the sacrifice of the will, thinking no one can tell it what to do with its self-determination of its existence. And, in that moment when a human being is told that they must accept Christ's Divine Mercy and comport with the Gospel to be delivered into the beauty of Paradise, the ego sees the sacrifice for the sake of resurrection, yet stubbornly vows that it will bow to no one. But, all will bow to Christ, the only Son of God, even the damned, because He is so great, so powerful, so holy and so beautiful. Anyone who rejects that beauty has no part in His Kingdom anyway.

Sunday, September 27, 2009
Virgin Mary

"My children, time will prove that success and good fortune will be your lot in life. You are giving Jesus your greater years, and He will deliver to you before you enter Heaven the best of everything that Eternity has to offer. This is My pledge. Today, you are blessed with My presence again to speak to you about the conversion of humanity in terms that you understand by virtue of My many messages from years before. Your hearts are so pretty, so simple; and heroic are your ways in the lineage of the Christ and the Saints in whose presence you shall soon bask with joy. You see the world through the lens of time, with dailiness and suffering, because this is the exile of men. I have told you before that it is not because you are yourselves inherently corrupt, but that Adam and Eve before you plagued the whole of humanity with the burden of mortality. Jesus has overcome it for you, and you are the beneficiaries already of the knowledge that your passage into His arms will ensure your lives forever. Think about all the people who have preceded you there. All the anonymous souls who have worked as you have, the Saints and commoners, the Popes, priests, nuns, deacons, and all who shared the sacrifice of the communal life. Pray often for the Poor Souls in Purgatory who depend on your petitions to help them, and God will hear you. He desires that the three stations of the Church be united by the one

Holy Spirit, and this means that you must pray for those who have died as they also pray for you. I come today with confidence that you understand why the world is in so much turmoil. I am the Mother of God. I see many desecrations that pierce My Immaculate Heart. I have witnessed these things for centuries. Your present circumstances, your ongoing difficulties are real, but some of them are only your perceptions; and they all will pass away, pushed into the Abyss by the Glory of God that is encompassing you now. Millions of pilgrims who visit My shrines in the eastern and western hemispheres wonder why I speak in such brief terms, why I do not simply offer them lengthy, substantive oratories about the condition of the world, the state of the Church, what the future will bring, and when the Triumph of My Immaculate Heart will be rightfully revealed. I know that it is difficult for you to believe, but the answer to their questions and the fruit of their prayers are in everything I have told you. You have published the Lord's response to their questions. You must be assured that this is true, and every day that passes is good; no matter how you feel or what your state of mind, you are moving toward the revelation to humanity what the Morning Star Over America came to say. I ask again for your patience while this process is underway.

My Special son, you are correct when you state to your brother that I did not come to you for no reason. All you need do is look at your books and your spirit is encouraged. I say to you now, please remember how powerful they are and will be to those who have not been exposed to them like you and your brother. You will see the miracle all over again when you witness their reaction to My intercession."

All of my personal writings which supplement the actual texts of Our Lady's words have been commissioned through Her expectations of me. She wished me from the beginning to synthesize and describe my growth, my transformations and understandings. She told me that my perspectives would be valuable and enlightening to anyone who was conscientiously seeking their own way out of the darkness. I have always hoped this to be true. Still, I maintain an invincible confidence that everything She has told me privately about our work will come to pass. It would seem that I spend a substantial amount of time admonishing unbelief in the subjects that compose my writing, even to the point of openly shaming pride and cowardice. I do this because "belief" is the front door of faith, and the impenetrable composure of the American mind requires a frontal assault on the rampaging ego that is holding that door shut. One cannot seem to speak kindly enough or grovel lowly enough in our day to get past the epicurean pride of the secular western mind. And, realizing that horror awaits them if they do not tender their hearts, it behooves any messenger to speak in a way that they might hear anew, even from the housetops. Far too many faith leaders are worried about being summarily dismissed if they speak too stridently. Our Lady will not let the Truth be held hostage by sinners who threaten to walk away. She has taught us not to be afraid of anyone who dismisses themselves with scowls on their faces. We must remember the Saints and Martyrs who endured far more than unsavory parting glances. Our Holy Mother asks how much has been gained in the last fifty years by compromising away the clear mandates of the Holy Gospel to the hedonistic onslaught of sinners? She tells us that we have gained nothing by compromising with evil for the sake of a false fraternity in sin. Diablerie consumed us anyway. Therefore, we must come to recognize that something was lost. Civility was squandered and honor based in the great devotion to Christ has been obscured. Every Sunday, the Catholic world declares with one voice, "We believe...." And, without taking that step into the realms of what is right and true, there is no courage; there is no openness; there is no bond with Heaven; there is no good will; there is no unity, and there is no progress toward any goal set out by the Mother of God to lead us to Paradise. And, there is no future. She does not compromise with my brother and me in matters of the Truth. Although we were relatively disciplined individuals at the outset, there quickly arose boundaries which we were never to cross again. In Her eyes, there is no compromise with the world regarding the parameters of the Truth because God's Will is the only will She serves. While Her presence radiates the beauties and gentleness of Heaven, She is not mocked or manipulated away from that grace. Her maternal instincts always magnify the spiritual discipline and decorum which advances and secures the atmosphere of the Holy Spirit. And, She has the power to visit that atmosphere upon us, sometimes at the expense of sacrifice and pain as our lesson. Yes, She can call for reorienting discipline if Her children are so out of bounds and inattentive that they require Her to do so. But that flavor of authority seems to never come from Her hand. It comes from the Father through His Son at the administration of the Archangels. Woe, oh woe, if one forces that occurrence. Children grow to be sons and daughters of God in Her household. This may be a shocking revelation for many because of the single dimensional caricature they hold of our Blessed Virgin Mother. They characterize Her motherhood as affirming of everything they decide to do and any way they decide to act. And in this, they are lying to themselves. There is a difference between skinning your knee and losing your soul to the fires of hell. We gain a fuller comprehension of this discipline by contemplating the Scriptural passage that states to whom much is given, much is expected. This is inclusive of the levels of comportment in holiness. I do not relate this aspect of spiritual discipline in any way to diminish the breathtaking compassion and endearing understanding that Our Lady manifests towards us at every moment. Even in Her discipline, the human soul cannot separate itself from the love that envelops and soothes us. I accent the discussion of discipline for our sake, we who must be determined in overcoming our sinful nature. We must surrender nary an inch of our identity to lewdness and dissipation. We must never scare away the dove of the Holy Spirit by maintaining familial spats. Every person can rise to dignity as royalty in God's Kingdom. We can be saints right now through our determined devotion and cleanliness of heart; set upon the higher things, enduring the attacks and distractions that try to rob us of grace and confidence.

Belief allows us to profit. One who does not believe in our Holy Mother's intercession profits nothing from it, which is truly a cause for sorrow. There is a difference in seeing the assistance of the Holy Spirit as a welcome intercession as opposed to an unsolicited intrusion. This has been the question that the Church has asked lost sinners since the Feast of Pentecost. If we think about this properly, we should realize that the Father deposed Adam and Eve from the Garden into exile on Earth, effectively preparing them for the organization of the Church Militant here. When they were exiled, it was not to any kind of structured secularism to which they were sent. Secularism is a way of living for those who do not believe in God. It is not inherent in those who are destined for Salvation; in fact, it is an impediment to those who espouse the tenets of Christianity. Not to oversimplify the issue, but it boils down to those who either believe in Christianity and those who do not. While we are not the person to judge the ultimate value of anyone's soul, the mandates of the Gospel allow a spiritual clarity into the content of others' hearts by the works and countenance they reflect into the world. By their fruit we will know them. Does that mean we judge them? No, it means we help them, especially by calling upon the graces of God for them through our prayers, fasting, and sacrifices. And, sometimes those sacrifices include strongly addressing illicit conduct and destructive agendas inflicted by them upon the body of humanity. Our Holy Mother asks that we ponder the concept of whether humanity is prone to accept the intercession of the Holy Spirit, or whether the mandates of the Gospel are little more than an intrusion on their right to private lives. Imagine for a moment the content of Our Lady's messages laid before people with multiple marriages and penchant for telling lies, infidelity in marriages, lording leadership over workers, and those immersed in materialistic ways. Ponder the message they receive when told about their future in the sight of the Cross, and what they will force against themselves when viewing their whole life at its end. Huge numbers become defensive, believing no one has the authority to address their private faults or make an assessment of how they live their lives. In other words, even though our reprimands are a reflection of Biblical citations and our responsibility to the spiritual works of mercy, the whole scenario whereby Our Lady would address the conduct of men is an unsolicited intrusion, an encroachment on their decision to ignore their past and pretend that none of their sinfulness is of any consequence. The concept of secularism is the phenomenon that is blocking humanity's view of the Cross. There are too many other distractions. Secularism even has its own communication hierarchy in print and electronic media that our Holy Mother has condemned on any number of occasions. What I am trying to make clear in all of this is that Her appearances as the Morning Star Over America include the proper and appropriate condemnation in union with the Holy Spirit on a wavelength into the American psyche that is not necessarily present in Her many other apparitions through time. We are a special breed in our secular, materialistic obstinance. There is great composure of identity and a naive confidence that we are creators of destiny in our own right. Our Lady said that the command of the Truth in our Morning Star works will make them more appealing to American Catholics and others who see the United States government as little more than an evil monster trying to devour the privacy of individual citizens. In the same way that most Americans see the Church as an unsolicited intrusion, we are now seeing our own government in the same way. Anything to be disobedient to the call for holiness; and in the case of the government, assistance for those in need is opposed because compliance is seemingly being forced by conspiring dictators.

When Our Lady speaks to humanity, She makes clear the dictates of the Gospel, applicable to all those who wish to be saved. And, this clarity causes dissonance in those who believe that everything they have done is merely a matter between themselves and God, forgetting the offense against so many whose lives have been julienned in their epicurean train wreck. Verily, how will the rich judge themselves in the face of so much human misery? Our Holy Mother inflects the unwavering Truth because She is seriously concerned about the preparation of sinners for Judgement Day when Jesus will tell the Father which souls are fit for entrance into Glory. God handed this power to His Son. God does not judge, but the Son is the sovereign determiner of who is worthy of redemption. Each time we make clear that human choices in life always incur consequences is a moment of great grace. This is why it does not matter whether it is a family member or stranger; in fact, sometimes our family members can be the bigger stranger. There are implications of judgement and immortality in all human conduct. Is this not the teachings of the New Covenant? Those who refuse to accept correction from the Holy Spirit, considering it to be an unsolicited intrusion, will learn the hard lessons that come with their rejection of the Christian Truth.   And, those who intentionally impede the Gospel being proclaimed to these languishing groups because of fear of causing the intrusion are a whole other lot of misguided souls. The Most Blessed Virgin through Her messages to the American people is attempting to direct everyone to the Sacraments of the Church through the humility that will induce our confessions and amendments; and in this, we should all see Her presence as a welcomed intercession.

Sunday, November 29, 2009
Virgin Mary

"It is a tribute to your goodness, My children, that you have come to pray with your Mother again today. We have for many years been speaking about faith and sacrifice, and you have been on an experience-oriented journey about the meaning of life. Indeed, it has not been an experimental journey, but one of experience and exposure to the pathway and destiny of human sanctification, conversion, and redemption that the Lord laid-out centuries ago in the Sacred Scriptures. You are living that vision for those who are yet blind, and you are leading them to the waters where their thirst for the identity of the soul is quenched. Today, it is My honor to speak to you about the true emphasis of that satisfaction as it applies to the world in 2010. Yes, you have prayed and listened to Me. You have heard the call of the Holy Spirit, urging you to patient obedience, and you have responded affirmatively. I hope that you will begin to see yourselves as participants in

the Salvation of your brothers and sisters, for without you, it would be practically improbable that anyone in your age would bother to listen. As you can see by now, it is not that they cannot hear, but that they refuse to lend their ear to the Truth that is impacting their face every day. Humanity does not know how suffering fits in the purification of the Earth. There seems to be a disconnection between man's understanding of eternal bliss and the sacrifices of mortals in exile. My Special son, you are teaching those who do not know that beauty is best perceived when seen through the lens of Creative Beauty, of the origin of life at the hands of God and the behest of His own Divine Love. You are seeing that agonies and torments exist in stark contrast to the peace and pageantry that is taught by the Church. Members of the faith are regularly called to operationalize their profession as they are chosen by the Lord to imitate the life of Jesus. This does not imply physical crucifixion, but it certainly points to the spiritual crucifixion of the human will. It is not in the peace of Christ that the most poignant reminders of redemption are found, but in His suffering and resurrection from the grave. Do you remember the biblical passage about the grain of wheat? Unless it falls to the Earth and dies, it cannot be raised again. This is the fact of human existence in the earthly domain. And, as you and your brother have been told many times, this is not the end of life, but its continuance in the Glory foretold. And, many people wonder how God chooses who must suffer. He does not 'choose' in terms that ordinary men and women understand, but He allows circumstances to prevail according to the self-will of men. In other words, He does not choose for someone who has inhaled tobacco smoke to suffer lung cancer. They do this on their own. He also does not choose which little children will become victims of sickness and disease in the way that one might pick a color. It is wholly dependent upon what occurs in their family or community that must be mitigated. At the end of time, it is those around them that will know that one in their midst suffered for the sake of their deliverance. This was the way of Jesus. He was crucified at the very place where He had been hailed as a King.

The point I am making is that these suffering people become part of the Crucifixion in a way that others who have known no suffering do not.

This makes them not only 'chosen' by the factors I have cited, but blessed in the lineage of the First Apostles. The whole world becomes their proving-ground. They are capable of making up for the deficits of people they do not even know. They bring mitigation for wrongdoings half way around the globe. This is the community in which they live: the entire world. This is the jurisdiction of the Universal Roman Catholic Church, and its seat is the Vatican in Rome. You see, therefore, that human suffering has a center. It evolves from and revolves around the Crucifixion of Jesus Christ. This is the lesson that most Americans have never learned. They fail to realize that their impudence, materialism, and extravagance are the origin of much suffering because they are blind to their own sins. They are told this in the Bible, but they will not read it. The message comes to them clearly in My worldwide apparitions, but they do not believe in them. They would hear about their wayward lives in the homilies of priests and deacons, but they will not go to Church. Therefore, since they will not open themselves to hear the message, Jesus deigns to take the message to them directly into their private lives. They search for purpose and meaning, and even higher powers, once they begin to suffer. They are even more apt to do these things when they see one of their loved-ones suffer. Yes, suffering is a sad portion of the human experience, but you know that it has its sanctifying mission. Jesus' suffering has saved the souls of men, and the suffering of mortal sinners takes those men to the foot of the Cross.

We are speaking at the last of November of 2009, and it would seem that many years pass without the message of redemptive sacrifice taking hold. Countless souls cast-off suffering as an innate part of life, a necessary evil that afflicts every age. However, we know that it need not be this way. You once included in one of your books the proposition that if everyone on Earth would pray the Our Father together, Jesus would return immediately. This is the sacred unity that is missing. Easter and Christmas come somewhat close for those who believe in Christianity, but you see many who choose to follow false idols and beliefs. The Lord asked of Abram that he sacrifice his only son, and Abraham took Him at his word. What was the result? 'Do not lay a hand on the boy.' He was rewarded for being obedient to God.

This is the same thing that can happen today. Anyone who is asked by the Holy Spirit to do something and they agree to it can be spared from the sacrifice simply because they agreed. You have seen this many times in your life. But, without that commitment, without that fiat that comes with faith, gruesome consequences result, and humanity wonders why such terrible things come upon them. I refer to My September 16, 2001 message concerning this phenomenon. Sinful man is the origin of the greatest catastrophes on Earth. You have studied and discussed the great world wars, the scourge of infanticide, and social debacles that erode the happiness of man. How ironic is it that sinful Adam has brought such darkness into the world, but his descendants decline to accept the perfect Christ who has brought such Light? I realize that I am somewhat preaching to the choir when I say these things to you, but they are basic but yet ignored by most people in the United States today. It is all about patriotic zeal and crashing the gates of the marketplace to procure the finest gifts and toys.

I have been watching you with apostolic joy as you write your next book. You have seen that you are capable of teaching, leading, and reprimanding lost sinners in the way of the Cross, and this is the Holy Spirit living vibrantly in you. I do not wish for you to believe that you are too critical of the masses when you reprove their conduct in the secular void. It is just that; they are devoid of conscience and holiness when it comes to the spiritual realms. Your prologues will open hearts and touch lives in the way of Saint Paul and the great Doctors of the Church.

I ask you to remember today all who have entered this first Sunday of Advent not knowing what the Incarnation of Jesus means to them. Imagine if the Church changed the name of the birth of Jesus from the Feast of Christmas to the Feast of the Incarnation. I am certain that it would have more meaning to secular men who see it as a holiday event to enhance the profits of merchants. You wrote 'On the Eve of Joy' in the sense that Peace has come among you. And, along with this Peace came Wisdom and courage, and service and Sacrifice. These comprise the Truth, and the Truth has been resurrected, claiming the freedom of all who believe."

Our Lady's intercession to my brother and me has been a process of refinement and maturity from the beginning. It could almost be characterized as the growing of roots which plunge deeper into one's being with each prayer that is said, roots so strong as to keep a towering oak upright in any storm. From my perspective, the entire process has been accelerated for me where multiple lifetimes of understanding have been compressed into two decades. In the normal course, Satan can stunt the spiritual growth of individuals through his attacks. People can live their entire lives never learning or accepting the gifts and graces of the Holy Spirit. Their lives are marked by stagnation and apathy. It is easy for people to give up the fight or backslide into indifference or outright evil works. It is easy for them to take flight into materialism and sensuality. Scripture speaks of the phenomenon where a person could have their house cleaned of many demons, but if they do not maintain vigilance, the devil returns with legions where the latter state is worse than the first. [Matthew 12:45] Hence, it can take a lifetime to make the smallest advancements in spiritual understanding when left to ourselves in a darkened world. With Our Lady's protection and guidance, our advancement in understanding spiritual matters, and the Truth itself, has been secured by measures of years from any debilitating effects, backslides, or subterfuges by the devil that could have inhibited the growth of our elevated sight. It must be known that suffering advances spiritual vision by leaps and bounds, but engendered within that experience of suffering is the susceptibility to cower and flee from the fight for our union in Jesus' Sacrifice. The Holy Virgin's motherly relationship with us augmented the protection we experienced to the advancement of our vision. She has raised us as Her children. It is not necessarily a unique gift because it is a product of the strength of one's faith and acceptance of Her as our Heavenly Mother. She asks everyone to engage that acceptance because She is here to assist all Her children. For instance, every person who embraces Morning Star Over America with a determined heart will experience the same motherly protection. The effect that occurred was that Satan assailed us with a continuous barrage of sinister attacks that we felt acutely as he tried to subvert Our Lady's work through the years, but we were holding Her hand through it all with access to Her vision, support and wisdom. Thus, we were able to transcend the uncomfortable events without diminishment and proceed into the higher realms so we would understand Jesus' suffering more clearly. Her intercession for us has been to unite us more deeply with Jesus' suffering through actual experience, all for the magnification of Love which is salvific; expanding and magnifying toward the dimensions of Mount Calvary. This is an important point. Our Holy Mother did not allow us to sidestep any suffering, but instead strengthened us as it rose to fever pitch as Satan tried to subvert Her intercession. She asked us to take-up the cross that our faith could sustain, then She augmented our faith so that the salvific nature of our cross could be increased and elevated into union with the Cross of Our Savior. This is why we bring our burdens to the Altar of Sacrifice in the Catholic Church. It is there that we unite everything with Jesus on the Cross who magnifies our very existence for the sake of the Redemption of the world. Our Holy Mother is the nurturing catalyst because She is always present with us with Her grace so that we will not fall or backslide as a result of our human weaknesses. She enhances our faith to levels that can withstand the most ferocious onslaughts, especially from the mystical realms. This is part of the meaning of Her repeated statement that mystical gifts only come through the diminishment of the flesh. And, what is it that keeps us so surefooted and willing to endure? Her Beauty. It is a reflection of Her Son, Jesus. Once one sees the Sacred Heart of Jesus as He hung on the Cross and the appreciation He had for all those throughout time who would adore Him for such a self-giving sacrifice, you take on your part as the Mystical Body of Christ with a great sense of gratitude and identification in your heart. It transcends everything about mortal life that could ever come, either to distract you or make you flee from the suffering. The human soul grows roots so deep in the Mystery of the Cross that we refuse to entertain thoughts that will not take us higher and deeper into our union with the

Perfect Sufferer. None of this precludes our feeling the biting pangs of sorrow and pain, loneliness and grief, or the temptations to abandon the path altogether. Satan will always be there assailing us until the Great Day. But let him come, because if we fall, we have access to the Sacrament of Reconciliation to lift us up again.

Saturday, January 30, 2010
Virgin Mary

"During the awesome beauty of this winter, we are speaking about thawing human hearts, softening them to the Holy Gospel, tenderizing their meaning and direction, and preparing them for the admittance of the Holy Spirit. My dear sons, I am truly grateful that you have decided for God your whole lives, and that you have again today come to pray with Me for the conversion of the lost. You know that these are historical times for the Church and for you. We must be careful to not lose sight of the majesty of your consecration to Jesus' Most Sacred Heart and to My Immaculate Heart as you greet each new morning. You have become accustomed to hearing and seeing the sarcastic cadence of the secular world that infiltrates the minds of those who are not predisposed to the spiritual realms. My Special one, your writing continues to awe the heavens. You have become capable of pouring-out your intellect about the Truth and your feelings about the way humanity ought to accept what the Kingdom of the Lord has to offer. You are so much like Jesus during His ministry, and your heart reflects the innocence that He never lost. My wish is for you to know that whatever the future brings, whatever blessings and obstacles come, I will always be with you. I have never lost sight of your desires to see the defeat of the wicked in your time on the Earth, and God the Father is completely aware of what this means to you.

My children, you are capable of becoming the pristine likeness of Jesus here in this world. If this were not possible, the Sacred Scriptures would never have been relevant. We have seen what prayer can do to change them, to enlighten the ignorant and correct the errant course of those who deny the existence of Heaven. My intention all along is to prove through you that those who cannot help themselves are aided by the intercession of the Church to learn their true inner-being. You have created a bibliography from which they can choose where to begin in discovering themselves. "At the Water's Edge" opens the door for the discussion that compares the Light of Heaven to the darkness of the Earth. "When Legends Rise Again" contrasts spirituality and realism. "White Collar Witch Hunt" reverses the slanderous attack against the priesthood. "Babes in the Woods" reminds all Christians everywhere that one must be mature in faith but childlike in nature, retaining the innocence of children who approach God openly and willfully. "To Crispen Courage" demands that human beings everywhere stand for something, to pull themselves into the acknowledgment that Jesus requires more than passive faith, but active spirituality that interacts with all the dimensions of the created world. It uplifts the Roman Papacy and reaffirms its infallibility before those who protest. We shall not forget "Supernal Chambers" because it consists of some of the deepest poetic theological thought ever committed to the page. Now comes My anthologies and the advent of your memoirs that will encapsulate the beauty of your entire deposit of works. All your books and writings advance the mission of the Church and the awakening of wayward sinners to the 'conscience' of the Gospel.

It is important for you to finish and publish the AD 1997-1999 book about My intentions for the world. This book also makes a more direct connection between Medjugorje and My appearances here as the Morning Star Over America. I am honored and pleased to be your Mother, and My Heart is filled with admiration for your mature spiritual faculties with which you perceive the mortal world. The genius of God is deeply seated in your being."

The Most Blessed Virgin has told us that it is very difficult to engage human beings with this message in a way that pierces their boundaries of acceptance. She asked me to consider how She first came to my brother and me with simple messages, small signs, and elementary requests. Then, She referred to the magnificence in the New Millennium messages after AD 2000, and asked how my brother and I would have responded had She begun Her intercession from those elevated plateaus. She said that we would never have been able to grasp the dimensions or insights in them that we now take for granted within the maturity that She has tailored in us. She secured our capacities of obedient faith and used them to construct a flowering representation of spiritual knowledge and elevation that everyone can now engage to find easier acceptance that Her intercession is authentic. She did not present great theological treatises that theologians would haggle-over for centuries. She could have, but, what would that have done to lift the hearts of Her simple children? Our Lady presented Her intercession so that everyone can progress through the same stages of acceptance in a much more accelerated fashion than experienced by my brother and me because time has now become so short. Archbishop George Lucas who was the Bishop of Springfield, Illinois during the personal unfolding of our work is the exception. He was exposed to Morning Star Over America as an ecclesial participant in the process, requiring his patient faith. He received the works of Morning Star Over America in realtime, in a timely historical sequence without the benefit of knowing how the intercession would progress, or when it would conclude. He portrayed great openness to the Holy Spirit and love for the Most Blessed Virgin. He experienced the progression of its unfolding, not knowing the majestic New Millennium messages in advance. Hence, his is the greater faith and the more expanded perspective than any of those who would come later.

Sunday, November 22, 2009
Virgin Mary
The Solemnity of Christ the King

"Today, My beautiful sons, I have come to pray with you for a world that is rife with distractions and corruption, for humanity that yearns for Living Truth, for the lost, aching and forsaken, and for everything you know to be imminent before the closing of the ages. My sons, we have put forth a deposit of works that can change the very existence of the universe. When the

Father says that the time is ripe, every creature will know Me. It is I who have borne unto mankind a Savior, and I will lead all who will be saved to the Cross. This is why it is imperative that you never stop hoping for that day, even if it shall arrive after your own entrance into Heaven, because the Earth needs The Word, and they will inherit it by all the workings of the Holy Spirit available to them. I only ask that you continue to allow the Spirit of Jesus to speak to His brothers and sisters through your bountiful heart. You are so sweet and deferential. You are filled with the expectation of the healing of the nations that I spoke about long ago. And, you have also seen that this takes time, mortal time, for people to awaken from their indifference. They are eventually reached and touched by the hands of immortality through such holy meditations as yours. To be sure, you have discovered that the Salvation of the world was finished on the Cross, and that it included your age from its inception.

When you ponder the idea of secularism, you surely must see its prevalence in places that you would not have otherwise thought. Why? Because you were raised in an atmosphere where Christianity was accepted innately. Could you imagine what would happen now if little schools around Illinois would stage a production about the birth of Jesus for Christmas every year?"

I responded, "It is sad that it is gone."

"My son, it is only temporarily gone. I must ask you again to believe Me when I say these things. They will arrive. You can tell that your nation is headed on a disastrous and destructive course. And, I am doing My part to help My children avoid the collision that will ensue. But to many, I seem foreign to them. Let Me provide an example. I ask you to think about everything I have ever said to you. Ponder all the complex messages, all the dissertations I have given you about the Church, the state of humanity in exile, the Sacraments, what other people are thinking in private, addressing your spiritual and physical needs, the corruption in America, and on and on. I have given you messages that have lasted for hours, and ones where you and

I were seated across from each other in a physical room. What if your brother had handed you the messages that appear in all of your books on February 22, 1991. What would you have thought?"

I said, "I would have been overwhelmed by them and would not have known how to engage him after that."

"Why?"

I said, "Because I would not have realized that I was a participant and as close to you as he was."

"Yes. And, have you now not created the massive works for the world because of your love for Me?"

"Yes."

"I am the Mother of humanity. I received My children on Good Friday knowing that none are given the Christian intellect to accept the dogmas and doctrines of the Catholic Church on their own. In effect, the original messages of your Diary are an introduction for the whole world to the manifestation of Morning Star Over America as though that world was just born. How do you speak to little children who are only beginning to see and hear? In short sentences, enticing words that make you curious, and in a way that helps you lend trust to the communication you are receiving.

Now, we are almost 19 years advanced in time, and you and your brother are embarking on opening humanity's collective heart in the way that I opened yours. However, you are going to present to them the mature manuscripts that I could have given you in 1991. What will this cause? Well, it is clear that it will require tremendous trust from those who will believe. Thanks to the way you composed your Diary, all who come to accept Me as the Morning Star Over America will be able to gain their formation of belief based upon your recorded experiences. What I am saying to you today is that they will not have to wait five or ten years like you did before the New Millennium messages broke the intent of My appearances here wide open. They will not have to forge the path of the highest faith because you grew along with your brother on their behalf in comprehending My purpose here. You have been the vehicle for the Mercy about which you speak. You are the origin of their conversion in the same way as the Apostles and Saint Paul. I raised you from the seed of infant faith to the grand and esteemed Christians that you and your brother have become. Now, you must consider how this applies to disseminating your works to people who have never even seen the words 'Virgin Mary' in their lives. Think keenly about this for a moment. You and your brother take for granted My role in human Salvation because you have been so close to the Truth. How will you react when someone says to you, 'the Virgin who?'"

I said, "I will try to generate a perspective for them based on where they are in Creation, and what they see compared to a greater perspective of the world."

"Indeed, this is what you must do. And, that is the miracle. Your testament to what you have seen, heard, lived, sacrificed, and believed is the miracle for modern man. If you had not recorded your twelve manuscripts, it would have been impossible for you to speak the miracle. Now, you can speak long after your audible voice is gone. You can sing the songs of life even though you may be in Heaven with Me. I am not suggesting that this is what will happen or that you will not have the personal venue to speak to crowds about your life, but you must not assume that the massive impact of your witness on My behalf is restricted to your personal accounts. Your writing is timeless and without boundaries, constraints or parameters. You sense the feeling of Eternity glowing from your writings, as well as My messages, because you feel the final victory already coming to you. Therefore, you cannot lose hope that your life here with your brother has been for the Glory of God. Think in the terms of a child just learning to read, and that child growing to become a great statesman. This is how My initial messages became the massive deposit

of works that you have today. If the world sees your Diary first, before they are bombarded with the barrage of New Millennium messages, it will be easier for them to accept. Do you see why?"

I said, "No one can accept that you would speak the way you have in your New Millennium messages compared to the way you have in all your other messages through history."

"Yes, this is the hill they must climb. Does it seem strange, however, that Archbishop Lucas did not have this problem?"
I responded, "He was a participant from the beginning, as it developed and unfolded. And, he has a different sense of its dimensions."

"Yes, now you can see how far others must travel to believe."

There seems to be many people who reportedly experience mystical phenomena who are not members of the Roman Catholic Church. This leads many to ask why we testify that the Church of Rome is the vessel of human redemption above all others, and that works such as ours only fall under the auspices of the Apostolic Church, especially under the grace of the Sacrament of Confirmation. In truth, there are phenomena seemingly outside the Sacraments of the Catholic Church, but we must be aware of the possibility of diabolical influence in them that requires keen mystical discernment. For example, does God allow people pre-figured visions of Heaven in near-death experiences on occasion, and periodically permit manifestations of deceased loved ones to bring comfort after their passing? Of course, but only according to His Will in knowing the environment of souls, how the person will sustain the gift, how they will judge themselves at the end of time after receiving them, and who will be edified and uplifted more toward the sacrifices for His Kingdom as a result. He will take every opportunity to save souls that mankind permits, but He will not throw pearls before swine. Sometimes simply having to endure the moniker of being delusional in the face of faithless pragmatists is adequate suffering to allow Christ to open the door to these graces. I am heartened by any gift the Holy Spirit wishes to dispense to famished hearts, but there are parameters of depth associated to the ones that we witness.   It is edifying for doctors and nurses to hear astounding miraculous details that could not possibly have been known from a patient whom they have just revived from the precipice of death, and further, to hear a testament to a land of light, beauty, bliss, and angelic beings enveloped in infinite love.   Many people who then hear such testimony through books and other media are uplifted as well after having someone confirm that Heaven just might exist after all. Testimonies of this caliber are the simplest and have their purpose, but they are truly limited in converting power, and can often be distracting to the greater revelations.   Then there are those who profess to be mediums who claim to be speaking to the dead or bear unrevealed knowledge of things about people's private lives.   These people are sideshows under the influence of distracting self-delusion, and even demonic spirits, if they are not outright liars about their supposed gifts. There is nothing redeeming in the image of Christ about their works. It is ironic that people so easily embrace these other testimonies, as they are splashed across television screens, but cannot bring themselves to accept the greater ones which bear the more beatific Light. What good does it do to be shown a vision of Heaven but reject the Suffering King who is the Light that sustains it? While these lesser revelations tell of a supernal land of milk and honey, they have relatively little momentum to sanctify and convert the world. Why? Because it is the higher gifts that magnify the Crucified and Risen Christ who is the Source of Redemption. These higher gifts are the Himalayas of God's mountain range of revelation. It is a gift to be reminded that Heaven is real. But, it is an honor and the highest endowment to share in the redemption of humanity.   The greatest and most comprehensive revelations are centered in the Sacrifice of Mount Calvary, that Love which descends like a plummeting meteorite unto every Altar of the Catholic Church at the Consecration of the Bread and Wine by a priest at the Holy Mass. While it is good to be reminded at times that there is a Heaven, it is far more beneficial to unite ourselves daily with the Holy Sacrifice that takes us there. That is the paradisial nature of the Holy Mass that the Catholic Church has been testifying to since the Last Supper. These highest revelations define the mystical lives of the Catholic Saints, and are rarely if ever seen outside the fueling fire of the Sacraments of the Catholic Church. Why? Because the Catholic Church is the destination to which God testifies by the acts of His Holy Spirit. It is the full revelation of Christ's Mystical Body arrayed in suffering. The lives of the Catholic Saints were solidly implanted in the Sacrifice of Jesus through the Most Blessed Sacrament. And, they surrendered their entire beings in obedience to the Cross in order to share Our Lord's redemptive sacrifice to make the Light known to the ages of men. They made themselves perfect manifestations of the Love of God that emanates from that pinnacle of human obedience. You do not hear that from anyone who was just revived from a near-death experience. And, the world asks, why suffering? Why dispense these lesser gifts at all which are mere flashlights compared to laser beams that shoot missiles out of the sky? Because there are so many people who are so far away from the idea of there even being a Heaven, so many people who are lost and suffering in such a pit with no logic, reason, comfort or hope, that the smallest flicker of light offered in the most comforting way will ignite their hopes that a joyful new beginning is in the offing; and in this, it is an act of Jesus' Divine Mercy for His children. If He shows them a spark, they will seek the raging fire, one step at a time closer to realizing the full magnanimity of His Crucified Son. The Eternal Father knows that the Wounds of His Son are too much for them at the moment, just as Our Lady knows that the New Millennium messages outdistance the faith of too many people without seeing the fertile field of the original Diary from which the messages grew. By seeing the recorded testimony of their progression and development, one can find an attachment to the process of sanctification, and not be forced to grasp an astonishing claim of miraculous intercession out of a vacuum that has no anchoring framework in organic reason or process. Our sanctification and growth in faith is a process after all; a process that is defined by how we are forged by the sufferings that are thrust upon us.

Sunday, May 10, 2009
Virgin Mary

"You are My children who utter the immortal refrains of charity and repentance to the Americas, and I intend to fully extend the fruits of your labors worldwide. Here, we have gathered to communicate about the modern world in ways that have never been heard by mortal men, and you should know that your work will not be in vain. My Special son, this has not been easy for either of you; there is no questioning the sacrifices you have made. You speak of what your lives might have been, what blessings would have otherwise come if you had chosen another path; and there would have been plenty. However, you have built an international foundation for upending the world and setting humanity on the course of righteousness. When you prayed that My messages would bear the awakening of lost sinners, I set out to tell them what they must know. I took your hands into Mine and knelt before you, holding your shoulders square before Me, and told you what to run tell your brothers and sisters throughout the world. I detained and distracted you from the workings of the material Earth so you could realize the purpose of your faith. And, you shall see in time that you delivered My messages perfectly. Thank you for thinking about Me on this secular Mother's Day as you do every year. No earthly mother can measure to the blessings I give you. We must ensure, however, that they are every day lifted-up before the Father. You must pray for their strength and spirituality so their children and grandchildren come to Me for the graces dispensed from Jesus in Heaven. As a crafter once said, "I have built you a good ship." His words, however, were no match for the danger of the world. On the other hand, I have given you a solid deposit of works to change the course of human history, and this voyage will be successful above all other sojourns.

I also wish to remind you and your brother what great warriors you have been over the past 18 years. Satan has been battering you ever since I woke your brother in the night in February 1991. His friend in Beardstown who said that he stopped working for Jesus because God would not keep Satan away from him told your brother that he would likewise give-in and abandon his work with you for the same reason. You did not surrender! Your brother did not surrender! You did not quit the fight or fall from the race. Satan has been lambasting you with physical, spiritual, psychological, and biological warfare for nearly two decades. The latter is the origin of your sicknesses. The first are your bodily injuries, and the second and third are the battering of your heart and mind. You have prevailed because you have prayed and trusted in Me. You have known about My power for many years, and I ask Jesus to amend the Earth according to all who call upon Me. As you say, it is the "relationship" that you and I have enjoyed that has made you strong over everything else in the world. Many are struggling to understand how God can come so close to someone on Earth. This is rather ironic given the fact that God became His own Son in that same world, according to the teachings of the Church. They know that it is either Me speaking to you, or they are living amongst the likes of Saints Thomas Aquinas, Augustine, Ambrose, and many other Doctors of the Church in the company of you and your brother. And, if you were them, which would you decide? Yes, they know what is happening here. And yes, there has never been a messenger who did not want to be believed by the Church sooner rather than later because it lends credibility to their word and immediate purpose to the devotion of time given to Me. You and your brother's lives have not been wasted. I have requisitioned special graces for the propagation of your Apostolate, and it will occur as you and your brother continue to live. It makes Me indescribably happy when I hear you speak about not truly realizing the power of your written works. You must understand that you have accumulated eleven, and soon twelve published works that have for the most part not been dispensed very far. Once they start moving, they cannot be stopped. It will take them time to read them, but they will not need to read them all completely before doing something with them. This is the miracle that the Bishops have been praying for."

The Most Blessed Virgin Mary calls to the world that She is in our company, speaking the strains of affection that the Lord holds in His Heart because He wishes us to remember that He is always looking over us. Her intentions everywhere and always are to pray about two issues that are important to Him so we can assist in the mission of the Church. Within the scope of the first, imagine what it means to Jesus to be welcomed into a human heart. The Holy Spirit takes abode in those who receive the Divine Love of God seriously and with purpose. Many hearts are closed because they are embittered by the experience of human exile, and others have been scarred by personal failures and tragedies beyond their control. We, as mortal creatures, are given birth to glorify Him. Many are given venue to praise His Holy Name to the nations unlike anyone else in their vicinity. And, still others are like Saint Paul on the road to Damascus, stricken from his horse in order to make a lethal sword out of a flailing butter knife. The point Our Lady wishes to be made is that there is a linkage between Heaven and Earth due to the immense communion shared between the human soul and the Spirit of the Father. It is immense because it is made possible by the willingness of the Holy Spirit to visit those on Earth, along with the receptive will of those living in exile to receive Him. She has told us that spiritual conversion is a process of refinement, not without obstacles and setbacks. This is to be expected. However, the most offensive act to God is that His line of communication between Heaven and a penitent might be completely cut off. One of the most reprehensible, offensive, grotesque, and blasphemous acts that a human being can perpetrate is to take their own life. Do we realize the number of young boys and girls who are committing suicide? And, others who are older that do not want to carry their share of the Cross? Our Lady has asked me to write about the efficacy of physical and mental suffering, that it is spoken about in the Gospel and by Saint Paul as filling the ullage in the Crucifixion. While there is nothing lacking in Jesus' Holy Sacrifice to redeem every human soul, those sufferings endured by His Mystical Body likewise make reparation for the sins of men. How can someone do this if they decline to live? What would the world have been like if Jesus had chosen to rather die of His own accord than to permit His life to be taken by ruthless sinners? Our Lady says that God the Father wants His creatures to live until conditions prevail beyond their control that take them unto their deaths. Suicide is a catastrophic wrongdoing, and we must pray that it ends. While the Church provides descriptive terms in the Catechism as a means of reducing the punishment for suicide, it is very much as offensive to Jesus as the scourge of abortion. The Mother of God has spoken to us of the cowardice of those who commit suicide. They are not the spiritual brothers and sisters of the Son of Man. They are quitters and traitors to the Salvation of the world. Everyone knows at least one person who has committed this act, and we must therefore pray for them all. Euthanasia is a demonic abomination; one of the prongs of the trident of the culture of death.

The second issue is that we see many horrid decisions and statements made by the American president and other politicians to scandalize little children, promote lust and impurity, violate the sanctity of developing children in the womb, scandalize the purity of school children, and fail to lead in matters of sexual morality. They are the people whom the American citizenry have chosen to lead the government, but they do not necessarily have the final word in matters of faith and morals before God. Even in this description, these lost souls are not as immersed in darkness as those who mock Our Lady's messengers and accuse them of speaking to evil spirits. There are tens of thousands of people in the West who think like this. They fight against other evils and believe that the only way to effect change for the good is to become evil themselves. So many display a rogue arrogance against the discretion, modesty, and scrupulousness about which Our Lady teaches. In far too many cases such as this, engaging them with the Truth causes them to become full of themselves, which forces them to the path of revenge against the Light. They ignore the suffering of others brought by their ignorance, and only care that people accept their interpretation of the world through their eyes of secular hatred. Our

Lady says that Christians must never fear engaging these people or the vitriol that they will launch against us.

It is always a joy for our Immaculate Mother to take part in our prayers for the conversion of lost sinners and the eradication of suffering that is imposed on the innocent because of the acts of the wicked. The Christian faithful of the world have much more praying to do before conditions around the world improve. And, in the midst of that prayer, we must remember that the miraculous intercession of Heaven's Queen has the power of the Cross in touching human hearts, not in an absolving way, but to give rise to the Truth in a world that is so saturated with lies. Even as we are seeing a massive movement in America to improve the lot of its citizens, the number of poor and diseased around the globe continues to increase. There have been occasions in past generations when holy people have turned their faces to the skies and asked the Lord how much more the world can take. These years are no different when it comes to this. What makes these times particularly more repugnant is that even with the facility of mass communication, sinners are still reluctant to propagate the message of the Gospel. It would seem that there should be a copy of Our Lady's Fatima, Lourdes and Medjugorje messages on every doorstep by now. Images of the Cross should be on every paper and electronic medium. But, we should never worry, though! Jesus will not be displaced by any man, and His Crucifixion cannot be eclipsed by any other mortal act. Humanity is growing and changing, as it has for millennia. Our intelligence in matters of faith and morals is widely enhanced from ancient days. Our Lady says that there are various forces that diminish men. Stress, toxins, and aging are the main three. She insists that part of the message of Christianity should be a calling for the purification of the heart and respect for our bodies as temples which bear life to its destination in God. We have learned that we are the Lord's temples, and we must remain chaste and pure during our natural lives. God's Kingdom is progressing toward Glory on the Earth. When we awake in the morning, we see a new day that seems so repetitive of the previous, but Jesus sees us taking another step toward the foyer of Heaven. Our physical labors and mental anguish often blind us from this; it takes the whole world away from seeing the inexorable movement of humanity to the end of times. We are taught that living is not for the moment, but yet it is comprised of our focus on the moment. That is why we have heard the saying that the years are short, but the days are long. Hence, there is time every day for us to pray for the blessings of Jesus, being confident that He hears us. We must petition Him for strength and perseverance in performing our life's work which can be in every way as powerful as the writings that our Virgin Mother has dispensed as the Morning Star Over America. I know some people in their desire to control and define the heavens exaggerate the poignance in Our Lady "closing" the composite of Her messages to humanity as the Morning Star Over America, because for them it implies that She has nothing more to say. Nothing could be further from the truth. She wishes every one of Her children to open their hearts to such a degree that each would accept Her mystical intercession in their own lives. But, remembering Saint Thomas, does it not begin by believing others? I have heard comment on not too few occasions where people have said that authentic messages from the Most Holy Virgin only encompass a few words here and there. To put it clearly, they are wrong; and it is very presumptuous for them to make such declarations. Our Lady has asked me rhetorically who they think they are, and She encourages them to read the books we have placed before them. There, they will witness a beatific experience that began for the conversion of a world that doubters such as them refuse to engage. Our Lady wishes us to be stronger, bolder, and more assertive in a good way, more in the image of the great Saints who lived striving to bend the world into the shape of the Cross. People of faith in Jesus should be sure of who they are, displaying an awesome confidence that could stare down battlefield generals and a cool demeanor that could explain why they never need fight again.

Our Lady calls us to gather joyfully in the pleasance of God's glory to pray for humanity in ways that are heartfelt and hopeful, knowing that it will bring swift healing to those of our brothers and sisters who are in pain. There are no words to describe the deeply held appreciation that She has for our doing so. There are scarcely terms to express what our dedication to Jesus means to Her. She is our most powerful intercessor to Jesus, while Saint Joseph is our most powerful canonized Saint. We must pray for everyone who is fighting against the darkness being perpetrated on the Earth, and remember them to the Father for everything they need. In this, Our Lady's work will take its shape, coming together in a mystical way that will provide the most awesome conclusion to human exile that we could ever have imagined. Our Holy Mother has given my brother and me months and even years to reflect upon Her intercession in order to fathom the unique and revealing depths of Her great grace and beauty. And in this, we have only begun to delve deeply into addressing the solutions to the social and personal problems that plague humanity. It is but a partial solution to describe what is wrong. Next, we must utilize the mission of the Church and Her two decades of messages to prescribe the activation and implementation of the solutions that will bring about the victory we seek. Humanity must become kind and return to innocence, open and receptive, and real and true to everything known to be authentic about the Kingdom of God through the Roman Catholic Church. Jesus is pleased with the heroic faith manifested by so many within the Church, in good times and bad; and He could not be touched more devotedly by our sincere affections for Him in the multitudinous ways His followers have tendered their sacrifices. Everything we will see in this life must be measured alongside His Crucifixion. It is as simple as this. Whatever our goals, everything we suffer and sacrifice, and even our best years must be compared to the confidence by which He lived. And, our knowledge of others' pain and sorrows should shape our own prayers, our own view of the world and the mitigation of the failings of men. The Church has done these things well for two thousand years, despite the ignorance and maliciousness toward it by those farthest from eternal deliverance. The key is to continue to progress toward the Cross compassionately, to address what we know to be erroneous about the actions of humanity without becoming embittered, but with courageous determination and lack of compromise. A hand set to the plough cannot look back. Our Lady is here to help; and all we need to do is act like Her. Think like Her. Love like Her. There is patience atop of patience in the Fruits of the Holy Spirit because God is Love. Love has no underside, no dark side, no pitchy slogans, no infatuations, no ulterior motivations, and no selfish whims. Love is not a pastime for fame seekers or self-indulgent profiteers. Human love is all about consecration and devotion, prudence, truth, compassion, holiness, and service. Love requires the company of a sympathetic heart and blameless mind. Love in the way of eternal redemption means little if not imparted to forgive one's enemies. Absolution is love's companion, its other self, its mirrored reflection in the physical world. Love without sacrifice is but a hollow shell, a mantlepiece, an idle instrument, a blurry image. Love is the definition of human perfection in heraldic form, the lifeline we cling to when we are submerged in pain.

We must think of eternal salvation as more than something that happens to us beyond death; it is a tangible institution in the here and now. In this sense, salvation is a preeminent domain beyond this world at the same time it is an ongoing redemptive process. Salvation is a synonym for our new reality at the moment we are taken into Paradise. Therefore, salvation is simultaneously a place, an event, and a description of a place and event. Another transcending word in our vocabulary is love, through which God reveals His desire to take us into His presence through the Crucifixion and Paschal Resurrection of His Messianic Son. Let it henceforth be forever told. We can offer ourselves to Jesus like snapping our fingers together. And, we can flourish in His grace as though waking from our sleep. There is a visible resolution to the obscure aspects of human thought and action that is clarified by focusing on what makes us think. We have a grip on everything we have done and desire to do when we take into account the internal framework in which human intelligence is formed. It comes from our receptivity to the wisdom of God. This is the way we foster revolutionary change and purge toxicity from our homes, villages, and neighborhoods. It is also how we barge through the doorway of everyone who hates us and demand respect for the Messianic King whose Cross and golden Scepter will bear our souls to the cherished succor of the endless ages. It is in this vein that we should prepare for that great moment. We must journey carefully, respond openly, listen keenly, right ourselves smartly, pray devoutly, and hope beyond the constellations that all the blessings we seek will come in our day.

We must be careful to never allow any stain of hatred to infiltrate our hearts. Hatred is a mortal sin. Not only does hatred reveal to humanity that we are an enemy of redemption, but that we are incapable of aspiring to the perfection of Jesus Christ. Hatred eats away at our soul like a parasite, like a gargantuan monster devouring what is left of our conscience. Anyone who hates his brother confirms that he does not want to go to Heaven. Those who espouse hatred are themselves indicted by the very virtuousness they reject. It is only by seeing life through the lens of complete love that we recognize how evil hatred is. Love is freedom, while hatred is incarceration. Love is sweet and warm, but hatred is bitter and cold. Let there be no mistake that it is possible to detest the actions of other men without hating their souls. Hatred is the ultimate act of depravity. We must never allow ourselves to become ensnared in the hatred that shrouds the human spirit from seeing the resurrection of life that comes through love and forgiveness. Humankind must realize that Satan is real and is the instigator of so much pain and darkness that is heaped upon the world. Every time we undergo a period of sadness or obsession with the arrogance of others, for example, we see what Satan has done to them. And, then we see what he is trying to do to us. His main purpose is to divide us, one from another, parishioner from pastor, priest from Bishop, all from the Vicar of Christ, and ultimately the Church from the Holy Gospel and its

Great Commission through time. The devil separates people into factions within societies, into groups within governments, nations from their agreements, and cultures of continents from any beneficent comradery with the whole of humankind. He dissolves holy alliances so he can further his cause of commotion and damnation. He has been ripping through America and around the globe, turning people one against another, destroying friendships, causing death and destruction, and inhibiting souls from taking refuge in the Roman Catholic Church. He takes revenge against any person who gives themselves to the obediences and obsequies that our Christian unity demands. And, in all this diabolical revelry, we know that he will not succeed, but he can surely make things miserable for us when we do not take rest in the grace of the Mother of the Church. Our Lady refers to us as being beautifully human, and that the key to our strength is to use our heart as a visor to the next moment when our thoughts turn to the defeat of evil, knowing that our ultimate happiness rests in our union with Jesus on the Cross. The entire caption of life exists in our unity with Jesus in the midst of His suffering for the Redemption of man. We are Children of the Resurrection when we embrace our suffering in union with Him. There is no doubt when we are absorbed and consumed by the Easter joy that infiltrates our heart. The Holy Spirit brings this to us, and this is why we are able to maintain our happiness amidst the most gruesome atrocities. Our sense of this transcending perspective is a product of our ability to see where we have been and where we are going. Time brings obsolescence to many things, but it cannot change the fact that we belong to Jesus in every age and through all human events. This is why the heavens are reciprocally happy for us, and it is the reason we are fully aware that our life of Christian faith is having the desired effects on repairing broken-humanity in ways that our meager hopes rarely burn bright enough to recognize.

The joy and peace of the Risen Son of Mary is upon us today and always! Hear the instruction and blessing that Jesus gives you through the entirety of your days, and keep in your heart Matthew

28:20 to give you strength and purpose. *"...teaching them to observe all that I have commanded you. And behold, I am with you always, until the end of the age."* These are not ordinary days because hundreds of millions of Christians around the world are doing as Our Lady has committed our hearts to know, that our future beyond time and destiny beyond the world has been achieved in the Paschal Mysteries. Easter has meant many things to each of us through the years, but it has always been a celebration of new beginnings. The Church in Rome performs its contract with the Lord during the Easter Triduum by offering the blessings from the Father in memory of Jesus' victory over death. Where could sadness have ever been located at sunrise on Easter morning? The whole world and its people's suffering was eclipsed by the knowledge that the pain and torment we have endured has a reparative purpose for the purification of those who will join us in Heaven someday. The Most Blessed Virgin has spoken to humanity under many titles. Some of them are Our Lady of Triumph, Our Lady of Eternal Victory, Our Lady of the Rosary, Queen of Peace, Queen of Love, Mother of Perpetual Help, Our Lady of Prompt Succor, and on and on. However, She has also been known as our Sorrowful Mother for a specific reason, and it is because so many of Her children are not working with purpose for the conversion of their hearts and the souls of their friends to the Holy Cross in which their sins have been annulled. She carries these sorrows even during the Feast of Easter. This is why She asks us to remember the millions of unborn children who have been aborted in the past, and the millions whose lives will be taken too soon in the coming days. Sinful humanity is scouring the Earth with its own inequities, needing the sanctification that She has commissioned us to speak about. We see and hear the news of fathers and mothers taking the lives of whole families, and then killing themselves. Deranged sinners attack entire groups of people with firearms and bombs, killing them by the dozens and hundreds. These crises do not stop just because the dawn of the first Easter has already broken, but they should. Millions of marriages are destroyed because of the lack of spirituality. Untold numbers of people are plunged into depression because their children have died, their homes have burned, they have lost their whole life savings; accidental tragedies and incurable diseases have struck them, their favored sons and daughters have been kidnaped, raped, and beheaded. All of this is more of the same sin that befell Adam, and Our Lady declares that it must end now! We must remain strong so we can transmit the Lord's message of hope, repentance, and redemption in Jesus' Sacrifice and Resurrection. The heavenly hosts are confident that we shall do this; it is utterly imperative and imminent. Our Holy Mother hopes for a bright future, and so should we through the great vision of our faith. She cries because Her other children seem so callous and disinterested. But, She reminds us that they turn deaf ears to the Spirit of God at their own peril. We must warn them, but they must heed the call.

These days are our great opportunity and gift to summon the Queen of Heaven to help us. She stands at the ready. We have welcomed Her Immaculate Heart and the strains of consolation to which we have given our hearts so many times. She promises to be at our side, and asks us to pray about what She would say to us in each circumstance, at any hour of day or night, whenever we feel any sadness, if we have a hint of doubt about what God might say in any situation. The Holy Spirit speaks to us clearly and with seminal clarity about what the future holds. Again, I refer everyone to the latter clause in Matthew 28:20 because we will find strength there. We hold to each other the same way She carries Jesus with Her through Her travels around the globe. And, we must know that the same Holy Spirit just mentioned will lift us from the throes of the Earth, if only we will lend God our heart openly and sufficiently. This is what has been said to all Her messengers and seers throughout the centuries, a college of humble Catholics that are making the difference that Jesus needs on the Earth. We know the power of prayer, for it was this power that took Jesus to gain new strength in times of trouble. Hence, Our Lady comes to comfort and bless us every day as if it were the first Easter that humanity had ever seen.

Sunday, September 6, 2009
Virgin Mary

"My little sons, contrary to what many believe, the primary purpose of your exile is not the crucifixion of the human race, but your refinement and enlightenment, your excavation from the wreck of Adam's error, your deliverance to the threshold over which you will pass when you die, on into the Glory to which you are given as members of the Church Militant. Yes, you have called upon the Hosts of Heaven, the Supreme Deity, the Church Triumphant, and all the advocates given you through your faith, and they have aided you in ways too large for Me to explain. When all is said and done, it is what you do for God through Jesus that matters most, how you kept your promises through untold sadness and sorrow, what obstacles you overcame in maintaining your loyalty to the Cross, and with what devotion you have loved all the Lord's creatures. While human life is never easy or simple, it is made bearable by your trust in the tenets of the Gospel, and I have come to assist in your mission of taking it to the Church. I pray for you, I weep for your agonies, and I ask My Son to affect you in ways that make you understand what the Roman Catholic Church has believed for 2,000 years. You already know the sufferings and sacrifices you have endured and made to remain faithful in your goals. There are countless people whose minds are like yours; they wonder when the gifts of God will finally be dispensed to the Earth to reverse the tide of evil that seems to be overtaking the course of future events and bringing such darkness into the world. My purpose here is not to make excuses about why reality seems as it does, but to help you place it into the context of the Faith Church and how you are playing your designated part in bringing to fruition its mission in your time. Consider all the Saints before you, the ones canonized, and the millions I have mentioned who have never been known. Each and every one of them lived and died here in this world to advance the holiness about which I have spoken for centuries. They were not hailed as great visionaries, but simple people with a common cause and higher domain. This domain was unseen because it began and lived inside their hearts, where the Holy Spirit forges great righteousness out of a material world that is otherwise nondescript.

Thank you for allowing Me to continue speaking to you here, even past the time when I have completed My specific messages for the rest of God's people."

Let us pray -

Lord Jesus, heal our broken hearts and feed our hunger with the fastness of your everlasting truth. Be with us when our temples fall, our warriors die, our cities burn, and our bodies break. Bless us today and evermore. Remind us that the human will is never deity-prone but pride driven, power seeking, blinded by the flesh, selfish when tempted, and stubborn in the face of outright sacrifice. Remain forgiving of your people despite our repugnance; be relenting when convicting us of sin. Rhyme our words with your Gospel commands; chime our simplicity with the Church of old, and pluck our heartstrings clean of the dust of good men's silence. Guide us to clear your pathway to the Earth; help us charm the angels, broaden our vision to see right through the crusty walls of human arrogance, to break them down and trample them underfoot. Give us the sheen of righteousness that will make our faces glow with unfeigned loyalty in the way of the Apostles who first walked with you. Preserve the souls of stouthearted Christians and pull us into the fires of your Kingdom, inflamed by your holiness, fanned by human suffering, felt by prisoners, and carried in torches the size of sky-scraping summits, closer to you now than ever before. Instill our spirits with harmony's peace through Creation renewed, with Nature emboldened and redemption assured. You can make one voice speak an orchestra's song, and nations pray in symphonies. One last request should suffice our needs. Dear Jesus, be there when we die in you! Come again in glory wearing your martyr's Crown, shining like a castle afire, taller than the oceans wide, Scepter held high and arms outstretched; Lord Jesus come again! Benevolence adorned and beauty beyond all imagining! Light like never before beheld with the eyes of mortal men, trumpets blasting and melodies aloft, Vatican choirs raising Judgement Day prayers, the sunup of the Blood-drenched human soul, the resurrection of undeniable love, and old hearts born again into new! This is where you have fought to be. Always absolving; forever blessing, restoring, revealing, retrieving and redeeming the humanity you died to save by your agony on Good Friday, by your Sonship with God, with your Sacred Heart moved by what you've seen us do with the Earth you hold in your hands. You raise it high and hold it steady; you bid your Church to bless it here and feed it there; you warm one precinct with the blazing sun while cooling another when the nighttime comes. This is why we pray, O Lord, to you who are worthy of the sanctity of your brothers dying in honor of the Cross, of your sisters beating their breasts, bewailing the casualties of this life, given to you from the foothills of the world to the heights of Heaven where you live and reign with God. Amen.

Monday, September 14, 2009
Virgin Mary

"*Thank you, My children, for pausing with Me again today as we continue our perpetual prayer for the conversion of the lost. You are here with Me at the proper hour, on the appropriate day in history, so I can tell you how profoundly Jesus loves you. There are no wrong days to bow and pray with the Mother of God. I have brought with Me today the blessings and good wishes of the Lord, and He asks Me to remind you that He hears your petitions for the healing and safeguarding of all people everywhere, especially your special petitions for the liberation of the captive peoples in Korea. We have exchanged a massive amount of words and ideas, My sons. We have spoken of the world the way it ought to be described, aptly giving emphasis to the issues that stand in the way of the progress of the Church. Today, I have come to bless you with Jesus' most proficient knowledge about what may come, and ask you to be reminded that there are good times and bad ones that comprise your human experience in exile. I have been giving you signs of My presence because you continue to pray the Holy Rosary every day.*

My little ones, the sun is arching farther southward as the fall days begin to come, and autumn will again give way to winter. The seasons do not pass for no reason, My sons. They are purposeful in your lives, much the same way as your feelings change, as you grow and mature in wisdom and faith. They are a means for you to measure the steadfastness of the existence of man through the colossal events that comprise your journey toward Heaven. I have said that Jesus is with you, though He never changes, and that He understands with emphasis the meaning of life's mysteries, your capacity to endure whatever comes, and your determination to hold true to His Sacrifice through your trials and tribulations. I have said on multiple occasions that the majority of human suffering is self-induced because of humanity's reluctance to see Creation through the gateway of the Cross. We are here together now as we have been for nearly two decades last passed, praying into being the refinement of the world's coarsest places. As a good Mother, I am feeding you the nourishment you require to grow as Christians, to rise as admirable disciples in the majesty of the Church, and to become leaders of the Marian laity that will ultimately change the world. Even as I have given all the messages to America that must be heard, you remain here to tell them what I came to say, what I ultimately did say, and why your friends and enemies alike must respond with genuine intentions. The Catholic Church must be ever-growing and faithful. It must reflect the Will of the Father in chaste flesh, sown to the Spirit, afraid of nothing, willing to charge the depths, and fascinated by the supernatural miracles that the Lord is dispensing during these eventful times. My Immaculate Heart encompasses you in grace so you can feel the warmth of My Motherhood wherever you work and play. Jesus wishes you to join all the heavens at My bosom for this comfort. Wherever you sense the power of His Resurrection in what you do and say, you will find Me there. Words and syllables cannot capture what you mean to Me. There are no poems or anthems to regale what you have given to God through your sacred years on Earth. I invite you to think about your relationship with Me in the context of the Angels and Saints who await your arrival in Paradise. Your days are simply repetitive and often difficult to bear, but they lean in the direction of eternity into which you have been baptized. This should give you hope and strength when life turns sour and your bodies begin to break. How often have I asked you to live one day at a time? Not enough; and I will repeat it until you understand.

Your lives here are a prayer of thanksgiving in preparation for the spiritual nutrition that I come to offer. I make you privy to the portals of the future as appropriate, and I divulge what is going to happen in the future for your joyful hope. Yet, Christ Jesus wishes you to live with the same faith as those who have never heard His voice, who have not known My place in Salvation history, whose knowledge about God is limited to their own questions as to whether He even exists. You are His advocates to your lost brothers and sisters in the same way that I am your representative before Jesus. The Holy Spirit binds us together with God's Sacred Love that is seen with the eyes of the heart, with the focus of humankind on the mission of the Church, with everyone finally understanding that your exculpation in Jesus' Crucifixion on Good Friday is as much about your acceptance of His forgiveness as it is the Blood that He shed that day. He offers redemption to all sinners, but it is they who must believe. This is My pronouncement of blessing upon Creation through the Son I bore for you. Until I speak to you again, I beseech you to awaken each morning with new resolve. Find your purpose for life in everything that is yet to come. As I have told you on many occasions, the conclusion of My public messages as the Morning Star Over America infers absolutely no diminishment of My presence here with you. Please practice human love in the way of Jesus' Divine Love, and you will commit no wrong. You may suffer in His likeness because of the brutality of the world, but you will be stronger for it. The Church will be holier; its light will shine more brightly, and its reaches will be farther-flung to touch all who have never heard about the Man-God to whom they owe their lives."

Roadblocks and Gatekeepers
Why Do They Stand in the Way?

"Christ Jesus, valor of Martyrs, we pray that you grace your flock with dignity and comfort those who are persecuted for your Church. Encourage the doubtful to seek their way into your Kingdom. Make human hearts the wellspring of your holiness the world over. Give paupers dominion over their lives, and make us mentors to wayward sinners who look for direction in their final journey toward your heavenly dawn. Amen."

There are so many ways to speak of our lives on Earth; so many perspectives to offer where we would see our existence here in a wholly more revealing way. But, it all boils down to how we wish to define ourselves before the scrutiny of the everlasting ages; how we will allow ourselves to be molded and changed for the better into the image of the highest ideals and mores that have ever been manifested in the annals of the millennia. Mankind has been one family of creatures from the beginning, a mortal contingent of sentient beings who have been given the power to envision and create, feel and decide; filled with curiosity and intrigue, endowed with both memory and foresight, gifted with the capacity to be heroic beyond the parameters of this life held sacred. Standing upright, we are mobile, can work with our hands, see to the horizons and into the vaulting skies; romantic and sentimental, yet commanding toward honorable goals on either end of a breath. We have demonstrated courage in the face of all that we see as offending our entitlement to survive, and still a species that responds to any love that is able to reach us in the inner sanctum where we live out our lives, hoping that pain and misfortune somehow pass us by. Where is this description in our daily lives? How is it that such great truth has been evacuated from our societal discourse? Why are our discussions and punditry not flowering from these holy premises? Our identity as the family of man is being obscured by the critic with an opinion, the pessimist with a prophecy, the capitalist with his greed, the ideologue with his movement, the secularist with an agendum, the feminist with an inferiority complex, the race-hustler with a grievance, the slacker with an entitlement petition, the politician with a crusade, and the atheist with nothing but a vacuous soul. Our dictionaries can be researched, and we would find several definitions for the word "culture." Most everyone today is looking out their front door, worried about our country, and using the word "culture" to circumscribe their fears. One derivation says, "the quality in a person or society that arises from a concern for what is regarded as excellent." Another states, "to grow (microorganisms, tissues, etc.) in or on a controlled or defined medium," such as when health scientists take samples from areas of our environment to their laboratories to determine just how contaminated they have become with infestation and disease. If we were to take a culture of our culture, would we find that we are cultured? In other words, if we made an honest assessment of our nation, would we find that the quality of our society arises from a concern for what is regarded as excellent in the eyes of God? If He were to swipe His petri dish of discernment across the landscape of our nation, would He find that excellence has grown there, or has it been overwhelmed by the septic diseases collected along with it? To put it clearly and simply, would He see religious pluralism, moral relativism and atheistic secularism as diseases that are engulfing the moral excellence that He is trying to cultivate upon the Earth that He created? Everyone with an ounce of faith knows the answer, but millions are in such a cavity of darkness that they refuse to admit this stark reality because it requires the wholesale reorientation of their lives to conform with the beatific excellence of God. Conversion, indeed! Hence, huge segments of our society are convinced that the Truth cannot really be staring them in the eyes or that they will accuse themselves before the ages for their non-existent contribution to the sacred vineyard of their Creator; and thus, they continue on their personal paths of contortion and denial. They have actually moved into a paranoid xenophobia about the greatest Truths ever revealed on this planet. It is the ultimate psychological inversion where Light has been replaced by darkness, which they believe gives vision and warmth. "When the light inside of us is darkness, oh how deep the darkness becomes." [Matthew 6:22-23]

Let us consider the nine Fruits of the Holy Spirit as described in the Holy Bible: Love, joy, peace, patience, goodness, kindness, faithfulness, humility and self-control. Does the secular world ever mention any of these? Does it show any interest in securing these qualities within our nation? Again, we know the answer. It is quite obvious that secularists are not even remotely concerned for the attributes of Christian perfection that make a nation cultured in excellence as God would have it. Why? One reason is because of the phenomenon of the "roadblocks and gatekeepers." In order to understand roadblocks and gatekeepers, we must describe the psychological arena where they function. Humankind has always been an inquisitive lot. From the beginning, we observe everything looking for consistency, pattern, and repetition by which we can define, circumscribe, subordinate and conquer. It is part of our inherent mortal nature. We are programmed to live, to survive, and are inclined toward peacefulness of soul through the satisfaction of our interior desires. We could go on for pages, highlighting the themes whereby we have ascribed definitions to things in order to place them into our service as we subdue the earth and propagate our happiness. For example, we call someone a friend whom we know we can count on, or an enemy if we cannot. But "count on" to what? That they act toward us tomorrow in the same advantageous ways that they have treated us in the past. We speculate whether we can be confident they are going to continue to be beneficial to us in the future. Are they going to affirm us or contradict us? This is the same theme with most of our "sizing-up." Are we going to be affirmed or contradicted? Are those around us going to unite with us in our beliefs or take stands against us? Are they friend or foe? Our pattern recognition and subsequent definition of things come from our desire to be confident that all future things will be of service to our personal interior satisfactions and inclinations. We want to be sure how we will be impacted tomorrow so that we can avoid every discomfort that could come our way. And, this is the key. In light of our primordial avoidance of suffering, we find the natural human inclination to subordinate everything we possibly can beneath our discretionary auspices because we know what suffering is, and we do not trust people whom we believe to be surely as sinful as we are. Case in point: If you will watch keenly the interactions between people, you will see that most people will not befriend those with whom they cannot find a peaceful interactive composure; hence, the great racial divide in America. If they do not have confidence that a person is not going to bring them suffering, they will begin a process of psychological subordination in order to influence a person into a relationship with more conscripted and predictable parameters. It is about power and not wishing to be bridled by any superiors. We sense that if we can subordinate, we have power and can thus diminish the possibility of our own suffering by executing control within the domain we have conquered. It is the reason for every act of mockery, every put-down, word of gossip, insult, office spat, playground affront and derisive statement. It is a psychological dance to define superiority because we are afraid of the consequences of inferiority. It is why so many young gang members are consumed with the idea of retaliating against any supposed sign of disrespect. They are trying to outrun their own suffering by becoming the most ferocious beast on the block. Is this not also the cause of the horrible uproar regarding immigrants who have crossed the borders of the United States in violation of the federal law? Are not those who are opposed fearful because they have lost control of their imagined future to this body of humanity which is altering the demographic customs and financial landscape in which they live? And, are not the people who are entering the country illegally also fearful that they may be "...obliged to respect with gratitude the material and spiritual heritage of the country that receives them, to obey its laws and to assist in carrying civic burdens," as the Catechism states? Are they not fearful that they may have to wait, or be denied entry altogether, should they submit to the lawful entry process of assimilation? All are fearful of subservience to conditions over which they do not hold control when they just want to live unfettered, peaceful and prosperous lives. And, in the irony of all ironies, Christ said that His yoke is easy and His burden light; and if we want to become the greatest, we must become bridled by the needs of the least whom we should serve and return to health, which includes immigrants who are fleeing failed states brought to their knees by corruption. Humanity is fighting a great contradiction: Trying to control a sinful mortality that will soon thrust each of us into a grave, and being asked to accept a subservience to Christ through His Church that will raise us from those tombs. We are attempting to outrun subservience while Christ is asking us to serve. That is why Christianity through the Cross of the Messiah is the great contradiction. The Sign that is opposed. And, how is it opposed?—One way is through roadblocks and gatekeepers.

There are two contradicting ethics or worldviews that are at war within our culture. One is defined and influenced by only the observable and measurable, by desires and whims, lies and subterfuges, and by advantage and profit. The other is enshrined in a comprehensive awareness of the interaction between the seen and unseen, between the past and the present, and then how we effect the future, notwithstanding any personal desire, measurable opposition or material profit. The first view is founded in self-centered epicureanism, defined by any common dictionary as being fond of luxury or indulgent in sensual pleasures; having luxurious tastes or habits, especially in eating and drinking, but also desirous of wealth and the power that secures it. The second view is a manifestation of selfless human nobility, defined by the highest ideals, principles and character of the human person, even at the expense of life itself. Our culture is overwhelmed by the first and famished for the latter because, in the last five decades, vast numbers have been seduced into rejecting the spiritual disciplines required to enamor their characters with greatness. Thus, they do not have sight beyond the material parameters of the world that would clarify their vision and give them a fighting chance of becoming a noble or even heroic contributor to the elevation of humankind in the lineage of the Saints. And in this, I do not mean an understanding of the most sublime unseen mysteries of the universe, I refer to the simple comprehension of Divine Love revealed to the ages by our Lord Jesus Christ. The only thing worse than the proverbial bull in a china shop is a demographic of spiritually blind individuals holding the reigns of the societal order while trying to outrun their personal sacrifices and responsibilities that would define their nobility in the family of man. It is like scrambling up a torturous mountainside using the heads and faces of everyone beneath you as footholds to thrust yourself higher. The spiritually-blind judge nearly everything selfishly to their personal advantage. They give away nothing of their surplus, let alone from their want. They surrender nary an item unless profit is forthcoming. They speak only of charity when calling for everyone else to perform its sacrificial works. They boast a spirit of thrift only to make sure there is enough left for them. They believe commodities are priceless when they are selling them, but a pile of worthless junk if they are forced into buying them. Is there integrity in any of this, or even a hint of the Spirit of God? Of course not. It is a duplicity spawned from minds that are afraid to allow entry to the spirit of the heart that would mollify and knead its perspectives into a leaven that would elevate the world into its greatest spiritual manifestation.

Most secularists perceive spirituality as nothing more than a mere effigy, something that at its core contains no real life. They train their eyes only on the avenues and overages that help them garner the fullest material benefit from what they believe. This is not the way of Christianity. We are servants, stewards, custodians, and facilitators of a living Kingdom belonging to the Son of the Blessed Virgin Mary, one that God shares abundantly with those who are courageous enough to defend it. Our lifelong struggles are about spreading the Gospel in the face of everything about humanity that opposes it. This is how we discover the true meaning of life, the reason for our trials, and the rewards that rightly belong to those who seek redemption. Christians are not out of touch with the practical world, but we are careful in discerning what is really worth pursuing, and ultimately worth building. Our nation is experiencing a collective refusal to accept the wisdom of the heavens revealed by the King of Heaven because we are distracted by the shimmering of the material elements of a world which will be consumed in His final justice. We are thrust into a battle for the earth's resources, lest the top five percent of the population would hold 99.9999 percent of the nation's wealth instead of only 75 percent, after which they would proclaim their great charity by piecemealing those resources to the rest of us as a reward for our indentured servitude to them in their capitalist wealth factories. We have solidified perspectives within our culture that are not remotely in communion with the highest aspirations and ideals of humanity at its best. This is why Jesus came to show us the way to Heaven, and sent His Virgin Mother as His grandest reminder. It seems that we no longer hold that redemption into eternal glory through the tenets of Holy Gospel is of any relevance before the day we pass from this life, whereupon we mistakenly believe that Jesus will simply forgive us and let us pass, no matter how despicable the lives we have led. It is a sobering thought to realize that mercy is ultimately only for the penitent. When people refuse to magnify the wisdom of the heart and surrender the mechanics and decisions of the mind to the sacrifices and responsibilities that would take us to the highest pinnacles of human excellence, nothing is left but to fight for the scraps scattered on the battlefields of materialistic conquest. We surrender to being a people that are always looking downward into the most base regions of our beings, wondering why life could not have been some other way. Truly, if people of noble conscience had not stood up to contest the atrocities of the corporate rich over the last 200 years, they would have polluted every waterway and stream in sight with toxic waste, filled the skies with clouds of chemicals that would have dropped every bird from flight, mowed down the last giant redwood on the planet, strip-mined every fruited field in the nation down to a lunar landscape, gunned-down the last buffalo to freely roam the prairie, killed or run into the ocean every Native American who hunted those buffalo, marketed lung cancer to every person from birth who could purse their lips around a cigarette, and literally hog-tied every worker to their station in firetraps with chains on the doors to keep everyone in, notwithstanding the possibility of a twelve alarm conflagration. This is not cynical or negative. It is a sorrowful testament to what Christianity has been fighting against for over twenty centuries because the rich are fattening themselves for the day of slaughter in the justice of God. Opulent wealth and power is the god of the rich, and they will compromise or bargain away every tenet of moral decency, fairness and respect to secure the golden calf before someone else does. They forfeit their immortal souls for the sake of material and financial gain. Our economic atmosphere does not have to be this way. The lives of the poor do not have to be futile experiences of simple survival. The rich do not have to be terrified that they someday might find themselves poor. The world does not have to be dominated. Our planet has a supernal dignity enshrined within its architectures by God, and our mad dash to extract profit from it is the "strip-mining" that leaves nothing but a wasteland.

Nevertheless, economic systems arise naturally as people interact for the sake of survival and growth. Agreements are made to contributions and fruits from those contributions. In the societal organization of any culture, it is natural that people be called to serve in positions that centralize and organize other groups of people toward collective goals. There will always be those who are the focal point of the ideas and needs of other larger groups. For example, a supervisor of multitudes of workers probably would not take his subordinates to a meeting with his superiors to report on their progress and specific needs when they could better spend their time continuing in their fruitful endeavors. But, does the supervisor serve the least? Does the supervisor, and indeed the entire hierarchy, advocate their subordinates' needs, especially that their human dignity not be infringed? Corporations are filled with leaders who would not dare lower themselves to do the grueling tasks that they obligate their workers to do, yet walk away with the spoils of their labors and accolades that belong to those below them. Our system of human management fails when leaders allow their spiritual vision to be overwhelmed and supplanted by the materialistic vision of the secular realm which is based upon nothing but autonomic greed. Profit is the overarching principle that provides justification for any conduct that bolsters it. Their assessments become either self-inflating at the expense of their workers or simply rhetoric to their superiors who really do not want to hear that they should have to realign their priorities to maintain the dignity of their workers. How many families have been destroyed by the stress of lording employers? One is too many. Too often, the virtuosity of Christianity fades to the more obscured levels of the interior human awareness, and the whisper of the conscience that calls out for us to do right by the heavens and our fellow man is supplanted by the bellows of fear that tells us to protect ourselves, our lives, positions, power, wealth, and future profits. This is when the gate starts to swing on its hinges. When gatekeepers do not see the triumph of their mortality in their unity with those who suffer, they surrender their obligation to lift-up and care for those below them because the altercation with those above them is too great. So, they harden their hearts, turn their faces, and continue their ascension up each step of their life's ladder, sidestepping their brethren who are wallowing in subservient positions. They become the roadblocks to the ascension of the Gospel into the higher echelons, and obstruct the transformation of the Earth as Christ would have it. This happens while Jesus Christ tells us something totally different about human elevation in His Kingdom. Christianity does not state that owners and senior leaders of companies are a superior breed of human being who are deserving of the windfall of wealth from the labors of other men. Nor does it state that the Holy Gospel of the Savior of humanity be relegated into an afterthought by the news media amongst their portrayal of human events as they worship materialistic capitalism. Indeed, how can the Mother of Jesus Christ appear every day for over 30 years in Medjugorje and it still be a non-existent story to the worldwide media? The gates are sealed to Jesus Christ in their secular kingdom of worldly wealth and power.

Sunday, October 18, 2009
Virgin Mary

"*My dear little children, please imagine a scenario where you could have approached the local newspaper and asked them to place the two most miraculous words in the English language on the pages. Virgin Mary. What would it take? What could be done by bribe or by force to seek mention of your messages and My intercession for the secular masses? You could scarcely have done this as was accomplished today if you had not dedicated so many years to your work. Let the record show that the words 'Virgin Mary' appeared in the book section of today's edition because you cared enough about the conversion of lost sinners to keep going. And, this is why I am here. I remain steadfastly with you to pray for the amendments to Creation that will refine the world in the themes of righteousness. We have given of the grace of the Lord, your own prayerful obedience, My willingness to help, and the invocation of the Holy Spirit that souls will be saved. My Special son, I cherish My moments together with you here, though you know that I am forever at your side. You saw a week of unimaginable heresies spoken and written by the enemies of the Church and of My messages, and even by priests within the Church. You are seeing the evidence of what I told you about in the past year. There is a collective movement afoot to emasculate the Church by its detractors and rogue members within. You know that these people will not prevail, but you know not yet what the Church will suffer before they are stopped. I wish to be clear about some things, some of which will seem rather rhetorical to you. First, the Medjugorje messages cannot be stopped. My mission there will never be impeded. The signs, miracles, and wonders that the Lord has planned for the whole of the Earth will not be blocked from standing strong against the indifference of this world. Even hatred against My seers is a signal of their authenticity, as you have watched My shrines be impugned by those who refuse to believe. This is why My Immaculate Heart is so consoled when I come to speak to you and your brother. You have never once turned your back against Me. Secondly, the Church hierarchy does not fully realize the multiple places that I am appearing in attempt to change the hearts of the lost. There seems to be too many reports of messages for the Church to keep up. However, after 28 years in Medjugorje, one would think that they would see the fruits for what they are. I have asked the Church to employ discretion and wise discernment in matters involving the paranormal, and they are being careful to do so. The Holy Spirit will eventually lead everyone who believes in God to also believe in the messages of Medjugorje.*

What wars must be prosecuted before then? This is the gruesome toil of living in exile. It is the grand play that is unfolding inside the universe where also you will find the Spirit of the King. You are not players on an imaginary stage; you are true activists, believers, servants, teachers, admonishers, and merchants of the Truth of the Holy Gospel for the unchurched around the globe. I ask you to understand that the fight against the greasy evil of Satan's lies is a modern one, an unfurling series of events that must be taken seriously."

Everywhere we turn, there are people who are holding the door of change closed in the face of Jesus and His Mother. And, most of the time, it occurs through the simple sentiment of indifference to the things that are holy. Where does holiness fit in our secular society? The phenomenon of the roadblocks and gatekeepers is an exclusionary downward force of submission at each rung of the societal ladder by those who reject Christ in contradiction to the liberating salvation of mankind. Our truest calling and outward signature must be to indwell the genius of Christianity into the framework of our social conscience, a deposit of righteousness so profound that it brings the wicked to repent of their sins and give their lives to the Cross. Messianic Salvation. It is all about the irreducible troth of human holiness dictated by Christ's Crucifixion, imbedded deep within the heart of man. The Messiah revealed a revolutionary ethic into the human domain as the foundation of His Kingdom. The greatest among us must serve, expecting nothing in return. What does it profit a man in his character to serve only because he was guaranteed unimaginable material wealth and power? Our country is filled with genius, placed there by the Holy

Spirit, that will never see the light of this age because so many roadblocks and gatekeepers refuse to serve the dignity of man unless they profit from these labors of others. Jesus unveiled the personification of Divine Love which He asks us to imitate to the fullest extent of our beings through every venue and medium that human beings can generate. Lift up the world! Make way for the parade of moral genius, and let us see what God will do! Those filled with the Holy Spirit see life in a wholly different way. They recognize more sanctified hierarchies and benevolent ethics. The world is upside-down to those who view life in the Light of God. The hierarchies are inverted! The greatest become the least. The mighty dive into positions of assistance seated next to their brothers. Kings and dictators liquidate their treasuries and toss them to the poor. Leaders become servants; the poor become heroes; earthly wealth is dispensed before it is eaten by moths, and worldly stations fade into cabooses detached from their engines to be left in the middle of the long forgotten wasteland of greed. Is this not what made Saint Padre Pio, the stigmatic Saint of the Church, say that he envied the suffering? Suffering for the sake of Christ, for human redemption, for the poor, for Love, this is the seed of everlasting reward! It is only in this. Portions of humanity through the ages, led by the examples of the Saints, have embraced this deific wisdom to differing degrees of success. And, to see what happens when we do not, we need look only at the dysfunctional puss oozing from the sores of our contemporary society? The rich who reside at the pinnacles of power reject the sacrificial nature of the Holy Gospel because it means they must sell what they have and give to the poor, forsake their lives of opulence, and live like the rest of humanity whom they are going to have to somehow convince Christ that they loved. But, we are stuck in a stagnant pond of greed where the same rich decide who will be elevated into positions of power throughout the subordinate domains of our culture. And, whom do they allow to ascend into their personal spheres to share their power? Yes, those whom they can count on to affirm and protect their power and maintain the security of their wealth and distinction. They are afraid of losing it all to the demands of the Gospel. Every person admitted to their halls of power must reject the Gospel themselves, or at least keep their truest Christianity securely in the vault of their private lives. Does not the Gospel say that the world will love its own? [John 15:19.] We must recall that it will not be that way for those who follow Christ our Lord. We will be hated because our testament to the elevation of humanity shakes the foundations of their material empires. Look at our culture. Does Jesus reign as our King, or is something totally contrary to the Gospel occurring? Through all the material pressure, the machinations of society from top to bottom have taken on the hollow distinction of becoming secular, or absent the benevolent orchestration of Almighty God. And, that is why we have begun to see the phenomenon of "prosperity gospels," where wolves in sheep's clothing proclaim what tickles the ears of those with wealth; that God wishes us all to be materially rich. Why would anyone value sacrificial charity when they are hellbent on securing as much personal wealth as they can stuff in their pockets? Do they just pass by the Scripture parable of the widow's mite [Mark 12:41-44], or how the rich man walked away sad when Jesus told him to sell what he had and give to the poor? [Matthew 19:21] Furthermore, in a world where Christ wishes His Kingdom to become visibly present, do not secular architects skew the definition of public and private to mean that Christianity must be relegated to the unseen portions of society only? Children can be taught the Faith in their homes, but all the societal influences and educational machinations of the rest of the world are aligned to bludgeon them to accept the anti-faith of materialistic secularism. It is not anecdotal that if a child goes to college with a sense of Christian faith, they will most likely graduate faithless with their good conscience shredded by diabolical disorientation, misplaced priorities, and atheistic indoctrination. Now, how does this happen? It occurs because the gatekeepers who call themselves liberal educators have had their Christian consciences destroyed long ago by secular humanist intellectualism. They have made themselves roadblocks to the Gospel of Jesus Christ, fighting for a progressive utopia that they do not realize will never come without the conversion of their hearts to the King of kings. The atheistic secular values they suborn destroy life throughout the world, one student at a time, one issue at a time, whether it be their advocacy for socialist domination, legalization of illicit drugs, abortion rights, divorce, sexual liberation, homosexuality, lesbianism, same-sex marriage, transgenderism, euthanasia, anti-Semitism, anti-patriarchy, and on and on. The family is under constant pressure from these destructive mentalists in nearly every arena their children enter, multitudes hearing nothing of the Faith that would form their souls with deific strength that would both save them from a life of spiritual desolation, and further, would give them the character to be of benevolent service to the weakest remnants of society in the darkest hours of life. When suffering comes upon them, as it does for most everyone, they have nowhere to place their grief. It is un-transformable. Marriages are then destroyed, children are aborted, human suffering continues unabated and unmitigated, bushel baskets are placed over every glimmer of light to be seen. People turn to the vices of life; drugs, alcohol, infidelity, pornography, gambling, materialism and distraction. Look at that list. Marijuana is headed toward national legalization; over-indulgent alcohol consumption is an American pastime; infidelity is commonplace; pornography is being all but mainstreamed to our national consciousness; gambling is promoted by the states to feed outrageous budgets; and commercial advertising is successfully conscripting our youth morning, noon and night into never-ending fads, all for the purpose of getting their money. Civil liberties groups file suit against any image of the Savior of the world that encroaches on the secular domain they believe exclusively belongs to them. They know the hypocrisy of their claims to support the U.S. Constitution while concurrently using any judicial and legislative technique to terrorize Christianity into the silence of the private sphere. Somehow, they believe the destruction of Christianity is worth the price of their national honor and coherent intellectual integrity. This is the legacy of the secular roadblocks and gatekeepers who are taking our country to the precipice of the judgement of God. The entrenchment of secular power, absent Christ's beatific light, is one of the worst impediments to the salvation of humanity because nearly all secular-minded gatekeepers impede the movements and development of our culture toward the elevation of Deific Love which will bring the deliverance we are all seeking. It becomes an arena defined by the scratching and clawing for power, a worldly ethic of domination where brother stands against brother for the spoils of the conflict; a runaway stagecoach where we are in hand-to-hand combat atop the roof, while the leads dangle beneath the horses' stampeding feet, giving Satan the opportunity to deliver us all to a smoldering pile of death at the bottom of cliff we just plummeted from. Yes, it is about wealth, but only to the extent that it services complete freedom from the sufferings that can come from others through life. This is why the deathbeds of the worldly titans are so beatific. Not even their wealth can save them then; and the only power they have in those moments is the power of the pauper to pray to their God that they be granted Eternal Salvation and the forgiveness of their many sins through time. It must be a hollow feeling for these financial moguls to ultimately realize that those circling their deathbeds are thinking more about how the fortunes left behind will be divided, instead of being concerned as prayerful intercessors, petitioning the Divine Mercy of Jesus upon them.

Now, it is true that an organized, structured society may need things such as gatekeepers for the organization of peoples toward mutually beneficial goals. We see gatekeepers in every business, in every workplace, in our educational institutions, our media, throughout our governments, and in our religious institutions. Each and every one of these levels of individuals is exercising power. The question is this; are they trying to avoid their own personal suffering by maintaining and extending their own prosperity and power? Do they have personal agendas in opposition to the Gospel? Are they taking the fruits of others' labors that do not belong to them? Have they become roadblocks to Jesus? Are they attempting to outrun their own personal suffering when

Jesus explicitly states that those who wish to be greatest among us should serve the least, even to the point of their own sacrifice and discomfort? It would seem obvious that our secular architectures of governance are truly more about just the opposite, the avoidance of discomfort and suffering, and controlling everything beneath their auspices, that it not burden them for one moment. Consider the public media again. Is not secularism the 'default' worldview of the gatekeepers who determine what is allowed to be heard through the nation's media venues? And, do they not function as roadblocks to the advancement of the Holy Gospel of their God? They would say, "Make some money and pay for your own venue if you want to preach your religion." Let us be honest. Only the rich can afford such venues, and they have become so by their rejection of the Sacred Scriptures. So, the only people who possess the resources to affect the public discourse are materialists who have an empire to protect, which is the reason they make themselves so prominent before the public anyway. Why does it cost so much money for the Truth to be heard? The answer is the other head of the beast. Profit. Yes, power and profit by those who have made themselves gatekeepers. These are the symbolic horns of the capitalist beast. They are the root of many other evils here in the United States. Would many people submit themselves to becoming subordinate to the autocratic power and control of others if they were unpaid? Would they sit in rooms cordoned like cattle and allow people they do not even know to exact judgements against them daily in the performance of their duties? Would men and women perform sexual acts for motion pictures if they were not paid? Would they refuse to do so if they knew that no one would purchase these wares? Where does that market come from? Yes, evil works. This makes power and profit the tools of Satan in America. A multitude of sins grow out of these temptations. Many people approach and say that without profit, large companies would not be in business. Without that business, they would not hire any employees. Without employment, millions would have no wages, no means to purchase food, clothing, and housing. Yet, there are American corporations that are sitting on trillions of dollars in wealth because they believe that they will reap insufficient profits if they spend it now, in this particular financial atmosphere. It is not about survival of an enterprise, it is about domination and conquest in an inhospitable landscape of empire builders. Does this not prove that profit is directly related to self-ingratiation? Self comfort? Is it not about preserving the engine of penthouse living, self-perpetuation, and fear that an even more ruthless beast will consume them. The Kingdom of God is about sacrifice, expecting nothing in return. It is about sharing and building up as a family. Indeed, if a corporation is sitting on huge piles of monetary wealth, why have middle class wages been completely stagnant since the mid-1970s? How and why has executive compensation ascended like a rocket over the past decades compared to those who have labored in those same companies creating those fruits? Could the anti-gospel be any clearer? Bigger barns, indeed! [Luke 12:16-21] And, the irony is that most of these executives are the most cordial, intelligent people you will ever meet. So, profit as a concept is not inherently evil until those who hold wealth do nothing unless an unreasonable profit is to be gained for their coffers. And, they increase their profits by canvassing every landscape in order to conscript as many buyers as possible, buying their competition, buying low, selling high, generating as much false hype as possible to manipulate the public consciousness, and also by categorizing their employees into lower classes than themselves so they can justify compensating their indentured servants at a fraction of the level that they heap upon themselves. For example, who conceived of the idea of giving pay raises based upon a percentage? After all, a three percent pay increase for a person making $50,000 a year is significantly different than a three percent raise for a person making $500,000 a year? Is it legitimate to proclaim everyone got the same raise? Well, they do it without shame, no matter how corrupt it is, and they further pile clandestine performance bonuses and stock options atop those same percentages, which causes the whip to be cracked so production figures look rosy. And, human dignity is stampeded throughout the whole selfish process. Have you ever met or heard of anyone in the United States that has said that they do not believe they should accumulate any more than a given level of wealth; or if they do, they must help the poor of the world with those riches? Or that executives should never make more than a given percentage above their subordinates? Corporations become larger and extend their economic imperialism as far as their profit margins will allow, and then say they are making some minuscule percentage on their investment. They claim tiny profit margins after they have taken the profits which they should be sharing with the workers who generated them; and they invest those profits instead in the expansion of their wealth, generating opportunities that only they profit from. The point is that there is no limit to the amount of social or international wealth they desire to accumulate under their autocratic control. This is what the European Union is all about. Does this not imply that the current concept of 'profit' is always a source of evil? It is the definition of avarice! But, Our Lady says that it need not be this way. The concept of 'profit' can be realigned to be more inclusive. Human beings should run in terror from opulent wealth. This does not imply a nation governed by the tyrannical dictates of a socialist government; it has very little to do with the nature of the government at all. It is a nation inhabited by countrymen who love one another, and are guided by honor and the wisdom of the Gospel where those blessed with material success voluntarily give of themselves and their lives that others may live with dignity. Lift up the world! Secure the blessings of liberty to ourselves and our posterity, indeed! It is about love and the Kingdom of God on Earth. Capitalism says that prices are defined by what the market will bear. I ask "which market?" Are the poor part of the market? Are prices set by what the poor can bear? No, they are set based upon the production inventory of a given item targeted at that segment of the economy with the disposable income. Does this not mean that the poorer you are, the farther you have to reach for something? Are not prices set at the highest threshold that the middle class can be marketed into paying? And, higher economic classes of people never have to reach for anything of consequence. It is all about bigger estates and opulent luxuries to them. I have never heard of a company that has built quality essential products and marketed them to the people with little money. The economic system will not allow it. The poor are simply told to get "un-poor" so they will be able to reach higher. No one should make the mistake of believing that I am opposing capitalism or advocating socialism. I believe everyone has an obligation to strive to contribute the complete scope and magnitude of their talents. I believe that elements of poverty can be a great incentive to change for the better for all of us. I believe in the responsibility of every child to grasp life by their own lapels to learn and believe, to forego disobedience and instead drink-in the wisdom of the mature, protect their virtue and integrity, inebriate themselves with humility in preparation to serve, to observe the lessons of history, study the language of Creation, and comply with the yoke of the Holy Spirit who tells them to be responsible before men and straight in their conduct. Yes, just like the Boy Scouts who are assailed for saying so. These precious moments of life should not be exhausted doing only enough to get by, dreaming of life's luxuries that fatten one's character for slaughter, or defining success only within the paltry dimensions of what exotic car sits in the driveway or the gansta-rhythm one can creatively intone. Once we get over worshiping at the altar of those who have denied everyone and everything to become rich and famous, it will be asked, who did we help? Who did we lift up? Who did we love? What did we change? Is the world closer to the image of Heaven as a result of our being given life? It is then that the world's great feats of invention can be put into their proper frame of reference. Has the iPhone encouraged anyone to become more holy? For all the eulogies hailing the vision of its inventor, he has now met the Messiah of the Cross and has been asked, "Who did you help come to know Me better?" The qualities of holiness, honor, fairness, and kindness are attributable to the thoughts and actions of those who understand virtuosity as magnified by the New Covenant Gospel. Cognitive intelligence does not necessarily imply true wisdom, but beatific vision sure does. Although the consequences of random genius sporadically change lives, it cannot reinvent them the way human love renews. Not all knowledge advances this reconciliation, and therefore cannot be equated with true universal power. The highest honor we can render Jesus Christ is to live His love with dignity and announce His presence before those who are walking in error. Look at our capitalist materialism. Man's definition of greatness is sorely out of focus when presented with the crystal reflection of God's testament to human perfection. What is it that God sees as greatness? A nun serving the poorest of the poor in the slums of Calcutta for well over a half a century. A Roman Pontiff demolishing an Iron Curtain by simply announcing the word "Solidarity" directly in the face of Communist oppressors. A mother sacrificing everything she ever owned along with the toils of her aching body to steer her children away from the seediness of life and into the virtuous arms of the Catholic Church. A technologist developing a device to ease the suffering of humanity, then giving it away so that no one would ever be deprived of its benefit. A drug company whose executives renounce personal profit so as not to become wealthy atop the suffering of others. A father attending daily Mass for years upon end as an example to his sons of what grace and commitment really mean. A movie star socialite renouncing the limelight and becoming a Catholic nun in order to dedicate herself to a life of prayer. This is greatness. This is what has changed the outcome of Creation before the final purview of the ages. It is what sustains the world from God's complete annihilation of our culture of sinfulness against Him. [Genesis 18:26-32]

We can start by remembering the Gospel Truth that says it is going to be nearly impossible, but for the Divine Mercy of Jesus, for the rich to enter the Kingdom of Heaven. Guttersnipes and street urchins. Ironic as it sounds, this is what many wealthy people have become these days, not by the measure of their assets, but by their self-imposed spiritual squalor. Millionaires living in mansions and jewelry-clad socialites walking down red velvet runways. They are segregated not only from Heaven, but from the grace of God too. Charitableness has escaped them for no apparent reason; they have no idea what their excesses are heaping on the suffering of the world. It is not as though they are not old enough to know better. Little children are cute when they make mistakes, but self-indulgent adults are expected to make reparation for theirs. This is not to say that there should be no reward for hard work or that we should adopt a socialist approach to governing the commonwealths. It simply means that we should be more 'social like' and not so closefisted in our charities. Thus, the profits of international wealth and industry can and should be shared—voluntarily, not by the coercive force of governments. The wealth can be redistributed to be more fair to those who work hard and follow the rules. The statement I just made is key to the matter. Those who work hard. Those who follow the rules. And, since our government hierarchies are as corrupt as the corporate organizations, who determines who works hard and who follows whose rules? The Gospel of Jesus Christ. Men and women must give their greatest effort, their best and most honest labor for a fair living wage. And, executives and leaders must renounce the delusion that they are worth so much more than their subordinate employees. You see here that the concept of profit is also affected by the relationship between the business and its employees. So, just from these sentiments, we can see the disoriented impact that secularism is generating even within our capitalism. It does not encompass the parameters to influence society to being anything more than a fight for the scraps from the tables of the rich, and it proscribes our ultimate descent into a society controlled by a government of the few who are in turn made rich because they affirm the secular power of the wealthiest among us. So, who are the gatekeepers in America? Those with power and wealth. Who has the responsibility to keep fairness and equality alive? The same people, those who are holding-out their wealth until conditions occur whereby they can earn even more profit. But, it is a two-way street. Those who are dependent upon the public coffers for sustenance must be truly needy.

It is uniquely easy to claim that one is incapable of offering a day's labor when he is just being slothful. The guide is the center of the heart, the deeply-held view that what is proper must always be sustained. What is proper is that business owners must be willing to live in the same place their workers live, not in gated estates sipping the finest wines, savoring the richest caviar, and vacationing in the farthest corners of the globe. The whole blame for the deterioration of the American financial system is the greed of those who were already rich. It has been about power and profit all along. The Holy Gospel has been shunned. The wealthy have been blinded by their own assets. This is not the definition of freedom. It is de facto thievery and corporate-government collusion. You see that there are so many frameworks and institutions that are interconnected in the secular void to the detriment of the transformation of the world into the Kingdom of Heaven. Public institutions and private entities are often commingled and inter-dispersed. They share the same goals with different drives and directions to reach them. They are comprised of secular individuals who are only looking out for themselves, trying to defend themselves against the suffering they see being inflicted upon the rest.   There is extremely little societal compassion. Where is mine? What is in it for me? And, millions of souls go to their graves every year believing that this is the proper way to live. We ought to spend more time dignifying other men by living more parallel to the sacred divines that Christ Jesus has established within us. Our hearts should be more endearing, our motivations more conciliatory, our actions more appealing, and our proclamations more attuned to the great hosannas declared by the heavenly hosts. Such pious love is the making of legacies and legends; it primes the teardrops at our weddings and wakes; it is the triumph in our pageants and our birthright in the new nativity we have inherited in the Cross.

I suppose it is beneficial to mention that it is not just the public domain where gatekeepers have impeded the advancement of the Holy Gospel. Would it not be proper to suggest that certain Protestant beliefs run contrary to the teachings of the Catholic Church? Many of them espouse homosexual unions, abortion, and are fervent advocates of capital punishment. One would not know that they believed in the same God. Most Protestant churches will not let you get anywhere near their flocks with the sacred impressions of the Virgin Mary, let alone allow you to proclaim your witness to Her miraculous appearances within their congregations. They shun the Holy Spirit and they know it, but refuse to admit it, thus they are a roadblock to any of their flock moving to receive the True Bread of Life. This can also be said about the many gatekeepers within the Catholic Church; those who summarily dismiss the wisdom of the Holy Spirit as if it is something they do not need. How is it that the Virgin Mary has been appearing every day since June of 1981 in Medjugorje and the Catholic Church is not thundering this truth through a billion unified voices? Again, it is the gatekeepers who have made themselves roadblocks because of their faithlessness. They are no more than secularists sitting on thrones of power, donned in the sacred vestments of the Church. This is not an indictment of the Mother Church of Christianity; it is a rebuke of the liars who claim position, power and authority, but whose cups of sacrificial faith are empty. Jesus said there would be wolves in sheep's clothing. We would more have our faith shaken if there were not. All of this is an impetus for each of us to review the landscape of our lives and either be awakened or at least more clear-sighted as to the force structure of society and how hearts attuned to the Love of Jesus are the solution to true freedom as we all so desire it. The wisdom of the Holy Spirit must be allowed to take over every seat of power within Creation through inspired human hearts. A recent news article says it all. Is it a manifestation of the Spirit of the Gospel for a billionaire to spend over a billion dollars building a replica of the RMS Titanic to retrace the path of the doomed luxury liner from Europe to New York? Can you imagine what Jesus would think if this man would have instead been moved by another news article; the one which stated that the poor in Manila root through garbage bags every night outside their local restaurants, picking scraps of chicken from discarded meals so they can place them in small baggies called "pagpag" to sell the next day for fifty cents apiece in the slums to their poorest brethren? This billionaire could have gone to Tyson Foods in Arkansas, emptied their production inventory, and proceeded to Manila riding at the bow of a flotilla of ships or been in the cockpit leading a squadron of C5A air-transports making land amongst these suffering people like an angel coming from Heaven to feed them all and leave them the resources and knowledge to never go hungry again. This is the disorientation of the secular world.   This is why suffering continues. And, the media of the United States ignore these disparate atrocities because their corporate owners are rich and would eject their anchors for shining such a light on their empires of darkness. Christianity is the only thing that turns this entire phenomenon on its head and transforms it into our path to human unity. And, if I were to petition the Heavenly Father, I would ask that He put this billionaire's replica of the Titanic on the bottom of the ocean again, at the exact same coordinates so the world might contemplate why.

What series of events will finally make us alter our perception of the path we are treading? Is it going to take the absolute collapse of our civilization before we realize what we are doing? On that day when the forces of realization are thrust into their psyche by fate, it will be too late for the secularists to extract themselves from the consequences they have brought upon us all. And oh, what a sad day that will be for them. The opportunity for all that could have been the definition of their lives, evaporating like a mirage disappearing in the desert. There will be no redemption for them that day when the legacy of these reprobates comes crashing down upon them with such force that they will wish they had never been born. Their lives of wanton disregard for the tenets of God's Kingdom will recoil into oblivion like the bottom of a window shade being popped and flying into a tiny scroll at the top. And, the light will be shining in their eyes so powerfully that their lifetime of rebuttals against Christian truth will be as vacuous as a decorated WWII veteran of the Battle of Normandy being approached by a drug-addled, long-haired, teenage drop-out who says, "Hey dude, I know how you feel, we re-enacted Normandy in our paintball war last weekend." What kind of response could this battle-hardened hero have to such pathetic drivel? We must begin to realize that human excellence is not in the mantra: Tolerance and Diversity. It is Responsibility and Unity in the highest ideals of the Sacrifice of Jesus Christ on the Cross of Calvary. Tolerance and diversity as advertised by secularists is a diabolical lie where they somehow applaud the delusional idea that it is a sign of greatness that we allow the contamination of our culture with every decadent matter that can grow, and when challenged, accuse us of some apartheid theocratic mentality of ethnic cleansing and religious fanaticism in the likes of Reverend Jim Jones of the Jonestown Massacre. They have wholesale adopted the damning mentality of the Antichrist. It is a phenomenon of actual diabolical delusion that these people find themselves in, and no power save the miraculous intercession of the Virgin Mary can break them from those satanic bonds. And, She will do so at the Triumph of Her Immaculate Heart where they will then be free to make the choice for Jesus in the light of full consciousness. It is then they will stand with shoulders heaving as they wail tears of horror at how deluded a people they had actually become. They will be fleeing to the foothills of our mountain ranges, looking for any mining tunnel they can find in order to crawl into those subterranean bowels, not for gold, but to hide themselves from the Judgement of God. They will see they killed over 60 million unborn babies in their mothers' wombs, scandalized and raped several generations of children with their pop culture, literally destroyed the gift of human sexuality, demolished millions of marriages through their mockery of the responsibilities of motherhood and hatred of God's patriarchy, disparaged and crucified the splendorous Catholic Church because of the homosexual sins of a minuscule few, forced the social acceptance of the abomination of same-sex marriages, applauded transgenderism and bodily mutilation, hissed at every display of Our Lord's Birth and Crucifixion within eyesight of the public, debased children's souls in liberal university indoctrination camps, financially destroyed the government by paying for sloth and insolvency, enslaved the population through financial usury by the richest among us, wielded mob justice and the inflaming of abject racial hatred amongst our people, made partisan cheerleading squads out of our revered news agencies, and plain ran the voice of moral decency out of town. We must come to realize that we no longer have to live our lives amongst the lowest common denominator of human corruption. We no longer have to accept the degraded and despicable as the definition of our culture out of some corrupt idea of freedom. Is it legitimate to have a conversation about whether it is even possible to sustain a nation of such disparate antagonisms where darkness is at a state of war against the Light? In truth, we are but a vague image of our once hallowed greatness. The liberal branch of our government has surrendered willingly into allegiance with Satan's immorality, while the conservative branch is making sure millionaires and billionaires are given every possible advantage, hoping they will be productive enough to take care of the rest of us as their indentured slaves. Secularism is a cancer, and those who embrace it are parasites feasting on a corpse. Maintaining the integrity of civilization is a job for selfless heroes, and we are raising far fewer of them than we did a few short years ago. But, Our Lady tells us all is not lost, even in the midst of such a dark night.

There is something to be said about the way we play the game and how we adhere to the rules that does not diminish who we are. Straight talk and feistiness are still in vogue, but we must never be ones for landing low blows, shin kicking, mudslinging, backbiting, showboating, hypocrisy, distortions or outright lies. Our reputation for true gallantry is always on the line. We sleep soundly at night because we have good consciences. Others sleep well because they have no conscience at all. The way we protect our world, conduct our affairs, embrace our friends, confirm our beliefs, structure our values, perform our duties, teach our children, and shoulder our weapons says more about who we are than our own modest impressions of the way history ought to be. There are no such things as factions or fissures in the Kingdom overflowing with unconditional love. We are led to absolution not by the northern star, but by a whole host of New Covenant luminaries guiding us through the night. Hail O' Risen Christ! Greet us with joy come the morning dawn! Creation sits in front of us, open and apparent, all of its material dimensions and subtle interactions. Every person can ascend the plateaus of awareness and grow in knowledge and wisdom of the world in which we exist. At each successive plateau, we widen our scope of understanding of the factions and forces that influence our lives. We learn and we categorize; we are influenced and molded; we define and cultivate the plateaus upon which we will found our existence. They are formed by an expanding breadth of relationships between ourselves and others, and also with the facets of our environment as we fluctuate and flow through time. What many do not realize is that there are ultimate plateaus in mortal life where our perspectives of the material environment peak, almost like banging our heads on a ceiling. But, Our Lady wishes to tell us that there truly is no ceiling, and that the difficulties we are experiencing are our impact against the veil between Heaven and Earth; and these difficulties can be transcended if we would but take Her hand and allow Her to teach us to ascend into the palatial realms of Paradise where we have shed the biases of the flesh, and are instead bathed in light, purity, virtue and peace. She sees as reality from Her plateau of envisionment what we consider as being only pipe dreams. She knows how good we can be. She knows we can leave behind all the fear and dive into the Sacrifice that will transform us into a people prepared to be granted the gift of Eternal Life. If Saint Paul taught us anything, surely it is that we should not cast aside as beasts and barbarians those who do not believe in redemption, for they are still lost creatures in search of identities, vessels waiting to be filled. But for all their eightpenny opinions, they might already know the truth. It seems that faithless men stand summarily alone, idle-toothed and hungry along Creation's margins, wondering why their brazen arrogance and prudish isolationism lead only back to themselves. They squint to see life's meaning through dung-shuttered eyes, ignoring everything catechetical that lends humanity Our Lord's transcending wisdom. They ingest a daily regimen of secular crassness and queer indiscretion lapping at their shorelines with tasteless pursuits, and still they starve. They invest in perishable goods instead of viable hopes; and they rely on clockwork, crankiness and kilometers to survive, but seem to go nowhere from there. They seat themselves at delectable banquets with exquisite fares and quaff the finest sloe gin, all the while impugning the heritage of Godfearing men, mocking the miracles that refurbish the Earth, and turning deaf ears to the dogged tenacity of Christian disciples who are warning them about their inevitable fate. It would please the heavens if we sheathed our indignation for now, for the slow piercing arrows of time will eventually strike them in the knees, pilfer their youth, cripple their pride, and expunge their last scintilla of doubt.

America, you are situated at the epicenter of one of the greatest miracles to ever occur in the world's western hemisphere, and you are worthy of the blessings you are seeking. It is clear that the darkness that surrounds us is from nefarious origins, and we must pray together to restore peace. Any fearful thoughts of inferiority and rejection are being forced into our national psyche by Satan. It has nothing to do with what we have done or failed to do. It has nothing to do with whether our prayers will be answered. We are being subjected to an onslaught of evil works, the likes of which we have never seen in our lives. We must understand that Satan takes advantage of our fears and exploits them to make us believe that Jesus is far from us, that He does not care how many crosses we carry, or that we believe that the Cross will not have the last word. We are witnessing things within our culture that have never happened before. Things such as these made the great Saints take moments unto themselves to question their own resolves, but we continue to take steps forward toward glory with the obvious power of the Crucifixion. And in response, Satan dispatches his dogs upon our motivations, our traditions, and our spiritual integrity with ferocity, looking for any way to stop the work of the Gospel, to bring us fear and paranoia, to cause us to question our role in human redemption. There is no more to it than this. We are under attack by evil, who searches for ways to enter our lives and culture to achieve his fiendish goals. And, whether we realize it or not, he has not succeeded because the valor in us keeps fighting back with all the grace of the Angels. Although much of humanity at large is broken, and oftentimes the sword of truth lay in shards in their hands, it is not so with us. There is so much verbiage flying in the air due to the convulsions of the spirit of man that Satan has caused that the context of our existence is skewed to make many believe that Christianity is on its last leg, post-Christianity they call it. Our Lady declares that the response from Heaven is soon to be so overwhelming that the masses of evil doers are going to be scurrying to the mountains in torrents to find one to crawl under to hide themselves from the justice that is going to reign upon them. Satan is losing that fight. We must be assured that he is still intent on placing a shroud over our heart so we cannot see our way clear around the paranoia that often comes with being bearers of the Gospel. Our Lady tells us that we need never concede to the evil that bombards us, and that She is confident that we will join the likes of Saint Francis and all the Saints in complying with and accepting what the Father knows we will wish at the end of time to have transpired for the propagation of His Kingdom. We will be given reason for the dancing that is about to ensue. We must stand with courage in the face of whatever comes our way, be it good or bad, evil or benign. There is an opportunity coming to regain what we once believed was lost. Even though we present ourselves as weak and selfish, we are a grand species of beings. Satan wants us to demand from God the answer to our prayers. He knows that we will not be happy until we can see into the future, absent the sacrifices for the Cross and everything we already know about the Church. Our happiness is staked in the world to come, in the Church, and in our work for Our Lady. And, the Son of Man is not going to allow us to be disappointed! God would never allow His beloved humanity to enter a game that could possibly be lost. And, we should always expect the unanticipated victory. We must be willing to risk it all for the Savior who gave everything and see our way clear to know that Satan is the one causing so much pain. There have been good days and not as good ones. We must know that Our Lord has always taken great pride in watching us stand again.

Imagine how Our Lady feels when She sees us so passionately begging for the love of our heart to be fed. She knows what that means. When evil doers killed Her Son, the devil came to Her and said that he finally took away the person She loved the most. However, She turned to him and said that he was deluded, that even though Her Son lay lifeless, He would rise again. That same Resurrection is calling to us to find the light in our soul that will convince the Earth that nothing in this world is as important as our dignity in Jesus—no fortune, health, fame, anything for which a mortal man might be proud. The light of our heart is there, but it is being impugned and disdained, it is undergoing a hailstorm of doubt and fear. This is our punishment from Satan for marching toward Heaven in lockstep with the miraculous intercession of its Queen. It is no more complicated than that. Our Lady knows the sacrifice of endurance that She is asking us to make. She knows that we are being placed in the cross-hairs of evil. She knows Satan's response to Her work. She has seen it coming since the day She stood beneath the Cross of Her Son; He who knew it would lurk through time seeking victims. And, in the final analysis, they both saw into the future that we would wail in pain in the image of Jesus' Passion, wanting to know where the kindness of God finally went. There is an Easter Resurrection in us, my friends, that we have not yet summoned because we are being blinded by the horrendous attacks of the devil. Our Lady prays that we never allow Satan to lay us low onto the ground. And, when the Light comes, the Saint in each of us will lift us back up from the ground, and Heaven's Queen will announce into Paradise, *"Attention all Angels, Saints, noblemen, and creatures of good will. My children of the exiled world have decided to fight! Peal the bells at Saint Peter's, and you Pontiffs of the ages, stand and applaud! They have ceased their doubt in their conviction; they refuse to permit the derailing of the most important mission of their lives, for years to come, until the Earth is through, until the Mass is finished, until the Son of God returns to claim His earthly Kingdom."* We may rise and fall again in the next days and weeks that are coming. They will not be easy. But, that is what makes it worth the cost. Call upon Saint Michael to cast Satan into the Abyss, along with all his evil spirits. And, when we write his death warrant, Our Lady asks us to sign it in Her Name.

The crucial concept is to take things one day at a time. Remember that our strength and happiness waxes and wanes, but we must keep our eyes on the outcome of the Plan of God to call evil to an accounting of its despicable works. Satan is a mocker; he laughs because he does not believe humanity can recover its soul. He simply thinks that the darkness is too much for us to overcome. This is how he has destroyed the happiness in millions of lives, broken up marriages, and caused untold acts of violence and carnage around the world. But, Our Lady's miraculous intercession prefigures his defeat. It is hard for a human being to imagine the power that the Virgin Mary possesses. In fact, it truly cannot be grasped by the human mind. We can look back through history at the carnage and destruction, the conquering of kingdoms by despots and the marauding of sanctified lands by invaders, the slaughtering of innocents, the genocide and death-camps, the starvation and disease, the sorrows and broken-hearted agonies, and it is almost too much for any one age to take in. We are presented with the evidence of human history and are almost forced to admit that Satan has won the lives of men and the storied outcome of this planet. And, in the midst of it, at the center of mortal history stands a Cross with a Lamb hanging on it and a beautiful Virgin Mother standing beneath it; the consummation of Paradise upon the fertile plains of suffering that wipes the horrific ages of men from the memory of Creation. This is the power granted Her; the ability to retake all that Satan has stolen from what the history of the world could have been. It is beyond human imagining, the humiliation a humble Virgin has thrust upon the Evil One of Hell. He is left with nothing to savor. All that he gained in time, he has lost in Eternity. The momentary flash of evil in his mind that he once relished through his acts in the mortal world has been replaced by an unending, permanent, everlasting peal of defeat that rings without end at seeing his kingdom taken from him and restored by Resurrection. All you unrepentant hedonistic revolutionaries, secular pagans, and moral relativists, this will be your defeat as well, because you wilfully serve the diabolical Destroyer! The Lord wants us to believe that He speaks to the world through the Spirit and Creation, that there is little difference between hearing His voice and actually feeling His presence. The latter is more ardently the way Jesus solicits our avowal. And, the Scriptures say, 'If today you hear His voice, harden not your hearts.' [Heb. 3:15] Here, we are reminded that Christ speaks through life's circumstances about our inner-feelings and the prospect of facing certain setbacks, crises, and even death by infusing deific Wisdom into our consciousness. There is no doubt that we are hearing God's resonance, counsel, consolation, and advice through Our Lady's miraculous intercession. He often requires from us mutually shared sacrifices to knit us together, not through some kind of staged theatrics, but by endearing faith; not by secular sentimentalism wrapped around populist politics, but by genuine holiness grounded in the Church. The real question is what will be our response? What will we give or lend to our own redemption? How does our faith translate into pious works? Jesus gave us an entire Crucifixion with which to prepare our answer, but God will not wait for an eternity. In Christ, we have the means to overcome the burdens of sin. We have through the Cross the ability to rise in dignity where Adam once fell in shame. So, let us anchor our destiny to that lodestar, come to our feet again, begin laying tracks toward the immortal horizon, and prepare to wrap our arms around the Kingdom that knows no end. It is what we do for others that shapes our lives in Christ, whether we recognize His calling in them or not. Our Lord is quite adept at depositing His presence in those who suffer; and we do well by listening to them. Here, we are taught fruit from prejudice, piety from indifference, truth from lies, and acceptance from rejection. There are incalculable ways to inherit this wisdom through the faculties of the Roman Catholic Church, many facets to the crown jewel of redemption, but there is only one Divine Love, one Holy Spirit, one Cross to which our own crosses are affixed like railcars to that train traveling through the desert. This is the essential message of the Woman meek and mild who has come to America seeking the demise of both atheism and secularism. Educators and psychologists often speak about the abstracts of human contemplation, those things we dwell upon randomly when our mind seems to wander or we lack clear focus in our perceptive thinking. It is during these moments when we are open to the influx of external forces as though our guard is let down. However, this is not always the case. Our personal identity and true innocence are best revealed when we set aside even temporarily our cognitive shields, at least long enough for the Holy Spirit to infiltrate what is ordinarily our impermeable state of being. This does not imply that we should not be aware of evil influences around us, but be open enough to accept what truth is being revealed from outside this world. There still seems to be some question as to whether we see human life with our eyes or through our eyes, or both, and so it is with our religious faith. Moreover, do we look for raw confidence in other men, a kind sense of understanding, intelligent emotion, courageous insight, or a composite of these things? Whatever makes-up our random reflections should include our flexibility to be receptive to God's overtures in the wake of our own assertive disposition. Only in this way will we recognize the difference between thieves and givers, gargoyles and flowers, fact and fiction, and love and hatred. May the Lord God bless everyone with His Sovereign Love. May the Angel Choirs usher the Holy Spirit into the lives of hardhearted men. May our faith be good and strong, authentic, true and loyal, that we pay homage to Christ the King through His missionary Church on Earth, where the just and sanctified venerate the Cross by which millions have already been redeemed, a sweet and timeless clemency that can never be annulled.

The Sacred Amalgam
The Difference Between Faith and Belief

"The soul living in us now, here on this Earth, has the same eternal qualities that we will take into Heaven. What changes is our worthiness; we must become more holy through our prayers and the Sacraments of the Church. We belong to Christ's perpetuity despite the waning hours. The spiritual conversion of man is an amalgam of our faith and our soul's redeeming love—always absolving, infinitely shining, and forever bound to righteousness."

Faith is the definitive articulation of Truth by the Creator of all things. It is the possession of the Almighty Father as Himself, given as a gift to humanity through the Life of His Messianic Son, Jesus. The essential substance of faith is Divine Revelation. Faith is Truth as God has spoken it. It is the absolute clarification of reality, encompassing both the seen and unseen. Faith is what is above all other manifestations of mortal existence. In contrast, "belief" is something that is decided by someone who chooses to accept and exercise that faith. Belief is a product and manifestation of human volition through the exercise of our free will. This is an important point. People do not have the free will to decide what faith is; they are only able to determine whether they will invoke the mechanics of belief and accept it. To have faith means there is a communion of the Holy Spirit with the heart of humankind. We accept and are melded with the immutable gift of God that has already been defined. Belief is the cognitive acceptance of faith, and it is this cognition of Divine Revelation that translates spiritual love into recognizable actions. People with faith, meaning people whose lives are impregnated with all that has been revealed by the Father, are eligible to tell the world that what they believe has been validated by God. It is like a billionaire saying everything that he has belongs to you, whereupon you take to the streets screaming that you are rich. A pauper who has never had a relationship with the billionaire would be errant to declare such wealth. Therefore, people who say that they believe in God, but who do not accept and practice Faith as defined in the Holy Gospel and the Catholic Catechism, are either delusional or outright liars and hypocrites. It is a simple matter of empirical deduction. There is no substance to support their mechanics of belief, thus they really have no belief at all because they do not possess God within them. Their belief is wisping smoke created by a delusional agent in their mind. This describes Roman Catholic politicians who accept abortion as a legitimate form of public policy, for example. Anyone who holds an office of public or private domain that exemplifies or holds power over those who are learning about personal and public morality has the responsibility to speak and act according to their faith, not just what they 'believe' about their faith. The teachings of the Church cannot be interpreted to improve one's standing in the public sphere with the electorate or improve others' perception about what kind of person they may be. Trusting in God and serving His Kingdom is not about stature, it is about measure. The difference in stature and measure is that the focus of stature is on the person, and the focus of measure is on the device being used to measure. Hence, it is not about what 'I' have done, but what others are able to see by what 'I' have said or shown to others. Therefore, the second contrast between faith and belief is that faith always extends outward by extolling the teaching instead of the person explaining the lesson. The obvious exception here is that Jesus is the lesson and the teacher, and equal emphasis should be placed on the Holy Gospel and the Second Person of the Blessed Trinity whose life and teachings are celebrated there. Indeed, this second contrast delineates the difference between faith and belief in that those who teach the Gospel are not proclaiming the text of their speech and writings to be of their own making, but from origins garnered throughout the whole history of Messianic human redemption. Our sensibilities regarding societal justice are skewed in our present age in that many believe that everyone is entitled to their beliefs as applicable and worthy of respect by everyone else. If that is the case, are the beliefs and ideologies of history's despots worthy of respect also? If not, what is the measuring stick that disqualifies those horrific beliefs? This leads us to the discernment of the beliefs of those who speak premises that are false and damaging to our striving for the highest faith revealed by our Creator.

A third distinction between faith and belief is that faith is timeless and immutable. The faith we have inherited is the same Faith that was given to the Apostles by Jesus and every disciple who has prayed to accept that Faith since the beginning of the Church upon the miracle of Pentecost. Beliefs, on the other hand, are amendable. They evolve over time, and often do. Beliefs are susceptible to alteration from life's conditions and the worldviews of the people who practice their beliefs. The reality of God as He has chosen to reveal Himself in history through the birth of His Son Jesus becomes operative and redemptive through our belief in it as our Faith. This is power, and is consequential to the imminent conclusion to the material world, while beliefs will never escape the world's confines. At the Second Coming of Our Lord, there will be no such thing as the concept of "belief" because Faith will be unveiled as Eternal Fact; immutable, unmovable, impregnable, inviolate, definitive, precise, and eternal, as it has always been. All conflicting beliefs opposed to the Faith of the Apostolic Church will be vaporized at the transfiguration of our Faith into Fact. Therefore, Faith is the father of mystical courage, and the beliefs of the children of that courage spread into new groups and societies to coopt listeners and seers to that original Faith, the primal Revelation of God, Himself. Faith is the mission; beliefs are the objectives employed to accomplish that mission. Faith is the mountain, the base of all things immortal, and beliefs are the sounding board for sharing that Faith with those with different beliefs in order to bring them out of their darkness. There is only one true, completed Faith in Creation, and that is the Gospel of the New Covenant, divinely secured in the bosom of the Roman Catholic Church. All other orientations and persuasions are only false beliefs that have no bearing on the future of humanity or how individual believers can affect the Will of God to amend the course of history. Jesus Christ is the Master of Faith and the King of all who believe in Him. This indicates the reciprocity between God and man, between Heaven and the human heart. Faith and belief are inseparable only in the context of Jesus Christ. Therefore, when we speak of the teachings of the Church and relate the mysteries of our Faith, we are speaking from our God-given knowledge of His very existence and desires. And, when we are rebuffed, derided, and disowned for asserting the sovereignty of the Truth over every other belief, we are merely confronting the darkness which disperses and destroys. Those who 'believe' other than what the Church teaches are denying their own eternity. They are little children who refuse to eat the nourishment that will sustain them through their spiritual lives, and they will die an unprovided death and be lost in the abyss for the everlasting ages. If they would feed on faith instead of their own beliefs, they would be able to grow, learn, prosper and prevail beyond the end of the world without need for anything else. Faith is a giant redwood tree that stands over and shades them. Faith is the lighthouse that guides them to the shores. Belief is that the giant redwood has characteristics that are inexplicable to them, while faith informs them that God put it there. Faith is the internal framework of moral conscience that comes from the Wisdom of Heaven. Belief is doing something only because it seems like the right thing to do, or that their forebears did it that way, or because they will be the very first to do something that way. Faith is the flag pole, belief is the flag. The flag would be no more than a rag on the ground without the pole. The pole is the often overlooked foundation that provides elevation and awareness to the flag. It places a meaning and witness above all other declarations. The pole is the standard to which the belief is tethered that gives definition to its existence. Flags are supposed to be on poles. Beliefs are supposed to be attached to the Divine Revelation of Jesus Christ, the Messiah. We have faith that the car will not quit, so we believe we will drive it on a 1,000 mile trip. Faith is the furnishing of the fires of conviction, and beliefs are consumed by that faith to make one's actions come true. It is endless. On and on. The Lord God responds to whatever you offer in His name. Faith tells us that He sees the candle we light. Belief says that He will be equally looking at it through our own eyes. All parameters of existence and dimension are transcended by the distinction between faith and belief.

Now, we must address the most important reason for this discussion. The secular world and non-Christians see Messianic Salvation as though it were a simple belief instead of the Universal Faith given to humanity, the Omnipotent Revelation of the Almighty Father. This is one of the greatest stumbling blocks of those who are waiting for great signs from God before they accept what the Scriptures teach. They are looking for something more believable instead. This is what has led to the whole gamut of detractors of the Church and its enemies who have tried for twenty centuries to bring the Church down. The Catholic Church cannot be felled; it is a manifest impossibility. No man or group of humanity has the power to bring extinction to the Apostolic Church. It is not only like trying to put out a burning skyscraper with a thimble of water; there is not even any water. The roots of the Catholic Church are located at the feet of the Throne of God. Mortal men cannot reach them there. Men on earth are not even as large as ants underneath the soil somewhere. They cannot ascribe for themselves even a self-identity or recognize themselves as self-evident creatures alongside the glory of the Roman Catholic Church. I am speaking about a Church of Faith that just happens to 'believe' in what it is doing. This is the Kingship belief that is fed by the Faith of One God, given to those who will accept Him as their King. The Catholic Church is embedded in the foundation of the whole created universe, and it is upon Saint Peter that this Church has been stationed. No organic or inorganic creation has the power to deny the existence, propagation, progress or eternal consistency of the Roman Catholic Church.

The Catholic Church is not simply a collection of individuals who happen to hold the same beliefs. Its spiritual essence and mystical qualities are not subject to or determined by its members. It is flawed and weakened by nothing. It has no comparison with any other religious beliefs in the world or through time. The Catholic Church is the clearest manifestation of God on the Earth. The Catholic Church is more crucial to the survival of man than all the aspects of nature and the world combined. It is clear that this is the Faith to which wise men turn during their waking hours. It is the food for the soul that keeps its future in Heaven from dying. The Catholic Church is the origin of the whole world's elegance and eloquence, its majesty and authenticity. The Church is the glittering sequine in all the heavens in which the planet Earth is only a subpart.   God sees the Roman Catholic Church suspended in space before He sees the world because He placed it there from Eternity. God sees righteousness brought forth in faithful people before He sees the plight of the poor! Look around and you will see ample evidence of this. Indeed, God sees the faith we practice in everything we do for the Most Blessed Virgin, for the Church on Earth, for our brothers and sisters, and even our accidental blessings of other men in the same way we might inspect a diamond the size of the Moon. Thus, Our Lady comes to give us Her introduction of what we already know about the providential majesty of the Roman Catholic Church. Why? Because we have an understanding between the Faith of Jesus' disciples and the believers who stray in other ways. It is true that Christian faith and believing in that faith are united in one place. However, belief without Christian faith has no place. It is irrelevant and inconsequential. It will die a vaporizing death at the final revelation of the Light. Faith has made all the difference in our lives. It is the reason we accept our sacrifices in honor of our King. It is the genesis of all that has ever been written and proclaimed about the Truth. It is the energizing fact of existence unleashed in the Sacrament of Confirmation. Faith is the seed of our growth in Wisdom in the things of perfection; and we will do well because Our Holy Mother will raise us well, to follow the Light and inhale the scents of Salvation from whence we were young children.

Now, what can be said of those who violate the teachings of the Church upon the justification that they are allowed to follow their conscience? If their conscience is not based on the Gospel and the teachings of the Catholic Church, they have no conscience. They are calling on a resource that is not really there, like standing on a floor that is seconds away from collapsing beneath their feet. If they say that they are following their conscience by committing to something that is against the teachings of Jesus Christ, they are actually channeling their own will, not the Will of God. It is this simple. And, their will can become the possession of the Antichrist who will dictate it. If someone believes in or practices and teaches something that is contrary to the Kingdom of God, they are already under the influence of the Antichrist. Politicians and others who defend and promote abortion have surrendered their consciences to Satan and are headed for the fires of Hell. They will not be able to withstand the Judgement. When a person says that something is farther than a country mile or faster than a New York minute, they intentionally make pseudo-assertions that a given distance is relative or time passes at different speeds depending on the location. We hear these kinds of false comparisons every day. This is the way people justify such wrongs as abortion and contraception. They say that they cannot afford to raise a child on their income, ignoring the fact that there are millions of willing families waiting to adopt and feed them. They buy into the evil pretense that just because they cannot support a child, the child must die. Birth control is another example. Instead of relying on the beatific conscience, that of corporeal chastity, they turn to illicit mechanical and chemical methods to nullify their responsibility to apply sound moral standards. Such are acts of slothful, faithless, selfish individuals who refuse to listen for themselves to what God would have them do. Abortion is arguably the single greatest example of diabolical darkness overwhelming a soul where the adherents still believe their consciences are telling them what they are doing is acceptable in the sight of God. This is why Sacred Scripture offers this admonishment: *"The lamp of the body is the eye. If your eye is sound, your whole body will be filled with light; but if your eye is bad, your whole body will be in darkness. And if the light in you is darkness, how great will the darkness be."* [Matthew 6:22-23]. Scripture speaks here about how belief separated from the Light of Faith blinds the conscience and thrusts man into the darkness to wail and gnash his teeth. Our Lady wishes to clarify the configuration of our faith in this world and the presence of holiness that the Holy Spirit asks us to possess and espouse. Her mission as the Morning Star Over America is to speak about our alliance with God to bring to humanity all that will make things right. Our Lady told me that everyone who has come into His presence through death has told Him when asked that the most intense impression they had about life on Earth is the battle between love and hatred. Love is the presence and actualization of the Father on Earth and in Heaven, and hatred is manifested by those who reject Him. That is why it is a lie to say that there is love at the foundation of same-sex marriage. There is only hatred manifested by those who reject the language of life in such a willful way. The language of Creation speaks volumes about its Maker. There is no actualization of the Father in same-sex marriage or any other homosexual union. Therefore, it is imperative that the Will of God and the will of mortal men become one through the process of conversion. Does this imply that they are originally separate? Is it possible that baptized Christians can exercise their will in contraction to the Will of the Father? The answer is yes, and this is the product of either intentional or unintentional thoughts, impulses and actions. There is nothing wrong or sinful about questioning the motivations of God, but it is not the best use of our faith. There is no doubt or question in faith. Hence, we see that questions about the Lord's motivations are more based in ascending levels of faith than in right and wrong. If we trust that God knows what He is doing; if we defer to His Sacred Will even when we do not understand, then our faith will be strong. It is often difficult to remember everything we are supposed to do in various situations, and this is why the Holy Spirit guides us; this is the reason the Holy Spirit will give us the words to say when our time has come in accordance with the Holy Scripture. Sometimes, the answers we seek lie in hidden places, sometimes they are more obvious.   This highlights the overpowering, cleansing, clarifying and redeeming purpose of human suffering. It indeed ratifies humanity's trust in the Father when accepted in faith.   The suffering of the Son and the suffering of His Mystical Body are one in the same sacrifice.   Yet, other matters are not as clear while they are simultaneously being prepared for clarity.   This is the process of life in the exiled world.   Human beings are creatures of insight, habit, judgement, renewal, expectation and culmination.   We are a complex amalgam, a mixture of anatomy, chemistry, thought, and disposition.   Each of us has drives that capture our attention every day, and these drives assist us in pursuing purposeful living.   All the graces and blessings from God that rain down from Heaven every day are completely obvious to millions and billions of souls around the globe, and Satan and his minions have yet struck blind the souls of further billions who are meant to see and receive them.   Those who receive blessings will always receive them as the Lord intends if they remain aware of the amalgam of His Will and their own, the synchronicity of their beliefs with the Divine Faith of the Church.   This is a Sacred Amalgam where humanity does not always seek answers or justification for earthly events that transpire in any given time.   This spiritual amalgam ties the love between God and men into one prenatal and postnatal unit on Earth and in Heaven.   Men are born and then born again.   They die and are resurrected.   These blessings are given through the amalgam of human faith and the reciprocal faith that God shares with those who believe in Him.   This concept of 'amalgam' has so many dimensions that they can scarcely be described.   The original amalgam is God creating us as His children in the beginning.   We have been under the Providence of His salvific care from the conception of our beings.   He knew He would have to come as Savior the instant He conceived a race of creatures called humanity.   The Sacraments of the Church are a manifestation of this salvific Sacred Amalgam.   God offers the Sacraments, and faithful men on Earth recognize them as such.   The Holy Eucharist even brings the spiritual and physical Communion between Jesus Himself and worthy communicants. The Sacrament of Marriage is an amalgam of two hearts, minds and lives into one holy union. This principle applies in all the Sacraments. And, the Sacred Amalgam is especially present when someone offers another person forgiveness because, in those moments, the Spirit of Jesus is acting through them. What is loosed on Earth will be loosed in Heaven. Forgiveness can only come from God! Satan never forgives; and if he says he does, he is again lying. Blessing a meal is another example of the amalgam of God and His people. The Church's recognition of the Saints is its witness to the Sacred Amalgam between God and man. Frankly, this entire discussion is rather simple. Faith, belief, conscience, light, and divine union. Our Lady characterizes these simple concepts so that we can recognize reference points on the pathway to strengthening our capacity to accept the perpetual amalgam of God with His children. Man is a wholly different creature without the Most Blessed Trinity, like a light bulb; filament intact, but no current, no light, no warmth, and no purpose. Imagine handing a light bulb to a king in the ancient world who had no inkling of electricity. He would see it as a fragile, but useless novelty...until it was plugged in! Our Lady's shrines such as Guadalupe, Lourdes, Fatima, and Medjugorje are great electrical outlets, and the power plant is the Roman Catholic Church. The Divine Faith proclaimed by the Original Apostolic Church generated Our Lady's miraculous intercession. God granted a Sacred Amalgam between Heaven and Earth, between the Mother of God and Her children, at the behest of the petitions being offered on every Catholic Altar throughout the world. The Catholic Church cried "Lord have mercy, save us all!," and the King of Creation sent His Mother at the close of the ages to announce His Divine Mercy in order to salvage all those whose names are written in the Book of Life. Then, He will come and wipe Creation clean.

The Didactic Consciousness
Moral Instruction

"Lord, let the depths of our suffering lead the world to greater light. Let humanity's sacrifices make us whole. Let decent men vanquish the evil ones. Let fairness prevail over injustice. Implant in us the distinction of accepting your miracles. May peace and good will be our final legacy. Amen."

The human psyche has a natural tendency toward stagnation within parameters of thought and engagement that are comfortable to the soul. However, these states of comfort are not necessarily the peace in which God wishes to enwrap His children. Numbness, indifference, sensuality, and gluttony can be states of comfort when compared to a relentless barrage of mental abuse or physical attacks. Drunkenness is even a state of comfort for some people. Even while these are seen as moments of respite by those who are suffering, none are the liberating fields of euphoric beatitude that the soul was actually created to experience. They are not of the refreshing and vibrant character brought by the awareness of our eternal identity and purpose. They do not answer the questions: Why was I created? What is the meaning of life? And, where am I going? For those who know nothing of the paradisial definitions personified by Jesus Christ, existence becomes a pursuit to define a personal plateau of ease, confined within the worldly attributes of cultures, marked by survival of the fittest, fastest and fanatical. For people who know only to seek their own comforts, any attempt to enlighten them about their eternal happiness is usually met with an unwillingness to even consider anything more than what they already believe. We call this incredulity. They see the testament of the bearer of the Good News as the fantasy of a religious fanatic whose call for sacrifice cannot compete with their agendum of worldly comforts. Now, I am not contrasting the differences where people find solace in a turbulent world so as to condemn anyone for where they might be experiencing life. My words are more a way of drawing a picture before anyone who might be seeking solace while trying to make sense of it all. Many people even of older years have not begun to look within themselves at their soul. They live confined in a bubble of awareness that has constricted their perception of the true dimensions of life. And, Our Lady is the needle! There are facilities in the railroad industry called "roundhouses" that locomotives and rail cars are driven into to be serviced. As these railway vehicles are driven into a roundhouse, they are parked atop a giant turntable that can be mechanically turned in a circle for the ease of their maintenance. Upon completion of any repairs, the turntable is rotated and the train is driven back through the door that it came in. Now, the parable. Millions, if not billions of people are spectators of life, sitting metaphorically on these trains. They are dining in club cars, being entertained in the card rooms, or heaving coal into the boilers. And, as they look from the windows, none seem to realize they are spinning on a worldly turntable. There are those who wonder why they periodically see the same recurring scenery pass the windows, but they never realize that it is the train that is stationary, spinning in circles, making no progress toward any destination. They have no idea that, beyond the walls of the roundhouse, there is a breathtaking heartland impressed with tracks upon which their vehicle can take them to places they have never dreamed. Consider sitting on this train. Does not the exit door of the roundhouse appear through the window once per revolution as the train spins on the turntable? For a moment, does one not see the tracks leading through the door, out across the countryside, and then begin to ponder what those steel rails may be for? This single idea: The realization of one's place in Creation is called "consciousness." And, what does one do once they realize they are on a train in a roundhouse and they see from the windows that there are tracks leading out a door into the sunlight? They begin to wonder how to move the train down those tracks. They seek out the pilot's cabin of the locomotive and search for the "didactic" manual that instructs them on how to make the progress they are seeking. Once they acquire the knowledge, they possess the instructional awareness, or the "Didactic Consciousness." The word 'didactic' is an adjective that means a letter or epistle that instructs others in moral Truth. A didactic letter is sometimes formal and oftentimes informal, but through it, one tries to persuade and enlighten the receiver about living according to the Gospel, according to the teachings of Jesus. When one knows we are presently living in exile, away from the paradisial garden of the Kingdom of God, and that Jesus Christ is the Savior of the World, still alive on the Altars of the Roman Catholic Church in the Most Blessed Sacrament, we possess the Didactic Consciousness that can rouse the conscience of an entire world because we know the moral Truth that is outside of time. Consciousness is the state of a person understanding his place in Creation, the way he sees his participation in the world according to measures of existence and purpose. "Didactic" basically means teaching or instructing others in a lesson, which in this case happens to be a moral lesson on how to move our existence toward the Kingdom of God. Therefore, a didactic consciousness is the condition of the human person along the lines of knowing moral Truth and instructing himself and others about the parameters of that Truth. The Lord is seeking this didactic consciousness in exiled men to come to the fore when the cultivating events of the future begin to unfold.

We have heard of the radical reorientation of the human person to the tenets of faith into an openness to the Will of God to establish His Kingdom here on Earth. This radical reorientation transforms the finite temporal perceptions of physical beings into infinite spiritual vision beyond the boundaries of time itself. Just as some people during sickness lose their sense of clarity of consciousness, no one is truly conscious unless they are aware of the morality prescribed by Jesus as their way of life, their purpose and mission of life, and their destiny for the whole of their years. All who hold to the teachings of Jesus have this didactic consciousness by virtue of their membership in the Church, their allegiance to the Cross, and their consecration to the Immaculate Heart of Mary and the Most Sacred Heart of Jesus. We are commissioned and ordained to teach and preach, enlighten, reprimand, console, bless and underscore the benefits of Christianity in the same way as anyone who holds a vocation. Moral instruction is instinctive to the didactic consciousness because there is no morality if the person is not self-aware that they exist there. The didactic 'consciousness' produces a clearing, much like a meadow in a deep forest, where the didactic 'conscience' echoes between the circumference of standing trees. One cannot have a conscience until they are first self-aware of their position in Creation before God who created them. It is a rather simple context in which you can lay your faith alongside that of your forbears and the first Apostles and early disciples. By the power of the Holy Spirit, we have inherited this consciousness and its accompanying conscience. For many people, especially baptized as infants and grounded from their childhood in the Truth of Jesus Christ, everything they have ever done since they attained the age of reason has been accomplished through their didactic consciousness; every morning that they have awakened, the decisions they have made about their private lives and their public image, the ways they approach friends and strangers, their unity with those who also believe, and the sureness about their state of holiness with which they retire for their sleep. All Christians have practiced to the best of their awareness the Faith to which their souls have been given. God knows this consciousness because He has implanted it within us, and He has assimilated our identity and intentions into the fullness of the Church Triumphant already before we depart the material world. It is to this state of consciousness that Our Lady has always spoken and appealed. The response and obedience of those who have accepted Her miraculous intercession throughout the world are its fruits. Our charity on behalf of Jesus in this world grows from our self-awareness that we have power with God and here in this life because we believe what the Bible says, and we accept the flourishing consequences that come from the Power of His Holy Spirit into the lives of His children. Many Doctors of the Church professed that they wished that their didactic consciousness could have grown by immeasurable dimensions during their earthly exile; yet their witness to it was stunning nonetheless. They did excellently, even though miraculous communication directly from the Mother of God to them was rare. The Holy Spirit was their Wisdom and guidance, and that was sufficient for their contributions to the Faith and the betterment of the world that existed before they were born. This is a supernatural dynamic that comes to and overwhelms all who relinquish their self-will to a sacrificial will that spreads the Holy Gospel and prospers the Kingdom of God. There is no weakness in recognizing the difficulty of this process. Most of our secular brothers and sisters are utterly separated from even the slightest comprehension of what a didactic consciousness even is. They are asleep in sin, and as such, they have no consciousness other than the allures of materialism, lust, and all the other perils of the world. They are 'sleep walking' through life as though they have trained their eyes on a massive billboard somewhere, while we see them staring at it as if to be mesmerized or in a trance. And, by rational deduction, they have no interior conscience that would speak to them of the error of their ways since the moral conscience flourishes in the didactic consciousness which they do not possess. Thus, they live in a state of ease about their debased lives. This is how someone can look at over sixty million children having been slaughtered through infanticide and have nary a movement of the heart that they are cooperating with the horrendous evil of Satan which will damn them at the revelation of God's judgement. They are completely unaware of their station before the purview of God's Will, and their consciences are as dead as their souls. This is their state of not yet being converted to the power of the Cross and the enlightenment that they should share by accepting the Crucifixion and the Resurrection of Jesus from the Tomb. We have seen television programs where certain actors and characters are walking around amidst other people, but they cannot be seen. This is the same principle. Those who are not converted cannot see what is right before their eyes because they are close-minded about faith and refuse to believe in miracles. This principle is not just reserved for those everyone would recognize as being outside the Church. It applies to all men and women, pastors, theologians, nuns, priests, bishops, and cardinals who are witnesses of Our Lady's miraculous intercession in our time and refuse to respond with all the power, authority and composure they possess. But, this will rapidly change because the Triumph of the Immaculate Heart of Mary is inevitable. They will be touched, they will move, they will give their lives to Her, they will rise just as Saint Paul on the Road to Damascus; and the world will become holier for their newfound faith in the powerful Mystery of the Church Militant. Even though the world is in turmoil, it is peaceful within the Immaculate Heart of Mary. Holiness reverberates in our own hearts as we reside there. Tranquility saturates the soul, and the growth of the Kingdom of God in us and around us becomes astounding; it is wholesome and unique, it is timely and reassuring. Our Holy Mother is with us, and She hears every Hail Mary we utter. She blesses us and those for whom we pray as together we wait in joyful hope for the Coming of the Lord as the Didactic Consciousness testifies. We must never be afraid to be proud of who we are and feel a deep sense of accomplishment about the holy consciousness that we possess. If one never becomes proud of their knowledge of the Truth through their didactic consciousness, they will never be set free. It is a pearl that is worth protecting. The Didactic Consciousness produces the maturation of wisdom from "Wisdom begins in fear of the Lord," [Psalm 111:10] to "Perfect love drives out fear..." [I John 4:18]

We must encourage secularists, atheists and others to reevaluate their many vested interests and ponder whether their opposition toward Christian religiosity is really as progressive toward our success as a nation as they believe it to be. The Almighty Father is allowing great mystical prodigies to be manifested through the Immaculate Virgin Mary in our time for the purpose of spontaneously combusting the Didactic Consciousness in all humankind. Once everyone realizes that God actually exists, our collective spiritual perception will awaken to where we stand before Him on this earthen globe and before His Eternal

Throne. The arena of the didactic consciousness will be splayed before us like an amphitheater mowed down in a rainforest, and the didactic conscience will begin to thunder. The Holy Gospel will come alive as humanity's only true testament in history, and will explode with the revelation of its prophecies regarding our deliverance into Eternal Life at the Second Coming of Jesus Christ on the Last Day. Man will find the meaning of life. But, before a conscience can be stirred, it must first be formed, built on the foundation of moral excellence which is consciousness in God. Exiled humanity cannot become good until it becomes aware, not through the dialectical frameworks that promote the world's practical knowledge, but by the genius of the Christian heart in union with its God. As our country now stands in its confrontation with authentic Catholic Christianity, the Church resembles a gentle spouse, battling a drunken family member who is rampaging in the twilight of consciousness after searching for ease at the bottom of a bottle of a mind-altering drink. And, every day as the world rotates and spins, the Light through the Eternal Doorway passes in front of their eyes—The daily Holy Sacrifice of the Mass. One day soon, everyone is going to be allowed to see that this recurring Light is actually the real world that we have been searching for our entire lives; and then our societies will know a peace that we never imagined could exist. Everything we yearn for; the good fortune we desire, and whatever we hold-out for comes through the same hope springing forth from the faith of our fathers, knowing that deep inside our best kept secrets is the recipe for fulfillment that God has implanted there. We will never see or capture it without Him. Without the love that comes from On High, we would be too shortsighted to envision the grandest of what life can be. We might become giants among men in all other ways, but if we fail to clothe ourselves in the raiment of the Father's saintly blessing, we will never shine like Jesus Christ. Instead of being stepping stones into Paradise, we will remain like scattered grains of sand, idle to the universe, with no wisdom or grace to foster a better world. Is this what the heirs of our Lord's Resurrection foresee? I don't think so. Christians expect far greater substance out of life than simple mortality, much more than the fiery arches of offensive weapons or the grim images of such things as school book depositories and hundred-year floods. It is possible to see how bountifully we are blessed. All Creation makes it known. The limitless brilliance of our Christian faith tells us that this is true, as does the eloquence of the heart and the laudatory meditations we submit to the Father by way of contemplative prayer. Everything we do in Jesus' name resounds His divinity within us, extolled and projected through our pious reflections, begotten by the undying wisdom that the Holy Spirit deposits inside us. Humanity could not escape the veracity of the New Covenant Gospel if we tried. Whether everyone accepts this truth is quite another matter. Those who believe in God understand that spiritual virtue has measurable effects. Things like order, friendship, charity and good will have both motion and direction; they are goal-oriented, even if unseeable with the naked eye. We all have different prayers, penchants, aspirations and talents, but these are part of the same contemplative daring that unifies the whole Church as one collective faith to seek the origin and purpose of life. Personal piety is even capable of discerning intent when given access to reviewable input. A photograph of a crescent wrench laying beside an apple means very little to us, but the scene of an automobile sitting on the shoulder of a freeway stimulates our relational thoughts to envision a larger comprehension of objects and actions. The car is a well-known method of conveyance belonging on the pavement inside a system of highways and intersections in a world and universe that sustain their own presence. It is somewhat akin to the parameters of the Holy Mass within God's boundless Kingdom. This is the way our entire religious ascension should be, a measurable expression toward an infinite destination with a specified outcome. In order to do this, we must ask Jesus to give humanity individually and as a single body of creatures a sacred heart like His, one 'corazon sagrado' as Our Lady of Guadalupe might say, that is inclusive and yet verifiably distinct, the way syllables and verses constitute the Sacred Scriptures. All of our holier attributes, peacemaking, positive energies, and constructive emotions are derived from this same indivisible goodness, this same didactic consciousness. We are poised for Salvation because God's Holy Spirit gives us hearts capable of faith. What does this mean? How do we focus on all things eternal while exiled yet today? Surely it is the combination of an inward and outward vision that helps us see invisible things like divine love, hope, peace of mind and a holiness that unifies us with all true believers around the globe. It is a redefining impulse that says that our lives can be beatific in the here and now. This is what Jesus told the Apostles. Live the message of redemption at dawn, and anticipate its fulfillment before nightfall arrives. This is not too much to ask of a world whose completion was wrought by the Passion and Crucifixion of one Immaculate Man.

We have learned that it is possible to become overly introspective, to be too self-examining about our own humanity, disallowing our heartstrings to sound unscripted melodies. We must try instead to live according to the Gospel message without expelling the spontaneity from our everyday lives. Even though we are yet exiled from the presence of the Father, we are not solitarily confined. We have inherited a freedom that most people have never even conceived. We are at liberty to presume how vast God's Kingdom can become because the didactic consciousness has no limits. We are free to harvest our victories at will and build our dreams on foundations as huge as thunderheads. We have the birthright to reclaim our heritage from the opportunists who are slowly trying to steal it. And, we have every reason to believe that we will win the watershed battles against the evil that is devouring this world because our Roman Catholic faith is poised to destroy it like lighted dynamite inside a glass jar. The key benefit of practicing Catholicism is being able to see life beyond the parameters of time and space, to circumvent corners, barriers and obstacles that cannot be easily overcome by those outside the Church. With this insight, we discover what was previously unknown about the framework of the world; we have the capacity to embrace everything conceivably good about humanity because Jesus the Messianic King helps us look beyond our faults, failures, and weaknesses with the same sacred keenness awaiting us in Heaven. What else can we see around those corners? Surely it is retracing our footsteps so as to straighten crooked paths, reestablishing our connection with hopes that slipped away, and reviving memories that lost their sheen through the coarseness of the years. Many people walk through life while straddling, kicking, gouging and tinkering around the edges of the greatest possibilities known to man, but they never quite get there because they refuse to accept the Savior who makes us whole inside Himself. For example, the entire middle eastern region of the world is a wasteland because it cannot recognize the preeminent greatness of Jesus Christ and His Sacrifice to make their lives one of faithful beauty and brotherhood with all mankind. One of the most ironic aspects of having spiritual faith is that it proves so many things; we are able to discern right from wrong before being forced there by a surplus of untimely mistakes. We can envision the prescience of the Creator through His enviable capacity to foresee our next moves, that He is willing to nullify our transgressions if only we will invest ourselves in Him. Christians learn to recognize not only the roots of human sin, but its effects deeply seated in the corruption of the physical world. In Christ Jesus, we are bound here by little more than the element of time, for surely we have already superceded our posthumous frames in the sanctity of the Cross, ascending like angels to deposit our sheepish spirits inside the heart of the Messiah who was crucified there. In truth, nothing can bring harm to anyone bequeathed to Him on the occasion of their passage from this life. To be reborn and regained in Our Lord's Crucifixion is the ultimate definition of joy; for now listless cities can thrive again, and fallen heroes can rise. Babes can sound the strains of Tchaikovsky, and the barren can birth their first sons. Organs can shake dust from the rafters; the skies can be strewn with jasmine, and things without luster can shine. God has spoken through the Trinity, and all who believe Him can hear. Anxiety has been rightfully destroyed; and humanity should not fret seeing cracked rainbows, fraying moonbeams or dulled mountaintops anymore because the whole universe has been created anew.

It is the goal of contemplative Christians to make their dreams more than just vague nighttime images, but to give them identifiable meaning and the capacity for life in the framework of the physical world. They represent the marriage of the Spirit and the hope of the human heart that is plush with divinity, that electrifies the whole Faith-Church with passion. This is the magnification of fruit-bearing supernaturalism that would remain otherwise undiscovered and unharvested within the realms of everyday existence. It is the freedom to pursue real perfection through the Holy Gospel without feeling pretentious. While practicing what we know to be mystical faith, we are oftentimes tested by the hollowness and difficulties of everyday life. What we accept in faith is always laid alongside what we desire the world to become. This is the connection between faith and genius, knowing they are one and the same gift for the consciousness of man. We cannot say that we walk by faith if we just stand idly by, flatfootedly holding it. We must become alive in it, inhale and exhale its fruits, and reach-out with courage to those who might chide us for embracing what the Holy Spirit has inspired us to believe. Jesus has set forth a priestly calling to every soul on Earth, a command to protract our holiness into the world so we can overcome our pride and prosper the Gospel of Heaven and the Sacraments. The whole idea of reading between the lines surely must have come from the Sacred Scriptures; not that we are allowed to infer anything from its text that God does not intend, but so that the chapters and verses become the heartstrings we pluck with our prayers, playing-out the melodies of righteousness, relying on the strongholds of love with which our faithfulness is upheld. The Lord forms our thoughts with lyrics about the way life is meant to be, and the Holy Spirit endows us with wisdom rolling off our tongues like honeydew in the midday light. We have always known that Christianity brokers the coalescence of all souls beneath the Cross to be immersed in the Sacred Blood of Our Lord's Sacrifice, but many are still uninformed about how that mystical experience translates into tangible spiritual action. It has everything to do with effecting our brothers and sisters' conversion through our knowledge and understanding of the redemption of Creation. And, it has even more to do with placing our own suffering into that same context as we commit ourselves and our families to the purification of the world. It is said that persistence in prayer is as great a virtue as prayer itself because God is pleased by our determination to stand by Jesus and invoke the Most Blessed Trinity. It seems that this is the only way to purify the world, by beseeching the King who reigns over it, turning to the spiritual realms to effect change in our physical life. We must trust that what we cannot see is as curative as anything we can touch with our hands. And, we need to recognize the value of rhythm, learning not only to hear the sounds of the world's daily charms, but to live by the echoing silence of the off-beats as well. We can in this way envision the face of Heaven in our prayers and imagine in these dark times what it means to rediscover our lost innocence. We are constantly bombarded by different levels of commonness every day, against which we contrast what ultimately become the more extraordinary moments of life. We reserve the right to defend whatever we wish as being more beautiful than most, higher than the rest, and better than anything else based on the value we place on our own insights and actions. If we saw ourselves before the backdrop of the Earth as Jesus sees us, perhaps we might more clearly understand that every person fashions and transcends his own thoughts and tendencies to reach those heights in ways unmatched by any other creature in the world. We often search for words to describe our dilemmas, ways to express how we feel about the condition of the world's soul–if it has one, so that we can find a means to inspire it, touch it, heal it, and comfort it. This is really what is missing among the nations. We are never wholly shed of sorrow because many of us have not completely opened to Our Lord's Resurrection. Our years are more about process than consummation. It is how we get to the destination that matters most, whether we make the right decisions that determine how fruitfully we live. Let there be no mistake; life is no vacation, but it need not be a toilsome experience in futility. We have credentials and principles inherent to all those who believe in God, and we can invoke them spontaneously at any moment, whenever circumstances demand it. Sacrifice is not so repugnant to those who know what redemption is, what it requires from us, what it foretells about the fulfillment of Christianity, what Jesus seeks through His own desires, and what miracles can be begotten if we trust in God. We share more than faith in the obedience of His love, but an identity that overcomes and overwhelms the undertakings of the world. When we speak about righteousness giving endurance, this is what we mean. If we spend our whole lives making judgements about the immensity of our suffering, we will become so disconcerted by it that we will miss the blessings it procures. Not all things facilitate the kind of changes we need, and this is why we must focus on how best we can see. World affairs and circumstantial events must be weighed according to how they positively affect our faith. It helps to know what to expect, and what we are searching for. If we see wood shavings scattered on a workbench, we can safely assume that there has been a carver there, and that he has just crafted something. We likewise connect the world and Heaven by what Jesus taught us throughout His life and by the Table of Salvation He has spread before us. The Lord ordains for humanity abundant new dawns pouring copiously over the horizon, a fabric of life that dries the weeping willows' tears, fosters friendships that never die, hope for the despairing, overtures yet unwritten, cantatas still unsung, stallions in the wild, infants bound for knighthood, timidity outdone by heroism, apathy slain by wisdom, steely moral courage, immeasurable depths of righteousness, the fascination of the Cross, freedom of the spirit, clarity of sight and sound, sustenance for the poor, strength for the frail, counsel for the wicked, truth that never wanes, confidence for the unsure, honor for the upright, stability for the wavering, fathoms for the shallow, dignity for the despised, faith for the lost, comfort for the mourning, victory for the honest, and grace for all things redemptive. It is here that the world must begin to live again, to feel the texture of life from the inside out, grasp the handhold of genius, and expand the vision of human love brought to perfection in Jesus' Sacrifice, leaping toward the future untethered from our fears. We thereby satisfy the cravings of Heaven and the eternal ages with our own sweet holiness. We gain access to the grand ballroom of Salvation en masse and Jerusalem restored by making our volition compatible with the obedience of the Saints and the excellence of the universe that touches the face of God. We die gladly in His Son because the Crucifixion takes our breath away and hands us back new life.

Let us pray:

Lord God of the Saints, hear our pleas for help. Let your sovereignty reign over the travesties of this world. Wipe the sweat from the brow of our exile, and make peace inundate our lives. We offer our honest confessions in exchange for your forgiveness; please render us your aid. As we witness the destruction of this world's unholy places, grant us the strength to trust you in all times and seasons. May we become acclimated to your Holy Will as your Kingdom spreads across our tortured domain. Help us be strong in the image of your Son, and grant us the awareness that we are seamlessly united in you. We ask this through Christ Our Lord. Amen.

What is Our Hierarchy?
Patriarchy, Feminism, and Abortion

"O' Lord, you are loyal to our well-being; you are our health and shield, our comfort and peace, our beatific assurance. We call upon you every hour for guidance and protection. We ask that you ratify our prayers in your love; we seek your encouragement when we are in doubt. We urge you to enter the exiled world with justice during these difficult times. Tend to those who are discounted and dejected. Console the afflicted. Heal the infirm. Shine your everlasting brilliance upon the dreariness that besets us from taking charge over our enemies with the tenacity of the Saints. Jesus, you are the hero of the Cross, and this is why we come to you. We will surely fail without you. We cannot carry the burdens of this life without the strength we gain from you. It is in this confidence that we are disposed to your blessings, and we ask that you touch us with your grace through the whole of the ages. Amen."

Sometimes the winds of change blow more placidly upon us, with a divine air of sophistication to their breeze; and this is when we are saturated with peace within and without, felt so coolly and gently that they could almost lift us entirely whole to the sovereignty of the altars. Even as the Holy Spirit speaks volumes in poignance and urgency at times, there are moments when we realize that the Lord dispenses His calmness with ease. And in this, we no longer wonder what human emotions are for. What must be said about our holiness is that even in our most excruciating hours, we painted the prettiest pictures of redemption in our hearts; we applied our rarest innovations against the strains of daily life, and we won our place beside Jesus Christ by a landslide and a mile. Remembering this high architecture is how we force our anxieties into the farthest voids and bring to surface the love and trust that are most worthy of our faith. Life is always more about how we feel than what we know; and our thought-lines are often calico and restless, unstable and disquieting, inquisitive, and sometimes merely faint. Many of us have not yet figured out what the Bible means by spiritual ingenuity. It certainly implies an explicit belief that someone eternal is watching us, whoever started this whole thing, whatever Creator fashioned the world so beautifully and anonymously, with such reciprocal simpleness and complexity, intricate detail and incalculable design, allowing the coexistence of such harmony and discord, discretion and error, inequality among its species, and such far-reaching extremes of sharpness, intelligence, dullness, and ignorance. Humanity is separate from other creatures in that we are communally aware of what causes our own demise; we have the capacity to know that we are not beasts in the wild, and we have the venue through orthodox faith to will into being our transition from this life through a network of parallels, morals, and conclusions that permeate organic flesh and help us reject illicit impulses. When we speak about prayer, we refer to the intersection of previously existing outer-limits, infinite and inexplicable, unseen and undying, with our measurable social and individual desires. It is the coalescence of our needs and preferences with the forces of dominion empowered to satisfy them. And, we know what to pray for based on the aforesaid ingenuity we have inherited from the deific hierarchy that gives us license to practice the principles and revelations aligned with its laws and doctrines relevant to our final redemption. In short, Heaven allows us to establish and ordain the protocols and metrics that best reflect the heart and teachings of its King. This is what prayer is for; we remain consistently connected like a lifeline to the Godhead we cannot yet see, instilling in us the ability to fix what is broken and suffice what is lacking in His eyes.

What do all these words mean? What does the titling of this chapter mean to us? Those three words, Patriarchy, Feminism, and Abortion? It is indisputable that they are integral components in the cultural battles we are witnessing that lie at the foundation of the civic transformation of America. Some claim this transformation is for the good, others believe it to be an abomination destabilizing our national fabric. How easy it is to see the intellectual arguments constructed by either side. And yet, amidst all of them is the truth, as all the rest fall away as worn-out rebellious palaver. Parenthood embodies a sacred duty that wisdom be invoked to clear away the distractions and misdirections employed by children, balancing them more toward the ordered disciplines of the truth than the wasteful wilfulness that consumes their opportunities for true happiness and self-reliant prosperity. Children can give excuses and twisted perspectives all day long to justify the illicit conduct they may be contemplating or have been caught participating in. Some of them are the most seasoned manipulators and salesmen the world has ever seen. My words about young people should not be construed negatively because I believe it is a fantastic gift from God for the human mind to be contemplative about given situations, and to ponder multi-dimensional scenarios. All children grow through periods where their minds mature and attitudes form. But, how they mature and what attitudes they adopt during this critical formation is of the most crucial importance. Children can be lost for a lifetime before the age of ten. The multi-dimensional capacities of every child are formed either in a hierarchical structure based on the order and priority of virtuous principle, or they are left in chaos amongst a collage of equal options to be selected from at the behest of whims that are personally advantageous to them in the moment. And, this is the point: a hierarchical structure based on the order and priority of virtuous principle. Wisdom comes when our thoughts are disciplined under the hierarchy of virtue. There is an order and a hierarchy to the definition of what is noble. For instance, the defending of the free will to choose is a noble endeavor, but allowing a murderer to choose to carry out the killing of their neighbor is not. In this, we can see there are instances where it is not noble to defend the choices of human beings. Therefore, we must never look upon the freedom to choose as an unassailable omnipotent right, because it is not. We must further ask ourselves what framework of thought provides us the ability to recognize that the freedom to choose to kill our neighbor is wrong. This framework of moral thinking is what is not being employed in our nation by tens of millions of people, depending on the issue. They have no moral framework by which they are guided, and it is obvious by the positions they take on issues, the actions they perform, and the laws they legislate. The freedom to choose is not a virtue, it is rather a capacity granted to us through our free will given by God, a morally neutral capacity that can be employed for good or evil. The freedom to choose is not sacrosanct as many wish to portray it. They do so simply for the purposes of violating every sense of morality and propriety that a human species could have cultivated into a civilized society. *"...for although they knew God they did not accord him glory as God or give him thanks. Instead, they became vain in their reasoning, and their senseless minds were darkened. While claiming to be wise, they became fools and exchanged the glory of the immortal God for the likeness of an image of mortal man or of birds or of four-legged animals or of snakes. Therefore, God handed them over to impurity through the lusts of their hearts for the mutual degradation of their bodies. They exchanged the truth of God for a lie and revered and worshiped the creature rather than the creator, who is blessed forever. Amen. Therefore, God handed them over to degrading passions. Their females exchanged natural relations for unnatural, and the males likewise gave up natural relations with females and burned with lust for one another. Males did shameful things with males and thus received in their own persons the due penalty for their perversity. And since they did not see fit to acknowledge God, God handed them over to their undiscerning mind to do what is improper. They are filled with every form of wickedness, evil, greed, and malice; full of envy, murder, rivalry, treachery, and spite. They are gossips and scandalmongers and they hate God. They are insolent, haughty, boastful, ingenious in their wickedness, and rebellious toward their parents. They are senseless, faithless, heartless, ruthless. Although they know the just decree of God that all who practice such things deserve death, they not only do them but give approval to those who practice them."* [Romans 1:21-32] Virtue is another word for moral excellence. There is order and priority in the hierarchical structure of the human mind and heart that supports moral excellence in our lives. In the one who chooses to kill his neighbor, there is no order or priority toward moral excellence within their mental hierarchical structure that precludes their intentions to kill. They do not possess an ordered sense of right and wrong to dissuade them from acting out their evil intentions. They are lost souls who are victims and accomplices of evil that is exacerbated from both the seen and unseen realms of the spirit.

This simple conversation is merely to bring to the fore the concept that each of us possesses a mental construction that is rooted deeply within our spiritual composure that has been formed in virtue, or not, that gives standing to our personal beliefs, how we respond to situations, indeed, what we defend as being part of allowable human actions in the arena we call society. Our country has an ever-expanding population of people who have never been exposed to, even from childhood, the molding influences that would give a principled hierarchical structure to their mental constitution, anchored in what is noble and virtuous. There is also another increasing portion of our citizens who may have been raised with a good foundation of moral virtue who have been stripped of it by the forces of darkness who are dragging our country into the abyss. It is not simply anecdotal that a child possessing a measure of Christian faith will have it eradicated from their thinking after completing a secularist, progressive education in almost any of the universities in the United States. Those who have been deprived the formation of their spirit, or who have otherwise had it stolen from them, do not have a breadth of understanding about their lives, the impacts they have on those around them, or the composure they need to withstand the temptations from the seedier personages they will encounter throughout their lives. Satan is lying in wait for them, knowing they have no armor to combat him. They are vulnerable to any of the many differing forms of evil when only one form may be necessary to destroy their soul. They have no moral excellence or compass, but only situational expedience oriented toward the satisfaction of their indulgent whims, the gratification of their sensuality, the greed of gaining profit, or their self-preservation at the time. Without a hierarchical structure infused with order and priority based on virtue, they have no basis from which to understand consequences and no visionary insight to extrapolate outcomes from the point of view of their judgement before the Son of God at the end of time. They truly have no vision, and thus, no wisdom. They are blind, and they are lost.

The Gospel of Matthew 7:24-27 states, "*Everyone who listens to these words of mine and acts on them will be like a wise man who built his house on rock. The rain fell, the floods came, and the winds blew and buffeted the house. But it did not collapse; it had been set solidly on rock. And everyone who listens to these words of mine but does not act on them will be like a fool who built his house on sand. The rain fell, the floods came, and the winds blew and buffeted the house. And it collapsed and was completely ruined.*" What is this "house" that the Holy Spirit speaks of in this scriptural passage? Is it not the interior hierarchical structure of the mind and heart that I am also referring to? When a person possesses the house built on solid rock, the foundations of the Gospel, the life conceived in the womb of a mother is of the highest order and most sacred priority in the interior hierarchy governing their actions toward that life. There is nothing that outweighs our devotion and responsibility to protect human life, even to the point of surrendering our own. This is the definition of nobility: To lay down one's life for those whom we love. This is also the definition of love. There is no greater composure of the human person than this. Those who defend abortion are completely dumbfounded about how to deal with the concept of pregnant mothers who are suffering terminal illnesses, declining life-saving measures in order to protect the child in their wombs until birth. They are giants of human greatness who surrender their own lives in the image of Christ that their child may live. Holy Heaven, what beauty, what structure, composure, conviction and devotion! Heroic and elevated into the pantheon of immortal grace! Perfect love is staring right at them, and yet, the defenders of abortion choose instead to damn themselves and continue in their ultimate hatred of human life. Those who possess either no interior hierarchy or a fatally disordered one, but instead exercise a freedom to choose from amongst their collage of supposed equal options, will generate justifications based upon any criteria which happens to fit their excuse in the moment. They are mentally unstable relativists who have no solid anchoring in either truth or virtue, but only in what profits them at the time. What is the excuse given by those who justify and defend the killing of the child in the womb? "The woman has the right to choose,"—as if she is omnipotent and possesses the right to kill a child. What are the excuses given for aborting a child growing in the womb of a mother? "I just can't have a child right now. I am too young. The father is not here to support me. I'm being forced by my parents. It will ruin my high school years. I won't be able to go to prom. I do not have a job. I do not have the money. I mentally cannot endure a pregnancy. I have too many children to take care of now. My parents will kill me if they found out. I haven't finished high school. I have to go to college. I am too old, the child could possibly have Down Syndrome. I was raped. My father sexually abused me. I wanted a boy, I already have a girl. My husband does not want another child," and on and on. Can we see the house built on shifting sand and what happens when the rains come? They grasp at vacuous justifications because of the realization that there is no solid rock beneath them. No order of virtue, no noble sacrifice, no priority of moral excellence, even to the point of choosing to kill the innocent child within them. And, the feminists applaud. There is no stabilizing hierarchical structure of virtue in any person who says, "It is more convenient for me if this child dies!" Definitive, clear, like a rock. ***Human life inherently embodies rights, and it demands its unequivocal preservation by its veritable existence.*** There is not one issue in the trenches of our culture wars that is not given greater clarity by our testament to the truth of the Gospel. Isn't it ironic that the most quoted passage of Sacred Scripture used by those who possess no interior hierarchy is the first verse of the same Chapter of Matthew 7:1, "*Stop judging, that you may not be judged.*"? "Do not foist your hierarchy of moral excellence upon me!," they say. Well, the terrible news for them is that it has already been laid upon humanity by the Crucified Messiah as the wage for entrance into Heaven. Our Holy Mother said to me that our response should be, "No, I am not your judge, but I am to tell you how you will soon be judged."

Dear Lord, maker of all good things, redeem us from our weaknesses; bring your mighty consolation into this world with vigor; give us the blessings warranted by our faith in you. Unleash your mighty powers across our land and damn the devil's works. Behold in us the desire to be one in you, to take upon ourselves the burdens you prescribe, to clarify our comprehension of your Gospel and make it triumph in our day. Accept our humble prayers and plant in them the trueness of your Spirit, that all the world will succumb to the Glory of your Sacrifice and awaken at your door. We ask this through Christ Our Lord. Amen.

So, where do we begin to rebuild and fortify the interior hierarchical structure of moral excellence within the American people? Could we begin by returning to the very pages of the Bible, beginning in the admonishments contained in the Seventh Chapter of the Book of Matthew? There, it speaks of discernment before judging others, pearls before swine, the answers to prayers, the golden rule, the narrow gate, the false prophets, the true disciple, and the two foundations. The truth borne within this short chapter offers a testament to the orientation we need when addressing the societal chaos being stirred by Satan between the citizens of our country. Truly, how does "*Do unto others as you would have them do unto you,*" square with a mother choosing to kill the child in her womb? What is she "doing" to the child within her? Would she wish God to do to her what she is doing to the life inside her? Her "choice" is anti-Gospel and anti-Commandment, and thus Antichrist; and the entire universe knows it. Look at the diabolic disorientation spread across and engrained within our country by this renegade abuse of the freedom to choose. A Supreme Court of the United States of America voted 7-2 in 1973 to surrender our nation into allegiance to Satan, and millions of feminists have been deluded into cheering for the stench of hell ever since. So many have placed their freedom into the hands of the devil, serving him without any realization that he is preparing their souls for eternal damnation the instant they die. We are living the consequences of failing to impress into millions of children an interior hierarchical structure based in courageous virtue flowing from the Life of Jesus Christ. Over 60 million children have been killed through abortion when every person in this country should have been standing in their defense from the moment of their conception in the womb. Rebuilding our interior hierarchical structure begins by removing any personal authority we hold over ourselves interiorly, and submitting ourselves in obedience to Christ in prayer. We must want to be remade in His image. We must tell Him that we wish to become a new creation, reconstructed in His grace, forgiven of our sins, worthy of being mounted like a diamond in the crown of His Kingship. We must tell Him that we are willing to relinquish our old selves, any attitudes contrary to His own. We must desire to be filled with Light, even if it means that we are rejected by the whole world and must suffer every day of our lives thereafter. We must reject any selfishness that calls us to forsake the sacrifices required to defend Christian virtue. We must be willing to turn our backs at times on our conveniences, fast from our pleasures, and extend ourselves in sacrifice for the betterment of our neighbors. We must be fluent in performing acts of charity, expecting nothing in return. In all these things lies human perfection as Christ lived it. If nothing else, we must be brutally honest with ourselves and eradicate the tendency to generate cerebral excuses for everything we know to be wrong. Yes, there is a Truth by which others can tell us what to do! As Christians, we must honestly approach Jesus and accept the true meaning in the words He spoke and the message that He declared to humanity through His Life, Death, and Resurrection. The hierarchy revealed by Jesus issues with clarity and power in the first two words that He uttered when teaching His Apostles to pray, "Our Father..." [Matthew 6:9] In this utterance, Jesus specifically reveals the Patriarchy of Heaven. Our Creator is our Father who is the Alpha of the hierarchy, the pinnacle of life itself and the beginning and end of eternal wisdom. Anything that attacks and disparages this universal supremacy of His Patriarchy over the Earth is foreign to the order and priority of moral excellence as Jesus revealed it.

Our Holy Mother reflected with me on the Patriarchy of God through an incident I engaged with a Roman Catholic nun. I do not relate this for any reasons other than edification. At one time, I received a daily reflection by email that, upon my research, was being distributed from a website run by a radical priest who is in continuous opposition to and contention with the Hierarchy of the Catholic Church, indeed the very teachings of the Church. He presents himself as a great mystical-thinking expert who in reality couches his deranged eccentricity in thought-provoking revolutionary language that titillates the sensibilities of those who eschew the orthodoxy of the Church, or those who know very little about the Faith of the Church to begin with. One particular day, his meditation was so completely out-of-bounds regarding the orthodox spirit of the Church that I forwarded the email to my brother with a message of how "dangerous" I believed the meditation to be, and how the priest's veiled heresy was actually soiling people's interior understanding of the truth. He was leading them astray. In other words, he was disruptive to the good ordering and clarity of a person's interior hierarchy. It was a perfect example of a wolf in sheep's clothing. Unbeknownst to me, I actually hit the "reply" button to the nun instead of the "forward" button to my brother, and returned my critique to the nun herself. And, what was the nun's response? The next day, she sent a meditation containing one of the most vile attacks by the priest against the Patriarchy of the Church that I had ever witnessed. Although I was disconcerted by my accidental sending of my reply to the wrong person, I was stunned by the aggressiveness of the nun in response. Our Holy Mother told me:

Sunday, October 18, 2009
Virgin Mary

"You did in fact respond to the sister at the behest of the Son of Man. It was no accident that you hit the other key. And, your brief essays in response were brilliant but not offensive. Let us take another look at the war about which I speak. What was the nun's response? To forward the worst heresy of the priest back to you. She looked specifically for what she sent after your communication, delaying what she actually intended for that day, in an attempt to show you that the femininity of God will prevail over any attempt of patriarchy that you might pursue. I wish for you not to become upset by this. In fact, you should be grateful that it was such a learning experience. Jesus is letting you see what is really going on inside the Church. Imagine this if you will. I have been Mother of the Church for 2,000 years, and I have never said anything even remotely similar to the heresy you are seeing. Stay the course of your work here with My messages, and realize that you have been given further evidence that what I have been saying is true. I told you about the problem of the emasculation of the Church. Strengthening and maintaining the patriarchy of the Church cannot come by mere words. Feminists and rogue homosexual priests will not respond to what they hear or read from a page. The spiritual warfare that I have mentioned is often fought out beyond the scenes, behind the sights of those who are causing the war. This is why I have given around the globe such phenomenon as Saint Gabriel's appearance to you and asked My visionaries to do inexplicable things. I ask all of you to pray most prolifically that humanity comes to understand that God sees the battles for the souls of men from the other side of time. He knows what weapons Satan uses against the Church and individual souls. He knows their origin, what damage they will do, and how they can be disarmed. We have had so much success in the battle against evil in this home that it would cause you to fall backward in surprise if you could see it with your eyes."

Our Lady continued by explaining to me the concept of real power, as opposed to getting into a futile quarrel with those who are not disposed to listen anyway. We will remember that Adam and Eve in the Garden were tempted by the serpent to become like God. And, what this meant to them was not that they would have some omnipotence that would only be seen by the elements of the Garden. They did not desire something that would only be pleasing to them. They believed if they had power, the kind of power owned by their Creator, they too could create according to their independent will. They were tempted with the desire to be like God in His creative attributes. And, when they fell to that temptation, what did God do? He banished them from the Garden. And, where did they go? They were exiled from the presence of God into the world below because they wanted to be like Him. Now, what is happening since the Sacrifice of Jesus on Calvary? The Father has promised the reinstatement of all believers into the Land of the Living if we do what? Become like Him. What an irony! This is where feminists initiate their flawed concept of God which is the origin of their error. They are told that they must become like the Father whom they are trying to describe as a woman. Their perceptions are tangled in the flesh of their gender instead of free and soaring in the spiritual grace of their Father. This is the work of the devil. And this is why men, along with the patriarchy, are the target of their emasculation. They see only flesh and worldly power. Our Holy Mother came to us in 1991 speaking about the restoration of the dignity of the Church, the subservient brilliance of all believers to know that God is the Patriarch of all created things. He reigns in His hierarchy as "Father." However, dissidents such as the nun I engaged and the priest whom she serves will not accept this truth because they refuse to be subservient to the King. They not only want the Earth to be called mother, and Our Lady to be seen as Mother, but now they want the Father of Creation to be seen as mother also, so they can have power to be freed from their sacrificial subservience to the Cross. They have prepared no room for Abba! They would rather have a queen with no king! They are not looking for subservience in love at all, but power so they can implement their will, based in their pride. This is exactly the failing of Adam and Eve. Let us refer this to the Sacrament of Penance where their humility might be reinstated and their vision restored. Confession to a male priest cleanses the soul to an infinite degree. But, what happens to those who deny the supremacy of the Patriarchy of God? They are not fully absolved. Additionally, if they partake of the penitential Sacrament at all, they abhor confessing to a man in a confessional. Is it any wonder that the number of those availing themselves to the Sacrament of Penance has plummeted at the same time that the ideology of feminism and their gospel of male hatred has flourished? They will bow to no man, not even if He is the Son of the Most High. Yes, souls are forgiven of the sins they confess in the penitential sacrament. However, if they do not confess their error about intentionally misidentifying the gender of their Lord, they are not prepared for entrance into Heaven if they die moments after exiting the confessional. Now, the Catechism of the Catholic Church declares that God is Spirit, and there is no punishment against saying that God is whatever you believe Him to be if it does not contradict the teachings of the Magisterium. But, in the midst of this seeming ambiguity, these people have decided to claim and accentuate feminine attributes for God as the backbone of their agendum because the Church has not declared God to be male. Yet, the Church has said God is Father, and Jesus has said that God is His Father. Everyone who heard Jesus understood and took to heart the paternal attributes of the unseen Deity that He was trying to reveal. Our Lady understood that God was the Father of Her Child. When someone says the word 'father,' does it not imply the gender of male? And, is this not what the Holy Spirit implants in the human heart? Regarding confession, the penitent must understand by the cohesion of the Truth with the human spirit and the language of Creation that the Father is the Patron of all Creation. He is male according to His creative powers, His Providence, and ability to hold sway over every creature great and small. He is male according to His Dominion and His authority. These are all characteristics that do not necessarily require a human body, although Jesus is the incarnation of them all. Now, what does Judaism hold about the Father of Creation? What did Saint Joseph and our Holy Mother, and all other believers hold about the Creator of all good things? That Salvation would be through the lineage of the male line of the House of David. The genealogy proclaimed on the Christmas Feast is the testament of the Holy Spirit to this. There is a perversion of the Sacrament of Penance for anyone who attacks the Patriarchy of the Church to believe that they receive complete absolution of their sins while embracing this feminist ideology. This particular sin has not been forgiven because it has not been recognized and confessed. Our Holy Mother told me this to temper my thinking regarding the all-absolving power of the confessional. It is not unlike someone asking for forgiveness for any other sin they intend to continue committing. Our Lady told me that God takes the issue of the male hierarchy extremely seriously. It is ingrained in substance in His Plan of Salvation from the very foundational structures of Messianic revelation. Feminist gender ideology is irrelevant to human Salvation and is of no redeeming value. The only reason that the Church teaches that God is not assigned a specific gender is because He does not maintain Himself in the realms of exile in a human body. But, Our Lady says that if He did, that body would be male, and Jesus is the proof as the reigning King, the Second Person of the Most Blessed Trinity of God. The logical question, then, is where does this leave the dignity of women? It is fully manifested in the Queen, in Our Lady, the Mother of Jesus; and if women fully imitated Her, they would act like Her and find the dignity they are searching for. There is no such thing as a second-class status foisted upon the Virgin Mary or women as Her daughters simply because God did not incarnate Himself as a female. All women have the capacity to become like the Virgin Mary in ways that men do not have. And, in uniting with this Maternal love, they can touch the heart of the most stoic male ever to breathe mortal or eternal life. In other words, God adopts a reciprocal subservience to women in response to the infinite grace of the Virgin because His Love is reciprocally infinite. God laid down His life through His Son for Eve so that now the Creator has creatures to comfort Him, even in those who once fell from that Grace. Women must become everything that the Son has been, and man must become everything that the Father and Son are now. The Son became incarnate through the Most Blessed Virgin. Thus, women must be nurturing and loving like Her. If anyone wishes to call this subservience in the way that it is known in castes and classes on Earth, they do not fully comprehend the meaning of the term, or they are deliberately characterizing themselves as victims in order to steal the reigns of power not given to them. Just like Eve! Women must become everything that Jesus taught the whole of humanity in the Gospel. They must become like Him in all ways holy, taught to Him by His Mother. I will tell you now, please spare me the attacks of being accused as a misogynist. That is just another of the power-mongering epithets hurled by the sinful Eves of this age. I have seen the True Lady of Creation and all the beauty and glory that women were meant to embody, if they would simply humble themselves. I love this Woman more than all feminists put together supposedly love themselves. I venerate God's definition of woman. Whomever attacks the Most Blessed Virgin and what She teaches is the misogynist, even if that person is a female. In truth, we see women as not only the receptacles of the holiness that is of God, but the feminine grace that He admires. They are not the warriors of the world, but the nurturers, healers, and wound-dressers of those warriors. They have a dual role to play to effect the principles of the King in their mission to be His comfort. Now, we can take this back to the beginning of the discussion referring to Adam and Eve. Since they wanted to be like God, and He said that they should not eat of the Fruit of the Tree, it was their disobedience that cast them out. It was more their disobedience that forced their expulsion than their desire to be like Him. This is why the world in which we live is restored to perfection by human obedience to the Will of the Father. Adam wanted to be a maker of creatures, so God placed Adam and his descendants on Earth to propagate new children all they wanted. However, He did this with the caveat that all of Adam's descendants must become like Himself in all other ways as well. Charitable, sacrificial, kind, persevering, visionary, and all other attributes by which the Father can be described. How would they know how to do this? What example would the Lord provide? Christ Jesus. He spoke of Him through the prophets, then sent the Messiah to live among them as His best example of Himself. If we wish to become like God, then we must imitate the perfections of His Son.

The impulse behind the disobedience of Adam and Eve was the deadly sin of pride. It is this same pride that keeps feminist dissenters from believing everything I have expounded upon here. They are making judgements about Creation, their existence, and the Will of God from a disoriented interior hierarchy, not based upon the order, priority and hierarchy of Heaven. This is the same pride that causes these same people to believe that abortion is acceptable to God, as well as all the other sins that are so offensive to Heaven. Pride makes someone say that they have the right to define the Father any way they choose, when in reality, they have less intention of contemplating the Father and His motivations than they do of forwarding their own selfish agendas, after wrapping themselves in the personal claim that their understanding of God allows them to do it. They claim to speak for all women on Earth, pushing into obscurity the great sacrificial women of history who imitated the Most Blessed Virgin Mary in all Her magnanimous solicitude. And, the dynamic gets even uglier. If everyone does not affirm their radicalism, they claim victimization and oppression by a medieval patriarchy of male domination; and the secular void of atheists, agnostics, and other Christian-haters become their best friends and jump on their bandwagon because Satan is the father who leads them all. Strange bedfellows, indeed. They soil the truth with their own blindness. Everyone must realize that the Father will actually tender His masculine Will to anyone who loves Him as Father. The God who gave life to humanity through the death of His Son gives majestic signs of irony to His children through the power of prayer. What would happen if someone who agrees with all I have said here wanted to see a young girl rise to the power of a king and conquer the whole of a country? God would answer that prayer, and He did. Saint Joan of Arc is the evidence. He answered the prayer. This does not imply that He wants sixteen-year-old girls to become battlefield warriors, but that we recognize that God can do anything He pleases. When He sent Joan of Arc to accomplish her mission, He did not necessarily have to create conditions where she said she was hearing voices from Heaven. He did the latter so humanity would know from where she received her power. She was compliant and confident. She spoke without apology about the directives of the King of Heaven. And, the world came down on her like tons of steel. They condemned her as a heretic; they even allegedly forced her to recant her testament of visions. Indeed, they even burned her alive. And, what was she doing? What was the purpose of her campaign? Validating the patriarchy of France! She was not trying to take the throne of the Dauphin, Charles VII. She was defending the male hierarchy that she loved, and ushering in the kingdom of her king. Now, centuries later, God asks of His female creatures not to imitate Saint Joan of Arc with physical weapons of war, but to spiritually don her same armor nonetheless, and hoist the same standard by which she claimed her place in the lineage of Saints as one of Christianity's most courageous and obedient Martyrs. Women must perform their maternal duties with one goal in mind, the conversion of humanity to the Cross of the Man. This begins by instilling within their children a hierarchical structure based on moral excellence, rooted in the majesty of the Patriarchy of the Roman Catholic Church.

The Patriarchy of the Original Apostolic Church is a visible reflection of the Father, maybe not in each Prelate individually at times, but collectively as a guiding and nurturing bastion of strength, longevity and composure that cannot be deposed by any force in Creation. The accusations leveled against it by those who lust for power and independence are only indictments against themselves, like children throwing tantrums on the floor, kicking and screaming because they are not allowed to partake of the fruit of the tree of authority. If anyone were to witness the standard by which Prelates of the Church are to be judged come the end of time, perhaps they would have second thoughts about their ladder climbing upon seeing the responsibility to which these leaders are going to be held to account. More of them will wish they had become martyrs as a result of their allegiance to Christ. They are responsible unto death, even on a cross, for the proclamation and preservation of the Patriarchy of the Father in the Church of His Messianic Son. They are responsible to manifest an unyielding love in communion with the Truth of the Ages, compromising the message of the Gospel with no one, never fearing to declare it to anyone, and defending the source of redemption that rests in the seven Sacraments, applicable to every person ever desiring a chance to reenter Paradise. They are to imitate the Father through His Son in all His masculine authority and sacrificial persuasion. And, what does this look like? The Father is of a unique kindness that is of old, of the Ancients and prophets, and also of the Messianic disciples and Apostles. His motions are graceful, which reveal the softness of His Sacred Heart. He is the kindness of heart from a man who is trying to describe an horrific experience endured by those He loves. He is truly compassionate to the people who approach Him, and often engages them with levity. He is humble, an adult who is as innocent as any child, but of such wisdom, foresight, power, and gentleness. He will lay-out his own feelings for any person He loves, at the same time He is often forced to say, "...I do not know this person" when the latter is screaming, shouting, and blaspheming at Him. His entire composure is one of affection, an endearing way to express His feelings, even while viewing the horrors of man's sins across the expanse of time that pierce His Heart to the core. And, He is yet a God who listens intently and sees past His own pain. He is capable of genuine lightheartedness. He has a good sense of humor. He can compartmentalize a great many wrongs that are committed against His reign. If this were not true, He would have pulverized the Earth by now, leaving pockmarks that look like the back side of the moon on every continent. He welcomes all sinners into His open arms as gently as a father accepting a newborn son into his embrace from the hands of his spouse for the very first time. In the whole of history, God has been reprimanding, collecting His people by sword and sorrow, sparing them the worst calamities, embracing humanity with empathetic strains, and willing to forgive even the most egregious errors. And, this is precisely what His Church, the Original Apostolic Church, has been doing since the Day of Pentecost when Peter stood up before the crowds in Jerusalem with a paternal gaze and testified to the Messiah whom they had just crucified. Peter spoke from a humble heart, but with stern command, because he knew by the power of the Holy Spirit that the urgency of testifying to the King of Creation outweighed his chagrin at having denied Him three times. This is the same with all "fathers" of the Church who must, in like stead, stand and deliver. Each of them would love to have the miraculous words that would greet the diversity of human hearts in a singular way that would reflect the seriousness by which the Father perceives exiled man, but also display the comforting Heart of the Father. Our Lady possesses these words! But, the diversity of mental hierarchies within the human race causes them to be so despised. Jesus said we would be despised just as He was for spreading the truth of the Gospel. *"If the world hates you, keep in mind that it hated me first. If you belonged to the world, it would love you as its own. As it is, you do not belong to the world, but I have chosen you out of the world. That is why the world hates you. Remember what I told you: 'A servant is not greater than his master.' If they persecuted me, they will persecute you also. If they obeyed my teaching, they will obey yours also. They will treat you this way because of my name, for they do not know the one who sent me. If I had not come and spoken to them, they would not be guilty of sin; but now they have no excuse for their sin. Whoever hates me hates my Father as well. If I had not done among them the works no one else did, they would not be guilty of sin. As it is, they have seen, and yet they have hated both me and my Father. But this is to fulfill what is written in their Law: 'They hated me without reason.'"* [John 15:18-25] The priests of the Church are pleading to His people at the same time that the message itself is one of awakening urgency, reorientation, conversion, dedication, and sacrificial love. Jesus has chosen shepherds who are easy to accompany on the journey of life, simple to the touch, slow to anger, forgiving as any saints, and cordial in every way conceivable. But, they are required to be steadfast in the Truth that has been handed to them in succession for 2000 years. This is the Roman Catholic Church; beaten, scourged, mocked, spate upon, stripped naked, ignored, and vilified, while serving the poor, healing the sick, forgiving the penitent, performing every good deed, marking out the path to deliverance so that mankind can be prepared to greet the Savior when He comes again in final judgement.

This leads again to the Sacrament of Confession to a priest. How do we suppose the Father receives the confessions of His believers on Earth? Truly, in every mannerism that I have just described. God listens in a special way to those who have humbled themselves and made the sacrifice of their ego to openly confess their sins in the confessional to His priests. The image of God being overly destructive, overbearing, and unapproachable keeps many from entering the Sacrament of Penance because they believe that their contrition will be futile. They do not believe they can start again as on the very first day. If the Father put on a spiritual face in the material world; if He were able to be seen with expressions and gestures, He would appear much like Pope John Paul the Great, audibly singing a beloved melody from his heart to his flock at one of his open-air Pontifical Masses, such as when millions turned-out in his homecoming visits to his native homeland of Poland. Our Holy Mother told me this so we will understand the 'who' of the God we believe in. He is aware of the failures and weaknesses of man. They do not cause Him to turn His Face in repulsion. He knows that sinful people make mistakes that cause others to suffer. He even knows that some sicknesses and injuries are self-induced by many in hospitals and recuperating at home. And, He knows that some of them turn their heads skyward toward the heavens and ask Him why He did this to them, as if the storm, wind, and waves of life were His fault. The Father tries through His best patience to tell humanity that it is our fault, it is our sin, which has brought so much misery to humankind. He has been there to help all along, but has been shunned. This is why we have seen fair-faced Popes delivering strong messages about faith and morals, specifically iterated so as to protect the dignity of those they are addressing. This is why Bishops have been so precise and delicate in the wording of their pastoral letters, position papers, and ecclesial instructions so as not to bruise the reed or dowse the wick. Yet, there is time for angry words, blunt truth, and the turning over of tables as well. The Father always attempts to change sinful humanity through diplomacy first, and sometimes He waits decades or centuries before sending chastisement upon the segment who chooses not to listen, often asking the good to suffer these castigations along with the wicked for the salvation of all. We know the fruits of the Holy Spirit. We must think about the contrast between someone admitting a wrongdoing to a father they know to be understanding as opposed to one who is always condemning. Nevertheless, far too many fathers are accused of being dictatorial by people who are unashamed of their sins and deserve the flaming wrath of God Himself. These unjust indictments are simply the generic catch-all rebuttal that is selected from a mind with no hierarchical structure based on moral excellence. They are unremorseful for their sins and ignorant of the suffering they perpetuate, thinking defiantly, "How dare anyone address little ol' me like that? Who do they think they are?" Well, their accusers are evangelizers of the Saving Gospel who have been charged to speak the truth in season, as well as out of season when the wood has become dry and ready to become kindling in the fires of justice. The hierarchical structure of moral excellence is a living and growing thing. Read Mark 4:30-32. *"He said, "To what shall we compare the kingdom of God, or what parable can we use for it? It is like a mustard seed that, when it is sown in the ground, is the smallest of all the seeds on the earth. But once it is sown, it springs up and becomes the largest of plants and puts forth large branches, so that the birds of the sky can dwell in its shade."* It grows more spacious within us as we open and allow ourselves to be reoriented according to its designs, encompassing so many perspectives on issues of importance, even those of our national culture.

Sacramental forgiveness is the grace by which we become reoriented. It draws the openness from us because it requires us to invoke humility before man and God. Let us look at the process of sacramental forgiveness. It is apparent that the priest is there with the dispensation that the penitent is seeking. He possesses the healing within his ordained authority of absolution. He offers Jesus' pardon by virtue of his vocation. The penitent is not confessing to the priest, but to Jesus through the priest, while the priest is subject before God for the seal of confidentiality of the confessional. Consider this. If Jesus absolves a person and wipes their sins from existence so that they have never occurred, a priest would be lying before anyone whom he would tell about a sin that was supposedly committed. God would say to the priest, "You have borne false witness against your neighbor, because I have no record of any sin by the child you slander." This is how fatherly and protective the Heavenly Father is to His penitent children. It is the basis for the seal of the confessional. It protects the truth of the restored sinlessness. Both child and priest are protected in their dignity from a world that refuses to forgive. The seal of the confessional protects the dignity of that truth. New Life, indeed! Confession to a priest is a subject of contention for many people in their relationship to the Church. The Church has endured tremendous criticism for claiming that perfect absolution of our sins only comes through the sacramental confession to a priest ordained under Jesus' authority. There are millions of people on Earth who do not comprehend the concept of receiving the Sacrament of Penance as opposed to their asking for simple forgiveness in the privacy of their prayers. They do not realize that the Sacrament of Reconciliation is as ingrained in the Crucifixion as their ultimate Salvation. The statement that I just made must be underscored because it is the key that will lead millions to reconsider their entrance into the confessional. Our Lady says that the Sacrament of Confession is the ultimate forgiveness, the pinnacle of absolution to which no other act of absolution can compare. It is what changes the history of human sin. It is relevant to Catholics and non-Catholics alike, although non-Catholics would never be able to receive ultimate absolution of all their sins because they have yet to reconcile their opposition to the Roman Catholic Church by converting and accepting their part in its sacrificial nature and redemptive disciplines. They are yet like the young man of wealth walking away sullen after Jesus tells him what he must do to achieve perfection in everlasting life. The soul that has received forgiveness, who is absolved in the confessional after honestly confessing their sins from the purview of an ordered interior hierarchical structure based in moral excellence (a good examination of conscience), walks away from that Sacrament with the same Glory that springs from Jesus' Resurrection. It is not just the Catholic Church that testifies to the power of actual confession of sin to another person. Many in the Protestant world are coming to realize the efficacy in openly unburdening the soul to another person and performing the confession of sins, although their practices take place simply between faith-confidantes or spiritual friends. The difference lies in the fact that neither of those companions possesses the authority to absolve the penitent *in nomine Patris, et Filii, et Spiritus Sancti.*

I have been trying to highlight the wholly unique hierarchical structure supporting the thinking of faithful Roman Catholics from which we prioritize and order our lives according to the inspiration of the Holy Spirit. That hierarchy is manifested in the universal structure of the Catholic Church, a structure everyone can see, and many rage against. Every social problem, violation of the law, illicit practice, every crime, lie, and act of impurity comes from a disorientation in a person's structure of thought, where those thoughts have not received the molding and guiding influence of the Holy Spirit. Quite simply, our country is floundering in spiritual disorder, chaos, and sin because vast swathes of our population have rejected Jesus Christ; and those who have not known Him are swept into compliance with evil because godless secularism has become the most visible force dominating our culture. We are drawing forth from what is in us. Out of the mouth, the heart is speaking. Our actions reveal the priorities in our soul. And, the desolate results are nearly beyond any evidence that we can voluntarily mend our ways. A wholesale reordering needs to commence, and commence it will at the hands of the Woman Clothed with the Sun who will assist in closing out the mortal ages. Can we imagine what this means for people who are completely solidified in mentalities foreign to the Gospel, or those who have knowingly rejected Christ altogether? Everyone has ingrained in their minds the images of the Twin Towers of the World Trade Center in New York collapsing on the morning of September 11, 2001; the horror, the screeching whine of jet engines, the ground quaking, the rumbling of a seeming monster, and the paralyzing fear watching them reduced to dust in the span of minutes. It was an event that shocked the mental constitution of every citizen of this nation, and indeed, multitudes throughout the world. And then, an ominous awareness arose in foreign countries across the planet, sending them into cowering fear; just how would this all-powerful nation of warrior patriots exact justice against such a gruesome attack upon its fatherland? Now, can we imagine a reckoning from God so intense as to shove our nation's response into an afterthought in human history? Can we reckon an awakening so gargantuan that the mental constitution of the godless, indeed everything they believe about themselves and their lives, the structure of thinking they naively believe to be their support and stability, collapsing beneath them like the implosion of those towers? Politicians who maintain their support for abortion until that moment will wish they had never been born, especially those who claim to be Catholic. This helps us understand what the Gospel is referring to when it says that people will cry for the mountains to fall on them and the hills to cover them. For anyone who is filled with pride and seemingly fortified by a cerebral life of worldliness, materialism and sin, their world is going to come crashing down into a smoldering heap. Our Lady appears because She knows that She can help. She wishes for us to be pliable in spirit so that She can engage a merciful dismantling of our incorrect thinking, that we not be startled into a terror that would cause us to forsake Jesus' Mercy. She wishes to help us build a house that is a fortress against any evil that Satan could perpetrate. She wishes us to release our tight-fisted grip on our beliefs and attitudes so that She can either perfect the ones we have or cultivate newer and fresher ones that will flourish under Her care. She tells us that we can be forgiven, but we must seek the absolution found only in the confessionals of the Catholic Church. We can avoid the atrocities and the holocausts, the wars and the desolate aftermaths. We can find a common bond with our brothers. Humanity can believe in Jesus Christ!

I have never believed that anything I could ever write and say would have an effect on encouraging anyone forward in holiness. Left to myself, my testament carries no more weight than the opinions of anyone else, not even among my fellow faithsians. I am a nobody in the hierarchies of social, worldly or religious power. I have no fortune, title, unorthodox talents, and nothing where I could produce a venue for myself that would make my declarations possess any authority that they stand out in order to be heard, let alone obeyed. I realize the paradox wherein it is commonplace to dismiss individual voices, each as just another in a world of nearly seven billion voices, while knowing there is a Truth that every soul needs to hear and accept. I should have no hope, and instead believe that my life has been wasted according to the estimations of the world. But, the voice of the Virgin Mary has power! She augments everything that She has told me to relate. Everyone can see that it is Her grace behind and supporting the testament of the Morning Star Over America. If someone believes a person could create a like testament without the assistance of the Mother of Jesus Christ, then I say, let him stand forward and bring his resume for scrutiny. The Roman Catholic Church is the hierarchical structure of divinity that is embraced in the human constitution as the True Faith. It is the perfect orientation of the constitution of the human person. The foundation of this Faith is the Incarnation of Jesus Christ in human flesh, risen up upon the pillars of the Sacraments, described by angelic Dogmas, carried through time in Divine Traditions, personified in the lives of the Saints and Martyrs, animated in the faithful, shepherded by the priesthood, fortified by the Angels, empowered by the Holy Spirit, electrified by the miraculous intercession of the Queen of Heaven, and ordered by the Patriarchy of the Father to whom the Son submitted unto Death on a Cross. Wow, what a Church!

Saturday, May 23, 2009
Virgin Mary

"Now, My dear little children, you have engaged the awesome graciousness of the Lord by taking time to pray with Me for the conversion of lost sinners. We are assembled to change things, to make reparation for the actions of the lost, elevate the dignity of the oppressed, ensure the conversion of the wicked, and share in safeguarding the life of the unborn. We have manifested so much good in the past eighteen years and three months that it would take the hand of evil a trillion eternities to even think about undoing it. This is why I keep coming to you, My Special and Chosen ones. I wish to speak about the Church in America and around the world in the context of the Sacred Traditions, for they are what you behold as having adorned the modern Earth with the sacredness of the past. We have spoken about all the contemporary liberals who want the Church to become more effeminate and less demanding about compliance with the Holy Gospel. You have read My messages of the past decade, and you know how strongly about this I feel. For those who believe what I have said, they will recognize the stark contrast between the historical Church and its skeleton that exists in some places today. There are multiple reasons why so many have left the Church and others have decided not to enter. The priests and other religious are slowly succumbing to the secular forces that every day impact their consciousness. They work in an environment of competition against fashions and fanatics, and they are not allowed access to the inner-hearts of those they see. All the reasons I have explained to you since the turn of the century are applicable, and yet we are slowly gaining the members of the Church back. You have

said that you are too close to your work to see the power and magnitude of its ultimate impact, and this is true to a degree. However, that closeness also allows you to see how far away others are from the saving Sacraments of the Church. As I have said, even when one enters the vestibule, they can sense the panoramic dynamics of Jesus impact them. They know that their souls have taken another step closer to Heaven by simply walking down the nave. The Grace that allows them to sense this beauty is contained in your books, and that same Grace will usher them to the Holy Mass in droves. I have said that I always speak of things in the future that you must hope to see, but I promise that I am telling the truth.

You are about to enter the hottest summer days when the world will seem even more alive and boiling over. This seems natural to you because of the many years you have seen. There are many impassioned practices by humans everywhere, but very little of this energy is focused on making humanity more holy. We have plans that will eradicate this condition. You are still yet young, and there are multiple ways that you can deliver My messages to those who need them. Jesus awaits the transformation of public officials, physicians, counselors, and the like to take heed of the Gospel message and incorporate it into their work. Imagine the emphasis of My messages in public libraries and town halls, and in waiting rooms and on street corner kiosks. There is no reason to believe that this cannot happen. We are patient together as the Church is motivated to discern what I have said, make pronouncements about the urgency of My call, and decide how best to embrace and promulgate this miracle they are seeing. When Jesus asks you to wait in joyful hope for His return, He implies that you understand what it means for others to somehow stop their motion and realize what you have been doing here for almost 20 years. It is amazing if you think about it.

This, My Special one, brings Me to offering My profound congratulations on the article you wrote about the president speaking at Notre Dame university. I will pray with you that it be printed, but even if not soon, you can incorporate it in other works. Indeed, if the atheists at the newspaper refuse to print it, they will be as guilty as you stated in your text.

I wish not to tell you what will happen because Jesus wants you to live your life, with all the hopes, dreams, surprises, and fulfillment that comes with it. You surely see by now that there is awesome daring in what you have thus far achieved, and the final goal is the conversion of the lost. The Lord will use any venue of His choosing to soften the hearts of humanity."

Letter to The State Journal Register
Springfield, Illinois
May 20, 2009

The recent Notre Dame university commencement ceremony brought our religious divisions into bold relief. Pundits filled the airwaves with secular and political opinions. Reporters scooped the diametric opposition between feuding camps. And, television companies generated time-slot filler between commercials to bolster their bottom lines; yet again this morning, we awoke to doctors using their God-given abilities to terminate the lives of unborn babies in the gestating confines of their mothers' wombs.

Our society is a house that is confused, combative and divided against itself over the issue of abortion, with many calling it murder, while others calling it reproductive healthcare choice, leaving human life snuffed-out in the breach. Every great religion encourages people to protect the precious child growing in the womb, even while being shouted down by throngs of women who refuse to consider anything but a way out of their maternal responsibilities and the perceived sacrifice of material comfort and financial ambition.

Contrary to what President Obama said at West Bend, there is no common ground between death and life; and notwithstanding the noble yet often heated debate, there will inevitably come a time for the truth to prevail. It may come through prophetic leadership or regrettably through horrific battles for righteousness, but mankind will be forced to concede that human life inherently embodies rights, and it demands its unequivocal preservation by its veritable existence.

There is a day in the offing when our more enlightened posterity will peer back through time with a perplexed gaze, much like we study darkened history, bewildered at the audacity of those who defended slavery. Our successors will be incredulous at how the atrocity of abortion could have festered in this land without substantial opposition. They will review media footage of today's mentally deranged feminists, faces contorted in rage, waving their placards and tossing their undergarments, bellowing their cadenced slogans; and they will be bewildered how such a gender could have become so lost.

Our moribund social legacy is already etched into history with the consent of nearly every First Amendment advocate. Our conviction as exterminators of innocent human life is inevitable by that age of moral sensibility. If this does not give us pause to measure what we are doing, what will?

Our contemporary civic vita is destined to reveal morally deranged throngs who legalized the slaughter of over 60 million children through medical infanticide with barely a whimper of meaningful opposition from anyone who holds a seat of public sway. In the midst of this moral blindness, the righteous are left to stand peacefully beside highways with their own placards, pray passively at the gates of abortion clinics, have their editorial letters either edited or disregarded by atheists, and endure mocking as fanatics because they dared to prick the conscience of those whose duty it was to preserve us from such iniquity.

Heroism, righteousness and nobility have always been defined by those who sacrificed themselves and their personal ease to defend our posterity. How many warriors have returned to our homeland afflicted, debilitated, and dismembered so their children would have a future marked by peace? They engaged battles that were not necessarily their own.

And, as if stricken by a bipolar disorder, we defend instead those who refuse to accept the moral imperative to sacrifice their comforts so their children may live. And, somehow our cultural elite spurn any meaningful deliberation about this ominous contrast and the definitive judgement of the ages which will convict us as surely as the sun gives light to the day.

Henry Clay, the 19th century American statesman, once spoke of his times and those who wished to obscure the moral outrage of slavery. *"It is not this society which has produced the great moral revolution which the age exhibits. What would they, who thus reproach us, have done? …They must blow out the moral lights around us and extinguish that greatest torch of all which America presents to a benighted world---pointing the way to their rights, their liberties, and their happiness.*

And when they have achieved all those purposes, their work will be yet incomplete. They must penetrate the human soul and eradicate the light of reason and the love of liberty. Then, and not till then, when universal darkness and despair prevail, can you perpetuate slavery and repress all sympathy and all humane and benevolent efforts among free men in behalf of the unhappy portion of our race doomed to bondage."

Henry Clay would have spoken thus to our age about those who would enshrine a woman's right to kill her unborn child.

- William L. Roth Jr.

The rise of a radical feminist ideology targeted against the patriarchy of God and the metastasizing of the concept of "freedom of choice," unhinged from the priority and order of sacrificial moral excellence, have been two components that have enshrined a culture of selfishness and death within our society. They are outwardly characterized by differing manifestations of outright evil throughout the diversity of our culture, but no more deified than in the fanatical claims to the right to slaughter children in the womb. Further, if you spend two generations, perhaps three, spewing hatred of men at every opportunity and accomplish a wiping-out of the paternal-maternal hierarchy of the family, is it any wonder that there is so little mutual love and virtuous stability left between husbands and wives, a catastrophe allowing divorce to plague our nation, tearing families to pieces and destroying the environment where children develop their hierarchy of moral excellence? I have not lost hope that abortion will end or that this subculture of defiant women will find their true dignity in their imitation of the Most Holy Virgin. Neither have I lost hope that children can once again become beneficiaries of the wisdom that would lead them to happiness, prosperity, and ultimately to their own noble sacrifices that would confirm their acceptance of the Divine Mercy of Jesus Christ as their Savior. The end of all abomination is inevitable. The flushing out of all that is evil will arrive in the coming Reckoning. My concern, as is Our Lady's, lies in the future of those who will not repent at having cooperated with such hideous evil, who forward lies of such aggressive darkness. The Good News is that all can be forgiven. All human sin can be wiped from the memory of Creation, but those responsible must repent and retreat from the course they are set upon. Having their own hierarchy of understanding based in moral excellence would tell them this. There is a very delicate bridge just past the veil of mortality that allows only the childlike of heart to cross. *"Unless you change and become like a little child, you will not enter the Kingdom of Heaven."* [Matthew 18:3] Sins are very heavy, and when sinners try to cross that bridge refusing to relinquish them beforehand, the bridge will collapse beneath their feet and they will plummet to the place of fire they confirmed as their choice throughout their lives. This is why Our Lady is so emphatic that everyone repent and confess their sins to Her Son, Jesus, who will take them away by the power of His Sacrifice on the Cross, after which His command will be to go and sin no more. The truth that Our Lady is trying to get us to accept through Her spiritual imagery is that the interior hierarchical structure is actually a "ladder," an avenue of ascension from the base instincts of our sinful human nature into the domain of noble saintly greatness that is our actual identity in the highest orders of the Kingdom of God. This ladder, if we but allow Her to construct it within us, provides access to the highest dignity, identity and purpose of the human person. The consequences of our sins fall away and the Earth will become a new creation, defined by a pristine nature enveloping our soul. We must build-up the hierarchy of Jesus Christ so that everyone has access to the sweet words of the "better angels of our nature" who flutter in delight above us, hoping to alight within the branches of our wisdom. Let it be known that cowering before darkness is not part of that betterment.

Our moral conscience, our didactic conscience, is the voice and inspiration of the Holy Spirit that travels down the ladder of our interior hierarchy from the highest identity of our being that is always in communion with God. But, those who enter into deep states of sin, usually through a life of omission and aggression, will render their conscience dead to them, because they have no ladder into the patriarchal domain of the Father. Everyone has seen examples where people have perpetrated heinous acts of gruesome evil beyond our capacity to even understand, who also portray a macabre sense of peace about themselves, a complete detachment from the higher orders of the human spirit such as empathy and compassion, even respect for human life. We see this vacuous psychological void in abortion doctors or Supreme Court justices in television interviews, speaking analytically and intellectually about these barbarous acts of outright infanticide as if they were simply the removal of a wart. Those who have no ladder allowing them access to the higher plateaus of their being are dead souls who have no life in them. Even when God works miraculously and transcends the distance with His moral voice of clarity, they ignore these powerful movements in their soul as being no more than agitating thoughts, summarily dismissing them as they have habitually trained themselves to do. They hear nothing interiorly of any consequence to the reality of their existence but the noise generated by the collage of their worldly self-will and egoism. Satan moves to own them and dictate their being according to his diabolical prescriptions which will ultimately damn them. And, in most cases, the devil does not spur these people to perform great visual acts of horror, such as abortion, he encourages them simply to remain indifferent toward things of the heart in the first order, persist in being purposely non-compliant with anything virtuous in the second order, and inevitably to become clandestinely aggressive toward

Christian faith with their wealth and power in the final order. Is it any wonder that the abortion industry is so well funded by successful people who also happen to be the most aggressive against the Catholic Church? Their souls are dead. They serve the beast. It is one great simmering cauldron of hideous moral rot that is headed for the furnace of eternal fire. They have no ladder of ascension within them by which God could draw them toward their own redemption. Hence, they will never see the Paradise of God. Our Lady said to me, "The indifference of one atheist kills more hope than all the tyrants who will walk the face of the Earth." So, you see, people who have no interior hierarchy based in moral excellence do have a voice within them sometimes, but there is no volume to the moral conscience that comes from the Holy Spirit that would allow the stark contrast to be drawn to bring them to convert their hearts.

Then, comes the miracles. Then, comes the reality of prayer. Then, comes Our Lady. She has spoken for centuries to humanity through Her messengers and seers, seeking our compliance with Her pleas that we pray from the heart. Prayer creates the ladder of ascension within us. When we enter into prayer with Our Lady, especially through the recitation of the Most Holy Rosary, the miracle happens. We clear the interior landscape of the secular collage, and in doing so, eradicate the "voices" that are generated by this world that distract us. Anyone can experience what I am speaking of by beginning to pray the Rosary and take note how many times our minds wander into thoughts having nothing to do with our prayers to God. These are the voices whose origin is in the secular collage, having nothing to do with the ladder of ascension. Prayer places us into a state of being separated from the world for a time so that we can open ourselves to become recipients of what is above in the highest potentials of who we were created to be. Prayer unites us with the realms of the Holy Spirit who gladly descends the thoroughfare of the heart that we have constructed for Him. Those who never take time to kneel before God and offer Him adoration from a bountiful heart are passing through life, forfeiting every opportunity for elevation into their identity as children of God. It is like an airplane rolling down a runway that never takes-off into the sky. It is failing the function for which it was created. It forsakes its truest identity. When we pray, the Holy Spirit forms us if we are coming of age, and recreates us if we already have been deeply impressed by the errors of the world. It allows us access to the Light beyond our passage from exile so that we can begin to see ourselves for who we really are—made in the image and likeness of God as His children. We have capacities through His Spirit that are considered superhuman by modern social thinkers. Consider again the pregnant mother declining life-saving care in order to protect her yet unborn child in her womb, and sacrificing her life in the process of giving life. See also where the secular world has conceded that sexual purity is beyond the capability of the human person. Societal pundits mock its mere mention, while we Catholics recognize that, through God's Spirit, we can respect our bodies as the temples of the Holy Spirit and remain conformed to the disciplines that make our lives fruitful in the designs of His Kingdom and the language of Creation. We are prosperous in grace while they wallow in obscenity and licentiousness. We can forgive when they scream for revenge. We can love our enemies when all voices around us say we must maintain enmity with our neighbors. We speak the Truth of human Redemption in Jesus Christ when every seat of power is telling us to reject Our Lord for the sake of worldly peace. These are all Godlike feats of grace that issue from the highest nobility of our beings that unrepentant sinners cannot justify or generate from themselves. Zestful living with a great sense of moral excellence means that we have learned to overcome our anxieties, emotions, and impediments through our unabridged trust in what we know Jesus Christ is capable of doing. He can turn the whole world upside down by snapping His fingers, but He wants our footsteps to ramp-up the beat. Our communication with Heaven is humanity's rosin on the bow of everlasting life and the means by which our thoughts and prayers are attuned to the mind of God. All we have to do is look around at the moral depravity of this world to realize that the good Lord Jesus must be the most patient individual who ever lived. I am beginning to wonder, however, whether that patience has finally worn thin. We as Christians should not minimize or trivialize what this might portend for an unsuspecting humanity and the exiled Church. It is all rather simply really. We were born into an exiled world with no hope of ever grasping our highest identity; doomed to never rise from our deaths into the pantheon of eternal greatness. Then, Jesus came. A baby in a manger belonging to livestock changed the entire history of man. Seats were pulled back from the Feast Table of Paradise by the Angels, and God declared to Creation with the mighty Heart of His Son for all us to come and sit down. He made it possible by His Death and Resurrection for us to be engaged and united with His Father once again, to be remade into His image and likeness through a merciful absolution of our soul and an enlivening of our spirit with His own. He gave us spiritual senses that we could employ to speak to Him, to hear Him, to feel His presence, to bask in His comfort, to recognize His Will, and to adopt His strength to remain in communion with Him in these realms of exile until we meet Him face-to-face. This is the framework of perspective that is the only authentic reality that the world has ever known. All the rest is worldly illusion that shall pass at the end of time. The most thoughtful Ancients sensed their supernal identity in their contemplations of existence. They asked probing questions about the composition of life and the meaning of their passing. Do we realize that they all sit back now and laugh together at how prescient they were of Jesus' magnificent grace? They knew better than today's loud-mouth speculators how special is the life of man, and that we are not just some passing phenomenon that will become extinguished with the closing of our eyes in death. Their hearts told them that there was something altogether greater than what their eyes would take-in before that moment. The blessed Prophets lived in longing need to share their otherworldly experiences, hearts bleeding with the knowledge of the great Unknowable God. The Almighty Father revealed His beatific character in His supernatural relationship with Abraham and Moses. He commanded His motives and prescriptions for barbarians and brutes to be elevated to thrones of decency and decorum. And then, the Son of God made it all clear and accessible to every breathing person by offering a Sacrifice that would shake the universe, hoping that we would be awed and humbled before an event that would destroy the meaning of time altogether. Nothing more apocalyptic, meaning revealing, can ever be accomplished by a human being than the events of Good Friday and Easter Sunday. With all due respect, what can any other religion contribute to this salvific spectacle? It was the complete Revelation of the Love of God as a human being, matched by no messenger, prophet, swami, rabbi, imam, or guru since; the ultimate definition of humanity that resides in us as our truest identity. We are children and heirs of this Love, and by invoking the power of faith in all that Christ revealed we can begin to see clearly within us the power of Heaven that we can draw upon in every moment to remake the face of the Earth. We see the hierarchy within us where God is paternal Love. Every single human being can see the Light of eternal existence in their heart. But, Jesus asks us to do more than simply see the Light. He asks us to become the light, to imitate Him by accepting the Cross upon which He died, and shoulder our own. Millions do not yet know that Jesus is the one whom they see in their heart as that Love. He is the Love; and everything the Church has attempted to accomplish for the last 2000 years is to reveal that Love to each person it encounters through the absolution it extends to any humble soul, and the admonishments it has leveled as a call for humanity to come out of the darkness. The Church has tried to defend Love anywhere it has tried to grow. And, it has been against anything that has attempted to impede or damage that Love. The Church is willing to fight when required because it stands for the truth that brings peace. It is the sole beacon of eternal life whose liturgical prayers are the grand staircase that we all must ascend. Internal ladders and grand staircases. These are the pathways to success, to the revelation of the perfect chosen race, the people set apart, consecrated in the Sacrifice of Jesus, His Blood flowing down and wiping away all that would separate us from the Paradise that exists as an emanation of His Love.

Let us pray:

Jesus, without your love we would be like ships out of water; with no foundation, no purpose or direction; our lives would be lightless and seedless, shed of hope and shorn of innocence. Our memories are but brief outlines of the way life used to be, while we scribble the margins with regrets about the way it should have been. We are still young foals and fledglings in your arms, little foxes gnawing at your door; and we search for moments that make things right, all the arts and elements that soften the hardened, smooth the gritty, square the corners, and round the edges. Our years in exile pass too soon, as if clicking through a turnstile; they slip away, so bereft of sanctification, they tend to blur into one. We pray that you will score us clean of whatever tarnishes our souls without leaving too many scars, without allowing our faith to become fodder for the world's worst cynics, without giving us apprehension that we have not done enough. You manifest our completion in all good things. You finish us finely and set us out like kindling across the Earth so in need of the fires of your love. Let us never resist your advances, come what may, during hours of joy or sadness, whatever clouds our eyes, whenever we are feasting in joy or fasting in hope. Help us remember you just as the Father has never forgotten us. Reap from our prayers a fortune of real redemption, and feed the hungry from the work of our hands. Most of all, dear Jesus, make us holy; make us pure and simple, pretty as flowers, fragrant, sweet, gentle, encouraging, satisfying, and sincere. Hear our confessions and cultivate in us everything that Heaven wants us to be. Rescind our dying and bless our living. Call us back to you when we are wandering; render us lame should we go astray; mute our voices if we speak in error, and give rise to the Kingdom taking root in our hearts. Amen.

Three Moral Majors
of
Roman Catholicism

I. Monopolist for Redemptive Revelation

"...(and) when the Son of Man looks lastly upon this world with eyes so fragrant and convincing, we will realize beyond any shadow that His gaze has validated our faith, that we have echoed the arpeggio of the ages that magnify our redemption in ways more replete than the heavens. Therefore, if we defy every obstacle and speel every mountain that stands between us and that faith, we will not only win the battle, we will enshrine the victory itself."

The Mother of Jesus Christ has spoken with me at length about many subjects related to the redemption of humankind, and how I might organize Her thoughts for delivery so that greater Light can be brought into the lives of men. She discussed with me three "moral majors" of preeminent Truth regarding Messianic Redemption as the Holy Spirit has wished to effect it. While it is obvious that the concentricity of the Church is important, and the Seven Sacraments are imperative for the purification and preservation of the human soul, they are not among the Three Moral Majors that She wished to be highlighted. It is not that the others are not moral imperatives, I am simply saying that there are three other majors upon which the Queen of Heaven wishes that we also focus our attention. The first of Three Moral Majors that can only be procured and provided by the Roman Catholic Church is that the Apostolic Church alone is the Monopolist for Redemptive Revelation. The Roman Catholic Church is the only entity commissioned by Christ to pursue a Monopoly of Salvation in the exiled world. There is no other savior than Jesus Christ. The Savior is Jesus Christ. Jesus Christ founded the Original Apostolic Church on

Saint Peter the Rock. No other church has the legitimacy to make this claim. This Rock cannot be protested against without offense to the Father. Jesus commissioned the First Apostles to indeed make apostles and disciples of all men and nations. Jesus told His disciples to work for the unification of all peoples in Him through His Crucifixion and Resurrection. He instructed Peter—the Foundation of the Church—to teach, preach, and apprise in His Holy Name. There was only one Saint Peter. There has been only one recognized successor living at a time since the original Rock of the Church. Saint Peter and the power of the Papacy has lived in each successor, handed-down through the ages by the invocation of the Holy Spirit. Hence, the term 'Monopoly' implies that all sinners must be reconciled with God through the Apostolic Church headed by Saint Peter and his successors to the exclusion of all other faiths and beliefs. Now, there is much more to this than the simple framework of the Hierarchy comprising the consistency of the Catholic Church through the epochs of time. Inherent in this one Church is the superstructure of all immortal 'being.' Those who stray from the Original Apostolic Church lose touch with the Immortal Being of God. Those who wander into other beliefs, or into none at all, are not fed by the Seven Sacraments, and they are therefore starved for Truth. Hence, this leads to Our Lady's ancillary discussion of the difference between evangelicals and evangelizers. The Roman Catholic Church is not considered to be evangelical for a specific reason, mainly because it is the Holy Spirit that calls lost souls to the Cross, made tangible and communicable through the Holy Mass, and not any one preaching person whose message is devoid of those Sacraments. There is no concentric Bread of Life in churches separated from the Original Holy Catholic and Apostolic Church, and this is the emptiness that resounds in the testament of evangelicals; the void that all of them see in one another as non-Catholics. Anyone can be a nice, caring, sharing person, even those who do not believe in God. However, being congenial and sharing does not make someone a Christian. Further, being a Christian in name does not make someone Catholic. The point to be made is that all the Popes, priests, and mystics throughout the centuries have attempted to prove that, without the Holy Sacrifice of the Mass, there can be no true allegiance to the Cross. The Holy Mass is the centerpiece of the Crucifixion that has saved those who believe. Hence, the difference between being an evangelical and an evangelizer is that the former is of ungrounded Protestant partisanship founded in protestation of the Holy Spirit, while the latter is the esteemed character of the Roman Catholic Church. I am not parsing syllables when I say this because the distinctions are notable. The former is a sectarian division, the latter is based on universal Truth. The Spirit of Evangelization emanates from a life in accourse with the universal Truth of God, while being evangelical is little more than babbling about a life which the speaker truly refuses to accept. Protestant ministers will never fulfill the command of Sacred Scripture to lead their flocks to the Eucharistic Bread of Life at the Altars of the Roman Catholic Church; therefore their evangelical rhetoric is hollow. True Christianity is Roman Catholicism, all who are in allegiance to the Vicar of Christ in Rome. I am not speaking about those who simply recognize who he is, or who consider him to be a good person and the like, but all who acknowledge that he is the Holy See for the world on behalf of Heaven, and all who thereafter take the necessary steps to convert to Catholicism of their own accord. Belonging to the Roman Catholic Church implies that you are the sacred property of God. The Catholic Church does not belong to its people, the people belong to the Church. We are the conscripted entity whom Christ died to save. And, while there are stringent properties and responsibilities inherent to this ownership, it also means that the members of the Roman Catholic Church simultaneously belong to God. Heaven is our inheritance, so we claim ownership of Heaven as we are concurrently repatriated to the side of the Father. This is indeed a beatific Monopoly. The Father and the Son have effectively set-out into the world through the Incarnate Being of Jesus and the invincible power of the Holy Spirit to claim all living creatures for the Will of that Father.

Let us consider what this Monopoly implicates for the future of men. There is no deliverance into Heaven without the Salvation obtained through the Monopoly. This certainly implies that anyone with full knowledge who wilfully denies this Monopoly is destined for Hell. And, those who would vainly attempt to compete with this Monopoly are committing blasphemy, and they are also destined for Hell. Anyone who would claim deliverance through the Savior of the World without first engaging and living His Commandments and Gospel is materially and spiritually separated from the Kingdom to Come. Ministers and preachers whose edicts and decrees lead the innocent away from the Truth, the Way, and the Life are destined for Hell. There is no bargaining or negotiating with God that could cause or bring Him to change His mind about His Monopoly of Messianic Salvation to make it instead some humanistic fraternity of pluralism where everyone is admitted to Paradise because they were nice to their friends. This is not what Jesus' life was about at all. No human person in body or spirit has the power to dissect or dilute the Lord's intention to deliver His Original Church intact into His presence upon the Final Judgement of Jesus Christ. The Catholic Church has by the sovereign power vested into its prayers the right to claim lost souls for Heaven and dispense eternal Absolution upon those who repent. The Monopoly of the Roman Catholic Church implies that the Church stands in the fullness of grace and light beyond the horizons of mortality with Jesus Christ at the Victory of the completion of the world. This sacred Monopoly permits the Church to unilaterally mandate theory, practical thought and conduct for those who profess to believe the Faith it evangelizes. The Roman Catholic Church can expel anyone who teaches or lives in ways that contradict the teachings of Jesus Christ, and it is not a sign of lack of mercy to do so. The Roman Catholic Church can invoke the intercession of the Angels and Saints in ways unknown to those who do not accept its tenets, and these Angels and Saints will respond. Yes, the Roman Catholic Church is a Monopoly in the physical realms, working for the unification of all men in the Afterlife without regret or apology, responsible to no other powers or principalities, answerable to no secular governments, and designed and destined to remain unified here and now, and in the Church Triumphant, for the multiplication of the eternal ages. The Church will never surrender to any other origin; it not only lacks the desire to do so, it does not even have the capacity to surrender to any other dominion.

Men and women who are the true evangelizers in allegiance to the Roman Catholic Church take an oath to be the Lord's agents and representatives here in this life. This is not a license, it is a commission that is capable of withstanding the onslaught expected from all enemies, adversaries, and detractors. While the Holy Spirit can speak through non-members of the Church, that same Holy Spirit will bring all to whom sacred knowledge is given to the foot of the Cross where the Original Catholic Apostolic Church is stationed and sanctioned. Let me repeat that this is a Monopoly. There are no other limbs or branches, no subcategories, elements, or sects, no other entities whatsoever that could be visualized or imagined as being complementary to the unity of the Church. The Catholic Church is one, and there are no others. The One Table of Faith rests within its circumference of grace. It is imperative for all mankind to realize that it is through these things that the Church has prevailed for 2000 years. Even made-up of sinners, the Church has completed a perfect mission. Its purpose is to refine those who call themselves Catholic, and convert all who do not. Therefore, the Monopoly of the Roman Catholic Church will deliver the Mystical Body of Jesus to the presence of the Father as itself. Just like the Transfiguration on Mount Tabor, Jesus is glorifying humanity through Himself, and humanity is elevated and perfected in Him as His Mystical Body. Our Lady asks for all who will eventually hear these words to dare not speak harshly about the Roman Catholic Church or those who have been commanded to defend her honor. She declares that miracles will be wrought at the invocation of the evangelizers, and we will see miracles of transformation abound in this life and the next. And yet, there is hell to come. There are bloodbaths and agony in the future of man. There are annihilations and outright onslaughts. But, the Monopoly of the Roman Catholic Church will be unfazed. The Church will not be deterred. The faithful will keep their faces to the wind. The true evangelizers will never lose sight of the grand Light of Redemptive Love. There will be snarls and growls from those who refuse to believe. They will plead with God's witnesses and call themselves victims of the devil, but if they do not change according to the words spoken to them, they will remain the devil's victims with no compassion to hide them. In the end, there will be no mercy on those who refuse to fight against the very evil that holds them in its grasp. Everyone has been given both the will and the willpower to escape the influences of Satan and choose to accept the salvific balm of Christ's Love. The Monopoly of the Roman Catholic Church gives eyesight and vision to those who will see. It grants Eternal Life. Everything else is just an illusion. All other enticements and persuasions are the work of Lucifer. Unrepentant sinners do not realize how utterly lost they are. They have not only abandoned God, they are betraying themselves.

II. Custodian and Steward of Apostolic Faith

"Masterful God, with divine reason we acclaim your holy name and dedicate this world to the Scepter of your Providence. Cleanse and remake us in your likeness. Deepen the furrows of our sacrifices that your Will might be embedded in our being. Help us become creatures of the light, willing to shed the darkness of our exile. Absolve us of our sinfulness and lift our hearts into the infinity of your love. Remember those who have died and restore them to everlasting life. Hear our petitions in union with your Immaculate Mother, and grant us the humility exemplified by her life. We ask this through Christ Our Lord. Amen."

We speak of duty and honor as inseparable tenets of the Christian conscience because they are like legs upholding the ladder of ascendance with which we grow in our acceptance of the Faith. Even young children learn what these dignified qualities mean from their brothers and elders so as to instill this discipline in them from a very young age. If a person is given responsibility, it implies that he is trusted to carry out the mission to which he has been assigned. This is how Jesus—the Head of the Church—came Incarnate into this world to commission His own followers. He has entrusted in our care the responsibility for transferring the knowledge of the Gospel throughout the ages, that it arrives back in His beatific library in Heaven intact and fully honored. This highlights the foundation of the Second Moral Major: The Roman Catholic Church has always been the Custodian and Steward of Apostolic Faith to which generations and centuries have dedicated their lives and the substance of their being. Taking custody. This implies taking control by power vested and applied from the Great High Priest on His behalf while He remains here with us in Spirit. Thus, what does control mean? Control leads to the stewardship. To be a good steward implies that we handle something carefully and thoughtfully, respectfully and with a firm conscience toward preservation. And, in order to do this, our stewardship must always be comprised of deference to the Head of the Church. Through the power of the Holy Spirit in our hearts, Christ Jesus serves the Church as its Master. There is no doubt that there have also been different opinions about the composition of the Apostolic Faith. There have even been contrasting definitions. The Apostolic Faith embodies the conceptual definition of the role of the Roman Catholic Church. It is both action and description. Here, we comprehend the meaning of custody and stewardship in both theological and practical terms. While the Catholic Church is the Monopolist that preserves the integrity and defends the dignity of the teachings of Jesus Christ, the Church also holds in its own hands the responsibility for never allowing itself to be assaulted or denigrated by any outside force. It cannot surrender its supernal monopolist authority to the democratic whims of any cohort of sinners or other manipulative totalitarians. Hence, the Church is its own shield against the wickedness and snares of the devil because the Church in all three forms is the Mystical Body of its Head. Now, in light of this preeminent premise for custodial leadership and dignified stewardship of the vineyard demarcated by Christ, it is important to place this basis in the context of time and space. This is indeed where the free will of pious men applies its own strength and vision, its own version of sacrificial love within the exilic parameters of the Earth. This is what makes humanity's free will a force for good. This free will need not be a hindrance in the conversion of the wicked and the ferreting-out of those who would do it good and might otherwise do it harm. Therefore, custodial leadership and dignified stewardship can only be procured through allegiance to the Cross and a firm affirmation in the Resurrection of Jesus from the Tomb. It is through these two keys that the lockbox of human redemption is made open to those pining to get in. It is this custodial power that Jesus handed Saint Peter when He declared that the Church would be stationed on him. Jesus knew that Peter, even though Peter had denied Him in the moment, would be a worthy custodian and steward for those times and our time. Saint Peter was a sinner. All the Popes have been sinners. But, their conviction in and proclamation of matters of faith and morals have always been infallible. This same infallibility of holy love is transferable to all who believe. All become custodians and stewards of the Apostolic Faith simply by practicing and believing in the tenets of the Roman Catholic Church.

The distinction being made is that the custodial leadership and dignified stewardship of the Apostolic Faith is not concentrated in anyone who is not Roman Catholic or in those who are not in harmony with the Roman Catholic Pontiff. It is head-centered as much as the Salvation of the whole of the world is head-centered. I say this not in the sense of intellectual scope, but rather, Apostolic scope in the lineage of the Saints. Jesus Christ is the Head of the Church in this world and the next, and the Pope of the Roman Catholic Church is the custodian and steward of the Apostolic Faith here in this life, dispatched and transmitted to all who are obedient to the Pope. This makes little popes of all who believe in the Roman Catholic Papacy. This is how a new Pope can be culled even from the ranks of the male laity. It could not be done otherwise. The Great High Priest Jesus Christ reserves the right to commission any man He pleases to serve as maintainer of the faith of many in a world of many. Please think about it in these terms. Jesus made Apostles of lay men. He ordained them as Bishops upon the utterance of His Word. And, He continues to instill in all who believe in Him the same genuine desire to uphold the tenets of His Gospel with equal measure.

And, what can be seen of this power? One great example is Saint Francis of Assisi. Saint Francis made a leader of himself by importing into his life the mission of the Church and tendering his own free will as a servant of the masses. This was done through his acceptance of the Will of God that supplanted his own. He grasped a share of the Apostleship of the Popes in his day and laid-down a record of piety and humility that has been unmatched by all but a few. We become custodians and stewards of the Apostolic Faith as members of the Roman Catholic Church. This cannot occur if one lacks commitment. It will not be made manifest if we choose to piece-meal our faith in Jesus according to the whims of other objectives. Like Saint Francis, we give our lives to Jesus altogether to the point that others look at us mesmerized at how one could be so committed to the highest possibilities of man without reserve. This is our appropriation of the power of Jesus Christ to be a force for good in the modern world, and it is proof that we are exhibiting Jesus' mandate that His disciples should go out into the world two-by-two and teach and preach the Holy Gospel with confidence. The point to be made is that when people hand their will over to God, they will be led by the Wisdom of the Holy Spirit instead of their own prerogatives for the way life ought to be lived. This offsets the fact that people are sinners. They become a new creation, imbued with divine Light and wisdom, and it is the way that the Pontiff can be infallible in the faith and morality of the Church, indeed of human life entire. The fact that humanity is imperfect is irrelevant here because all men and women are in the process of being perfected in Jesus, who is the Head of the Church. It is as though we become aware of the true power of our Baptism, Confirmation, and the Sacrament of Confession by seeing for ourselves that we have been set free from sin, and are on course, living the new perfection that we have inherited. Here again, this is power that can only be appropriated by practicing Roman Catholic people. Why? Because the custody and stewardship of the Apostolic Faith has been deposited there. It is the Christological cornerstone of the Monopolist nature of the Catholic Church, described and applied in operational terms. As I have written before, the Catholic Church teaches what it believes, because it believes what it teaches; and it has the sovereign right to testify that it moves through time and space with the authority of the direct Will of God.

III. Vessel and Visionary of Theological Truth

Our Lady's Immaculate Heart is deeply filled with eternal triumphalism when She comes to speak because She is inspired with happiness at seeing Her children moving into the vestibule of Heaven where we can be reunited with Her forever. We must realize that we bring Her ecstasy when we are admiring of Her Son and affectionate toward Her. Our spiritual consecrations to follow the teachings of the Catholic Church and the dignity of Jesus' Sacred Heart and Her Immaculate Heart set us aside as among the most dignified souls in the material world. Our faith encompasses not only what the Catholic Church believes, but everything we believe that complements and augments its mission, its mystical grace, and its everlasting joy. This is the magnification that Our Lady sings of in Her Magnificat. Therefore, She wishes everyone to know the Third Moral Major: The Roman Catholic Church is the Vessel and Visionary of Theological Truth. Even as She has instructed us that the first two Moral Majors are not complicated to understand, neither is the third, although it contains all the attributes of this trinity combined, and therefore is simultaneously comprised of the first and second Moral Majors. It is not unlike the Most Blessed Trinity itself standing alone as one deific purpose, as the Godhead is concurrently comprised of three distinct parts. Having said these things, Our Lady submits that we can imagine that Theological Truth is inclusive of the Church's Monopolist role and its role as Custodian and Steward. The Vessel and Visionary of Theological Truth is the Church's overall mission. Every facet of contact between God and man and Heaven and Earth is harbored in and protected by its existence, its perpetual existence; and its connection to the higher plateaus and infinite ages begins here for all the faithful. Moreover, it is not practical to divide the Church's composition as Vessel and Visionary as though they are somehow exclusive of each other. This vision comes from the Deposit of Wisdom that has been granted by the Father through the

Son, and the Church receives this Wisdom as His Vessel. This is one of the reasons that the Vatican is referred-to as the Holy See. This is the Visionary aspect of the Church under the leadership of the Pope, who is the Vicar of Christ. We could speak for hours about theology and its cerebral dimensions, but this is not the point. The fact that the Theological Truth has been deposited into the Roman Catholic Church, and only the Church, is the point to be made. There are countless implications to this definitive proclamation. People ask whether the Holy Spirit works through Protestant denominations, and whether their faith and good works are in alignment with the Eternal Father. The answer is that prayer and good works come through the suffering of the Roman Catholic Church. God inspires prayers and good works wherever they may be seen because He sees in Heaven the sacrifices of the Catholic Church and responds to its prayers. Good works can be performed by both people of faith and those who practice no faith, but the Spirit that is initiating those works is being called upon them in answer to the prayers and penances intoned by the Catholic Church. And, in saying this, it is made clear that those who possess the Apostolic Faith can commend themselves to intercession before God for the accomplishment of conversion and good works, knowing that their duties and sacrifices are founded in and resultant from their identification with Jesus on the Cross. [John 16:26-27] We become animated vessels and visionaries of the theological truth characterized and unified in its wholeness as the Mystical Body of Christ.

Hence, the terms Vessel and Visionary are reserved as two-pillared descriptions of the Theology of the Roman Catholic Church. The latter flows from the first at the same time they are each interchangeable. Something so profound and beyond mortal parameters is difficult to describe in the same way that the Most Blessed Trinity is not easy to describe. It is necessary to make clear that the Catholic Church is the genesis of exemplary action in the way of Jesus for all humanity, and those of other denominations who act likewise are repeating the example of the Original Apostolic Church. They are imitators of the original. One is the sound of grace, and the other its echo. The reason Our Lady has been very careful in drawing these kinds of distinctions in Her other messages to the world is because the process of the cultivation of the Earth is delicate. All that is beautiful is growing amidst the weeds. She does not want to drive others away who would be offended by the thought of their faith in Jesus not appearing authentic. She knows they are doing the best they can at the moment. We must remember that She is trying to draw all men to the Holy Eucharist without granting Satan an opportunity to confuse Her children anymore radically. While one does not set out to increase someone's faith by telling them that the power of their faith judgement is wrong, it must not deter any true evangelizer from annunciating the Truth that sent Our Lord to the Cross. Most of these people have simply been misled by their forbears and have taken upon themselves the cloak of pride in their families' legacies. Indeed, when these people see others with no faith at all following the teachings of the Catholic Church with honesty and authentic conviction, they will be more inclined to convert themselves. Notice that I am not saying that non-Catholics who believe in God and pray every day are bad people; they are simply misled about a beatific truth that Satan has been working day and night for millennia to obscure. This is the reason they must begin to think of Jesus' Original Church as the Universal Church under the guidance of one Vicar. If they rouse themselves from the protesting platitudes which define their environment and their doctrine, then study this in the context of the whole world, they will begin to see. History will teach them. The writings of the Saints will instruct them. The Angels will hover before and above them to advocate for their assimilation into the Catholic Church where they will be pronounced on Earth and in Heaven as participants in and recipients of the Faith that Jesus ordained upon His Resurrection, Ascension, and Pentecost. Jesus told His Apostles and disciples that they were and had become the Vessels for all that would be known about Salvation in the Cross. He sent them as sheep amongst wolves. He asked them to 'see' as He saw

Creation, and to transform that vision into discernable action based on the Theological Truth enshrined within the Church that He commissioned in an Upper Room filled with fire.

Hence, it is obvious that there is only one Faith. There may be other beliefs, but only one Faith. And, this Faith is anchored upon and has flourished from the Theological Truth that has been deposited in the Roman Catholic Church by the Holy Spirit. This is an irrevocable Moral Major that humanity-entire must come to know and accept. And, as we can see through our empirical lives; our lives of experience and interaction, humanity is yet sorely divided and out of focus. The world is not attuned to the Theological Truth that Our Lady declares. We have heard the term 'vessel' before. We have heard such titles as 'singular vessel' and 'vessel of sacred knowledge.' This is the thesis of the existence of man's awareness that the Lord wants to save the souls of lost sinners. He wishes to fill up men's lives with heavenly purpose instead of secular effects. God mandates from His Throne that all who know and accept Him turn to The Son for this guidance. Other implications include the fact that generations of detractors are going to be difficult to dismiss. However, it is more a disposition than a dismissal, a screening-in process rather than screening-out. It is about welcoming rather than ostracizing. Imagine if someone came before us and said that another seer had said they heard from God that the Roman Catholic Church is an imposter, or the harlot. We would rebuke them and call them the devil in an instant. This is the same way that it is horribly difficult to pry Protestants and those of other religions from their positions outside the Church. In their exiled human perception, everyone is conscripted in darkness; no one has the Light; no one has authority; no Vessel of Truth exists, no entity possesses legitimacy. They do not even trust one another. But, if they would look for legitimacy in what the Catholic Church is saying, they would realize by the power of the Holy Spirit that the Queen of Heaven is that legitimacy; and Her miraculous intercession is their Sign. This great Matriarch, the Mother of God, is the Universal Mediatrix who birthed the Church of Human Salvation in the Second

Person of the Trinity for the whole world. This gives Her the standing, authority, Wisdom, power and desire to set the record straight. Our Lady cannot be defeated, and She tenders to us Her resolve to defend the Catholic Church and arm us with facts to uphold the Three Moral Majors to the physical world. She cannot be opposed because She has never come into the world as a prophet. She has never claimed to be the Messiah because She is not, and neither is any other man than the Man whom She bore. Enemies of the Roman Catholic Church everywhere believe that the Lord God can speak only through a man. She is the exception that they cannot ignore. And, how does this make Her different from all previous female seers and visionaries? She is not a sinner; She has never sinned, and She gave birth to the sinless Messiah as a Virgin Herself. There are no other women who can ever claim this distinction. There is but one Mother of God, and it is this Mother who is speaking to the world now from the Spiritual Keep of God's Divine Kingdom. Yes, Vessel and Visionary of Theological Truth. This is the Patriarchy of the Roman Catholic Church, whose Mother is the Virgin, given to the exiled world in the image and likeness of God the Father, the Divine Patriarch, the Master and Creator, the Father of the Alpha and the Omega.

God's Signature of Transcension
His Embossment of Authenticity

"There is nothing quite so rewarding as an accomplishment that revolves around the coming of our dreams, or a visionary beginning, or the permeating melodies of new worlds conquered and friendships renewed. There is nothing more satisfying than opening someone else's eyes, softening hard feelings, soothing aching wounds, declaring an end to war, hitting the highest notes, treading where no one has walked, or restoring lost faith. There is little that can take us to eternal happiness than the things we achieve in the name of redeeming grace. These are the designs and purposes that make us who we are in Jesus, and Jesus in us. These are the intricacies of the excellence we have found in His Paschal Resurrection. This is the conclusion of the book of life's mysteries where everything unknown to man is fully revealed."

God's divine signature of revelation is embossed in His act of transcending from the unseen Kingdom of His Glory into the recognizable parameters of our seeable exiled condition. It is a condescension from our perspective, and a "righteous claiming" of His Dominion from His. The signature of that transcension bears the name Jesus Christ, who is the Messiah and Savior of humankind; God became Man through the veil of mortality. This same signature of revelation is present in all that He does. In each of the seven Sacraments of the Catholic Church, God transcends the veil and makes Himself present in glorious and wholly revelatory ways. In the Sacrament of Holy Orders, the priest becomes "in persona Christi," a recognizable and verifiable personification of the character of the Savior during the Holy Mass through the ordination of authority upon him. In the Sacrament of Matrimony, the unity of the Son of Man in the Most Holy Trinity is made manifest materially in the bond that is consecrated upon a man and woman. And, in the Holy Eucharist, Jesus Christ becomes physically present under the appearances of the consecrated bread and wine. In each of these, God pierces the veil and is made manifest in the exiled world as an act of His signature of revelation. This same transcension occurs in each of the other Sacraments as well. The seven Sacraments of the Roman Catholic Church can be called the Seven Great Transcensions because they are the seven openings to the Heavenly Firmament that illuminate the authentic path of Redemption back into the Kingdom of Paradise, and each is affixed with His veil-piercing signature. So, the mystical signature of God is always a reflection of the entrance of Jesus Christ into the world through the womb of the Most Holy Virgin. Therefore, when we see signatures of transcension bearing the scents of Our Lady's immaculate grace, we must take notice because God is rejected and the Holy Spirit is violated when people are presented these revelatory signatures and either dismiss or refuse to accept them. In each case, the person refuses to invoke the faith to allow the transcension to occur "for them," and in succession, for those who might be edified and converted by the display of their faith. They slam the door to God at the veil of Creation and disallow Him entrance by refusing to cooperate with His salvific intent, leaving Him relegated only to the unseen parameters of Creation. Where after, they complain that they never see any evidence of God because He never answers any of their prayers. You see, He is never allowed entrance to their actionable lives, nor allowed to influence them with His grace because they refuse to recognize His signature when He does. God comes to humanity on His terms, not ours, for the preservation of our faith. For example, when the Protestant world rejects that the Most Blessed Sacrament is the actual Flesh and Blood of their Savior, they reject the transcension of God. But then, they progress even further. They contort the scriptural passage which proclaims, "Unless you eat the flesh of the Son of Man, you will not have life in you," to justify their rejection, stating that Jesus was simply speaking in metaphorical terms. They not only dismiss the signature of God at the doorway of seeable Creation, but refuse to partake in the authentic Bread of Life; and in effect, they deny in their age and time the revelation of Jesus Christ in the Flesh altogether. The same faithless phenomenon often occurs in our relationship with the Hosts of Heaven, the Angels, and the Communion of Saints. The authentic actions of the Holy Spirit, such as Our Lady's miraculous intercession, the mystical protection of the Angels, or the intercessory wonders of the Saints declared in their elevation ceremonies, bear this same signature of transcension where Heaven comes to Earth, heralding the imprint of Christ becoming Man. And, the Protestant mind-set dictates that they amputate these actions of God at the perimeter of their frail faith by relegating them to boweries that they believe to be unworthy of their reverent attention. They demarcate borders to their personal kingdom which they refuse to invoke their faith to see past. They cannot see the mystical regions beyond their physical vision, and they decline to invoke the faith that would bestow upon them the sight which transcends the acres of their biases. A self-imposed blindness veils their true vision past what their mortal temperament can see. Then, God comes knocking at the gate they have erected at the boundary of their worldliness, such as our Holy Mother's contemporary apparitions and messages, and He is turned away as if He were some illegitimate beggar who could be offering nothing they could possibly want. It is not just those of protestant disposition who are afflicted with this deficit. The Immaculate Virgin Mary has experienced tremendous difficulties throughout the generations when trying to encourage Her many Catholic Prelates to open the doors of their personal faith and accept the procession of Her Queenship down the nave of Her Son's Church in the full regalia of Her stature. It is doubtful that there has been even one of Her transcensions that has been accepted in faith from the outset in reflection of Her Fiat to the Archangel Gabriel.

The Queen of Heaven is standing at the gate of every breathing man, pleading with our consciences to let Her pass into our lives through the majesty of the Hierarchical Church. She wishes to process into the world to rally into the unity of God's greatness a people who seem not to wish to congregate toward anything holy. Faithless intellectualism and outright prideful indifference are destroying the grace-filled opportunities dispensed to our generation; and we are the poorer for it. It is the reason you hear such flippant retorts as, "Well, no one is required to believe in the intercession of the Mother of Jesus." It is such an easy slander when standing in a crowd of sinners who do not want to believe anyway. Our Lady's Immaculate Heart cringes at these words because She knows the ire of Her Son has been raised by them. What more must He do, She would ask? People such as these are failing to consider that they are witnessing the imminent closing of the ages, and Her major intercessions are the beatific events that have been specifically held in the treasury of Jesus' Divine Mercy since the day He died, waiting for their dispensation during the end of times. I declare that now is the time to believe! Ignore the malcontents and the gatekeepers. Run down the roadblocks; tear down the walls. There is a better way for the flock to be spiritually cultivated; and it is through the discernment and interpretation of these end-times mystical revelations; their acceptance, and their elevation; and it begins with belief, not impenetrable skepticism; not stoicism and claims of prudence dripping with cowardice. Time is short; courageous faith is of the essence. Our compliance with the Holy Spirit begins with respect rooted in faith in God, not in waiting for the giant faith of little people to shame us into believing. Imagine how many millions of people in the world would have bent toward conversion had religious leaders all over the Earth believed and taken it upon themselves to celebrate the great graces of Medjugorje through their congregations and secular venues over the past three decades, instead of being the reticent bystanders they have been, coming to the show only in time to see the final act. Will Jesus Christ be triumphant anyway? Of course, but that victory will not be savored pleasurably by those who are the modern-day doubting Thomas's. What spiritual heroism could possibly warm their souls at the Triumph? God solicits participation with the designs of His Spirit. He is burdened to see His children adopt a wait-and-see attitude, as if it were His responsibility to convert and convalesce the continents. He left the vineyard in our stead. He grants the tools and the techniques. And, He promised the rains of His grace to help our work flourish. Our Lady's miraculous intercessions are His deluges. Should we not be building aqueducts to the most parched regions of aching souls? Yet, there are stewards who stand with arms crossed with their noses in the air looking at the storm front saying, "Just let it rain, God knows our neighbor's fields are dying; He will move the clouds over to them to get their share." It is our charge to make disciples of all nations, and present them with His life-giving waters. He promised to grant the necessary gifts to assist us, and is fulfilling that testament. God is speaking to humanity through Our Lady's miraculous intercession for our sake, not His. He already knows who has listened, who participated, who humbled themselves, who magnified Her presence, who laid their soul on the line and accepted the ignominy and scorn of the doubters for His Mother's success. And, He knows who did not; the lackluster, the indifferent, the stoic, the panderer, the mediocre, the compromiser, the distracted, the hell-bent, the prideful, the arrogant...and the coward. He has been dispensing great tools of cultivation all over the world, and those placed in charge of the vineyard have been telling everyone through their indifference and shameful demeanor to ignore them because, "It is not required that someone use any of those tools in our vineyard." That is how shameful "We do not need..." really is. I have grieved deeply for over two decades, knowing how Our Lady's Immaculate Heart is burdened by those who refuse to respond to Her affections and Her guidance, and share them with those who are in so much need. I do not want The Chastisement to come, but I am comforted knowing She will be with us nonetheless during the trials we will endure because we did not collectively listen and obey. The world could have been converted by now, but so many neither listened nor participated with the powers and venues they possessed. It is saddening that She is required to endure the arrogant dismissiveness that is prevalent in many quarters of the Church, the stoic disinterest in evangelizing Her salvific cause, even among some of the higher echelons of Christianity's leaders, particularly within the Protestant sects. We must remember that Christianity is made up of sinners who, if they fail to cultivate their interior vision with an openness to the Holy Spirit, often become as blind as the worst of atheists; a state that is truly damaging because it is the manifestation of the wolves in sheep's clothing that Our Lord cautioned us against following. How then can we become confident amidst a belief that is oftentimes weak? How can we trust? Whom do we imitate as our examples? It is easy if we widen our vision past the parameters of the current moment in time and gaze at the panoramic scope of the Roman Catholic Church throughout all of history. When we look to the Original Mother Church with an intention of conforming ourselves to it more seamlessly, it is to the history of Christianity whose origins are in the Cross of Calvary. It is not so much that we look for a Cardinal, Bishop or priest with whom we happen to identify in our sensibilities, we must instead unite our beings with the history of sacrificial devotion that still lives in the Church Triumphant. How is it possible for a person to be scandalized by the failures of an individual Bishop or Cardinal in the current time if our vision is gazing upon the thousands and thousands of holy Bishops and Cardinals from ages past standing right next to them, who support them notwithstanding their weaknesses? We look toward the Saints who most certainly did believe in divine intercession, beginning with Our Lady when visited by the Archangel Gabriel. How did She respond? "Be it done! FIAT!" At that moment, confidence in the Glory completely drowns out and obliterates the temporary moment of uncertainty in mortal time. God is the clarity over mankind's indecision, and it becomes as clear as crystal at the first act of honest acceptance. For every sinner within the Church who refuses to see and believe, there are thousands of great lights who do believe, who are open to the works of the Holy Spirit, who do lead in the sacrificial way of the Cross, and who are obedient to Our Lady in these times of Her great calling. Follow them into the Sacred Heart of Christianity, and ignore the rest of the stragglers! Ignore those who have no use for the Virgin Mary! God has placed leaders within the Church, even in our time, who are the pride of the ages of Saints, who have the courage of warriors, the intellects of veritable geniuses, the piercing vision of history's mystics, and the patient endurance of the Lamb of God on His Passionate Way of the Cross. Therefore, even if we witness a trainload of missed opportunities, rejected graces and outright denial of God's transcensions, we must know the integrity of the leadership of the Roman Catholic Church remains as intact as Peter's inaugural oration in Jerusalem on the first Pentecost that lifted up three thousand into the realms of belief in the matter of minutes. Why? Because there still lives that communion of Saints who precede us, marching into that Kingdom, who are themselves beckoning and leading us to the Paradise on High. The life of every good Roman Catholic throughout history is a boulder in the ramparts of its mightiness, growing stronger and more indestructible by the moment. Every sacrifice through the ages, the patient endurance of mockery and derision, every great step forward in faith, every testament in the face of martyrdom, each act of penance, the holy labors of families, every decade of the Rosary, each catechumen who has said "I do," the innumerable acts of kindness toward enemies, every word spoken in defense of the Truth, and every little person in the generations of our Marian shrines who has humbled themselves before the assistance of the Queen of Heaven make up the composition of that unassailable Kingdom on Earth where Jesus still lives and breathes, seeking the maturation and victory of man over sin through His indomitable Spirit. Even if we were to witness the ultimate desolation of the Roman Catholic Church on Earth in our generation, the abomination sitting where he should not be, and every member of the Magisterium betray Our Lord; even this colossal human failure would not possess the power to destroy the Church founded by Christ, because its sanguine legacy is already secured in the ages by Christ and His Saints who would swoop down from the celestial vaults and resurrect His earthly Kingdom in one gigantic revelation. The enemies of Roman Catholicism and Her Divine

Traditions through the ages truly do not know how weak and vulnerable they actually are. They are gaining nothing but a larger and more precise dose of humiliation reserved for them at the Triumph of the Immaculate Heart of Mary. It is then and there that they will all be transformed into glory in one giant Pentecost to our joy or discarded into the abyss to our triumphant jubilation. We pray deeply and sacrifice patiently, hoping for the former in our imitation of the Divine Mercy of Our Lord Jesus. What makes Christians such excellent little creatures is that we are willing to forego the known for the unknown; we stake our fortunes on the faith of a billion anonymous fathers; we speak and conduct ourselves in ways considered awkward by practical men, and we have founded our future on the coattails of a Covenant that was etched in stone and ratified in blood long before we were born or had the opportunity to shape it. The enemies of the Cross are tinkering. They are no match for the Roman Catholic Church; they will never reach a formidable mass; their undertakings are unequivocally futile; and they will ultimately convert and die as martyrs in the battle for lost souls while feeding the flames of righteousness or remain as they are and be consumed as heathens by the inferno of justice themselves. This is the crux of the message espoused by Pope John Paul II the night he was elevated to the papacy, imploring humanity, "Do not be afraid!" Believers have a whole history's worth of engorged promises fulfilled by Popes, Cardinals, Bishops and visionaries, proving that our efforts have never been in vain.

"What we see through the lens of mortalism, Heaven sees with beatific envisagement. The breezes' touch combines the seen and unseen worlds. Hence, a waft of air is akin to angels' breath. When we are consecrated to obedience, God lends us sacramental power, and the Church remains His plenipotentiary."

Sunday, November 1, 2009
Virgin Mary

"*My dear sons, these are the moments in time when you will remember that you have practiced perfection in the obedience to which Jesus calls you, that you have seen and heard the summons in your hands resounding through your consciences, that these years you have given to God have meant the difference between a world discovered in His Grace and one adrift in the backwaters of its own indifference. Each time I appear in this place, it is God's signature of approval that you are living for Him. You must never forget this, My children. You have forged new paths and blazed new trails with this obedience because of the gift of faith you were accorded upon your baptism. My Special son, you repeatedly refer to the content of My messages in your works, and rightly so, to prove that I am aware of the intricate details of the conversion of lost sinners. I know what they need to be awakened. I carry the candle of light, and I ring the bell that tells them about Salvation in the Cross while they sleep in the darkness. Now, as this day has come when the Church specifically recognizes the canonized Saints, you are unified with them in heart and mind. You have referred to them in your own writings. You have even spoken to them while awake and in your dreams. They have interceded for you in miraculous ways because they want you to succeed. While it would be impossible for Me to list all of them here in the time we have allotted, I ask only that you remember that they are aiding you through the perilous trials of life. And, each one is mindful of your penchant for achieving your goals with passion. Just as you were once given some of the Angels' names, you must know that each Saint is with the Angels in company, that they see your lives on Earth with extraordinary distinction. The Lord allows them to intervene when all else seems to fail. I once told you that Saint Joseph is the most powerful Saint of all. Indeed, he has accompanied Me throughout the universe; his spirit is attuned to the heaviness of the years, and he remains your steadfast friend as you and your brother continue your mission.*"

Have we ever stopped to think about the co-dependency that we share with the Church Triumphant in Heaven? It seems rather contradictory, really, that anyone whose soul lives in Paradise could actually yearn for our inclusion and integration into what is already their glorious experience in perpetual bliss. The whole matter comes down to what the Saints desire as their concept of Heaven. If it includes living eternally alongside someone in particular, surely the Father through the Son will provide for them. After all, this is what it means to have the intercession of the Communion of Saints. Their prayers mean just that. It is what they deserve, indeed their right, to have us next to them as they concelebrate the timelessness of the heavenly skies. For what vibrance would the Faith Church on Earth have if not for the Church Triumphant? We are converted by the Holy Spirit through the gift of human faith, and we are redeemed when that same faith leads us to accept our final redemption when it comes. This faith allows us to see the Blood of Jesus on the Altar from the Cross, and it provides living proof in our hearts that the promises of Christianity are true. All we need do is believe and profess. This is the essence of being commissioned through the Roman Catholic Church to be chosen and elected, to be fully reliant on Our Lord's Resurrection that we cannot yet see to restore our life. We know that this is true because our hearts of faith are filled with the sublime Truth proclaimed by the New Covenant, and the Holy Gospel lives in and through us by virtue of the presence of Jesus inside us both spiritually and sacramentally. The boiling pot simmers down to reveal the unity of the Church here on Earth, the Church Suffering in Purgatory, and the Church beyond the gateway of Glory. For over twenty centuries, the authentic voice of Christianity has attested that the Chair of Saint Peter is the center-point of human conversion, the emerald city of God's enlightenment, and the golden bridge linking earthbound sinners to the Crucifixion of Jesus Christ. When the Holy Spirit speaks revelatory strains of faith and morality, the Pope's lips pronounce their urgency. Along with the Church hierarchy, the Roman Pontiff has outfitted the world with steeples that mean something. Throughout each Pontificate, we are schooled in the sacred principles of religious virtuousness by the way we present ourselves as Roman Catholic Christians and what we can glean from others about our personification of the Gospel transcripts. This is the impeccable proof of our orthodox faith. We feel a mutual companionship with other Christians in our supposition that they have been branded by the same suffering that first begot the purification of the world. What a thought! We have discovered even more common ground with Jesus Christ. Certain people are specifically chosen to endure pain and torment so that other people can live beyond the immortal horizon. Our Bishops and the Princes of the Church have been these people in an intimate way for two thousand years! And here, we humbly submit that we are as deserving of the same victorious blessings that Our Lord heaped upon the believing Apostles during His brief ministerial mission on Earth by our lives of communion with those who have been commissioned to mark time in their stead. This is the inimitable wonder of the Crucifixion and Resurrection, and this is what we live for every time we wake in the morning with as much Christological fervor as that which accompanied us to sleep the night before.

So, why so much emphasis on our recognition and acceptance of God's signatures of transcension when a Deposit of Faith stands so obvious within the Catholic Church? Because it is our responsibility to heed the call of the Holy Spirit of that Deposit with dignity and obedience. It is not an intellectual Deposit, but an Eternal Deposit that mystically actualizes and animates the human person to be in communion with all divinity, subject in obedience to the Will of our Creator in the moment. The Virgin Mother told the Archangel Gabriel that the Lord's Will must be done, in the moment; and in our day, we must reflect Her Fiat. The final Redemption of man is rapidly approaching; and believe it or not, when it is struck upon the Earth, we will wonder where the winter has gone. Jesus assists the righteous lot of humanity with His grace to remain focused and strong during these days of our exile, awaiting the response of the greater world. But, we must evangelize it with action, word, deed, agenda, devotion and courage! Christianity provides a brilliance and a perception which allows us to possess and control an ability to persevere that cannot be diminished by our disapproval with the slow passing of the days. History will prove that Our Lady is right; humanity entire will acclaim Her. We will someday look into the face of our own mortality and wonder why we ever questioned the pace of the hours and the fleeting of the years. It is obvious that things such as this are difficult for us to see at times, but we will someday turn to the Most Blessed Virgin and say that everything She ever told us during our time on Earth through the voice of messengers and the rebukes of prophets was correct. The reason we become frustrated with the element of time is because we rarely see the effects of Jesus' mission in the same magnitude that our hearts conceive them. Most everything He gives the world is in the lives of private people whom we rarely meet, and in Sacraments that are veiled as outward signs of inward Grace. Our faith is good, but it is tested. Without these conditions, would there be any need for faith? Our lives and consciousness swim daily around all the actions and reactions that comprise the human experience. Imagine with over six billion people living on Earth all the words that are spoken, physical acts that take place, the billions of tons of food consumed, the measure of oxygen breathed, and on and on. And yet, even in this, all of it is finite. When someone says that there are countless people doing something, they are speaking in hyperbole. The only immeasurable substance about our lives is our attributes that connect us with the Kingdom of God. Our faith, trust, love, service, humility, contrition, and all the virtues that identify us as Christians are part of the infinity to which our souls shall rise, come the end of time. Here, we are embedded in a physical world for a length of time. But, we will one day be able to see the parameters of these higher things as well. There are so many trees rooted in the soil, a numerable assemblage of animals and birds, and the hairs on our head. We have the gift of amenities that we take for granted not because we are not thankful, but because they are likewise below our feet and otherwise out of sight. We drink water from a mechanical system created by architects and engineers. It is miles long, and it serves millions of people in our locale alone. However, it is absolutely measurable to the very last inch and drop.

Everything that is fabricated by men contributes to the seeable, touchable world in which we live. We enter the grocery store and see the culmination of thousands of hours of human labor. The products were grown, processed, packaged, transported, and shelved there for us by people we have never met. God sees them. Jesus knows what they are doing. The Angels hover around them with curious interest. Indeed, the automobiles we drive, the buildings in which we work, play, and sleep are there because of the millions of hours of planning and labor invested, given to the whole of humanity through the grace of God. The point to be made is that there must be more than this. There must be Providence guiding the handiwork of men and their intelligence, their ability to place hammer to nail, pen to paper, eye to scope, and heart to inspiration. This is the creative instinct that makes us a developed species more than the beasts in the wild and the fish of the sea. We were taught by Mosaic revelation that we are to serve the world and be its stewards; and that the world belongs to us, we to God, and therefore all Creation to Him. When others speak about a circle of life, they do not imply that we return posthumously as something else. At least those who believe in Jesus rightly decline to accept the theory of reincarnation. The word that we must remember is "resurrection." Once we have been lifted from the darkness of death, we will no longer wish to have anything to do with the old Earth unless we hear the uttering of prayers from those who remain there. All the Saints we hail and imitate during our lives commit themselves to basking in God's Light for thousands of Earth years, but only a moment to them. Their first priority is to know that they have been saved. They look into Jesus' Face with awe and thanksgiving that nearly wipes away their entire identity in favor of magnifying the Son of God. But, God allows them to keep their individual identities, and remembers before the heavens their sacrifices in union with Him. And then, they become present in the reason they sacrificed, and they turn their thoughts to we who remain, hoping to hear petitions from the exiled world pealing like cathedral bells for their assistance before God. This is why we are asked to invoke their names and seek their intercession. The communication between us and the Saints is initiated by our prayers. They hear them the same way we hear the dinner bell or the echoing of songs from the steeples where we worship.

The intent of Our Lady's messages, indeed Her many intercessions, is not to call us away from the world where we are obligated to commit our greatest sacrifices, but to draw us to a realization that we are wrapped in the Grace of God right where we are. In spite of our taking for granted all the constructs and products about which I have spoken, we are going somewhere. We, the Church, are making the difference that Jesus procured for us on the Cross. This is where His greatest lessons were taught. We see with our eyes of faith what Divine Love means in sacrificial terms. When we see a beautiful woman wearing a diamond necklace, she is there, and it is on her only because the Son of Man allows it. He would rather the resources be used to feed the poor and lift-up the sick and brokenhearted, but He allows it because God's creatures are indeed beautiful. They will suffer no negative judgement when they see the poverty of His Birth from the other side of time, except for the guilt that they impose upon themselves. This is what Our Lady's lessons and messages have been about. She has called all in America and around the world to the Holy Gospel where we learn about discretion and modesty, about tending to the poor and dying. She has said to the people of this land that there is more to life than what materials we procure and how we expend our assets. Hence, we see that we have even more reason to know that the messages of the Morning Star Over America are more urgent than ever, with the devaluing of human life by our elected leaders, our economic system in shambles, the popular people in entertainment morally bankrupt, the Church impugned from all directions; and the story goes on from there. My key thesis is to tell everyone that none of these things really matter. Why? Because we have hope, and we are completing the Will of God that will expunge what we see from the annals of history; the world will be written anew! This is why we accept divine intercession and are trusting in everything that the Holy Virgin has said. What we can expect in the near future is the proverbial unexpected. Every Christian has seen how Jesus opens and closes doors according to His knowledge of how His Kingdom is progressing. If He deigns that men should cry, they shall each weep rivers of tears. If laughter and dancing are in order, He will strike the opening chord. Assigning ourselves to His Will is what He desires; this is our prayer for the reconfiguration of everything on Earth, and beneath and beyond it.

In March and April of 1991, my brother and I were praying in the midst of Our Lady's grace, when I asked Her to send the Holy Spirit into the world, whereupon my brother saw doves aplenty flying into the hearts and lives of those I had mentioned. Although I did not see this with my physical eyes, I saw it through a magnificent vision in my soul, simultaneous to his mystical declaration. We both knew from the center of our hearts that those for whom we prayed would receive the graces of our petitions. We trusted, not knowing the future, not realizing that our diary and a dozen other books would come, not having the benefit of foresight to realize the magnitude of the work that She was commencing for the conversion of the lost. Beyond the sight of the secular world, Our Lady weaves together the handiwork of God in our lives, a pipeline of holiness beneath the surface. Hard work and the sacrifice of long years have sufficed the changes that will come pouring now into the future, dramatically and historically. My brothers and sisters of faith, through all the life we are treading, through every hope and heartache, all the disappointments, battles we are weathering, and darkness of the heart, we are still accomplishing the goals that Our Lord set forth for us. We are shining like diamonds in the furrows of the Earth, and our spirits cannot be impugned by the calling of our detractors to another way of life. We must not feel trapped in the lives we lead. It is not in the purview of Our Lady's mission to tell us what Jesus has planned in minute detail, for what benefit would that be to our faith? But, it gives Her overwhelming satisfaction knowing that we stand by Her Son through all the disappointments and awesome heaviness that come upon us, particularly as retribution from others for believing in Her magnificent intercession. She has been calling the world with emphasis from Medjugorje, along with other places, for a reason. And, She conscripted my brother and me into serving Her grace, isolated here in this place for the purpose of completing the deposit of works that She set-out to dictate from the foundation of the world. All recipients of Her miraculous intercession are normal human children from whom She demands the highest moral standards. Our minds and thoughts are not out of the ordinary. Our expectations for prosperous and fulfilling lives are inside the parameters of those who are close to the Father. Even in our prayers, our narratives appeal to the finer side of Jesus, not for coldness and indifference that He might lend to those who spurn Him, but warmness and unity in the completion of the Will of God. Surely, we must know that Jesus hears our calling upon Him. He realizes that we bear our share of the Cross in us for the reparation of human sin and the conversion of the lost. And, so do all those who believe. Our Lady makes no illusions about a world that could be shorn of the gladness that we will find in Heaven, for all that is of Heaven can live in our hearts today. If we do not understand this, surely we will never pray. She promises us that She will ask Jesus to answer our prayers according to the Will of God, and more importantly according to that which will make us happy, believe more in His charity, move closer to the Truth of the Gospel, and open our hearts and lives to receive the sufferings of our brothers and sisters to lighten their burdens. We have spoken with Our Lady for these years for more reasons than to place our works and desires somewhere that Jesus will not see as readily as He might recognize Himself in a pauper on the street. She calls upon each of us to maintain the civility and dignity of heart that identifies us as Christians, no matter what the future holds. Yet, we live in a world where too many do not pray at all, some who casually wonder if Jesus is there, and others who are genuinely communicating with the Grace in His Sacred Heart. Our Lord hears us when we say, 'please, please, please.' He knows what it means to live a lifetime of rejection. He understands the feeling of wishing to be embraced by humanity in a spiritual way that perfects the heart of the giver as well as instills fulfillment in the heart of the receiver. Our Virgin Mother will not steal God's thunder and tell us how Jesus will answer our prayers, but we can be assured that She pleads as deeply and sincerely as the most passionate prayers of men ever uttered for Him to affirm our wishes into being. She stands united with us in whatever we desire from Heaven in prayer. It is not impious for us to sometimes feel betrayed by God. Everyone knows that there are some things He has not done through the centuries of the existence of men. The Lord knows that we are not just any creatures, but His faithful legions, who are the courageous warriors who set our feet on the battlefields of His vineyard, praying with His Queen every day and every week for the conversion of wicked men. Therefore, this Queen again asks us to join Her in saying, 'Let us see what our Lord God has planned for the Triumph of His Kingdom!'

Saturday, August 17, 2013
Virgin Mary

"The art, the theater, the pageantry, the eloquence... Welcome to My Immaculate Heart, My little sons, where you live at all times and in perpetuity. Your confidence in My intercession is both beneficial and benefactoral. You have the means to tell humanity about the greatness vested in you, about the holiness by which you have always lived, about your faith that is tested every day. It pleases Me dearly that you have exposed yourselves to the grace of wisdom raining down from Heaven. We know among us that we are making a difference in fashioning the Kingdom of the Lord here on Earth to be the likeness of Heaven.   How do I know?   Because the multiplication of wars tells Me so. The fact that so many are fighting against

evil is reason enough for Me to believe it. Today, I come more happy to this place than you have ever heard Me. I am more jubilant, more sufficed in gratitude, and more assured of the atonement of humanity with the Father in Heaven than I could have previously thought possible. It is true that the Roman Catholic Church is under siege from the inside and outside; it is being tested as your faith itself is always tested. My little sons, you are pouring forth into the vastness of the world your allegiance to God in ways that will be ultimately revealed to all. Your prayers, books, testimonies, memoirs, and strength of endurance are all proof that your role as warriors for the Cross is becoming evident to all. Even though the _____ may never overcome their questions about The Morning Star Over America; even though they may turn away the messengers of the Lord, they will eventually proclaim here and to the world, 'Surely this must have been the Spirit of God.' There is no losing here, My little ones. Positions of employment and stations of power come and go, but there is no diminishing the aroma of the Spirit of God, there is no dismissing the Truth. You have yet to become fully aware of the indelible mark you are leaving on the faithful here in this exile, and the impact you are having on those who do not yet believe. My joy is incapable of being measured; My awareness of the success of the Church has never been more pronounced. Remember the writer who said, '...up again, old heart; there is victory yet for all justice.' This is the way I live; it is the way I ask you to live. My little sons, where I place My eyes is where I am given impressions of how this world will conclude. I speak of My physical vision and spiritual foresight. I see people standing tall and proclaiming their faith, their self-confidence, their trust and acceptance of the Lord's proceeding Kingdom, their daring in conquering everything that tries to diminish their faith in God. There is a stalwart erectness of the conscience of men that has been handed-down through the ages to this age, to you and all who believe, to the ones who are willing to look upward and outward in ways that expand the Gospel into foreign lands and mountains. I see smiles everywhere. I see sensations of expectation for the Second Coming in what priorities faithful men embrace.

My Special son, My joy here today exceeds My previous messages because we are closer than ever to the Return of Jesus Christ, the King. I am not worried anymore that My children will fail. Many of them may fall, but they will never fail. And, it is perhaps not possible that you can see the forthcoming glory with your eyes, but your heart and soul are capable of discerning its color nonetheless. You can sense the streamers of celebrations to rival the Earth's rainbows. And, your spirit can feel the warmth of the Holy Spirit in whose light you are bathed. Indeed, you can touch the immensity of God's power by your grasp on the Holy Rosary. And, as I have said, you can sense the aroma of life beyond death, and even death itself, in your anticipation of entering the final days of this world as it has been foretold. I stand ready with My arms opened wide. The Angelic Hosts have trumpets in hand. The drum corps are poised to strike their first cadence. All of this is nigh at hand, and the world seems completely unaware. Nigh at hand implies that the years do not matter anymore. Today matters. What you do on this day, not what you did yesterday that has already been forgotten, not tomorrow that may open with Jesus descending on a cloud, but today. What happens when you open your eyes on each new dawn is what should matter to you at that time. Do you know why? Because the Lord scripts your existence here in the same way that He prescribed your creation from the beginning. He hands this power to you. He gives you and all people the ability to shape lands of peace and oceans of calm. He does not strike down the wicked in all cases because He wants to see His soldiers fight. He is engaged in the battle for souls in advance of that one final day. Not all of the wicked will be condemned; not all the wicked will convert. The separation of the sheep from the goats will proceed in earnest once everyone has taken their side. This is the motion and commotion of the cyclical seasons of life. Here today, I am again proclaiming that the conversion of lost sinners is occurring in massive numbers; you simply do not see them or hear about them on the news. This grand manifestation is not imbedded in internationalism, not in politics or partisan gain; it is found inside each human heart that is open enough to acknowledge and accept the Will of the God of Abraham. This God mandates that His people espouse decency and purity, chastity and charity, and prayer and penance. This is the Lord who commands that humanity must be baptized in water and purified by fire. Yes, this is the same Father of the blessed who has deigned to hand His own discretion to those who love and believe in Him.

My Special son, all this is a charitable thing. It is about sharing the warmth of Sacred Love; it is about touching others and allowing others to touch your heart. This is the primary essence of My messages that deal with empathy and compassion. This Sacred Love is always about understanding what other men suffer, what offends them, what heals and restores them, what makes them want to live. This is the same Sacred Love that has imparted in Christians the ability to see life beyond its present problems and ongoing obligations. Not all blight is malevolent; some is cleansing, enlightening, and purifying. Not all suffering is what it seems; it is beautiful in its conclusive realms. This is the message of the Cross. I ask you and your brother to remember this. I desire that you see the suffering of other men and your own suffering as the delight of the Angels as they perceive the Calvarian Cross. When the Lord speaks about repentance, He speaks about the capacity for exiled men to become heroes in the likeness of The Christ, like the Saints and Martyrs, like the little people around the world who walk with canes and ask only that others allow common decency to have a chance. Believe it or not, even as you and your brother are conquerors for Jesus, you are among these little people. You do not rage against the darkness like slayers, even though you certainly could. You do not make demands of God as though you are His equal. You do not destroy neighborhoods and cities; you do not burn the devil's barns just because you can. You are like Jesus. You know where and when to stone Satan's dogs. You, like God, are masters of timing. You realize that your prayers are more powerful than most American citizens are willing to believe. So, why would I not come in joy? I see colorful surfaces prepared to receive the burden of the years. I see a breathing, enlightened humanity poised for victory. Yes, and this victory has already begun. It will not spool like data into a queue; it will fall upon this Earth like a billion lightning strikes. It will fall men from their horses before they ever knew it was there. It will lift-up the poor and turn the world upside down; new rules, new priorities, fairer skies, and happier times. This is the victory that I have always described to you, that I have always told you would breathe triumph and elation on you in ways that you could not possibly have foreknown.

This is the same way that I see the upcoming release of your first memoir; genius in the material realms. It is the inscribing of the faith of your fathers in a 21st-century work. It reveals the content of your heart in ways that have been previously untold. I am overjoyed about this! I am here to say on this day and always that nothing can remove your revelations about God and your union with Him from history or eternity, those that you have packed into your extraordinary book. This is the stuff of miracles; it is the reason men throw their fists into the air and dance in place because their soul cannot stand still. You know that this is true; you cannot deny it; you would not try. Jesus feels what you feel, and He touches with His hands everything you have created. He runs His palms across your life and feels gratified that you have shaped your 'being' into the likeness of Himself. He sees as I have told you that I see. And, this makes Him realize that the performance of lordly holiness is emanating from you. I have said this to a scarce number of people in the past 2,000 years. When the poet asked his listeners to heed the call, to embrace the concept of, '...up again, old heart,' he was saying that life's burdens and worries can be overcome by the justice of God. The daily mantra of negativism is not a true description of what is really going-on in this world. Listen to Me! Hear what I have to say about the actualization of justice happening around the world. There is a sleekness, a newness, a powerful freshness to the Kingdom of God that He is injecting into your everyday lives. If you allow Him, He will internalize this fact into your conscious awareness in ways that has sustained His Christians for centuries onward. Remember, I am not promising that there will be rose petals covering the pathways on which you will walk. The skies will not be wholly shed of dark clouds and thunder. There will be drawn blood and bruising. There will be deficits and disappointments aplenty. But, you already know the outcome of the war. There is a purpose for it all. Thank you, My Special son, I offer you My richest blessings for making My intercession into *this world so filled with joy. I will speak to you again. I love you. Thank you for having responded to My call."*